CYBER CRIME
Issues Threats and management

CYBER CRIME
Issues Threats and Management
(In 2 Volumes)

Cyber Crime: Issues and Threats
(Volume-2)

Editor
Atul Jain

ISHA BOOKS
DELHI-110 033

Cyber Crime: Issues and Threats

ISBN: 978-81-8205-106-5 (Set)
ISBN: 978-81-8205-108-9(Vol. 2)

Reprint 2015 in India by
Isha Publications
B-69, New Gupta Colony
Near DDA Market
New Delhi-110009

Printed at: Chawla Offset, Delhi

Contents

Preface

Computers and the internet are powerful information tools. By their very nature they facilitate almost instant exchange and dissemination of data, images and materials of all types. However the new technologies also present new criminal opportunities or new crimes. Denial of service attacks, viruses, unauthorised entry, information tampering, cyberstalking, spamming, pager-jacking, dumping or phone-napping, and computer damage are relatively new types of offending or undesirable behaviour that did not exist in the pre-computing environment. Likewise, the development of computers has created new opportunities for services theft, manipulation of the stockmarket, software piracy, and other thefts of intellectual property.

Security of the global information systems is challenged increasingly by nontraditional threats from adversaries, both old and new, not only hostile regimes, but also international criminals and terrorists who cannot defeat us in traditional theatres of battle, but search instead for new ways to attack by exploiting new technologies and the world's increasing openness. Globally, cyber crimes constitute more than $15 billion in damages every year. Government and military networks are only one target of cyber attacks. The vast majority of network resources, estimated at up to 90 per cent, are owned by the private sector and are believed to be more susceptible than most government controlled assets.

Many states have enacted cyber crime laws. Those laws, however, were confined to a specific territory and were frequently outdated. Perpetrators of crimes have thus gone unpunished. The Cyber Crime Convention, an international treaty designed to police cyber crime through international cooperation is a welcome and long-overdue start towards addressing the exigent circumstances evolving from the Internet revolution.

This book provides an authentic and comprehensive analysis of the threats of cyber crime. The issues of cyber security are also discussed. It will serve as a valuable reference tool for investigators, researchers, students and all related with computers and internet operations.

Editor

1

Understanding Cybercrime

Cybercrime has become one of the major challenges to the future law enforcement. As Information and Communications Technology (ICT) becomes even more pervasive, aspects of electronic crime will feature in all forms of criminal behaviour, even those matters currently regarded as 'traditional' offences. It will also feature in many transnational crimes involving drug trafficking, people smuggling and money laundering. Cybercrime will present police and those involved in the broader criminal justice system with a range of challenges, including forensic issues. As most of us are aware, world has been avid in its uptake of technology and is among the leading nations in terms of key measures of Internet infrastructure, penetration and activity. This rapid increase in the use of computer technology has facilitated countries' participation in the emerging Information Economy but also increases its exposure to electronic crime issues.

Technology, particularly ICT, is becoming more and more pervasive in our society. The use of the Internet will continue to evolve and grow in many areas including:

- — Electronic commerce;
- — Online banking;
- — Drug stores with prescription services;
- — Health care services and records; and
- — Education.

Of particular relevance to those interested in crime issues is the potential for huge increases in fraud. Fraud has already been found to be the most expensive crime.

Technology has weakened the integrity of many identifiers currently in use – birth certificates can be reproduced using desktop publishing software; counterfeit passports and counterfeit smartcards can be purchased over the Internet. Easier access to these false identifiers facilitates a range of fraudulent behaviour, including tax evasion, immigration malpractice, fraudulent claims against social security and health insurance companies. It also assists in hiding the proceeds of frauds.

The computer has become an integral part of our way of life. However, as our dependency on ICT increases, so too does our vulnerability. This vulnerability and associated implications for investigators was clearly demonstrated in recent times with:

- — The distributed denial of service attacks on Yahoo, eBay and other major Internet players;
- — The 'Love Bug' virus (or ILOVEYOU worm);
- — The reported denial of service attacks on the St George Bank in September;
- — The recent hacking of Microsoft where an attacker apparently gained access to the source code for a future product;

— The large scale theft of over a million credit card details from various US cybercommerce sites by Russian and Ukrainian crime gangs;

— Attacks on government websites in the US, UK and Australia by Pentaguard in January 2001, said to be one of the largest most systematic defacements of worldwide government servers on the www; and

— The largest identity theft case in Internet history involving 200 of the 400 richest people in America listed in Forbes magazine, which was recently discovered in the US.

Nature of Cybercrime

The barriers to participating in criminal activity appear to be dropping and there is also a proliferation of individuals who are capable of countering IT security measures. For instance, it was believed a few years ago that only several thousand people in the US had the capabilities to launch a cyber-attack. Today, it is estimated that there are 17 million such people in the US alone.

People who commit computer crimes vary widely in skills, knowledge, resources, authority and motives. In addition, motives are said to include greed, need (to solve personal problems such as gambling debts), inability to recognise the harm done to others, personification of computers (seeing computers as adversaries in a game) and the Robin Hood syndrome (seeing corporations as so rich that stealing from them is morally justified).

None of these motivations are really new. An element of novelty does reside however in the unprecedented capacity of technology to facilitate acting on these motivations. It would seem that people who would not dream of stealing or maliciously damaging other people's property in real life have no qualms or second thoughts in relation to the opportunities and challenges presented by the Internet.

Global connectivity means that havoc can occur, in a very short timeframe, throughout the world. The abuse of computer technology may threaten national security, public safety and community well-being, and devastate the lives of affected individuals. A long list of traditional offending has been greatly facilitated by technology advancements such as mobile telephony, the Internet and encryption. Furthermore, new criminal opportunities or new crimes have been created by the development of electronic media.

Denial of service attacks, viruses, unauthorised entry, information tampering, cyberstalking, spamming, pager-jacking, dumping or phone-napping, and computer damage are relatively new types of offending or undesirable behaviour that did not exist in the pre-computing environment. Likewise, the development of computers has created new opportunities for services theft, manipulation of the stockmarket (through ramping up of stock prices and 'pump and dump' schemes using the Internet), software piracy, and other thefts of intellectual property.

Because many telecommunications networks, such as the public telephone network and the Internet, are now connected globally, there is an international dimension often added to the offending. It has been suggested that with modern mobile devices such as laptop computers, mobile phones and modems, crimes can also now be committed anytime anywhere, with the potential scale of the crime scene and the impact of the offending potentially the entire network-connected world.

Electronic crime is variable in its manifestations, so it is difficult to discuss in terms of aggregate incidence and impact. This inability to accurately define the nature of the problem is not helped by the fact that currently no statistics on computer crime are maintained by Australasian police.

Unfortunately, definitive information on the present extent and impact of electronic crime is not available. A significant amount of this crime is simply not reported and some may not even be detected. This non-reporting is in part because of a great reluctance to notify incidents to law enforcement authorities so as to avoid any potentially adverse impact on consumer confidence or share prices, or perhaps because of a lack of confidence in law enforcement to deal with such issues in a timely or effective way.

The nature and particular features of electronic crime will pose new and unique challenges for investigators. Consider for a moment, the impact of:

— Anonymity;

— Global reach (including issues of jurisdiction, disparate criminal laws and the potential for large scale victimisation);

— The speed at which crimes can be committed;

— The potential for deliberate exploitation of sovereignty issues and cross-jurisdictional differences by criminals and organised crime;

— The volatility or transient nature of evidence, including no traditional collateral or forensic evidence such as eyewitnesses, fingerprints or DNA; and

— The high costs of investigations.

The challenges of the digital age for law enforcement are numerous and diverse, and include:

— Bridging multijurisdictional boundaries;

— Retaining and preserving evidence;

— Acquiring appropriate powers;

— Decoding encryption;

— Proving identity;

— Knowing where to look for evidence;

— Tackling the tools of crime and developing tools to counter crime;

— Rethinking the costs and priorities of investigation;

— Responding to crime in real time;

— Coordinating investigative activities;

— Improving training at all levels of the organisation;

— Developing strategic partnerships and alliances;

— Improving the reporting of electronic crime;

— Enhancing the exchange of information and intelligence;

— Acquiring, developing and retaining specialist staff; and

— Avoiding 'tech-lag' (or ensuring access to cutting edge technology).

— Policing is certainly facing a formidable challenge in the area of electronic crime.

Tools of Cybercrime

There are said to be some 30,000 websites that post hacker codes, which can be downloaded to break passwords, crash systems and steal data. One only needs to read Jeffery Deaver's latest novel, 'The Blue Nowhere', to obtain an appreciation of the tools and methodologies of the skilled hacker or cyberstalker. Moreover, one study recently found that of 3 million sites tested world-wide, about 80% displayed a vulnerability that could be exploited by tools readily available on the Internet.

The cybercrime tools freely available at the internet are:

— *Anonymous re-mailers*: Machines on the Internet configured to receive and re-send traffic by replacing the original source address of the sender with the address of the anonymous re-mailer machine. Used by intruders to mask their identities.

— *Internet packet filters or 'sniffers'*: Software that allows intruders to intercept network traffic.

— *Nukers*: Software tools used by intruders to destroy system log trails.

— *Password crackers*: Software that allows intruders to 'break' encrypted password files stolen from a victim's network server.

— *Scanners*: Automated software that helps intruders identify services running on network machines that might be exploited.

— *Spoofers*: Software tools that allow intruders to masquerade as other users.

— *Steganography*: A method of encrypting and hiding data in graphics or audio files. Used by intruders to spy, steal, or traffic in information via electronic dead drops, for example, in Web pages.

— *Trojan programs*: A legitimate program altered by the injection of unauthorised code into that program causing it to perform unknown (and hidden) functions to the legitimate user/system owner. Intruders use them to create undocumented 'backdoors' into network systems.

Threats to Global Information System

The new information and communication technologies (ICTs) have empowered individuals, corporations and governments to grow, learn and prosper. However, as with most new technologies, there is a downside. Although their motives are very different, both political activists and terrorists can use the global connectivity of the Internet to launch their attacks. Governments too can use the same tools to wage war on one another. No information system or computer network is hack-proof, therefore awareness of the problem and vigilance in security practices are critical steps in protecting government and private sector systems.

Security of the global information systems is challenged increasingly by nontraditional threats from adversaries, both old and new, not only hostile regimes, but also international criminals and terrorists who cannot defeat us in traditional theaters of battle, but search instead for new ways to attack by exploiting new technologies and the world's increasing openness.

The borderless technology can enable a Chinese hacker to compromise a server in the Netherlands and use it to launch a Denial of Service (DoS) attack against Amazon.com, a U.S. company. Traditional notions of national security focus on keeping the borders secure, even military operation begins by looking at a map. The map of the Internet knows no borders, it is worldwide, and the first thing that hits you as you look at the map is that there are no oceans, there are no mountains, there are no natural barriers.

Government and military networks are only one target of foreign cyber attacks. The vast majority of network resources, estimated at up to 90%, are owned by the private sector and are believed to be more susceptible than most government controlled assets. Vulnerable systems are in all sectors of the economy, such as the government, military, hospitals, power and water utilities, telecommunications, financial markets, corporations and the air traffic control system.

The three most common global threats to network systems are: hacktivism, cyberterrorism and cyberwarfare.

Hacktivism

Hacktivism is a mixture of political activism and computer hacking. Hacktivists are skilled hackers, but unlike the hacker who is motivated by simple curiosity or malicious intent, hacktivists are attempting to convince the world they are practicing civil disobedience.

Hacktivists are a special breed of hackers and crackers who attempt to call attention to an issue with a virtual call to arms using intrusions or creating technology to advance a political of social cause. He/she may be a political activist, reformer, or even soldier. Hacktivist attacks range from embarrassing their targets via Web site defacements to outright economic sabotage.

To understand hacktivism, one must first understand its roots in hacker culture. Hackers are a community of sophisticated computer users, mostly young male, who use a variety of tools to gain illicit and generally illegal access to computer systems. Over time the term "hacker" has come to mean specifically those who use their computers skills to engage in intrusive or disruptive activities.

Hacktivism is unlike traditional forms of political activism in that the method defines the movement, not the movement's purpose and group identity. The distinguishing factor of hacktivists is their command of technology which unites them.Traditional political activism is produced when identity and purpose form into a movement, which then finds methods to forward it cause.

Hacktivists are born of hackers seeking group identity and a movement to exhibit their methods, hacking skills, thus leading to a sense of purpose. The methods of hacktivists – DoS attacks, FloodNets, site takeovers, etc. – are inextricably linked to the hacktivist movement because they are what define the movement. In and of itself, hacktivism is not necessarily a global threat to information systems.

However, in reality, hacktivists' activities are not limited by national borders and most well known hacktivism actions were played out on the international stage. The hacktivist community regards the 1998 hacking of Mexican government web sites as the first recorded political action of hackers, the first "hacktivism."

A U.S. hacker group, the Electronic Disturbance Theater (EDT), organized the hacking in retaliation for the 1987 massacre of indigenous Zapatistas in Chiapas, Mexico by a pro- government paramilitary force. Prior to EDT's action, an Italian group, the Anonymous Digital Coalition, used email to issue a global call for cyber attacks against Mexico.

Hacktivism is not always a harmless annoyance, like simple web page defacements or email bombings. In June 1998 another well-known hacktivist attack was initiated by members of Milw0rm, a hacker group whose global membership is united only by the Internet. Two members, JF of England and VeNoMouS of New Zealand, boasted of their hack as they were interviewed by Internet Relay Chat (IRC) by James Glave of *Wired* magazine. The two broke into the systems at India's Bhabha Atomic research center in Bombay. They were able to seize control of six servers for several days and downloaded thousands of pages of email messages and research. The documents contained analysis and discussion of nuclear testing from India's five recent test detonations.

To verify their claims, the hacktivists forwarded several Indian documents to Glave, although he did not receive a response from the Indian government or the research center to his request for authentication. The group is also targeting nuclear research facilities in Pakistan. One month later as part of their global anti- nuclear protest, the Milw0rm hackers were able to deface up to 300 web pages on web servers around the world, including The World Cup, Wimbledon, The Saudi Royal Family, even actress Drew Barrymore. The normal home pages on the compromised servers were replaced with a picture of a nuclear mushroom cloud and an 800 word anti-nuclear manifesto. They started by saying, "This mass takeover goes out to all the people out there who want to see peace in the world." They continued, "The year is 1998, we should be moving towards worlds peace in the millennium, and nuclear warfare [and] testing is NO way forward. It can destroy the world."

Numerous politically charged skirmishes and government actions throughout the world provide motivation for turning hackers into hacktivists. The ancient dispute between the Israelis and Palestinians is spilling into the twenty- first century; the intifada is becoming the inter- fada. Israeli and Palestinian hackers have taken the Middle-East struggle into cyberspace, targeting each others' servers and network infrastructure. The two groups are not alone in the conflict as American and Arab hackers have taken up sides on the issue.

On October 7, 2000, Israeli and U.S. hackers assaulted the Web and email server's of Lebanon's Hezbollah guerrilla group. A spokesman for the group knew what had hit them; he said, "This is a well known method used to kill websites. This is Israeli technological warfare." Not to be outdone, Palestinian hackers and their supporters have hacked back. In November 2000, messages were intercepted from a group known as GForce Pakistan detailing plans to hack ATT's Web services network because of the firm's Israeli relationships. The group of Palestinian supporters also had targeted numerous sites of Israeli and U.S. affiliation.

Cyberterrorism

Cyberterrorism takes the act of Hacktivism one step further; rather than simply calling attention to a cause, the cyberterrorist actively attempts to harm, destroy, and possibly, kill. It may be the convergence of cyberspace and terrorism, and can be defined as "politically motivated hacking operations intended to cause grave harm such as loss of life or severe economic damage."

At the present time cyberterrorism remains only a theoretical threat. No significant cyberterrorism attacks have been launched against the U.S. or other western nations. This is one more way in which the act is different from hacktivism, which has become widely practiced. Nevertheless, the lack of attacks has not quieted many in government and industry from their warnings of a coming digital Pearl Harbor.

Richard Clarke, chairman of the President's Critical Infrastructure Protection Board until January 2003, has been proclaiming the rallying cry for cyber security. His concern was that many in the U.S. government and industry were apathetic to the dangers of cyberterrorism and made a point of saying the issue is when, not if, foreign terrorists launch a massive cyber attack on the U.S.

At the Black Hat computer security conference in 2002, Clarke said he believes his role to be that of a digital Paul Revere and stated, "We're (the Federal government) going to spend $20 billion on security in fiscal 2004 through 2006. If a cyber-war comes – and come it will – we want to be prepared."

On the other hand, some are not convinced cyberterrorism is currently a threat. The current discussion of a digital Pearl Harbor and a digital Paul Revere has prompted critics to coin a new term, digital Chicken Little. Others have simply dismissed the cyberterrorists' methods as "Weapons of Mass Annoyance." Scott Blake, Vice President of Information Security at BindView Corp. in Houston, TX, believe Clarke's rhetoric is designed to play on the ignorance and fear of the public and politicians. Blake feels terrorist want to create the shock of a psychological impact to perpetuate fear, even more so than inflicting actual damage. He says, "If I'm a terrorist, I want pictures on TV. You don't get that if you knock out the stock market's computers."

Many others agree with Blake and have provided various explanations for their doubts about cyberterrorism. Jackson states:

> The Internet and associated networks are insecure, as everyone knows. Yet this infrastructure is so distributed that trying to seriously damage it is like throwing rocks at the ocean. Individual targets can be successfully attacked, but we are so accustomed to information glitches at the bank, at the office and at home that workarounds are common, even expected. The typical result is inconvenience.

As with any emotionally and politically charged discourse, the truth is probably closer to the middle of both arguments. The doubters express valid points; no cyberterrorism attacks have occurred in the U.S. and successfully accomplishing such an attack would be difficult. On the other hand, supporters of cyberterrorism awareness point out that just because it has not occurred, does not mean it cannot occur. Certainly, if the U.S. Postal Service can be used to inflict terror, computer systems can as well.

Berinato explains there are two clear threat categories of cyberterrorism: physical infrastructure and critical data. The threat to physical infrastructure is that critical systems would be compromised, such as power grids, dams, water and sewer systems, air traffic control, pipelines, and global positioning satellites. Attacks to these systems could result in massive destruction and most certainly death. However,

Berinato believes the threats are much greater for the nation's critical data systems, such as the Federal Reserve network, Social Security databases, industrial research, and military systems. Although physical destruction and death are not very likely is such an attack, catastrophic economic turmoil is possible. A well financed and proficiently trained terrorist organization could also launch cyber attacks in harmony with traditional physical attacks.

It is known that Osama bin Laden's al-Qaeda terror network made wide use of technologies such as the Internet and encryption software to communicate, raise funds and spread their message. The U.S. government also believes al-Qaeda has been training recruits in computer hacking to prepare them for cyberterrorism strikes. It is estimated al-Qaeda spent approximately $2 million preparing for the September 11, 2001 attacks, so financing development of a cyberterrorism is certainly within their means.

Terrorist organization have three levels of proficiency: simple- unstructured, advanced-structured and complex-coordinated. Simple- unstructured groups possess basic hacking skills, but rely upon tools others have created. They do not have a command and control structure nor are they skilled in target analysis. A good example would be the loosely knit Palestinian or Pakistani hacker groups. Advance-structured groups can perform more structured attacks and most likely have the skills to create or alter hacking tools. These groups have a command structure, can analyze their targets for weaknesses and can learn new skills. The most dangerous cyberterrorists are at the complex-coordinated level and possess the ability to cause mass-disruptions with sophisticated tools. The complex-coordinated organizations have a highly structured command and control and are very capable in their activities. Based on data at the time of the September 11 attack, al-Qaeda appeared to be between the levels of advanced-structured and complex-coordinated. The distinguishing characteristics between the three levels of cyberterrorist groups is sufficient time to develop the group structure and money to fund operations, both of which al-Qaeda possessed.

Cyberwarfare

Cyberwarfare is similar to cyberterrorism in its goals; however the participants are no longer terrorist organization, but rather sovereign nations. The U.S. is not alone it its effort to add cyberwarfare capabilities to its arsenal, and although difficult to confirm, reports suggest Russia, China, Israel, France, North Korea and India all are actively pursuing the technology. It is generally believed China, Israel and Russia are currently the most advance nations in cyberwarfare techniques, ahead of even the U.S.

Military leaders throughout the world are becoming aware of the potential warfare capabilities of technology while at the same time understanding the need to protect their own systems. Cyberwarfare, also called information warfare by the Pentagon, can be used as part of broader military strikes. Another likely use of cyberwarfare would be as a warning shot to dissuade another nation from entering a conflict, whether in the real or virtual world.

Cyberwarfare has great appeal because it allows one nation to strike another with no risk of loss of life to the attackers. The successes of the U.S in the Iraqi campaigns of 1991 and 2003 have demonstrated to most nations that they cannot expect to win a shooting war against the U.S.

Most nations, with the exception of Russia and China, do not have the weaponry, manpower or technology to compete with the U.S. in traditional warfare.

Cyberwarfare levels the playing field. Smaller nations with few resources see cyberwarfare as providing them an arsenal to compete with the world's few superpowers, a "low-cost alternative to initiating real violence." North Korea is one such nation; poor, isolated and under the constant watch of U.S. soldiers and reconnaissance efforts. Although the U.S. military will not confirm it, South Korea's government openly speaks about the North's cyberwarfare training center. According to South Korea, the school, known as the Automated Warfare Institute, was established in 1980s and is producing one hundred cybersoldiers per year.

Obstacles of Cyber Security

The internet is decentralized and diffused among thousands of private sector entities that are guided primarily by the profit motive and market forces. The burden of security falls on the private sector, not the government. Measurement of the cost of security failures and the potential risk to critical infrastructure is difficult and often exaggerated. However, no one disputes that the security of the network of computers that form the backbone of the information age is poor—poorer than it needs to be. The nature of this computer network, the speed with which it has arisen and the technology that underlies it explains how this situation came about.

Technical, legal, commercial and organizational issues stand in the way of better cybersecurity. These obstacles are in part the legacy of technology and policy developments as the Internet emerged over the 1990s, and they reflect the challenge of melding a new thing - the Internet and cyberspace - into laws and organizations not designed for it.

Technology. The millions of legacy systems that form the Internet are an obstacle to greater security. Security was not seen as a concern until much of the "infrastructure" for computer networks was in place. The Internet is a collection of open, unencrypted networks. Technical standards have focused on ensuring easy compatibility among diverse systems and on network reliability. There is no widely accepted standard for security.

The environment is one of rapid growth, diverse, evolving technologies and no common approach for security. Previous government policies discouraged the use of encryption to build secure networks. The result is a porous structure of unsecured systems. Some network "solutions" aggravate security problems, as programmers or systems administrators build network management tools like "Back Oriface" into servers and PCs without users' knowledge - these network management tools make remote administration of computer networks easier but can also create major security vulnerabilities that can be easily exploited by hackers or other unauthorized users.

Making better security products available is one area for potential solutions, if people will buy them. Industry-led technological solutions, such as the development of PKI and authentication technologies, protocols like IPSec or IPv6, – may provide a solution as these more secure systems over time replace less secure ones. The use of open source software could also improve security, by allowing thousands of testers to look for bugs and propose fixes.

Legal Issues. Security depends on enforceable laws, and establishing legal liability for security failures is crucial for better security. Contracts can assign liability, but are not sufficient for the larger problems created by an open, global network. Assigning liability has been very difficult (often, the failure is the work of unknown parties). If no one is liable for a security failure, there is less incentive to improve. Software manufacturers are not (to date) liable for errors in their products. Service providers have not been held liable for failures to provide service or for allowing a third party to launch attacks from or through their systems. Corporations are not liable for failing to take adequate steps to ensure network security.

The conventional legal solution to security failures would be to sue the perpetrator, or to assign negligence (and thus liability). This does not work when liability cannot be established. Contract law offers a partial remedy to this problem through the use of contracts between service providers and companies that explicitly assign responsibilities for security. More and more firms are using contracts to assign liability and this may emerge as a key incentive for improvement. Assignment of liability for security failure is a necessary step to ensure that the private sector will make precautionary expenditures.

Conventional legal solutions are also not adequate for deterring or punishing cybercrimes. Cybersecurity poses a new set of behaviors not neatly addressed by existing laws. Most countries lack an adequate legal framework for the deterrence and punishment of cybercrimes or rely on an uneven patchwork of legislation. While the Council of Europe's Cybercrime Treaty offers the possibility of strengthening legal frameworks in a number of countries, it has attracted criticism from industry and privacy advocates.

Improving cybersecurity also requires some resolution of the privacy problem. There are three parts to the privacy/security nexus. First, there is a close connection between security and ensuring the privacy of data on your own computer - preventing unauthorized persons from using the network to access files on your computer or plant programs on your computer. Second, ensuring the privacy of your data on someone else's computer is a security issue. Even if a site has a good privacy policy, if their security is bad and unauthorized users can get access to data stored there (such as credit card numbers or medical data), privacy has been compromised. Finally, measures that protect privacy (especially anonymity) on the Internet can complicate the task of increasing security.

Privacy safeguards can work against basic security technology implementation. Some measures that could make the Internet more secure can also greatly reduce privacy. Anonymity on the Internet, valuable for privacy, allows hackers to evade liability. While newer Internet protocols will help increase security and trust, the U.S. needs to consider the trade-offs between privacy and security. Government involvement can help define these trades, to help achieve a balance between security and privacy.

Multilateral Issues. The Internet is a borderless phenomena and cyberspace does not fall within any national jurisdiction. There is already extensive literature on how individuals or governments anywhere in the world can easily launch an attack on U.S. infrastructure or networks, and this attack can pass through several other countries in the process. This poses problems for assigning liability and for the enforcement of laws.

Efforts to improve cybersecurity can be taken on the national level, but these must be complemented by multilateral efforts. The U.S. briefly explored, but did not pursue, multilateral cooperation in talks held by the Presidential Envoy for Cryptography, and the Council of Europe Cybercrime Treaty is a useful vehicle for developing coordination. However, the U.S. may face difficulties in developing broad cybersecurity coordination, given concerns over national security issues in Europe.

Multinational cooperation in making computer networks more secure is essential, given the global nature of the Internet and to avoid "balkanized" solutions. As with the Y2K program, there must be an effort to educate other governments. This includes acceptance of interoperable standards and development of adequate civil and criminal law. A useful first step would be to assign the responsibility for working on multilateral coordination of cybersecurity to an agency in the U.S. government.

Market Issues. In a perfect market, the private sector would purchase adequate security and private sector firms would offer the products needed to build it. To date, this is not the case. In fact, it is legitimate to ask if there has been "market failure" when it comes to cybersecurity. Market obstacles to security reflect difficulties in assessing risk and liability, and grow, to some extent, out of the legal and technical issues. If companies become concerned about the potential risk to their networks or if courts can assign liability for attacks, demand for security products and services will grow rapidly.

The Health Insurance Portability and Accountability Act of 1996 (known as HIPAA) and the Gramm-Leach-Bliley Financial Reform Act, by creating responsibility for privacy and security, have had this effect and are driving demand for, and use of, security products.

The Act requires the Department of Health and Human Services to develop standards and regulations for transmission and storage of health information that identifies individual patients. These will standardize the exchange of electronic data for certain administrative and financial transactions and protect the security and confidentiality of electronic health information. The requirements outlined by the law and the regulations promulgated by DHHS are far-reaching - all healthcare organizations that maintain or transmit electronic health information must comply, and the law provides for significant financial penalties for violations.

The intent of HIPAA was to protect privacy, but it also affects security procedures. There is no common standard for the security of health information that fully meets HIPAA requirements. HHS developed a security standard with input from standards groups and industry that is technology- neutral and scaleable.

Health organizations that transmit or store electronic health information must conduct a risk assessment and develop a security plan to protect this information. They must document these measures, keep them current, and train their employees on security procedures. The security standard is divided into four categories: administrative procedures, physical safeguards, technical data security services, and technical security mechanisms to prevent unauthorized access to data transmitted over a communications network.

Section 504 (a) of the Gramm-Leach-Bliley Act establishes a federal standard for financial privacy. Financial institutions are required to have written privacy policies that must be disclosed to customers. The disclosure of a financial institution's privacy policy must take place at the time a customer relationship is established and not less than annually during the continuation of the relationship. In addition, consumers can opt out of having private financial information shared with most third parties without their permission. Federal and state regulators are to establish comprehensive standards for ensuring the security and confidentiality of consumers' personal information. The privacy provisions apply to any company engaged in financial services, whether affiliated with a bank or not. GLB covers finance companies, insurance companies, securities dealers, and even travel agencies. Many of these entities may not yet be aware of this.

Network security products can be costly and difficult to implement for anyone who is not an expert in security technology, and there are few such experts relative to the demand for their services. Security also remains a secondary consideration for many in the software industry – witness the number of products that contain software tools like "Back Orifice," to allow remote access to computers for customer service, but which also create serious vulnerabilities for unapproved access.

The weakest link in a computer network determines security. This can include computers on your own network or a computer that can access your network. While many organizations now see the security risks posed by their computer networks as important, their security is interdependent with the consumer side of the network. For example, the penetration of Microsoft appears to have occurred through an employee working at home. Consumer systems remain the weak link. Systems that provide for "always-on" Internet access are particularly vulnerable. Companies believe that consumers will pay little or nothing for security, but this may be less of a problem if security becomes embedded and transparent in consumer applications.

The traditional response to market failure is government intervention. Intervention could include some combination of direct or indirect subsidies or tax relief. Government could also target these subsidies at key sectors that have greater leverage to move the larger market. Government action could also include enacting legislation that would limit liability, using Federal Purchases and Standards to move the market in a particular direction, or exhortation by government officials for the private sector to voluntarily take certain actions. There are also negative incentives, where the government could use regulations and penalties to encourage certain forms of behavior.

Insurance Issues: Insurance markets arise where there is advantage from pooling risk. Cyber security is a logical candidate for insurance, and some perceive an opportunity in this for government action. Insurance requirements can drive private entities to take steps to mitigate risk, and insurance will play a role in improving Internet security. How large a role depends on how the insurance market is constructed and, possibly, the degree of Government involvement as an "insurer of last resort."

Currently, Internet security breaches could overwhelm the private reinsurance market. The worldwide reinsurance market is worth $10-20 billion, but a single attack or Internet event could lead to losses exceeding this amount. Insurance works poorly in spreading the risk of an event when losses are "correlated". Some see an opportunity in this: the Federal government could become the insurer of last resort but, in exchange for assuming this liability, it would require insurers and their customers to meet a certain level of security.

Reinsurance has budgetary implications for the government. Poorly constructed insurance markets can create unmanageable liabilities for insurance providers. Two key issues for insurance as a tool for the management of risk in cybersecurity are "adverse selection" and "moral hazard."

"Moral hazard" means that the insured person reduces precaution or allows people to undertake risks that they would otherwise avoid. If parties do not bear the costs of a failure to improve network security, they will have no incentive to minimize risk. "First party" insurance, where an entity buys insurance for its own losses, could reduce incentives to improve Internet security by creating "moral hazard," For example, flood plain insurance actually encourages people to build on flood plains, as they do not bear the risk of damage. If an insurance company will reimburse you for any loss from a cybersecurity failure, you will do less to reduce the risk of failure.

"Third party" insurance, where an entity buys insurance to cover the risk of damages to someone else, avoids the moral hazard problem but depends on good actuarial data, something we do not yet have for Internet security. "Adverse selection" occurs when insured people hide information that would be pertinent to the insurer in estimating the likelihood of loss. The lack of reliable actuarial data makes adverse selection a real risk for Internet security. Avoiding these problems requires good actuarial data and the ability to make those who are negligent bear the costs of security failures. Federal participation in reinsurance makes sense only in a market that avoids moral hazard and adverse selection.

An effective insurance market for cybersecurity has other requirements as well. An agreed measure of what is good network security is necessary for insurance companies to say that the policy holder has in place a level of security sufficient to show reasonable care. British Standard 7799 (BS7799), a widely recognized security standard covering continuity of operations, system access control, physical security and network management, is the leading candidate for a common standard. However, audits of how well a company has implemented BS7799 can vary widely and take months to complete.

HIPAA offers another set of standards that, with some modifications, could be used by other industry sectors. Most insurance policies also exclude "force majeure" events, such as acts of war, which could pose a problem for the Internet where it is sometimes difficult to distinguish between an act of war, terrorism, a crime or a fifteen-year-old prankster. In addition, for insurance to be effective, there would have to be some change to the "intentional acts" exclusion that is a feature in many insurance policies. It excludes coverage for claims stemming from intentional acts, but surveys show that between 70 and 80 percent of all Internet security incidents come from internal sources.

For insurance to be attractive there would have to be coverage for intentional acts While in the past insurance markets were not willing to write policies for Internet security failures, this is changing. Few companies are willing to write policies for business interruption loss. In part, this reluctance reflects the lack of good actuarial data, which makes it very hard for companies to estimate risk and the price that should be charged for insurance. That said, some companies report that applicants for insurance have quadrupled – and these applicants are seeking new policies, not extensions of existing policies.

The most sophisticated clients are not only buying coverage at catastrophic level, but they are requiring their business partners to have this coverage as well. The growing trend to outsource network management and security will also shape the insurance market.

There would have to be better actuarial data so that the degree of risk could be calculated (including the degree of risk that could be associated with different security configurations). The lack of a definitive estimate of the actual damages that could result from systemic network failure also poses serious problems for insurance. Public estimates of cybercrime damages vary widely and often include a range of damages such as theft of laptops and loss of intellectual property from Napster downloads. Insurance (and reinsurance) requires a better idea of the costs associated with various kinds of security failures and their results.

Government action could help remove some obstacles to the use of insurance, such as the lack of actuarial data, lack of security standards and problems with the assignment of liability. Government action could address the problem of correlated losses by subsidizing the reinsurance market, and the provision of reinsurance could allow the government to set standards for security.

Helping an insurance market emerge more rapidly or more smoothly is different, however, from providing a de facto subsidy as an insurer of last resort. Subsidies for a poorly constructed insurance program would actually impede security enhancements. Even the act by the government of exploring with the private sector the standards, costs and nature of insurance programs might benefit cybersecurity.

Organizational Issues. Since 1996, the U.S. response to cyber threats has been robust. The President's Commission on Critical Infrastructure Protection, established in July 1996, was the first national effort to address the vulnerabilities created in the new information age. The cornerstone of this response is the May 1998 Presidential Decision Document 63 (PDD-63), which lays out overall guidance for critical infrastructure protection. PDD-63 established a National Coordinator for Security, Infrastructure Protection, and Counter-Terrorism, located in the White House, whose responsibilities encompass cybersecurity. PDD-63 also established two new agencies, the Critical Infrastructure Assurance Office and the National Infrastructure Protection Center, to work with the private sector.

A "National Plan for Information Systems Protection buttresses PDD-63 by focusing on domestic efforts by the Federal Government to protect critical cyber-based infrastructures. Information Sharing and Assessment Centers (ISACs) were created to share information, and expertise. In addition, the Administration has pursued a number of related initiatives to improve network security, including the selection by the National Institutes of StandardsTechnology of a new and stronger encryption algorithm (AES) to replace DES, a Public Key Infrastructure (PKI) effort, and the creation of a Federal CIO Council. As part of this larger effort, the Administration relaxed its controls on encryption exports in September of 1999 to encourage the use of strong encryption.

These steps are beneficial, but like many other problems that cut across the responsibilities of traditional agencies in the last decade, the solution was to place a National Coordinator in the White House. However, responsibilities within the government are diffused in a way that could challenge even the most energetic national coordinator. This organization could be simplified and centralized.

A new Administration may want to reconsider assignment of responsibilities. The CIAO provides an essential coordinating function with the private sector, and if it is not continued, it must be replaced. Responsibility for information sharing about viruses or network attacks is critically important for security.

The current US approach could be improved. NIPC, while performing an essential function, has had difficulties in sharing information about network attacks in a timely fashion. Because of the constrained imposed on the sharing of law-enforcement information. For example, NIPC learned of the Love Bug attack early in the morning on the day it occurred, but did not notify the public until four hours later.

Law enforcement needs a centralized center for investigating network security attacks, but information sharing is a different mission with different requirements. Information sharing on computer attacks may also be an area particularly amenable to outsourcing to nongovernmental entities.

The private sector also has organizational issues. Managing network security risks is not yet an essential part of corporate governance. Some industry sectors are moving rapidly to address security issues without government involvement. Credit card companies and their participating merchants, banks, investment firms and others are making strides to operate more securely.

The leading edge on improving security appears to be the financial sector, but it is not clear how far its improvements will percolate into other sectors absent further change. A requirement for discussion or even rating of the security of a company's computer networks in annual reports would have stimulate security, as would consideration of security as part of the provision of insurance. Linking network security management to profit ands loss statements would raise the profile of the problem and create incentives for addressing it.

Some believe that government can affect corporate governance through an approach to cybersecurity like that taken to address the Y2K problem. While security is an ongoing problem and Y2K was a single event, the Y2K model may offer suggestions for moving ahead. The primary function of government in Y2K was as an organizer and educator.

The Y2K effort gathered and disseminated information, organized multinational networks for addressing the problem, shared information on best practices and worked through public-private partnerships to raise awareness. Regulatory changes in some sectors also had a marked effect.

The Securities and Exchange Commission had a galvanizing role in Y2K preparations, as did similar actions by banking regulators. Companies had to show publicly and to their regulators that they had taken adequate steps to protect against Y2K disruption. Similar SEC requirements for companies to report the steps they are taking to protect themselves from a cyber attack would improve the security of computer networks.

Cybersecurity in Perspective - Public Goods and Collective Action. A public good gap is a market obstacle of particular interest. A "public good" provides benefits to an entire society with very little incentive for any one person to pay for it. Since everyone benefits equally from a public good whether they pay for it or not, there is little incentive to pay. Provision of public goods is usually a government function.

Network security measures that protect critical infrastructure could be another public good. Securing the infrastructure benefits both those who pay for the improvements and those who do not. To the extent critical infrastructure security is a public good, there will be less incentive for the market to invest in it.

A gap would appear if the level of security necessary to manage risk for the commercial sector were not sufficient to protect critical infrastructures. The level of risk that a company might find economically reasonable might still allow for vulnerabilities in critical infrastructure networks. This would be a case of market failure where government incentives may be necessary.

A level of Internet security sufficient to protect critical infrastructures is also a "collective action" problem. Collective action problems arise when multiple parties have to behave in a coordinated way to get a positive outcome. For networks to be secure, the thousands of individual participants in the Internet must each improve security. Their own security depends on the choices made by others on the network. Several approaches that seem to offer possible avenues to resolving the collective action problem for Internet security issue involve reputation, tort and insurance. A "reputational" solution would involve the creation of a public rating of security by third parties and would create visibility and incentives for firms to improve security, especially if these ratings affect eligibility for insurance or were potential areas of liability for corporate officers. Other firms would not want to do business with companies identified as having poor security. The market can generate solutions to collective action problems, or they can be solved by legislation and regulation, or by some combination of the two. Orchestrating a collective effort to improve cybersecurity might be a good place for legislative action.

In thinking about cybersecurity, we might want to consider several scenarios. In one, security will improve through market forces, as better products come on line, as new standards and protocols become available, security will innately become better. Greater use of "Open Source" products will allow bugs and errors that could damage security to be found, publicized and repaired. The increase of outsourcing and the growth of larger server farms will improve security by distributing targets and centralizing responsibilities and needed skills.

The development and extension of contractual bases for security will allow parties, in the business-to-business context, to allocate risks by contract, so that penetration or failure of a computer network would result in enforceable financial penalties against service providers. In turn, service providers would seek insurance.

A second scenario would take these same trends but find that they were inadequate or too slow. Government intervention would facilitate these private sector developments, call greater public attention to them, and help ensure coordination with other governments. In some instances, the government could find incentives to accelerate or expand improvements for some critical sectors.

A third scenario would modify these trends by adding ill-considered laws and regulations, that would actually inhibit improvements to cybersecurity or misdirect work into less effective paths. Government must be aware that actions taken to fix one aspect of the cybersecurity problem could have unforeseen and damaging consequences.

A more careful analysis, based on public good and collective action models, suggest that we might be able to split this problem. These models predict that firms will pay for some level of improvements to security, but have little or no incentives to pay for improvements above that level. A simple guess would be that we can probably depend on market forces to improve network security overall - economic self interest and consumer concerns will probably drive business and organizations to build in security, and this will create demand for the IT industry to build and offer better security products.

What is undetermined, however, is whether this level of security, while adequate for commercial activities, will be sufficient to protect critical infrastructure. The degree to which commercial security improvements will be inadequate may differ from sector to sector - utilities may be willing to accept a lower level of network security than will the financial sector, for example. It is also not clear if the market response will occur in as timely a fashion as we need to meet national security requirements.

Given the technical difficulties of building security products, and given the legacy of a network built on millions of unsecured products, we need to ask whether in the near term government will need to take action in specific infrastructure sectors identified as critical and not secure. It is in this area - critical infrastructure sectors that have less incentive to improve security to the level needed for critical infrastructure protection- that incentives might make sense.

Some believe that market forces and the evolution of the IT industry will improve security, and others believe that the government must take a more active role. To some extent, this is a difference of degree - there are some activities that all agree the government should pursue - but in some fundamental areas, notably the question of whether the market has failed and that government must create incentives for the private sector, we are far from a consensus.

Combating Cyber Threats

Although national governments and the United Nations have proven powerless to stop war, especially cyberwar, they can provide law enforcement tools to fight hacktivism and cyberterrorism. The United Nations is aware of the problem, and has passed numerous antiterrorism resolutions, but none deal with the specifics of cyberterrorism.

The European Union is promoting the e-Europe 2002 and e-Europe 2005 initiatives to provide Internet access to the majority of its residents. However, the E.U. recognizes that cyber attacks are more likely to occur within a wired Europe. A proposal to create the European Network and Information Security agency is currently in progress and will serve to foster coordination and interoperability among the computer security agencies of the member nations.

The U.S. government has attempted to address the issue with legislation that provides severe penalties for cyber attacks. The USA Patriot act was signed by President Bush on October 26, 2001 is response to the al-Qaeda attacks of September 11. The act gives law enforcement greater powers in pursuing cyber criminals and terrorist, but many privacy and civil liberties groups vehemently opposed it saying it strips away many of the rights of U.S. citizens. Additionally, the Cyber Security Enhancement Act was added to Homeland Security legislation in November 2002. The bill goes beyond the USA Patriot act in its cyber security scope, even providing life sentences for convicted hackers operating with terrorist motives.

Role of Law Enforcement Agencies

The broad reach of the Internet, which connects millions of people worldwide, presents a number of unique challenges to law enforcement in the fight against cybercrime. Technologically sophisticated criminals can exploit the Internet's speed and distributed nature to commit crime and wreak havoc without regard to geographic and jurisdictional boundaries. A single perpetrator is able to anonymously take advantage of millions of vulnerable computer neophytes with relative ease. Law enforcement's dilemma is further complicated by the rate at which technological innovations evolve.

The nature of cybercrime necessitates that law enforcement overcome institutional resistance to information sharing. Improving existing relationships and forging new partnerships, inside and outside of law enforcement, will improve every po-lice agency's ability to exchange information in an expeditious manner. In so doing, law enforcement will be in a better position to investigate crime.

Attracting qualified candidates in the field of cybercrime and computer forensics is difficult given the higher salaries offered by the private sector for similar skills. This amplifies the challenge for law enforcement agencies that seek to blend the stability and deployment flexibility of sworn personnel, with the technical expertise of civilian analysts. In addition, this rapidly expanding and evolving field requires personnel to receive training on a continuous basis in order to keep pace with the cybercriminal.

Fighting cybercrime requires a coordinated approach, which unites local resources with those at the state and national level. Government must work cooperatively to ensure that statewide initiatives to fight cybercrime are not duplicative. The governments must fit into a coordinated national plan, which ensures that staffing, equipment, and training resources are maximized, and provides a mechanism to share vital information. The federal government should work cooperatively with states to develop statewide initiatives in an effort to advance a systematic approach.

The international ramifications of cybercrime suggest that the governments should develop funding guidelines promoting the adoption of a coordinated, statewide approach to address the growing threat of cybercrime.

Many of the crimes that law enforcement confronts everyday are beginning to appear in the digital world. Criminals have adapted to the information age very quickly. More and more traditional crimes such as those involving narcotics trafficking, gambling, auto theft, homicide and assault, stalking, child pornography, fraud, and identity theft are facilitated by the use of technology.

As criminals continue to utilize these evolving technologies, it is imperative that all levels of law enforcement are able to adequately respond to this elusive threat. The US Computer Crime Unit currently has five primary areas of responsibility—including forensic analysis, computer network and information systems security breaches, Internet crimes against children, fraud and identity theft, and training and research—challenges faced equally by law enforcement agencies statewide.

Forensic Analysis

Forensic examination of digital evidence can be crucial in the investigation of crimes facilitated by the use of technology. A growing number of investigations involve crime where critical evidence is stored on digital media such as computer hard drives. Whether the case is criminal, civil or administrative, processing digital evidence requires technically skilled personnel with specialized training and equipment. As the volume and complexity of casework grows, it will become increasingly important for additional resources to be allocated in a more efficient and effective manner.

Since 1997, the Computer Crime Unit has received more than 600 "containers" of evidence for forensic analysis. A container of evidence could consist of hundreds of removable media, a laptop computer, or a network server containing multiple disk drives. At present, there are 150 containers onsite awaiting processing. Requests for analyses are received daily, with urgent and time-sensitive cases receiving top priority.

Accordingly, evidence in important investigations is analyzed and completed in a short period of time.

However, low priority cases tend to have slower processing times due to the sheer volume of cases and available resources. It would take approximately 18 months to clear just the pending cases at current staffing levels, if no additional cases were received.

The fledgling discipline of computer forensics is at a point where the lack of accepted standards and procedural uniformity has prompted independent responses from a myriad of law enforcement agencies at the State, Local, and Federal levels. If this haphazard approach continues, defense challenges could call into question the credibility of computer forensic analysis due to the lack of standardization. The science of computer forensics must evolve to meet the same standards of evidence that have been established for other forensic disciplines such as fingerprinting, ballistics, drugs, and DNA.

Standardized operating procedures in the field of computer forensics are established and incorporated into the training of forensic examiners across the world. Population, geography, type and level of crime, as well as existing resources need to be evaluated prior to developing future computer forensic laboratories. The activities of all laboratories should be closely coordinated to ensure the development of generally accepted standards. At the same time, individual laboratories must be linked to the investigative mission of their respective region.

Protection of Information Systems

The reliance on computer interconnectivity has increased the risks associated with the Internet and computer network use. Malicious and unlawful cyber attacks in both the private and public sectors are becoming increasingly prevalent and of greater concern to mainstream society.One of law enforcement's newest challenges is responding to attacks on public and private sector computer networks and information systems. Those at greatest risk are the networks and systems linked to state and national critical infrastructures, including information, communication, finance, energy, and transportation.

As society begins to accept law enforcement's role in our connected world, it is increasingly likely that law enforcement will become the "first responder" to cyberbased attacks. This will require the use of specialized technical and investigative personnel with a sound understanding of computer technology and advanced forensic analysis. Coordinated public sector resources must work with private sector interests and must be available in multiple jurisdictions in order to effectively protect our vital infrastructures.

For example, in the State of New York, a the law enforcement agencies have established a multi-agency initiative focusing on addressing cyber-based vulnerabilities. The New York State Police and the Office for Technology have worked in concert to develop a plan to address the increased risk of network and systems intrusion. The plan calls for the development of endto-end detection and response capability thus enabling the State to identify and analyze attacks on government-owned computer networks and initiate appropriate technical and law enforcement measures when required. The plan also calls for the State to make every possible effort to ensure that an individual's liberties and privacy rights are protected.

Protecting Children from Internet Crimes

The threat to children from predators who hide their identity behind the veil of technology is greater than ever. Law enforcement in every state must act swiftly and decisively to protect innocent and vulnerable potential victims. As a result of a preexisting multi-agency initiative, New York State was one of the first to receive a federal grant from the Office of Juvenile Justice and Delinquency Prevention (OJJDP), which created the NYS Internet Crimes Against Children (ICAC) Task Force. This dedicated multi-agency initiative—comprised of the New York State Police, Attorney General's Office, and Division of Criminal Justice Services—investigates computer-enabled crimes that exploit children. In addition, the task force works to promote standardized investigative techniques, trains law enforcement personnel, and enhances public awareness. By cooperating with 30 similar task force operations nationwide and local agencies that have received ICAC satellite grants, the NYS ICAC Task Force has been able to successfully investigate, arrest, prosecute, and incarcerate predators who target children.

Ever increasing caseloads—currently more than 1,000 active ICAC investigations in New York State alone—require more cooperation and centralized coordination. Mechanisms for coordinating and sharing information about undercover operations within each state must be improved to ensure officer safety and the efficient use of law enforcement resources.

A recent federal evaluation of the ICAC program made several recommendations. One critical recommendation addresses capacity building for both forensic analysis and training in response to the growing number of reported cases. The forensic needs and investigative skills required in ICAC investigations are the same for other crimes involving the use of technology, and must be addressed in coordination with efforts in other program areas. Another recommendation proposes that a major ICAC grant be directed to each state. Quickly identifying, arresting, and prosecuting these predators will protect potential future victims. As the volume of cases grows, we need to ensure that there is a centrally coordinated point of contact in each state to advance multi-jurisdictional investigations.

Fraud and Identity Theft Investigation

Fraud investigations involving a "petty crime" are often indicative of more serious and far-reaching illegal activity. The ease and speed of the Internet can be used to facilitate fraud, enabling criminals to commit crimes with relative impunity. Scams of this type can be quickly replicated and disseminated worldwide.

Victims of these techno-crimes are now able to report fraudulent activity on a secure web site administered by the Internet Fraud Complaint Center (IFCC)—a joint initiative between the FBI and the National White Collar Crime Center. Complaints are then forwarded to all law enforcement agencies that have jurisdiction. The early success of this IFCC program illustrates the willingness of the public to report fraudulent activity to the proper authorities. Already more than 1,000 complaints have been referred to the New York State Police, and it is projected that this number will grow exponentially as IFCC continues to promote its program and increase its capacity to receive complaints.

Cyber criminals are now preying upon individuals as well as businesses. The Internet is a venue that can be used to obtain extensive personal and financial information that, if in the wrong hands, can be used to perpetrate crime. Recently, there was a case in New York City where an unscrupulous individual used the personal information of more than 200 of the wealthiest people in America to fraudulently obtain credit or services in the victim's name. This high-profile case is just one example of the identity theft complaints that law enforcement receives on a daily basis.

Training and Research

The demand for highly trained and skilled personnel to investigate computer-enabled crimes is tremendous. This problem is compounded by the rapid advances in technology, which make continual training a necessity. In addition, there is a shortage of qualified instructors available to deliver law enforcement training in this area.The Computer Crime Unit has provided instruction to thousands of law enforcement personnel throughout the State. At the same time, other law enforcement agencies are engaged in similar training programs. Consequently, duplicative training programs are emerging without coordination. These training efforts must be streamlined in a cooperative manner with delivery channels that result in highquality instruction and training.

The United States Department of Justice currently funds the National Cybercrime Training Partnership—a consortium of experts from government, academia, and the private sector. New coursework is being developed based on the knowledge, skills, and abilities required today in the field of computer crime. One goal of the partnership is to identify existing, government-owned training and make it available at the local level in each state. Through "train the trainer" and distance learning programs, and in cooperation with academia, these modules must be incorporated into law enforcement training and academic degree programs.

Fair Use Practices

Fair use is an affirmative defense to a claim of copyright infringement.It is a privilege, not a right. More specifically, it is an equitable rule of reason, which permits courts to avoid rigid application of the copyright statute when, on occasion, it would undermine the purpose of copyright. The primary objective of copyright is not to reward the labor of authors, but to promote the Progress of Science and useful arts. To this end, copyright assures authors the right to their original expression, but encourages others to build freely upon the ideas and information conveyed by a work. Courts apply the four fair use factors with this over arching purpose in mind.

The fair use factors are discribed below:

The purpose and character of the work: The first factor in the fair-use analysis, the purpose and character of the infringing work, has two primary facets, whether the use serves a commercial purpose, and whether the new use is transformative.

— *Commercial Use*. Commercial use of copyrighted material cuts against a finding of fair use. According to the Supreme Court "the crux of the profit/nonprofit distinction is not whether the sole motive of the use is monetary gain, but whether the user stands to profit from the exploitation of the copyrighted material without paying the customary price. This standard does not require courts to make a clear-cut choice between two absolute choices – i.e., making a dispositive decision of whether a use is a "commercial" or "non-profit" per se. Rather, the commercial nature of a use is a matter of degree, not absolute. This places the question of commercial use on a continuum between two extremes: (1) a use that serves a non-commercial purpose by a non-commercial entity charging no fee whatsoever, and (2) a use that serves a commercial purpose by a commercial entity deriving its revenue directly from a fee charged for the copyrighted material.

— *Transformative Use*. "The goal of copyright, to promote science and the useful arts, is generally furthered by the creation of transformative works."For this reason, "the more transformative the new work, the less will be the significance of other factors, like commercialism, that may weigh against a finding of fair use."What constitutes a "transformative work" is not subject to exacting definition. However, as a general rule, if the new work "merely supersedes the objects of the original creation,"it is not transformative, but if it "adds something new, with a further purpose or different character, altering the first with new expression, meaning, or message," it is transformative. Transformative uses add new information, new aesthetics, new insights and new understandings. Such uses may include criticizing the copyrighted work, "exposing the character of the original author, proving a fact," or representing the original work in order to defend or rebut it.

The nature of the copyrighted work : The second factor, the nature of the copyrighted work, recognizes that there is a hierarchy of copyright protection in which original, creative works are afforded greater protection than derivative works or factual compilations.Also, the fact that a work is published or unpublished is a critical element of this factor.The use of published works is more likely to qualify as fair use because the first appearance of the artist's expression has already occurred. Thus, a finding of fair use will be couched between two extremes. Use of an unpublished, creative work weighs against fair use, while use of a published work relating factual material weighs in favor of fair use.

The Amount and Substantiality of the Portion Used : The third fair-use factor considers the amount and substantiality of the portion used in relation to the copyrighted work as a whole. "There are no absolute rules as to how much of a copyrighted work may be copied and still be considered a fair use."Rather, this factor has both quantitative and qualitative components, under which courts have found a use to be unfair where the material used formed a "substantial percentage" of the copyrighted work or where the material was "essentially the heart of" the copyrighted work.In applying this standard, the Supreme Court has held that this factor "must be examined in context," focusing on whether the extent of copying is "consistent with or more than necessary to further the purpose and character of the use."

Effect on the Market Value for the Original: While courts frequently identify this as the most important element of a fair use analysis,the legislative history cautions that it "must almost always be judged in conjunction with the other three criteria."In addressing this factor, courts "consider not only the extent of market harm caused by the particular actions of the alleged infringer, but also whether unrestricted and widespread conduct of the sort engaged in by the defendant... would result in a substantially adverse impact on the potential market."The Supreme Court has stated, "the only harm to derivatives that need concern us... is the harm of market substitution."While a "work that merely supplants or supersedes another is likely to cause a substantially adverse impact on the potential market of the original," courts have held that "a transformative work is less likely to do so."

The advent and spread of Internet technologies challenges the courts to maintain a balance between the free flow of information and the protection of intellectual property rights. Application of the fair use doctrine is one way courts endeavor to strike the proper balance. Merely browsing a web site containing copyrighted material may, theoretically, constitute copyright infringement. As one court has stated, "when a person browses a web site, a copy of the website is made in the computer's random access memory (RAM), to permit the viewing of the website's material. And in making a copy, even a temporary one," copyright's reproduction, distribution, and public display rights are potentially violated.

However, courts have acknowledged that while browsing may, on its face, infringe on copyright, it will, in most foreseeable cases, be a fair use.Courts have held web sites and other Internet service providers liable for infringements conducted through various Internet-related functions such as linking, media streaming, file sharing and storage, the maintenance of electronic bulletin boards, and posting. Fair use, however, was successfully invoked in a case involving the use of low resolution, "thumbnail" copies of photographic images. Notwithstanding the low number of successful fair use claims, courts appear to be applying the fair use factors in a technologically neutral manner. That is, the new digital environment has not caused the courts to abandon or significantly deviate from traditional fair use analysis.

Fair use factors in the context of particular internet technologies are decribed below.

Linking and Framing

"Linking," a ubiquitous Internet function, comes in two varieties: outline links and inline links. When a user clicks on an outline link, the browser displays a new web site. When a user clicks on an inline link, the browser pulls content – e.g., an image file, textual material, or audio stream – from another web site into the linking site for performance or display. "Framing" is substantially similar to inline linking and occurs when material from a link is displayed within a "frame" or window border of a page on the linking web site. The use of these technologies to appropriate copyrighted material raises a number of issues.

Outline Links. An outline link that connects a user to a site containing infringing material may further infringing reproductions, performances, distributions, and displays by others.If a linked site contains infringing material, the link may give rise to secondary liability for contributory or vicarious infringement on the part of the linking site, particularly if the linking site is promoting the copying, transmission, public display or public performance of material at the linked site. To the extent that the linked material is not infringing in itself, the reproduction, distribution, performance, or display that results from the link may not be authorized, and therefore may constitute an infringement in its own right.

The fair use doctrine may apply to many outline links, because it is likely the case that many site owners will want their material disseminated as widely as possible. However, where a link causes harm, fair use may not be appropriate. For example, unauthorized links may burden the linked site's server by increasing traffic to the web site. To the extent that the links pull in users that the linked site is not targeting, the owner of the linked site could argue that such traffic is unwanted and prevents the distribution of copyrighted material to its desired audience. Specific kinds of outline links, such as deep linking, may raise other issues.

Deep Linking. Most web sites have a "home" page to which all subsidiary pages are linked. A home page is akin to a front door that users open to gain access to the web site's contents. Often, a web site's commercial applications, such as advertising and other commercial solicitations, are displayed as the user enters the site's front door and proceeds through the first few subsidiary pages. A deep link can bypass a web site's introductory pages, and therefore its commercial applications, sending a user directly to the site's content or particular service.

In *Kelly v. Arriba Soft Corporation,*the lower court, in dicta, commented on the use of deep links by a "visual search engine." The court noted that deep links provided by a search engine specializing in finding, indexing, and referring users to images on the Internet would not violate the reproduction or public display rights of a photographer, whose photographs were made available by the search engine. The court acknowledged that the search engine's links allowed users to bypass the plaintiff's "front page" and thereby made it less likely that users would see all of the plaintiff's advertisements and promotional messages. However, this, the court noted, was insufficient evidence of harm or adverse market impact for an otherwise fair use of the plaintiff's copyright material.

On appeal, the Ninth Circuit Court of Appeals addressed the material issues of this case, which involved the search engine's practice of inline linking to and framing of the photographs, as well as its use of low resolution, thumbnail images to depict the photographer's images. These aspects of the case are discussed immediately below.

Inline Links and Frames. Inline links and frames appear more problematic than outline links, in general, and deep links, in particular. As this technology allows a web site to appropriate copyrighted material by pulling content from another site into its own, an unauthorized inline link or frame may infringe on the right of reproduction, display, or performance, or may constitute the creation of an unauthorized derivative work.

*Kelly v. Arriba Soft Corp,*discussed above, involved inline linking and framing by a visual search engine of copyrighted photographs. In response to a user's query, Arriba, the search engine, displayed the results of its search as a series of "thumbnail" images. As discussed above, Arriba would then deep link its users to the full sized images.

However, before Arriba had initiated this practice, a user could click on the thumbnail and view the full version within the context of the Arriba's web site. The Ninth Circuit parsed the case into two distinct issues. The first concerned the reproduction of the photographs as thumbnail images. The second involved the use of inline links and frames to display those images within the context of the search engine's web site.

The search engine's display of the full-sized images was held not to be a fair use.Under the first analytical factor, the court stated that pulling the images into the search engine's web site did not serve a different purpose or add new expressive elements to the photographs. The practice harmed the photographer's existing market by discouraging traffic to his web site, where he sold advertising space as well as books and travel packages. In addition, the use harmed the photographer's derivative markets. For instance, he could sell or license his photographs to other web sites or to a stock photo database, which then could offer the images to its customers. Accordingly, the court held that the unauthorized inline linking to or framing of copyrighted photographic images was not a fair use, but constituted an infringement of a copyright holder's public display right.

Thumbnails

"Thumbnails," imprecise copies of low resolution, scaled down images, are widely exploited by web sites. Generally, a website will use a thumbnail as a reference device, and embed a link in the image, which will, in turn, send a user to a high resolution, full scale version of the image. When used for this purpose, a thumbnail of an image may potentially infringe on a number of exclusive rights, including the reproduction, distribution, public display rights, and, arguably, the right to make derivative works.

Only one reported case, *Kelly v. Arriba*, has addressed copyright issues related to the creation and use of thumbnail versions of copyrighted images. In *Kelly*, the court found that the use of thumbnail images implicated the photographer's reproduction right, but was, nonetheless, a fair use.While the use of the images served a commercial purpose, the search engine neither used the images to directly promote its web site nor tried to profit by selling them. As the search engine did not directly benefit from the images and did not use them in a "highly exploitative way, the commercial nature of the use only slightly weighed against a finding of fair use."

The thumbnails also served a transformative use, since they "were much smaller, lower-resolution images that served an entirely different purpose than [the] original images, [functioning] as a tool to help index and improve access to images on the Internet...."For similar reasons, the court found that the thumbnails did not have an adverse impact on the photographer's market, but would enhance his market by creating a demand for the larger images.

Streaming Media

Streaming provides access to a wide variety of visual and musical works, allowing users to listen to retransmissions of radio programs, concerts and other musical events and services, as well as view music videos, television shows, movies, cartoons, and other transmissions of visual content. A single transmission of music or video can simultaneously infringe on a copyright holder's reproduction, distribution, public display and performance rights, in addition to the right to make derivative works.

In Video Pipeline v. Buena Vista Home Entertainment,the defendant, Video Pipeline, created and streamed movie trailers to its clients, video retailers, for exhibition to their customers. The court held that this practice infringed on the plaintiff's reproduction, public performance, and distribution rights, as well as its right to make derivative works. The streams were not defensible under the fair use doctrine. The court found that the use furthered a commercial purpose, since the service derived a direct financial benefit from the streams – its sole purpose was to advertise and promote video rentals. Moreover, the use was not transformative, since no new "creative ingenuity" was involved in preparing the previews, aside from "snipping and clipping."

Even though the length of the previews were usually less than two minutes, whereas the length of the motion pictures was over one and a half hours, the small amount used did not sway the court to find in favor of fair use. From a qualitative perspective, the court found the previews relied too heavily upon the "expressive value" of copyrighted works – e.g., their themes, plots, character, and overall premise. In doing so, the clips went to the heart of the copyrighted works, coopting their essence. Accordingly, despite an indeterminate finding on the question of market impact,the court rejected Video Pipeline's fair use argument.

Peer-to-Peer File Sharing

File sharing refers to a process in which devices controlled by end users, known as peers, interact directly with each other to transfer files between them, rather than using an intermediary, such as a central server, to transfer files. Music, literature, motion pictures, photographs, and other examples of copyrightable content can be traded over a file sharing, or "peer-to-peer" network. These networks are architecturally diverse.

The design of some file-sharing networks employs a central server to house a publicly accessible and searchable index of files available over the network. Other designs eliminate centralized servers altogether. In these systems, a user joins an immediate community of peers and searches within that community. The user's query goes through the immediate community first, and if it is not satisfied, the query then goes to another community of peers.

When peers engage in the unauthorized trade of copyrighted material, the copyright holder's reproduction and distribution rights are implicated. The Internet service that provides for the functionality of these networks may be held secondarily liable for the infringing acts of its users, even though it does not reproduce, store, or directly distribute copies of the infringing files on its servers.

In *A&M Records v. Napster*,various record companies brought an infringement action against Napster, an Internet service that facilitated the sharing of digital music files among its users. The files themselves–the infringing material–always remained on user systems and never passed through Napster's system. However, Napster maintained a central server that indexed the contents of the network. This feature allowed users to search for particular files of interest and to initiate a peer-to-peer transfer of those files. This functionality was the basis for holding Napster secondarily liable for the infringing acts of its users.

Rejecting Napster's argument that the users were making fair use of the record companies' copyrighted material, the court emphasized that the use was commercial because the users of the network received for free what they normally would have to buy, namely, compact discs. It was not transformative, since the service added no new creative or expressive elements to the copyrighted material. Moreover, the court held that the service not only harmed the copyright owner's existing market for the sale of musical compact discs, but also raised barriers to the copyright owner's entry into the same market.

Posting and Storage

Making copyrighted works publicly available over the Internet raises obvious copyright issues. The most common means of doing this is by storing copyrighted works on publicly accessible servers or by posting copyrighted material on Internetrelated services, such as bulletin board services or web sites. These uses can violate a host of exclusive rights, but may, in some circumstances, constitute a noninfringing fair use.

Storage of Digital Files. In *UMG Recordings v. MP3.com,* various record companies sued an Internet company, MP3.com, for storing personal MP3 music files created from personal copies of compact discs sold by the plaintiffs.By opening an account with MP3.com, an individual could store his or her MP3 music files on MP3.com's central servers for play at a later time and place. MP3.com argued that the copying necessary to provide this service was a "fair use." Rejecting this argument, the court found that copying the recordings to facilitate their retransmission through another medium was not a "transformative" use, nor was it a time-shifting transformative use (e.g., video taping a television program for viewing at a later time). The court also held that the recordings at issue were at the core of intended copyright protection and the amount copied was excessive. Most importantly, the court concluded that MP3.com's business model had an adverse impact on the recording companies' market for selling compact music discs as well as on other derivative markets.

Web Site Postings. In *Veeck v. Southern Building Code Congress International*,the Fifth Circuit Court of Appeals held that an unauthorized posting of copyrighted "model codes" for municipalities and localities infringed on the owner's reproduction and publication rights. Without the defendant's permission, plaintiff posted defendant's copyrighted model building codes on plaintiff's nonprofit web site.Regarding the plaintiff's fair use argument, the court noted that when "use of a copyrighted work is noncommercial, defeating a fair use defense requires 'proof either that the particular use is harmful, or that if it should become widespread, it would adversely affect the potential market for the copyrighted work.'"

The potential harm to the defendant precluded plaintiff's asserted noncommercial fair use of the copyrighted codes, since the "posting of the codes on the Internet could prove harmful by reducing the defendant's market and depriving it of income used in its socially valuable effort of promulgating and revising model codes."*Bulletin Board Services* (BBS). A number of early infringement cases on the Internet involved the unauthorized posting of copyrighted material on electronic bulletin board services. A bulletin board service (BBS) is a computerized version of bulletin boards found in stores and other public places where people can leave messages. Generally, BBSs are run by local computer user groups. Essentially, a BBS is a host computer that is accessible by direct dial and can operate independent of the Internet.

However, many BBSs also have web sites which connect the BBS to other similar services and interested users.

Los Angeles Times v. Free Republic,a recent case, involved a bulletin board that posted the entire text of many news articles originally published on two newspapers' web sites. The purpose of the posting was to encourage BBS members to add commentary and criticism. The newspapers sued for copyright infringement.

The BBS operator sought summary judgment on its fair use defense, which the court rejected. The court found that the market for viewing articles online, for selling copies of archived articles, and for licensing others to display or sell the articles would be adversely affected by the availability of verbatim copies on the defendant's web site. Although the web site was non-commercial and promoted critical comment, the defendant failed to show that verbatim copying of the articles was necessary to achieve its purposes.

In a related issue, the court in Religious Technology Center v. Netcom On-Line *Communication Services* determined, on summary judgment, whether an Internet service provider (ISP) that allowed a BBS to reach the Internet was liable for the infringing activity of the BBS's users.While the court rejected a theory of direct copyright infringement, it held that the ISP may be held secondarily liable for the infringing BBS postings it stores and disseminates over its servers.

On the question of whether the ISP had a valid fair use defense, the court determined that while the provision of Internet access is commercial, it "also benefits the public in allowing for the functioning of the Internet and the dissemination of other creative works, a goal of the Copyright Act."The court went on to conclude that because the Internet service provider's "use of copyrighted materials served a completely different function than that of the [copyright holder], [the first] factor weighs in [the Internet service provider's] favor."Turning to the third prong, the court found that the service provider "copied no more of the plaintiffs' works than was necessary to function as an Internet service.

2

History and Evolution of Cybercrime

Information technology has become the best tool to foster instructional practices in educational institutions. Computers and the Internet are powerful information tools. By their very nature they facilitate almost instant exchange and dissemination of data, images and materials of all types. This includes not only educational and informative material but also information that might be undesirable or anti-social. In many colleges and universities of the developed world, email has become the preferred means of communication and many provide Internet access for staff and students.

However the new techonologies also present opportunities for crime, much of it just traditional crime using new technology tools. There is no commonly accepted definition of what computer crime means, however for the purposes of this information we identify a number of roles computers can play in crime. Firstly, a computer can be the target of crime, for example, when someone is intent on stealing information from, or causing damage to, a computer or computer network. Secondly, a computer can be the tool used to commit an offence, such as fraud or the distribution of child pornography. Thirdly, a computer stores evidence, and even though the computer is not directly used for criminal purposes this evidence can be of great value to criminal investigators.

History of Cyber Attacks

The idea of theft is as old as the concept of privately owned property, and an element of almost all societies is dedicated to taking as much as possible of what isn't theirs—by whatever means they can. As soon as it was widely recognized that computers store something of value (information), criminals saw an opportunity.

But just as it's more difficult to target a robbery victim who stays locked up in his own home every day, the data on closed, standalone systems has been difficult to steal. However, when that data began to move from one computer to another over networks, like the robbery victim who travels from place to place, this data became more vulnerable.

Networks provided another advantage: an entry point. Even if the information that was of value was never sent across the wire, the comings and goings of other bits of data opened up a way for intruders to sneak inside the computer, like a robber taking advantage of the victim's housemates who leave the doors unlocked on their way out.

In the early days of computing and networking, the average criminal didn't possess either the necessary hardware or the technical expertise to seize the digital opportunity of the day. Computers were million-dollar mainframe monstrosities, and only a few of them were in existence.

An aspiring cybercriminal could hardly go out and buy (or steal) a computer, and even if he did, it's unlikely that he would have known what to do with it.There were no "user-friendly" applications; working with early systems required the ability to "speak" machine language—that is, to communicate in the 1s and 0s of binary calculation that computers understood.

The cybercrime problem emerged and grew as computing became easier and less expensive.Today almost everyone in industrialized countries has access to computer technology; children learn to use PCs in elementary school, and people who can't afford computers of their own can use PCs in public libraries or on college campuses for free, or they can rent computer time at business centers or Internet cafés.

Applications are "point and click" or even voice-activated; it no longer requires a computer science degree to perform once-complex tasks such as sending e-mail or downloading files from another machine across the Internet. Some of today's cybercriminals are talented programmers, but most are not.Advanced technical abilities make it easier for cybercriminals to "do their thing" and cover their tracks, but these abilities are by no means a job requirement.

During the period of standalone computers ENIAC was a behemoth, requiring more than 1500 square feet of floor space—more than many of today's "starter homes."This gigantic machine used more than 17,000 vacuum tubes and could do about 1000 calculations per second, compared with the millions of calculations per second attained by compact, inexpensive modern PCs.

ENIAC was quite an accomplishment, but the good doctors involved in its development didn't rest on their laurels. In 1949, they introduced the Binary Automatic Computer (BINAC), which stored data on a magnetic tape. Shortly thereafter, they invented the Universal Automatic Computer (UNIVAC), the first commercially marketed computer, under a grant from the U.S. government.

When the first UNIVAC was delivered to the U.S. Census Bureau in 1951, it was the size of a room and cost $1 million.The manufacturer eventually built 46 UNIVACs for government and business customers.The UNIVAC used magnetic tape, which was faster than the IBM punch card system that was its direct competitor. These early computers had some inherent security advantages:They were huge and expensive, they were standalone systems, and most of the world didn't really know what a computer was, much less how to use it.

It wasn't long before scientific types were enamored of computers.The Programmed Data Processor (PDP-1), developed and marketed by Digital Equipment Corporation (DEC) in the 1960s, was the first computer used for commercial time sharing. Because numerous people and businesses were using the same computer, the data and programs stored on it were vulnerable.Thus the first doors to hacking were opened—and despite the efforts of systems administrators, security product vendors, and law enforcement, those doors have never been closed since.

Evolution of Cybercriminals

In the 1960s, the term *hacker* was used to refer to someone who was considered a "real programmer," who had mastered the computer systems of the day and was able to manipulate programs to do more than they were originally intended to do. In the late1960s and early 1970s, hacking became associated with the radical underground ("yippie") movement and took on an antiestablishment flavor. Law enforcement agencies began to arrest *phreakers* for tampering with the phone system.

In the 1980s, the FBI made some of the first high-profile arrests of computer hackers (including that of Kevin Mitnick, who became something of a "martyr to the cause" in the hacking community). Movies such as John Badham's *WarGames* in the 1980s and Iain Softley's *Hackers* in the 1990s brought into the mainstream the concept of the hacker as a brilliant and somewhat romantic figure who breaks the law (but usually for noble purposes).

Hacking in the modern sense of the word—as applied to someone who breaks into systems, usually remotely—couldn't have come into its own without the network. However, we mustn't forget that networks existed long before there were computers. In the 1940s, when the first real computers were being developed, today's huge global telephone network, the construction of which began in the late 1800s, had already been steadily growing for 60 years.

The first electronic hackers broke into the phone system to make long distance calls without having to pay for them.These telephone network hackers became known as *phreakers.*Yet another term that originated during the early years of electronic communication is *cracker*, used to describe someone who "cracks" a system's security; this term now often refers to someone who specializes in cracking passwords.

An MIT student named Stewart Nelson, who figured out how use MIT's computer to generate the tones to access the phone company's long distance service, was one of the first known phreakers. Some especially talented phreakers were able to reproduce these tones merely by whistling, but most phreakers used a device called the *blue box*, which was a tone generator set to reproduce the 2600Hz frequency.

Today's phone systems don't use the 2600 tone for long distance access, but there is still an active contingent of phone phreakers who take advantage of the complexities of modern systems to find new ways to exploit the telephone system technology to their benefit.

Phreakers

John Draper, a U.S. Air Force veteran and engineering technician for National Semiconductor who went by the alias of Cap'n Crunch, is generally credited with designing the original blue box after discovering that the toy whistle included in boxes of Cap'n Crunch cereal could produce the 2600Hz signal that granted access to AT&T's long distance service. Draper was arrested and served time in a California minimum-security prison for this infraction. According to legend, he held seminars while in prison, teaching other inmates how to hack the phone system. He was later arrested again in New York.

Steve Jobs and Steve Wozniak, who later founded Apple Computer, are reported by several sources (including Wozniak himself, who worked for Draper prior to meeting Jobs) to have made and sold blue boxes in the early 1970s.

The British phone system had its own phreakers, dating back to the time when the "Toll A" hack was discovered and exploited to make free long distance calls. Later, British phreakers constructed "bleeper boxes" that served the same purpose as the blue box in the United States but used different sets of frequencies.

In addition to the original blue box, phreakers constructed a number of other devices to outwit the phone system.The *red box* replicates the tones that are produced when coins are deposited in a pay phone, and a *black box* allows calls placed *to* the phone to which it is attached to be made free of charge. Not all phone phreaking was done for the purpose of circumventing long distance charges.

Manipulation of the phone system was also popular with people engaged in other criminal activities, to cover their tracks when conducting illegal business over the phone.The *cheese box* was devised to connect two lines at a location in such as way as to allow bookies or drug dealers to receive calls from another remote location and go through the cheese box to disguise the number at which they were actually located.

A huge wealth of information about phreaking is available on the Web, including detailed instructions for "wannabe" phreakers.The phreaker "attitude" (disdain for large corporations such as the telephone company and a belief in the "right" of those who are clever enough to rip off these corporations) formed the basis of the later hacker subculture. Many of the first computer hackers began their criminal careers as phone phreakers.

Network Hackers

In the 1970s, the first affordable personal computer, the Altair 8800, became available. The machine was sold as a kit that the buyer had to put together, and it didn't do much once it was built because the owner also had to write his or her own programs for it. Nevertheless, the Altair gave birth to hacking as we know it today; this device made it possible for individuals to own their own computers and learn to program.

Other relatively low-cost computers followed; the Commodore 64 was a popular "toy" that introduced many youngsters, mostly teenage boys, to the joys of programming and, later, full-fledged hacking. Radio Shack's TRS-80 (affectionately known as the *Trash 80*) and the original IBM PC brought more powerful computing to people who were eager to find new ways to exploit the systems' capabilities. But it was the PC network that really opened the floodgates for all hacking that followed.

The first computer "networks" were not actually made up of networked computers. Rather, they consisted of one computer—a mainframe—and many terminals that connected to the mainframe, ran programs on it, and accessed its files. Although these terminals were networked in one sense of the word, they were "dumb" terminals that possessed no processing power of their own.This mainframe time sharing linked multiple users and allowed them to share files and printers. It also allowed early hackers to access the files of other mainframe users.

Disadvantages of mainframe computing included the high cost of the computer and the single point of failure that it represented. If the system went down, no one on the network could do any computing, since the terminals they operated were dumb. *Minicomputers* (such as the DEC PDP and VAX and the IBM AS/400) were created as lower-cost, more compact alternatives to the full-fledged mainframe, but these machines still relied on dumb terminals and worked in essentially the same way as the older devices.

Eventually, the search for a better way led to the development of smaller, less expensive computers (then called *microcomputers* and later called *personal computers,* or *PCs*) that could sit on a desktop.With each worker having a full-fledged computer on the desktop, there was much more fault tolerance than with the mainframe; if one computer went down, everyone else could keep computing.

However, workers missed some of the advantages of the mainframe environment, such as the ability to easily share files with others."Sneakernet"—copying files to a floppy disk and physically transporting the disk to another computer—was the workaround, but that system didn't work so well when the users who wanted to share files were in different parts of the building or the files were too large to fit on a floppy.

The solution was to connect the standalone desktop computers in a network, providing the resource-sharing benefits of mainframe computing with the fault tolerance of decentralized computing.

Networked PCs give us, in many ways, the best of both worlds.They also give the hackers among us a way to access our information, whether we want to share it or not. In the 1970s, researchers at Xerox's Palo Alto Research Center (PARC) developed Ethernet, which still forms the basis of most local area networks (LANs) today. DEC, Intel, and Xerox got together in 1979 to create Ethernet standards (originally called DIX after the company names) to make it easy for vendors to create compatible products.

In 1983, the Institute of Electrical and Electronics Engineers (IEEE) released the 802.3 specifications based on thick coaxial cable and called 10Base5. Ethernet gave companies a way to link their computers easily and relatively inexpensively, especially after the IEEE developed and standardized a second version based on thin coax (10Base2) in 1985. Networked PCs began to emerge as a popular alternative to mainframe computing (or in some cases, an addition to it) in the 1980s.

In addition to networking PCs together at one location to create a LAN, PCs could be used to link to one another from remote locations using a modem and a telephone line.This led to the advent of the *bulletin board service (BBS)*, a computer system equipped with one or more modems so that users can dial in and download files from it or post messages to a "board" to carry on public virtual discussions. Ward Christensen and Randy Suess developed the software for the Computerized Bulletin Board System (CBBS) in the 1970s in Chicago.They described it in an article published in *Byte Magazine* in 1978.The system was a huge success, and BBSs sprang up all over the country.

Early hackers and phreakers seized on the BBS idea as a way to communicate with one another and share their tricks and techniques. Most boards included both the public forum and e-mail service between members of the BBS. Although many BBSs were legitimate "places" where computer hobbyists could gather and share the software they'd written themselves or discuss issues of the day, the BBS had a natural appeal to the criminal element.The BBSs spawned the first large-scale method of distributing *warez* (hacker jargon for pirated software), often computer games. Other BBSs specialized in sharing of pornographic pictures and/or stories.

Early BBSs were slow (2400-baud modems were top of the line at the time) and expensive unless you were lucky enough to live in the same locality as your cohorts or you were a phreaker who didn't pay for long distance calls. It was often difficult to get connected because most BBSs were operated out of someone's home on a limited budget, so the average systems operator, or sysop (the person who ran the BBS), didn't have a large number of modems and phone lines.While some sysops ran these systems for fun, many (especially those who dealt in pornography) charged members a monthly or annual fee to connect.

Some BBSs are still in operation today, but the popularity of these forums began to decline in the 1990s, when Internet access became commercially available at an affordable price and the graphical nature of the World Wide Web made the BBS systems with their ASCII drawings seem hopelessly outdated.

Online Services and Cybercrime

Back in 1957, no one could have foreseen the communications system that today connects friends, relatives, business partners, and strangers all over the world. In 1957, President Dwight Eisenhower authorized the creation of the Advanced Research Projects Agency (ARPA) in response to the launch of the Soviet Union's first artificial Earth-orbiting satellite, Sputnik.

ARPA's first project was to develop a satellite of its own for the United States; it was not until years later that the agency began to work on computer and networking technology. In the 1960s, as the cold war with the Soviet Union continued, the government considered the possibility of nuclear war and how to maintain communications if the unthinkable occurred.This is where ARPA's involvement with computing began.

Dr. J.C.R. Licklider was appointed to run ARPA's computer technology project in 1962. He was largely responsible for building the beginnings of a wide area network connecting government/military and university sites, using redundant links so that if one node was taken out, messages could still get through by taking a different path.This network, based on packet-switching technology developed in the 1960s, was called the *ARPANet*.

The first node of the network was installed at the University of California at Los Angeles (UCLA) in 1969. Additional nodes were installed at Stanford, U.C. at Santa Barbara (UCSB), and the University of Utah, located at Salt Lake City.

In the early 1970s, e-mail—which today is still the Internet's "killer application" in terms of popularity—was invented. Gateways were devised to connect networks using different architectures, and specifications were developed for what would become File Transfer Protocol (FTP).

By the end of the 1970s, Usenet newsgroups had been established, and the first interactive multiple-user sites, called *multiuser dungeons*, or *MUDs*, had appeared. By that time, the ARPANet had been up and running for over 10 years, although it was still limited mostly to university and government sites.

In the early 1980s, the TCP/IP suite was defined as the standard for communications on the ARPANet. Soon after, name servers were created to handle the translation of "friendly" computer names and paths to the IP addresses computers use to route messages to one another.

William Gibson's sci-fi novel *Neuromancer,* published in 1984, coined the term *cyberspace* as a description of the online world. At that time, no one had any idea just how crowded cyberspace would soon become.

The worldwide network was steadily growing, but in 1986 there were still only about 5000 hosts (computers) on the Net. About this time, the National Science Foundation (NSF), which maintained the Internet backbone, established five supercomputer centers, which resulted in a dramatic increase in available connections. The next year, 1987, the number of hosts had risen to either 10,000 or 28,000 (depending on the source you consult), and a year after that, the NFSNet backbone was upgrade to 1.544Mbps (a T-1 line). By 1989, all sources agree that there were over 100,000 hosts on the network.

In 1990, the ARPANet ceased to exist, and the Internet was born. In actuality, ARPA had already been split into two parts in the 1980s: Milnet (for military use, which was integrated into the Defense Data Network) and the NSFNet, which handled civilian communications. NSF upgraded the backbone again, to T-3 speed (44.736Mbps).The NSFNet grew into today's commercial Internet, and by 1992, there were over 1 million Internet hosts. In 1995, NSFNet gave the backbone services to interconnected commercial network access providers (NAPs) and became a research network again, establishing the very high-speed Backbone Network Service (vBNS) that connected the five supercomputer centers.The commercialization of the Internet had begun.

During the early ARPANet days, security was both a major concern to the military contingent and almost a nonissue to research scientists, who were more interested in what the technology could do than in securing it)—hence the splitup of the network.The small number of nodes on the network limited the scope of the threat posted by security breaches.

In the early days of the commercial Internet, getting online was not necessarily an easy proposition. Unlike today's operating systems, the operating systems in use (mostly Windows 3.*x*) didn't come with the Transmission Control Protocol/ Internet Protocol (TCP/IP) stack built in; also not included was the software required to make a dialup connection to the Internet and use its applications (Winsock).

The correct software had to be downloaded, complex text configuration files had to be edited, and it took a certain amount of technical savvy (not to mention patience) to put it all together and successfully log on to the Internet. In addition, users had to log on through the first commercial Internet service providers (ISPs), which were often brand-new ventures launched by a couple of nerds on a shoestring budget, working out of an apartment.These entrepreneurs generally didn't provide user-friendly setup CDs to configure the settings for you, as most ISPs do today.

There was, however, an easier way to get online: the online service. Companies such as CompuServe, Prodigy, and AOL offered access to their network "communities." Once logged onto the service, users could download software, post messages to bulletin boards, find information on a wide variety of topics, and waste amazing amounts of time in chat rooms or holding private conversations through instant messaging.

The big lure of these services was ease of use.They provided a disk that usually installed the proper software automatically and configured users' computer settings, so users didn't have to know anything about much of anything to get "connected."

In their early days, the services were excruciatingly expensive by modern standards; in the 1980s it cost US$25 an *hour* to connect to CompuServe. Prices dropped in the early 1990s to around US$3 an hour, and eventually the services went to unlimited usage plans that cost less than US$20 a month. The online services were *not*, in their early days, ISPs. Rather, they were private wide area networks (WANs) in which members interacted with each other but not with the "outside world" of the Internet—they were similar to BBSs on steroids. Later the services provided e-mail gateways so that their members could exchange e-mail with others outside the private network.They also added access to the World Wide Web.

Today, most online services are also ISPs. Even though ease of use associated with regular Internet providers has increased dramatically, many "Net newbies" still find the online services easier to use.This ease of use attracts criminals (along with legitimate users) who are not particularly technically proficient.

Another benefit of the online services that attracts criminals is the anonymity they offer. Generally, if you set up an account with a regular ISP, you're assigned a user account name and an e-mail address based on that name. It's possible to get the ISP to change your account name, but it's a lot of trouble and can't be done too frequently. Services such as AOL allow users to create secondary "screen names" that they can change whenever they want, making it easier for a criminal to change identities and cover his or her tracks.

However, in 1988, a *worm* (a selfreplicating program) was released on the Internet and attacked computers running Berkeley UNIX, spreading all across the United States, infecting thousands of computers and shutting down a large portion of the Internet.This was the wakeup call; Internet users suddenly realized that some in their midst harbored malicious intent. Many more virus attacks and hacks were to follow.

By 1991, e-mail users had begun to consider the possibility that their Internet communications would be intercepted. Philip Zimmermann released an encryption program called Pretty Good Privacy (PGP) that could be used to protect sensitive messages. PGP was also used by criminals to hide evidence of their crimes from police.

The first cyberbank, called First Virtual, came online in 1994, opening up vast new opportunities for hackers. Also that year, researchers began work on the "next generation" of the Internet Protocol, called IPv6.The primary purpose of the new version was to address the anticipated shortage of IP addresses using the current IPv4's 32-bit address space, but another concern addressed by the new protocol version was to be IP security.

In 1995, the U.S. Secret Service and the Drug Enforcement Agency (DEA) obtained an Internet wiretap to help build a case against suspects who were accused of producing and selling illegal cell phone cloning equipment. In 1996, Congress became concerned about the amount of pornography that was being exchanged over the Internet and passed the Communications Decency Act (CDA), which was later declared unconstitutional. Meanwhile, a cracker was able to shut down the Public Access Networks Corporation in New York using a hack attack that was described in *2600 Magazine.* A "cancelbot" launched on Usenet destroyed over 25,000 newsgroup messages, and in the same year, U.S. Department of Justice, Central Intelligence Agency, and Air Force computers (among others) were hacked.

In the next three years, many more government agencies and prominent companies had their systems hacked, including the U.S. Department of Commerce, UNICEF, and the *New York Times*. eBay, Microsoft, and the U.S. Senate Web sites also fell victim to hackers.The Melissa virus caused company email servers to shut down.A fraudulent Web page that was designed to appear to be a Bloomberg financial news story resulted in the shares of a small tech company increasing 31 percent in response to the false "news."

As we entered the 2000s, a huge, distributed DoS attack shut down major Web sites such as Yahoo! and Amazon.Apache, RSA Security, and Western Union were hacked, the Code Red worm attacked thousands of Web servers, and the Sircam virus hit e-mail accounts all over the world.

However, malicious code and hack attacks comprised only a small portion of the overall criminal activity that in some way used or depended on the Internet. From the infamous "Nigerian letter" scam to the use of the Net to plot the September 11, 2001, terrorist attacks, crime was running rampant on the network —and still is today.

The new millennium brought with it the growing popularity of new and exciting technologies, such as wireless networking and low-cost, high-speed "always on" connectivity options through Digital Subscriber Line (xDSL) and cable modem.These technologies have become available in increasing numbers of places. Unfortunately, these technologies also provide new opportunities for cybercriminals, for a number of reasons, which we explore here.

Vulnerabilities of New Technologies

Most of us are much more security-conscious today than we were a decade ago, in regard to both our computers and life in general. Certainly there are more security products on the market today than there were a few years ago. Lawmakers all over the world have "cracked down" on behaviors such as unauthorized access that not long ago weren't covered by criminal statutes.

We seem to have all the most important elements for reducing the incidence of cybercrime:We have the laws; we have the tools; we even have the widespread awareness that is sometimes the most difficult component of a crime prevention effort.Why, then, is cybercrime not only *not* going away, but steadily increasing? An important reason for the increase in cybercrime is the whirlwind pace at which new technologies are being developed to make our computing experience more productive, easier, faster, and more fun. However, convenience and performance often come with a price, and that price is security.

Cybercriminals love new technologies, including:

— Broadband

— Wireless

— Mobile computing and remote access

— Sophisticated Web technologies such as Java, ActiveX, and so on

— Fancy e-mail programs that support Hypertext Markup Language (HTML) and scripting

— E-commerce and online banking

— Instant messaging

— New operating systems

Cybercriminals also love standardization. If everyone uses the same operating system, or the same Web browser, or the same e-mail client, or if all vendors adhere to the same specifications, the potential attacker has much less to learn and a much larger playing field. Let's discuss why these new technologies and the standardization of computer and networking technologies are so dear to the heart of the cybercriminal.

Broadband Technologies

Broadband technologies such as xDSL, cable modem, and satellite Internet services have made Internet users' lives easier, but they have also made it easier for hackers to invade those users' computers and networks. Because individual computers attached to broadband networks such as cable modem or DSL behave more like computers attached to a network than like individual computers that use telephone lines to dial into the Internet, it is easier to exploit the technology to gain unauthorized access. As a consequence, broadband users need to be much more security conscious than dialup Internet users.

A network is vulnerable to an attack from outside only when it is connected to an outside network.When most users and companies were connecting to the Internet with analog modems or dialup ISDN connections, their vulnerability to attack was limited because the system was available to outsiders only during a session. When you finished doing what you wanted to do on the Net, you disconnected and your system "disappeared" from the Internet. Additionally, most ISPs use Dynamic Host Configuration Protocol (DHCP) to assign IP addresses to dialup users.This means that your Internet-connected computer gets a new IP address each time you hang up and reconnect.

DSL and cable are referred to as "always-on" technologies. You don't have to dial up a connection each time you want to get onto the Internet; instead, you stay connected 24 hours a day, seven days a week. This makes it quicker and easier for you to access Internet resources. It also makes it easier for you to run a server, allowing other authorized users to remotely access shared files on your system. Because your IP address generally stays the same, since you don't disconnect, these authorized clients can find your server more easily from one communication session to the next. Of course, powering the computers down breaks the connection (and "shuts the door" to potential hackers). However, today's computers are made to run continuously (and except for some peripherals such as the monitors, generally run better and last longer when they do), so many technically savvy users never turn their systems off.

The problem with 24/7 technologies is that they make it easier for *unauthorized* folks to access your system, too. Your exposure is much greater because you're "always open for business," giving a hacker more time to mount a brute force attack to guess your password or figure out which TCP/UDP ports might be open and vulnerable. Furthermore, because your IP address stays the same, it's easier for these hackers to return to your system next time they want to do a little virtual breaking and entering.

Another advantage of broadband is the increased connectivity speed. Unlike an analog modem that's limited to 56Kbps (and practically speaking, less than that due to federal regulations and line considerations), DSL and cable companies offer high-speed downloads and often higher upload speeds as well.This means improved performance on your end—but if your service offers a high upload speed, it also means an intruder will be able to snatch your files more quickly.

Luckily, in terms of security if not usability, most broadband services are asymmetric.That means that upload and download speeds are not created equal; typically for consumer accounts, the upstream transfer rate is limited to 128Kbps by cable companies and anywhere from 128Kbps to 764Kbps by DSL providers. Even with these limitations, however, upstream speed is generally at least twice that of an analog modem—a boon to hackers downloading data from your computer to their own.

The problems linked to high-speed 24/7 connectivity and high-speed data rates associated with consumer broadband technologies also exist with traditional 24/7 high-speed business solutions such as T-1. However, because most T-1 lines are connected to companies that employ IT professionals, it is more likely that security measures are in place to offset the security risk.

The problem with cable and DSL is that these technologies have brought high-speed, always-on access to home and small office users who can't afford the high cost of T-1.These less sophisticated users are also less likely to be aware of the security risk or to have the technical expertise or budget to implement the proper level of security. Most small offices and a growing number of home users run Network Address Translation (NAT) software of some type to share Internet access with multiple PCs on a small LAN.This provides a small measure of security to the systems on the local network because NAT assigns private IP addresses to the NAT client computers.These addresses are not visible on the

Internet. However, the NAT host computer that is directly connected to the Internet is exposed.

If you have a computer that uses a broadband Internet connection and the computer is *not* connected to a LAN and is not functioning as an Internet server, one step you can take is to be sure file and print sharing is not enabled on that computer. Another common security hole on Windows systems is called an *IRDP vulnerability*. This is caused by the ICMP Router Discovery Protocol (IRDP) that is enabled by default on Windows machines that are configured as DHCP clients. IRDP isn't needed when the DHCP server specifies router information, but hackers can use it to add default route entries that will then override the default route that the DHCP server provides.You can disable IRDP by editing the Windows Registry.

Some cable users have found that when the NIC used to connect to the cable modem was installed by the cable company (or by the user),Windows automatically binds the card to both TCP/IP and the Microsoft Networking service. Having this interface bound to Microsoft networking opens their systems to others on the cable segment. Which is more secure: DSL or cable? Cable is a shared connection (that is, everyone in your neighborhood is part of the same network segment). In essence, this creates a local area network.That means that your neighbors have access to your system, much as neighboring computers on any LAN have access to one another.

As on a regular LAN, there are ways to protect yourself from your LANmates. The Data Over Cable Service Interface Specification (DOCSIS) standard for cable modems provides some measure of security because modems that comply with this specification support data encryption between the provider's hub and the user's computer.

Data is *not* encrypted between the provider and the end destination (that is, when traveling over the Internet), but this standard does help to address the "neighborhood segment sharing" problem, since others on your cable segment will not be able to read your data if they intercept it. Cable networks that use DOCSIS standards also prevent your computer from announcing its shares to the network using NetBIOS protocols. Be aware, though, that a hacker could still connect to your computer if he or she knows your computer name or IP address.

DSL users are connected directly via their phone lines to the telephone company central office (CO).Thus DSL provides fewer vulnerabilities to hackers—but this does not mean a DSL connection is a secure one. No one should use a broadband Internet connection without also using a firewall to protect from outside intruders. Firewalls can filter both incoming and outgoing data and block open ports to cut hackers off from their usual entry points. A firewall can be either a hardware device or a software program that runs on the Internet-connected computer.Microsoft's newest desktop operating system,Windows XP, even comes with built-in firewall software.

Wireless Technologies

Wireless technologies are emerging as the Next Big Thing in computer networking for the twenty-first century.The IEEE's 802.11b specifications provide standards for wireless networking at 11Mbps using spread-spectrum radio transmission. A newer specification, 802.11g, allows for wireless communications at about twice that rate: 22Mbps.This specification gives mobile computers the ability to boldly go where no Ethernet cable has gone before—and still stay connected to the local network and/ or the Internet. Microsoft's latest operating system,Windows XP, includes built-in support for 802.11b wireless networking. Setup of a wireless network is easy using the XP interface.

Bluetooth is a wireless technology designed to enable a wide variety of portable devices, such as personal digital assistants (PDAs) and mobile phones—as well as more traditional laptop and notebook computers—to connect to the Internet. Unfortunately, the ability to access a network without any physical connection makes it that much easier for hackers to do the same, because they don't have to worry about "plugging in" to the cable. If a network includes a wireless access point, it is vulnerable to outside intruders even if there is no remote access server or Internet connection on the network.

It's important to understand that most are based on radio transmissions that go out over the airwaves. For example, Bluetooth devices transmit in the 2.4GHz spectrum.This is an unlicensed range, so anyone can transmit and receive on it. Transmissions over the airwaves can be intercepted, and 2.4GHz antennas, amplifiers, and transceivers are readily available.The signals can be picked up hundreds of feet from the access point; high-gain antennas increase this distance. All this is fodder for the cybercriminal.

It's not quite as bad as it sounds, though.Two types of spread-spectrum radio transmission are supported by IEEE 802.11:

— Frequency Hopping Spread Spectrum (FHSS)

— Direct Sequence Spread Spectrum (DSSS)

The first type, FHSS, uses *frequency hopping,* which means the signal "hops" or changes from one frequency to another. This means a hacker can't just tune into a set frequency and listen in, as you can do with narrowband radio broadcasts that use a fixed frequency.This provision gives only a small measure of security, however.

DSSS uses a redundant bit pattern for each bit of data that is transmitted (called a *chipping code*).The purpose is to make the signal more resistant to interference and provide some fault tolerance; if some of the bits get damaged during transmission, the redundancy allows for the original data to be recovered.

The 802.11 wireless standards actually do provide for security measures, such as authentication and encryption. Unfortunately, the encryption used by these technologies is weak and can be broken relatively easily. Small handheld devices, such as mobile phones, have limited memory and processing power.This means larger encryption algorithms that require heavy processing can't be used.

A program named AirSnort that runs on Linux exploits the weaknesses of wireless encryption to discover the WEP encryption key simply by passively monitoring the wireless network.The fact that WEP uses static keys (rather than more secure dynamic keys that change at regular intervals) makes this technology especially dangerous.

The weakness of the encryption algorithms aside, wireless encryption covers only the transmission between a user's computer and the wireless gateway that connects the wireless network to the Internet.When the data reaches the Wireless Application Protocol (WAP) gateway, it must be transferred from the wireless network to the wired network. In order to do this, the wireless communication, which is in the form of encrypted Wireless Markup Language (WML), must be decrypted and then re-encrypted in order to be transmitted on the cabled network. The data is vulnerable during this "encryption gap."

Another problem is that even though the data is encrypted, the source and destination addressing information is not. Finally, encryption is not necessarily enabled by default when wireless networking components are installed. According to a BBC News broadcast of March 8, 2002, an informal survey conducted by i-sec discovered that 67 percent of networks in the survey had encryption disabled.

According to an article, Exploiting and Protecting 802.11b Wireless Networks, published on the ExtremeTech Web site in April 2002, security tests were conducted using a Yagi antenna on the deck of the Ziff Davis office building in Manhattan.Testers were able to find over 60 wireless access points, and an astonishing 79 percent of them did not have encryption enabled. Similar vulnerabilities were found in Jersey City and Silicon Valley. The practice of driving around with a portable computer that's equipped with a wireless NIC, searching for wireless network signals, is called *war driving* (a term coined by security expert Peter Shipley) or *drive-by hacking.*

Organizations and individuals who use wireless technologies don't want to give up the convenience, but they are recognizing that extra security precautions are necessary.One way to add security to wireless networks is the use of hardwarebased security devices such as smart cards; users are not able to access resources without swiping the issued card through a card reader.

Other wireless security measures that can be implemented either by wireless device manufacturers or by wireless LAN (WLAN) administrators include:

— Moving wireless hubs away from windows and toward the center of buildings

— Ensuring that wireless encryption is enabled

— Disabling broadcasts on the network's hubs

— Changing the default settings such as the Service Set Identifier (SSID) and the default password on the wireless access point or router

— Limiting the number of wireless access points can also make the WLAN less vulnerable to unauthorized access

— Assigning static IP addresses to wireless NICs and disabling DHCP on the wireless router

— Security auditing, in the form of a media access control (MAC) address tracking system that can be used to track the devices that access the wireless network

— Installing a firewall between the WLAN and the wired LAN

— Putting the wireless access points in what is known as a *demilitarized zone* (DMZ), also referred to as a perimeter network or screened subnet, and configuring wireless users to use a virtual private network (VPN) to create a secure tunnel into the network

— Treating the wireless network as though it were a public network and not sending sensitive data over it without taking precautions (such as using another encryption method along with WEP)

Mobile Computing Technologies

Over the past decade, the high price of portable computers—laptops, notebooks, and handhelds—has steadily dropped while the processing power has come to equal that of desktop machines.This trend has been great for on-the-go businesspeople, who can now continue to work when they're on the road, with little loss in productivity. Often, getting the work done requires access to the corporate network, and accordingly, most of today's laptops come with built-in modems and Ethernet ports.

Travelers can dial directly back to the remote access server on the company LAN or dial up a local ISP and "tunnel" back to the corporate network through the Internet. More hotels are now providing high-speed Internet services, to which you connect via your portable computer's Ethernet port or PCMCIA (PC Card) NIC. Once you connect to the company's LAN via one of these remote access methods, your computer becomes another (temporary) node on that local network, and remote access technology allows you to perform any task you could do from a wired workstation on site.This is great for employees who must be away from the office—but it's also great for hackers looking to come in uninvited.

Every point of access on the network creates one more vulnerability. A remote access server provides a point of access, as does a VPN server. Of course, mobile computing also provides an additional security consideration:the possibility that the entire computer will be stolen.You might think this isn't a security problem if you don't store sensitive information on the portable's hard disk—but what about your VPN or remote access software configuration, which would allow anyone in possession of the computer to connect to the company network?

Although a password may be required for network logon,many users set up their systems to "remember" their passwords so they won't have to take the time to type them in each time they connect, thus defeating the purpose of password security if someone else takes possession of the computer.

Mobile computing presents some special security concerns. User authentication is one of the biggest. Unlike the corporate environment, where there are security guards, surveillance cameras, and fellow employees to physically recognize the presence of suspicious strangers around the computer systems, a user connecting remotely to the network offers no assurance that he or she really is the person whose credentials are being used.

There's one more reason cybercriminals love today's powerful, lowcost mobile computers: Now they *can* take it with them. Lightweight, compact computers are much easier to transport to a "secure" location such as a pay phone, from which a hacker can initiate a hard-to-trace online session, or to take on "drive-by hacking" expeditions to find wireless LANs to which they can connect surreptitiously.

The first line of defense in mobile security is physical security of the portable computer.There are many laptop locking devices on the market. Mobile users should be instructed to keep a close watch on their computers, especially in airports and other crowded public places.You can buy hardware devices that will emit a "homing" signal and software programs that can be set to automatically dial in or contact "home base" through the Internet the first time the computer goes online after someone uses an incorrect password.

Various means are available to address the mobile user authentication problem. For example,Windows-based remote access servers offer the ability to configure user accounts so that *callback security* is required.This means that a specific telephone number is associated with that user's account.When the user dials into the network and enters the username and password, the server doesn't provide immediate access. Instead, it disconnects and calls the user back at the specified telephone number and only then allows access to network resources. This means that someone who has stolen a user's laptop with "remembered" passwords will not be able to access the network unless the hacker is also calling from the user's home or other previously specified location.This system works well for telecommuters, who usually dial into the network from their homes.

It is less useful for traveling employees, who might be calling from a different hotel each day. Similar systems are available that, instead of hanging up and calling the user back, identify the caller's number through caller ID and check it against a list of approved remote user numbers. If the number is on the list, the user can access the network.This would work better than callback for users who dial in from several different fixed locations.

Windows remote access servers allow you to set remote access policies that control whether remote connection attempts are authorized. Another method of authenticating remote users is the Remote Access Dial In User Service (RADIUS) server. RADIUS is a security protocol that supports multiple authentication methods and allows encrypted transmissions between client and server. RADIUS allows administrators to place limitations and restrictions on the tasks that a remote user can perform once that user is logged onto the network, based on settings for that user account. RADIUS can be used to centrally manage multiple remote access servers or VPN servers using the same set of policies.

Other measures that can improve the security of remote access connections include:

- Use of dedicated application access so that the remote user connects to a specific application on the network server using proprietary protocols. This means the connected user will not have access to any other network resources.This system works well in cases in which remote users need to perform only a specific task, such as checking e-mail.
- Use of two-factor authentication. In this system, two separate components are required to successfully access the network: the first is *something* you know, and the second is something you have or something you are. In addition to providing a password (something you know), you must also provide a hardware token, smart card, or a biometric identifier such as a fingerprint (something you have).
- Deployment of callback security for telecommuters and other remote access users who connect from the same location all the time.
- Use of encryption for sensitive communications over public phone lines or through the Internet.

— Use of remote access policies to restrict what dial-in users can do on the network as well as the days and times of day they can connect and other parameters.

Remote access opens company networks to employees, partners, and customers —and to unwanted intruders. It is important to take extra security precautions at every point at which your network can be accessed from the outside.

Web and E-Mail Technologies

Today's World Wide Web is a different "place" from that of 10 years ago. In the early 1990s, most Web pages consisted of plain text and graphics.The limitations of HTML and the slow bandwidth of most Internet connections dictated that Web designers follow the "keep it simple, stupid" caveat. Today it's a whole different ballgame.Web sites flash and dance.

Increasingly sophisticated presentations and interaction are possible with technologies such as Java and Visual Basic scripting and ActiveX controls. New markup languages such as Dynamic HTML (DHTML) and XML provide opportunities for Web designers to push the envelope.The prevalence of high-speed connections makes bandwidth-intensive Web applications feasible. But once again, one man's (or woman's) feature enhancement is another's security hole. *Scripts* are programs that run when you access Web sites in which they are embedded.What the program does is up to the programmer. Most Web scripts serve useful, harmless purposes; for example, a Java script can produce visual effects such as falling snow or animated text. Applets and scripts can also create calculator tools, chat interfaces, games, or clocks.

Malicious programmers, however, can use these technologies for their own nefarious purposes.Although there are many kinds of attachments,Web page components, and other aspects of Web and e-mail technologies that can present security risks, the most worrisome are those that can actually run code and do things on (or to) your computer.

In most cases, this kind of material—sometimes known as *active content* because it can run itself on your machine—is benign and is designed to perform specific tasks to manage or update a page display, run an animation, perform a calculation, and so forth. But active content can also include malicious code that can do all kinds of nasty things to your PC if allowed to run unchecked.That's why most security experts recommend that users (and network administrators) screen active content. By far, the safest security policy is to refuse to accept active content. However, this alternative could also prevent you from being able to use features that you need that depend on active content.

Other strategies include requiring the active content to show valid credentials before being allowed to run or accepting active content only from specified (known safe) Internet locations or addresses. If written by a malicious programmer, active content can introduce viruses, worms, back doors, and all kinds of other questionable code and access points to your systems and networks.

This same problem (along with a few others) that applies to Web browsers also applies to today's sophisticated e-mail client programs that allow the display of HTML mail, running of scripts embedded in mail messages, and sending of attachments. Here again, active content—which makes sophisticated presentations and interaction work—opens the door to potential security breaches.

Scripts and controls can be used to perform tasks on your computer without your knowledge—including monitoring your communications with others or deleting key files on your hard disk. Java and ActiveX give programmers a way to run any program they like on your computer. Malicious code can emulate a login box request and send the password credentials you enter to the hacker, all without your knowledge.

There are many ways that your Web browser can be exposed to malicious code. Following links from other Web sites or clicking on links in e-mail messages or newsgroup posts can take you to a page that runs a malicious script.

Protection from Malicious Code

Because of these very security concerns, a number of mechanisms have been developed to protect unwary Web users from potentially dangerous content. Code can be digitally signed to verify that it is from a legitimate vendor and thus safe to download. Most modern Web browsers allow you to select the level of security you desire.You can disable Java and/or ActiveX, or you can set the browser to prompt you when a script is encountered so that you can make the decision about whether to run it based on your trust (or lack thereof) in the site.

For example, the Microsoft Internet Explorer Web browser allows you to either select a predefined security level (Low, Medium Low, Medium, or High).The level selected determines whether unsigned ActiveX controls will be downloaded and whether you will be prompted before downloading any content that is considered potentially unsafe. If none of the preset security levels works for you, you can also create your own customized security settings. Because the Web is one of the most-used Internet applications, it is important to ensure that you don't expose your system and your network to a hack attack through the code that is run by your browser.

Protection of E-Mails

All of the same risks that are inherent in Web browsers that run scripts and controls surface again when you use an e-mail client that allows you to receive messages formatted in HTML, which can have the same sorts of malicious code embedded. In the early days of e-mail, programs were simple and messages were basically text only.This system provided much less opportunity for security breaches, but it also limited the usefulness of e-mail communications.When it became possible to send files as attachments to messages, the doors opened to a new risk. Initially, attachments were usually photos (.jpg, .gif, etc.) or text files that were too large to include in the message itself.

The problem arises when an attachment is or contains an executable program. Files with .exe, .com, or .bat extensions are obvious examples, but there are many other files that can run code, infect your system with viruses, and otherwise do great damage.These files include screensaver files (.scr) and link files (.lnk). Registry (.reg) files can edit the Windows Registry, and .url files can open Web pages that run malicious code. Document files (such as Word .doc files) can include macros, which are simply small programs; virus writers have taken advantage of the powerful Visual Basic for Applications (VBA) support in

Microsoft's Office applications to create macro viruses that can infect your system if you open the macro-containing document.

To avoid the problems associated with modern e-mail programs, you might want to configure your e-mail client not to display a "preview pane" (which displays messages, including HTML messages, without you having to click on them to open them), install an antivirus package that checks both incoming and outgoing mail for viruses, and take care not to open e-mail attachments with suspicious extensions unless you are absolutely certain of their origin.

In the case of most e-mail–distributed viruses, once a virus has infected a machine, it automatically sends itself to everyone in the victim's address book, appearing to be a message from the victim.This means that you can't assume an attachment is safe just because you recognize the name in the "From" field of the message.

In recognition of these problems, e-mail programs are building in more security —sometimes so much that the functionality of the mail client is severely crippled. For example,Microsoft Outlook 2002 by default will not allow you to open executable file attachments, even if you are absolutely certain of the file's validity and safety.This restriction might be fine for the "average" user, but not for people like software developers who need to send programs back and forth on a regular basis. Luckily, you can get add-on software that will allow you to change this overprotective behavior if it's a problem for you.

In many cases, the correct application configuration can save you a good deal of grief. For example,Microsoft Word now allows you to set security so that the system will prompt you before running any macros. If you open a document that shouldn't have macros and get the dialog box asking you whether to disable macros, elect to do so and you can read the document itself without running the potentially dangerous code.

Threat to E-Commerce and Online Banking

E-commerce, online banking, and related technologies have resulted in millions of dollars of financial transactions taking place across network connections. Perhaps the growing popularity of online shopping, banking, stock trading, and other financial activities is best summed up by the title of an article published by Nua about a Penn State study of Internet activities: *Sex out, E-commerce in.* The study indicated that Internet users as a whole are spending proportionately less time each year searching for sexually oriented material online and more time on business and financial transactions.

The open nature and wide scope of the Internet make it a perfect forum for conducting business; transactions can be conducted between a business and a customer across the street or across the globe.Those wide-open cyberspaces also expose both seller and buyer to risks that aren't present, or at least not to the same extent, in face-to-face transactions. When buyers must enter their credit card information to make a purchase, they are rightfully concerned that the information could fall into the wrong hands. Some would say that providing this information to a Web-based vendor is no different than giving it out over the telephone—but that philosophy doesn't take into account the difference between a telephone connection and an Internet transaction.

A phone call establishes a temporary dedicated private circuit directly between the caller and recipient;

although it is possible to tap into a telephone line, it is relatively difficult and expensive. Information sent via e-mail or a Web form travels over the very public Internet and goes through a number of nodes (servers and routers) along the way. It is vulnerable to interception and, unless the information is encrypted, could then be used to make unauthorized purchases.

The Internet also makes it easy for criminals to exchange this illegally obtained information. Lists of stolen credit card numbers are posted in newsgroups that are frequented by criminally minded individuals. In fact, the incidence of credit card fraud in online transactions is significantly greater than that for more traditional purchase methods.

According to a paper on credit card fraud published by the National White Collar Crime Center (NW3C) Research Section, estimates put the overall percentage of credit card fraud at about .08 percent of all credit card transactions, but the same source estimates fraud accounts for 3 percent to 5 percent of all those transactions conducted online.

Credit card purchases are not the only online financial transactions that expose consumers to risk. An increasing number of busy professionals are turning to the convenience of online banking for depositing and transferring money and paying bills. Although one might assume that banks, of all businesses, would be certain to have adequate security measures in place, a number of serious security holes have been discovered in some online banking systems.

In 2000, a flaw in the software used by an online bank based in Palo Alto, California, allowed anyone to open an account and then use that account to transfer funds from other customers' accounts without their permission using the account and routing numbers for the victim's account. Barclays Bank in the United Kingdom has reported security breaches in its online services that allowed customers' account information to be displayed to others. Similar problems have haunted other online banks around the world.

Today it seems that almost any financial transaction—from buying Girl Scout cookies to financing a home loan—can be conducted online.Any time you send sensitive information across the Net, you need to be aware of the risks. Last November, a computer security firm discovered a security flaw in the software that many mortgage brokers use to process loan applications.The flaw resulted in the display on the Internet of applications filed by hundreds of consumers, exposing such information as their Social Security numbers that could be used to steal their identities.

Protection of E-Commerce and Online Banking Transactions

Protecting e-commerce and online banking transactions must be a joint effort involving everyone who participates.The "protection triad" includes:

— The IT professionals who run the e-commerce or bank servers

— The consumer who uses e-commerce or online banking services

— The law enforcement community

The role of the IT professional is to secure the servers that are used for financial transactions, using technologies such as firewalls to keep outsiders from breaking in and stealing confidential information and strong encryption to protect the data when it travels from customers through ISPs to the server. Consumers must also be made aware of the dangers of online transactions so that they can take precautions, such as never giving credit card numbers and similar information online unless the Web site or form is a secure site. Consumers need to understand how to secure the home or office computers that they use to conduct online transactions, because their passwords and other personal information can be stored on their own local hard disks, and how to properly configure security options on their Web browsers.

Law enforcement agents must understand the scope and nature of the online fraud problem and should be educated in what information to gather, how to track down and preserve the evidence, and federal and private resources that can provide guidance and information in handling these types of cases. Jurisdiction, as always, is an issue.

The U.S. government established the Internet Fraud Complaint Center (IFCC) in May 2000 to provide an avenue for victims of online crime to file complaints and submit information to a centralized source rather than having to figure out what law enforcement agency has jurisdiction in their particular situations.The IFCC is operated by the FBI in partnership with the NW3C.

Instant Messaging Technologies

Instant messaging (IM) gives Internet users the ability to communicate in near real time with others anywhere in the world. It's an application that inspires a lot of passion:You either love it or hate it. Some people consider "IM'ing" a time waster and an intrusion, but others happily spend hours at home and work communicating this way. It does have advantages even in a business environment; you can get immediate questions answered without waiting for e-mail to go through or paying for long distance telephone calls. Convenient as it might be, instant messaging software (AOL's AIM and ICQ, Microsoft's MSN Messenger,Yahoo Instant Messenger, and others) poses serious security risks, along with providing criminals an easy way to communicate with one another to plan or discuss their crimes.

By default, most of the IM products are configured to stay active all the time, running in the background, and broadcast that the user is online even when the program interface is closed.This wouldn't be so bad except that the IM software also allows for sending of files between users, which means it's not that difficult for a knowledgeable hacker to use this open channel to transfer viruses hidden in Trojans or other unwanted "gifts." Other IM programming flaws can be exploited to execute malicious code as well. For example, some versions of AOL's ICQ and AIM programs were subject to a "buffer overflow" error if the application was sent more code than it could handle; this error allowed hackers to download malicious code to the targeted computer. Although this particular problem was fixed in subsequent software versions, it is impossible to know how many people unknowingly continued to use the flawed version of the software after the problem was revealed.

In February 2002, two bugs were reported in Microsoft's MSN Messenger software: one that exposes names and e-mail addresses on the victim's contact list and another potentially more dangerous bug that can allow a hacker to take control of the program and perform tasks on the user's computer by exploiting a security hole in Internet Explorer known as the *Document.Open ()* bug. Although IM vendors are pretty good about releasing fixes for these security flaws when they become known, new exploits are continuously being found, and many users don't update their software often.They could remain unaware of the problem until they are victimized.

Network administrators and other IT professionals should stay current on these issues by subscribing to security newsletters and regularly visiting security bulletin Web sites.They should then work to educate the users in their organizations about security vulnerabilities and see that updates and fixes are installed when they become available. Another possible security problem is the IM log that records the content of online discussions.These could be accessed by a hacker, exposing private conversations. In fact, IM vendors generally admit that their products are not secure and, in their end-user agreements, they recommend that you not use them for sensitive communication. Nevertheless, many business users discuss personnel matters, financial and budgeting decisions, marketing strategies, and other confidential information via instant messages.

Another problem with IM software is that there is no reliable authentication mechanism to verify that a person sending you a message across the Internet really is who he or she claims to be.Anyone can set up an IM account using a false name and information. For this reason, instant messages are also a popular way for pedophiles, scam artists, and other criminals to make contact with their victims and get to know those they target for their crimes.

Protection from Instant-Messaging Security Flaws

The best way to avoid the security problems inherent in instant messaging is not to use the programs or to use them only when necessary and never for sensitive or mission-critical communications. Many businesses block the ports used by IM software in their firewalls to prevent employees from using the programs. If you must use IM, here are a few things you can do to reduce the risk:

— Block file transfers and game-playing capability at the firewall.

— If users only need to communicate with others within the company, administrators can install IM programs that run on the intranet, reducing exposure to the Internet.

— Users should close the program completely when not using it.

— Users should not accept messages from people they don't know.

— Some IM programs allow you to block the display of your IP address to recipients. If you don't completely trust the person with whom you're conversing, you might want to enable this feature.

— Turn off message logging or, if you need to keep logs, move the files to a location other than the default and encrypt them.

Like the other technologies we've discussed, IM software can be used for either good or evil. Because the programs were originally designed for recreational chatting, security hasn't been a high priority, but if you use instant messaging in a business environment or on a home machine that has sensitive data stored on it, it's important to consider the security ramifications.

New Operating Systems and Applications

User demands and rapidly increasing hardware capabilities result in new operating systems being released every few years. Each new incarnation includes nifty new features, and in many cases, the new versions are more stable and faster performers than their predecessors. It seems as though users hardly have time to learn one operating system before it's time to upgrade.The same goes for productivity applications; once you upgrade the operating system, you often need a new version of your word processing or graphics software to go with it. This system is great for the software companies, which get to make a lot of new sales, of course—but it's also great for hackers, for a couple of reasons:

— New software, especially operating systems that include dramatic changes such as Microsoft's Windows 2000 or Apple's Mac OS X, never comes out of the box perfect, regardless of how many tireless hours of beta testing went into it.Version 1.0 is almost always at least a little buggy, and hackers can often exploit those bugs.

— Even if the software *is* perfect, users are not yet well acquainted with it and could misconfigure it in ways that open up security vulnerabilities.

Thus cybercriminals are happy when you upgrade to the latest and greatest. It opens up a window of opportunity for them before bugs are reported and security patches released—and before users learn to configure the new systems for best security. There's not a lot you can do about this, other than perhaps foregoing the temptation to be an "early adopter" of every new software program that comes along. Even if you wait for version 2.0 or later, you'll still have to deal with users' learning curve. Network administrators should be especially wary and monitor closely for security breaches during the period immediately following major upgrades or the rollout of completely new software.

Standardization

It might sound like a contradiction to say that cybercriminals love the new and different and then turn around and say that they love standardization, but it's really not.What we mean by standardization is everyone (or a vast majority) using the same operating systems, applications, protocols, and hardware. Standardization makes things easier for hackers because they don't have to learn how to manipulate dozens of different types of systems.

When a product becomes a standard, it also becomes a favorite target of hackers, crackers and virus writers. Users of Windows operating systems are more vulnerable to attack than users of other systems in large part because the vast majority of computer users run Windows. It's common sense: If you want to do the largest amount of damage with a virus, you write one that targets the most popular operating system. You don't see many hackers out there working on how to crack OS/2 Warp (IBM's client operating system that has a very small percentage of the desktop market). It might not be a coincidence that many of the existing OS/2 client deployments are in the banking industry, a business that needs all the security it can get.

Standardization makes possible networking and computer communications on a large scale, but it also makes it possible for hackers to do their damage on a large scale. Standards are good in that they make computer hardware and software work more smoothly, but if your business deals with particularly sensitive information, one way to make your systems less vulnerable is to go with a proprietary rather than an industry-standard solution.

Cybercrime in Educational Instistutions

For further and higher education institutions, hacking, fraud and theft, copyright abuse, obscene content (including child pornography) and harassment are obvious areas of concern in the control of computer use. Also the confidentiality of emailed information can be lost when an email is intercepted (either through illegal hacking or legitimate monitoring); when it is inadvertently sent to the wrong address; or when it is simply read by an unauthorised or unintended person.

People have tended to see email as casual communication like perhaps a telephone call. Things may be written in an email that would never be put in a letter, but, unlike spoken communication, there is no emphasis, so the message can be more easily distorted or interpreted as offensive. In addition emails, unlike private letters, may be regarded as published information originating from the institution. As a consequence, liability for its publication may attach to the institution.

Cybercrimes used against education institutions include the following:

Hacking

Hacking has been defined as "Deliberately gaining unauthorised access to an information system." A variety of motives lie behind hacking attacks and not all hackers and virus writers pose the same threat. The vast majority of incidents are nuisance attacks rather than serious, malicious assaults, but victims of the former may still suffer financially (e.g. through computer downtime). Perpetrators can be from the traditional criminal world exploiting the power of the new tool, disgruntled employees using their inside knowledge, the curious and thrill-seekers treating the medium as a challenge and those engaged in industrial espionage and information warfare.

The cost and inconvenience involved in a hacking incident can be substantial. The handiwork of some hackers, or "crackers" as they are known in the computer industry, has had disastrous results. In May 2000 the "love-bug" virus crippled at least 45 million computers world-wide and caused millions of pounds worth of damage.

Denial of service attacks: Denial of Service (DoS) is the name given to attacks involving hackers preventing the normal flow of Internet traffic to a web site or e-Business.

Telephone-related hacking: Telephone hacking is illegal access into an organisation's telephone system by a person to make, for example, free long-distance calls. Breaking into phone systems is called "phreaking". Many people do not even know that it is possible to hack into an organisation's telephone system. One much publicised victim of telephone hacking is New Scotland Yard, which it is claimed lost £1 million. Hackers accessed its telephone system through the organisation's DISA (Direct Inward System Access) facility on a PBX. DISA is a facility which enables employees, who are working at home or travelling, to call into the corporate telephone system, enter an authorisation code and gain access to system features or make long distance calls.

In UK, the Computer Misuse Act 1990 (CMA) was introduced primarily to deal with the various guises of computer hacking. These anti-hacking laws created the following offences:

— Obtaining unauthorised access to computer material;

— Unauthorised modification of computer material; and

— Unauthorised access with intent to commit or facilitate commission of further offences.

Maximum sentences for these offences range from six months imprisonment and/or a £500 fine to five years imprisonment and/or an unlimited fine. The Computer Misuse Act 1990 (CMA) has been successfully applied against the range of offences for which it was envisaged. However, the Act predates the enormous growth of the Internet and it is not well suited to deal with some misuse including a denial of service attack. Instead, in England and Wales, such an attack might be prosecuted as an offence under the Criminal Damage Act; in Scotland, the attack could be prosecuted as the common law crime of malicious mischief.

In addition the Telecommunications Act 1984, s.43 makes it a criminal offence to use a public telecommunications network to send 'grossly offensive, threatening or obscene' material, and a 'public telecommunications network is widely enough defined to cover Internet traffic which goes through phone lines or other cables.

Computer crime has an obvious international dimension. It can involve persons and acts in different countries. Jurisdictional difficulty has been addressed in the CMA in that an offence will have been committed if either the accused, the accessed computer or the unauthorised modification is in the domestic jurisdiction.

Almost all hackers can be deterred with common-sense policies. Although conventional wisdom has it that the largest threat is often from within an organisation i.e. - employees / students, it is essential that any computer network has properly configured firewall protection as well as intrusion detection and other filtering software.

Fraud and Theft

Computer-related fraud can be defined as private gain or benefit by:

— altering computer input in an unauthorised way;

— destroying, suppressing, or stealing output;

— making unapproved changes to stored information; or

— amending or misusing programs (excluding virus infections).

Given the nature of electronic fund transfers - one often quoted estimate is that the United Kingdom's currency reserves could be transferred abroad in 15 minutes - it is a matter of considerable practical importance, especially because there may be a jurisdictional issue where the proceeds of a fraud are moved outside the United Kingdom. One of the most common type of fraud is the illegal use of credit card numbers belonging to other people.

Fraudulent activity is not substantially altered by the use of data communications. The computer is simply a modern tool by which the crime is carried out. Computer Fraud as defined by the Audit Commission can be divided it into 4 categories:

1. *Input Fraud* — Entry of unauthorised instruction, alteration of data prior to entry or entry of false data. Requires few technical skills.
2. *Data Fraud* — Alteration of data already entered on computer. Again requires few technical skills.
3. *Output Fraud* — Fraudulent use or suppression of data. Less common than input or data fraud but evidence is difficult to obtain.
4. *Program Fraud* — Altering or creating program for fraudulent purposes. This is the real computer fraud. Requires technical expertise and is apparently rare.

In the UK most cases involving computer-related fraud have been prosecuted under existing criminal legislation and this has been adequate to cope with these offences. However applying traditional criminal concepts to acts involving intangible information has meant that some amendments have proved necessary to resolve issues of applying existing definitions to the new technology. For a fraud to be deemed to have occurred it was necessary that a 'person' had to have been deceived. Where the machine was deceived to obtain a service no 'person' as such was deceived.

The Theft Act 1968 required that property 'belonging to another' must be obtained for fraud to occur. In a mortgage fraud case where the accounting data recorded in the accounts was altered this did not constitute the obtaining of property 'belonging to another' and necessitated the creation of the offence of 'obtaining a money transfer by deception'.

Theft of Information — whether information might be regarded as property sufficient to found a charge of theft has also caused a lot of debate. Misuse of information is generally considered a matter for civil rather than criminal law. With recognised forms of theft, the conduct has two elements. The owner loses possession and the thief acquires possession. In the case of Oxford v Moss, Cr App R 183, Moss, a student at Liverpool University, discovered and removed a copy of an examination paper he was due to sit. As it was part of his plan that the original paper would be returned the issue centred on whether his conduct amounted to theft of the confidential information contained in the paper. There was no loss in the traditional sense to the owner of the property - Liverpool University. Moss was acquitted on the basis that confidential information could not be regarded as property.

The significance of this is now somewhat reduced in that the offence of "unauthorised access" in s.1 of the Computer Misuse Act 1990 provides a method of tackling a similar computer based "theft" of information.

Gullibility Scams -Internet pyramid schemes: Despite the fact that many of these schemes have been around for years, the Internet gives criminals the ability to reach millions of innocent people who are tempted by the prospect of easy money.

Pyramid schemes are usually just get-rich-quick plans that focus on the recruitment of new members and the multi-level marketing of products. The formula usually requires the person to make a small up-front payment after which it is claimed they can make thousands of pounds.

They usually never receive the promised products or the expected pay-off.

Intellectual Property Offences

In the UK generally civil remedies will provide compensation to wronged intellectual property rights holders and most of the copyright criminal offences, contained in s.107 of the Copyright, Designs and Patents Act 1998, are concerned with commercial activity. However, one of the offences covers the act of distributing an article otherwise than in the course of business to such an extent as to affect prejudicially the owner of the copyright. In addition encouraging the copying of software for sale can lead to the criminal offence of incitement.

Breaches of intellectual property rights will frequently involve no loss of tangible assets and often the rights holder does not know that they are a victim until a defendant's activities are specifically identified and investigated. According to s.107 a criminal offence is committed if a person knowingly sells an infringing copy of a protected work without the licence of the copyright owner. In the UK, criminal penalties for companies and their directors can include unlimited fines and up to two years in prison.

In the United States in May 2000 the rock band Metallica filed a civil law suit against Yale University, Indiana University and the University of Southern California and five additional unnamed universities as well as other defendants alleging that the universities' failures to block access to 'Napster', the music sharing search facility, made them liable for contributory and vicarious copyright infringement. It is of course easier to file such a suit than it is to achieve a successful result. The outcome will be awaited with interest by many institutions who provide email and Internet access.

ECriminal proceedings for copyright infringement are not common but there have been a number of successful convictions and software pirates are likely to be imprisoned and / or heavily fined. In the United States criminal cases involving intellectual property are tracked by the Department of Justice at the website. Other forms of criminal law may also be relevant such as trade description law, forgery and the deception offences. Clearly by appointing Peter Knight, a specialist in covert operations, surveillance and criminal intelligence as its new Chief Compliance Officer in August 2001 the Copyright Licensing Agency (CLA) is making it plain that detection of copyright infringement is its new priority. Offenders may now be more likely to find themselves being pursued in the civil and criminal courts.

Pornography and other harmful offensive content

The availability of hard-core pornography, including material aimed at paedophiles, has helped to give the Internet a bad name. Firstly there is pornography directed at adults which is illegal for adults to read or view according to the rules of a particular legal system. The material most universally accepted as falling into this category is child pornography. Secondly there is pornography or other sexual material which is not illegal for adults to access, but may be considered harmful or upsetting for others including children to see.

Storage and transmission of material which is considered obscene is a criminal offence under the Obscene

Publications Acts 1959 and 1964. The traditional approach of UK legislation has been that it is acceptable to possess obscene material in private as long as there is no attempt to publish, distribute or show it to others - particularly for gain. However in the case of child pornography, which in its nature features the sexual abuse of children, Parliament has taken the view that the phenomenon is so heinous that possession as well as circulation should be criminalised. The primary Acts here are the Protection of Children Act 1978

The CJA 1988 makes it an offence for a person to have any indecent photograph of a child in his possession (s.160), on top of the pre-existing offences of taking, distributing, showing or publishing such a photograph. A child is defined as a person under the age of 16.

The test for 'obscenity' is set out in the Obscene Publications Acts 1959 and 1964 in s.1(1), and it is defined as material which tends to 'deprave and corrupt' those who are likely, having regard to all relevant circumstances, to read, see or hear it.

The offences are created by s.2, of the Obscene Publications Act 1959. It is an offence to publish an 'obscene' article whether for gain or not; and this is further extended in the Criminal Justice Public Order Act 1994, ss.84-87 which deals specifically with 'Obscene publications and indecent photographs of children'.

In Scotland, where the Obscene Publications Act does not apply, the Civic Government (Scotland) Act 1982 makes it an offence to publish obscene material and prosecution is the responsibility of the Procurator Fiscal Service.

The Obscene Publications Act 1959 does not extend to Northern Ireland. Obscene material is generally dealt with under the common law offence of publishing an obscene libel.

An interesting recent development centres on the US company Metropole News Group which runs 70,000 websites with some 7.8 million pages downloaded per month. A Director of Metropole, Stéphane Perrin, (a French citizen) was arrested in London and charged with three offences under s.2 of the Obscene Publications Act, 1959 and 1964. His conviction and 30 month sentence is under appeal and the indications are that his defence will raises key questions about the Internet and freedom of expression.

The European Commission has called for increased efforts to protect minors in the context of new media services. The Community's Safer Internet Action Plan also encourages initiatives such as the development of rating and filtering systems and the establishment of "walled gardens", i.e. portals where the operators guarantee the quality of sites which can be accessed through them.

The problem of illegal, harmful, distasteful or offensive content on the Internet is of course not restricted to pornography. Internet content exists which contravenes the rules enacted to prevent the making of anti-religious statements, the making of racist or inflammatory statements and the making of politically subversive or seditious statements. The BBC reported in June 2000 that David Copeland, the notorious nail bomber of a gay pub in London, had discovered how to make bombs from the Internet.

The hasty removal from U.S. Government websites in the aftermath of the terrorist attacks of September 11th in New York of all types of information including environmental data indicates that even apparently harmless information could in certain circumstances represent a danger.

The Internet Watch Foundation (IWF) was launched in late September 1996 to address the problem of illegal material on the Internet, with particular reference to child pornography. By using a classification system in order to enable users to customise the Net to their own requirements and providing a hotline to encourage whistleblowers it is hoped that self regulation can take the place of censorship of the Internet.

The Internet is an international medium and although views will differ on how it should be managed in other ways, all countries should be able to agree on legislation for child abuse and pornography. Balancing the need to protect minors with the need to maintain freedom of expression is continuing to prove to be difficult.

Harassment

Internet harassment has become a concern for many people. This form of harassment includes directing obscenities toward others, as well as making derogatory comments based for example on gender, race, religion, nationality, sexual orientation. This type of Internet crime can take place often in chat rooms, through newsgroups, and even through the sending of hate email to targeted mailing lists. Unsolicited email messages and advertisements can also be considered to be forms of Internet harassment where the content is offensive or of an explicit sexual nature.

Under s.1 of the Malicious Communications Act 1988 it is an offence to send an indecent, offensive or threatening letter, electronic communication or other article to another person and under s.43 Telecommunications Act 1984 it is a similar offence to send a telephone message which is indecent offensive or threatening. Both offences are punishable with up to six months imprisonment and/or a fine. Because the Malicious Communications Offence is more wide ranging than the Telecommunications offence it is more likely to be charged by the Police than is the Telecommunications Act offence.

Cybersmearing is essentially using the Internet as a medium to defame or criticise an organisation or individual, often by ex-employees. The reach and accessibility of the Internet makes it a very powerful tool in this respect.

Software piracy

Software piracy is a boom business. The theft of software, the copying of licensed software without permission, and software counterfeiting continue to be risks for all organisations. Further and Higher Education Colleges are as vulnerable as any organisation. It is a crime which can be punished with imprisonment and a fine. Software piracy is not only a matter for the police; it can also involve customs officers, trading standards authorities and advertising standards authorities, as well as civil actions for damages. It is important to bear in mind that, even if it is individual employees who are obtaining and using illegal software, an Institution and it office holders can be held liable. Ongoing auditing and tracking of software use is essential in any large organisation in order to ensure continued compliance with software licensing agreements.

Obscene publication

Storage and transmission of material which is considered obscene is a criminal offence under the Obscene Publications Act 1959 and 1964. It is clearly easier to gather and store offensive material over the Internet and use college servers as a repository for this material than in the paper based world. The key issue for Colleges is that such material may already be stored on their company's systems without their knowledge.

Student and employees as victims of Cybercrime

Some identifiable areas of difficulty include:

— online harassment in terms of race, gender, sexual orientation, religion, age, ethnicity or disability

— racist and xenophobic propaganda,

— cyberstalking, bullying at work

Precisely what duty of care an educational institution owes to its students and staff in regard to the use of information technology and crime is somewhat uncertain. It is suggested that a Health and Safety policy will address these issues when they occur outside the IT area and it should be ensured that such a policy extends to the situation where a student or member of staff experiences or is exposed to content that is hateful, racial or ethnically objectionable.

Students and Employees as offenders

As offenders, students and employees may do the following crime:

— infringements of copyright

— computer-related fraud,

— violations of network security

— illegal pornography

Monitoring and policing of users is a sensitive area. Interception of users communications can be acceptable to investigate or detect unauthorised use of telecommunication systems. Employee contractual terms should spell out what is acceptable. In addition a focus on acceptable use in training and awareness raising exercises will encourage an environment that does not tolerate misuse.

Prevention

Many Educational institutions now routinely monitor staff and student emails and the sites that they visit online. If these users see that vigilance is demonstrated by the organisation in policing the use of email and the Internet this may have the effect of reducing the likelihood of Internet harassment and abuse. Under the legislation Regulation of Investigatory Powers Act 2000 employers are entitled to intercept email to investigate or detect unauthorised use of their telecoms systems. There are no reliable statistics available on the full scale of computer-related crime. The estimates vary wildly and the number of intrusions detected and reported up to now, probably under-represent the scope of the problem. Below are some extracts or summaries of survey reports from the UK and the USA which give an indication of trends in computer abuse and crime. The signs are that criminal abuse of computer networks is a substantial problem and that it is increasing in volume.

The incidence of Information Technology abuse within the UK has been reported every three years by the Audit Commission since 1983. Based upon surveys of both the public and private sectors the reports provide a snapshot of the level of IT abuse, the reasons for its occurrence and the risks that organisations need to address. Confidence in the technologies that are influencing the way we live and work is being eroded. Organisations must address the issues contained in this report if the explosion in the use of new technology is not to be matched by a similar increase in IT abuse.

In the 2001 survey by the Computer Security Institute (CSI), 85% of the respondents detected computer security breaches within the prior twelve months. More than 70% of the respondents cited their Internet connection as the point of attack, compared to 31% who identified their internal systems as the source of attack. Some examples of attacks and abuses on the rise:

— Forty percent of respondents detected system penetration from the outside.

— Thirty-eight percent of respondents detected denial of service attacks.

— Ninety-one percent detected employee abuse of Internet access privileges. Only 79% detected net abuse in 2000. Ninety-four percent detected computer viruses.

As providers of email and Internet access to large numbers of students and staff FE & HE Institutions may face potential exposure in a number of areas.

No institution wants adverse publicity either relating to abuse by its computer users or abuse perpetrated on its IT users. While further and higher education institutions work long and hard to build up brand and reputation, it is quick and easy to shoot them down via the Internet. The growth in "hate sites" as they are known particularly in the United States is an Internet phenomenon. Often run by disgruntled former employees or students a target institution can suffer enormously both in terms of public relations and resource deployment in resisting the attack.

Going forward many further and higher education institutions regard IT as the primary channel for information dissemination. A major consequence of incidents of IT crime and abuse is the likely reduction in confidence in information technology itself and its ability to perform that role. New legislations 1 ew ways of working increase the risk of an inadvertent breach of the law by an institution putting an onus on those office holders directly involved in IT to keep up to date with legal developments.

There are tried and tested preventative measures that are common sense and are relatively easy to apply. If students and staff are to be made aware of do's and don'ts then practical and easily readable IT security policies and protocols must be widely available. The regular review and updating of IT security procedures and processes and the application of these on a day to day basis does help to reduce the risk of IT abuse.

Can an institution be held responsible for crime and abuse committed by it's users? What onus is on a further and higher education institution to prevent crime committed by its computer users? The general rule is that an organisation is only answerable for its own acts. In some circumstances, however statute may impose liability on an employer for the acts of persons under its direction and control. Vicarious responsibility permits the attaching of responsibility for an offence to a person who did not intend to commit the offence, was not reckless, and who was not aware of the circumstances of the offence.

Further and higher education institutions are under an obligation to ensure that the activities of its computer users are conducted in accordance with the statutory regulatory framework. That responsibility cannot be avoided by delegating the day to day running of the business to a third party or to a technology unit. It is fair to expect that there are proper procedures in place to ensure that those with the day to day responsibility are (a) aware of the regulatory framework and (b) the importance of abiding by that framework.

Security

In order for FE and HE Institutions themselves not to be a victim of criminal behaviour what steps should be taken? What can Colleges and Universities do to protect users from crime perpetrated by means of computer networks including the Internet? What role can Colleges and Universities play in preventing crime on the Internet and ensuring continued confidence in electronic telecommunications?

One answer to these questions is security. There must be a reliable and secure IT network underpinning Internet use. Getting the balance right between providing information resource tools to students and employees and providing a secure study and employment environment requires constant vigilance.

While the Internet has clearly brought great opportunities for the education sector, it has also brought increased vulnerabilities including increased exposure to legal liabilities for the use and abuse of Internet communications by students and employees — cyberliability. As more reliance is placed on IT systems, it is vital that effective and workable security policies are established and implemented and reviewed regularly in an effective manner.

A vast amount of information on network security and protection techniques is available to guard against the latest intrusions both criminal and non criminal. Every modern organisation with a computer network must have an information security policy. Security in any system should be commensurate with its risks. According to the ISO/IEC 17799 standard, assessment of risks involves systematic consideration of the following items:

— The business harm likely to result from a significant breach of IT Security, taking account of the potential consequences of failures of information confidentiality, integrity and availability.

— The realistic likelihood of such a breach occurring in the light of prevailing threats and controls.

The UK Government stands firmly behind the information security standard and it is one of the key benchmarks used in its approach to protecting critical infrastructure.

Employers do have a right and sometimes a duty to make sure that their computer systems are not being used for purposes unconnected with work such as child pornography. It needs to be clear that security is taken seriously and that the computer network is liable to be monitored.

In the UK the National Hi-Tech Crime Unit, which became operational in April of 2001, is a multi-agency approach to tackling problems raised by the use of computers and the Internet for criminal activity of various types. The Unit, based in London, is comprised of representatives from the National Crime Squad, from the National Criminal Intelligence Service (NCIS), and from HM Customs & Excise. It aims to forge links with Computer Crime Units in police forces and other law enforcement agencies throughout the country.

The signs are that criminal abuse of computer networks is an increasing problem. There is a need for effective substantive and procedural laws coordinated at global, or at least at European level, to protect the victims of computer-related crime and to bring the offenders to justice. At international level various organisations have co-ordinated or harmonised activities against computer crime. One European Union initiative has concentrated on trying to ensure that minors will not be able to access harmful and illegal content carried over the Internet.

The Convention on Cybercrime adopted by the Council of Europe (CoE) on 8 November 2001 is the first international treaty on crimes committed via the Internet and other computer networks.

Dealing particularly with infringements of copyright, computer-related fraud, child pornography and violations of network security it also contains a series of powers and procedures such as the search of computer networks and interception. The main objective is "to pursue a common criminal policy aimed at the protection of society against Cybercrime, especially by adopting appropriate legislation and fostering international co-operation."

The Convention is the product of four years of work by Council of Europe experts, but also by the United States, Canada, Japan and other countries which are not members of the Organisation. On 14 February 2002 the

CoE has released its first draft of a protocol to the recently signed Convention on Cybercrime. The protocol deals with "the criminalisation of acts of racist or xenophobic nature committed through computer networks."

The terms of the draft protocol would make it an offence to, for example, post a message on a web page which threatens a serious criminal offence against a person or group of people for reason of race, colour or religion. Co-operation at this level is of course the most powerful way of ensuring a consistent international approach to the problem of Cybercrime. It is anticipated however that the United States eagerness to uphold its Constitutional principle of free speech may lead to some conflict before final agreement.

The controversial retention of traffic data by service providers and law enforcement practices related to traffic data retention generally was the subject of the recent EU Forum on Cybercrime session in Brussels on 27 November 2001. Some Member States are taking legal initiatives requiring or allowing service providers to store certain categories of traffic data, not needed for billing purposes, after the provision of the service but which are considered useful for criminal investigations. The conflict with data protection safeguards is obvious.

3

Cyber Warfare

The term 'cyber warfare' can be defined as any act intended to compel an opponent to fulfill the national will, executed against the software controlling processes within an opponent's system. It includes the following modes of cyber attack: cyber infiltration, cyber manipulation, cyber assault, and cyber raid. Let us define each of them:

— *Cyber infiltration:* Penetration of the defenses of a software-controlled system such that the system can be manipulated, assaulted, or raided.

— *Cyber manipulation:* Following infiltration, the control of a system via its software which leaves the system intact, then uses the capabilities of the system to do damage. For example, using an electric utility's software to turn off power.

— *Cyber assault :* Following infiltration, the destruction of software and data in the system, or attack on a system that damages the system capabilities. Includes viruses and overload of systems through e-mail (e-mail overflow).

— *Cyber raid:* Following infiltration, the manipulation or acquisition of data within the system, which leaves the system intact, results in transfer, destruction, or alteration of data. For example, stealing e-mail or taking password lists from a mail server.

Cyber warfare is the conduct of military operations according to informationrelated principles. This does not define the full degree of capabilities now possible in cyber warfare. Limiting the scope of cyber warfare to "information-related principles" does not describe what happens when an enemy disrupts the electrical power grid of a nation by hacking into the controlling software.

Information is not only at risk—the fundamental control of the civilization is. As technology progresses, this "fundamental control" will devolve into networks and software-controlled electronics. This transition has already occurred in aviation. In the past, 100 percent of an aircraft's performance and capabilities were defined by hardware—the physical makeup of the aircraft. Today in the most advanced aircraft, 75 percent or more of the aircraft's performance and capability is absolutely dependent upon the software. Without software, aircraft would not be controllable or reach the desired performance capabilities. In some cases, through software, aircraft performance is gaining limited independence from physical configuration.

Software dependence and hardware independence are growing. For example, modern aircraft fly by wire, their engines are controlled by wire, and their weapons are fired and dropped by wire. Systems that in the past were entirely hardware with mechanical control are being replaced by software with software control. Software defines the strength of modern systems, and provides a basis for the integration of many disparate items through networking. These networked software systems are under attack today, and the attacks are increasing.

In US, the current doctrines and instructions of the Department of Defense (DoD) do not adequately cover the scope of cyber warfare. The following all handle information warfare as a discrete part of a military system: Joint Publication (JP) 3-13, "Joint Doctrine for Information Operations"; JP 3-13.1, "Joint Doctrine for Command and Control Warfare"; and instructions such as DoD 5000.2-R, "Mandatory Procedures for Major Defense Acquisition Programs (MDAPs) and Major Automated Information System (MAIS) Acquisition Programs." Current doctrine does not address software as the major element of a military fighting system; yet as the above discussion shows, many software and software-controlled systems cannot be separated from the system being developed.

The F–22 weapon system is an example of a software-controlled aircraft system that contains and communicates with integrated information systems. The F–22 is not a closed system; external information systems update and integrate F–22 combat operations during flight. Through these external connections, not just the information systems but the basic software systems of the F–22 can be attacked. Current information warfare doctrine in the Joint Pubs is mainly concerned with security of external C^4I (command, control, communications, computers, and intelligence) systems integrated on the F–22, but softwareintensive systems make internal systems of the F–22 vulnerable to cyber warfare attack. Our doctrine must account for these vulnerabilities and provide methods of offense and defense. Definitions for building future weapon systems and in cyber forces doctrine and recommended methods to incorporate them follow.

JP 3-13, JP 3-13.1, and DoD 5000.2-R focus on information systems and not software-controlled systems; definitions these documents provide are not sufficient to describe the full range of cyber warfare. The CERT® Coordination Center does provide a strong set of common terms to define cyber system security for the DoD, but these terms do not discuss military doctrine or national security. Furthermore, these terms focus on current methods of defense against infiltration and attack; they do not focus on future cyber force capabilities.

Targets of Cyber Warfare

Any military system controlled by software is vulnerable to cyber attack. The first step in any attack is cyber infiltration; all systems that incorporate software are vulnerable to cyber infiltration. Actions following cyber infiltration can affect organizations via the transfer, destruction, and altering of records—cyber raid. Software within systems can be manipulated—cyber manipulation. Systems controlled by that software can be damaged or controlled—cyber manipulation. The software itself can be copied, damaged, or rewritten—cyber assault.

Military C⁴I Systems

Military C^4I systems are particularly vulnerable, and are the primary focus of DoD cyber-related doctrine. JP 3-13 and JP 3-13.1 both provide doctrine for information-related warfare. C4I systems are a very complex mix—from radios to radars, mainframes to personal computers. Military C^4I uses interfaces through the Internet, base and organizational local area networks (LAN), modems, civilian and military communication systems, navigation systems, and radios in all frequency ranges.

Military C^4I systems are extremely vulnerable because they interconnect. Cyber infiltration can enter at many points and potentially affect a myriad of systems. These systems and their interactions are so complex that any modern military organization is unlikely to trace the full potential of any single cyber infiltration. The possibility exists for cyber attacks of every type, and the results can be catastrophic. For instance, nuclear weapon control systems are incorporated into military C^4I. As demonstrated by recent incursions in DoD networks, databases, and Web sites, almost any dedicated foe can engage in cyber attacks against military computer systems. Since military computers are the core of national C^4I, successful IA and UA against such targets pose a national security peril.

Weapon Systems

No current DoD doctrine adequately covers cyber attacks on military hardware systems such as aircraft and vehicles that require software to operate. The F–22 is a cyber-controlled aircraft.Infiltration and degradation of the aircraft's systems directly or via its C^4I connections can be as devastating as shooting it out of the sky.

Cyber infiltration of the C^4I system providing data to modern aircraft allows an avenue for cyber raid, manipulation, and assault. Because many systems like the Global Positioning System (GPS) automatically update aircraft information and intelligence, they can allow undetected infiltration of the aircraft.

Intelligence, navigation, and communication systems are integrated to each other and input and output to a host of other aircraft systems—the flight control system (through the auto pilot), propulsion system (through the auto throttles), radar system, master warning system, and environmental control system.

Using the correct control sequences, inputs, or reprogramming, an infiltrator could produce any level of systems damage, from driving the aircraft off course to overwriting the flight control software.

Vulnerabilities

The first rule in identifying cyber warfare vulnerabilities is that any software-controlled system that can accept an input can theoretically be infiltrated and attacked! This means all systems that accept inputs are vulnerable. Fundamentally, cyber systems can be infiltrated in two ways—by physical and signal inputs.

Physical Infiltration

Physical infiltration is made through the system hardware. For example, the on/off switch, keyboard, mouse, cockpit controls, flight controls, and removable media provide physical inputs into a system. The first line of defense for a software-based system is to secure the physical inputs and outputs of the system. If these are not secure, the system is not secure. Any system can be compromised if a cyber attacker can enter the facility, aircraft, or vehicle and directly infiltrate the system. The cyber infiltration can be maintained afterwards by the installation of repeaters and remote input devices on the hardware. For example, electronic bugs on phone lines are a common method of surreptitious surveillance; modem and LAN lines are equally vulnerable.

An easy method of physical infiltration is to use a spare LAN connection on a hub or route. Using common network parts, a connection can be made directly, or through a Radio Frequency (RF) transmitter (wireless connection) from the LAN to an infiltrator's computer. These infiltration methods are only discovered by careful system audits or visual inspection.

Signal Infiltration

Signal infiltration comes through existing indirect or direct connections to a system. These connections are typically LANs, infrared (IR) devices, RF connections (radios), and modems (phone lines). Any system with an external connection can theoretically be infiltrated. The number of potential entry points is limited only by the number of direct and indirect connections into the system. For instance, a system with an Internet server is vulnerable to cyber infiltration from any computer connected to the Internet. An isolated network with a modem is vulnerable to any computer that can call into it. These input paths are used to infiltrate the system and then assault, manipulate, or raid it.

Physical infiltration may be protected by physical security: walls, fences, restricted areas, identification, guards, etc. Signal infiltration has similar defenses, but these are incorporated within the software or hardware itself (for instance, passwords, coded signals, firewalls, terminal identification, isolation, and system monitors).

The second rule of identifying CyW vulnerabilities is to expect every softwarecontrolled system to be the objective of an attempted cyber infiltration. Even isolated systems can experience cyber assault through a computer virus brought in on a contaminated floppy disk. Because cyber attacks are largely unpredictable, all systems must have some degree of protection, and the level of protection must be commensurate with the likelihood and consequences of expected attack.

Every vulnerable system needs proactive and effective virus-protection in place. Assume U-actors will be influenced by I-actors. The anonymity of the Internet makes it possible for a cyber operative to pass on information about passwordcracking, system phone numbers, infiltration techniques, and programs to U-actors.

Many U-actors are young, immature, and unsophisticated. They don't understand the ramifications of their actions. However, some attacks that appear unintentional may be made by Iactors, operating through U-actors on the Internet. The recent cyber infiltration of information systems by California teens trained by the Israeli hacker "Analyzer" is an example of this mentoring relationship.

I-actors can easily influence the direction of attacks by providing system access numbers and system passwords. Trojan horse programs written and passed to Uactors achieve an entirely different result than the U-actor intended. The outcome, from the perspective of the I-actor, is the same as if the attack had been made directly. Because passwords and infiltration data are shared by U-actors across the net, the I-actor's mission package is likely farmed out to more than one U-actor, or data may be passed through multiple Uactors.

This ensures many attacks on the same target and further muddies the trail back to the source. This also means organizations that detect attacks and neutralize them should be prepared to receive the same attack over and over again. In addition, organizations that detect attacks must share data on the attacks immediately with other organizations.

Defense Mechanisms

The exploitation of system weaknesses and social engineering are the primary avenues of attack against cyber systems. System weaknesses and social engineering techniques take advantage of computer and human limitations to steal and bypass signal and physical defenses, mainly passwords and machineto-machine authentication.

Unfortunately, the largest part of signal and physical defenses is based on identification and authentication codes—passwords. Passwords can be stolen, bypassed, or obtained by deception (and in theory, any password or authentication can be cracked). Until a different method of protection is invented, dependency on password identification and authentication guarantees that all systems will be in some degree vulnerable to cyber infiltration.

Use dedicated and redundant security to protect cyber systems. Twenty-two security methods are compiled below. Each method is described, along with some specific examples to accomplish it. This list is intended to provide a starting point for decision making and risk analysis; in some cases, especially systems integration and offensive methods, these suggestions run counter to current DoD policy and practice. These methods are intended to provoke thoughtful examination of all cyber security options to allow a tailored approach to military cyber systems development. To provide the best defense, these techniques must be customized, combined, and layered with one another. In every case, cyber systems should be set up so U- and I-actors can get into decoy sections of the security network. This allows identification and containment of the infiltrator. Only when infiltration is identified can it be solved.

Inactive Defense Methods

Physical security is the primary means of cyber system protection. Without some degree of physical security, all of the defenses mentioned below will fail.

Isolate all critical systems. Provide no system inputs outside of a physicallysecure area. Many agencies handle classified systems this way; the systems themselves are physically isolated from any other inputs or systems. Isolation of critical systems also reduces damage caused by cyber infiltration.

Put critical operations under manual control. Critical functions should not be controlled directly by software. For example, an electrical power system should not be turned on or off through software. To be effective, the capability must be entirely eliminated from software control. For example, in a water utility, any setting that could cause water contamination should be manual so the system cannot be breached electronically. MIL-STD-882, "System Safety Program Requirements," is used by the military to classify critical functions. A basic rule for all critical cyber systems is that systems should be manual, when possible, so critical functions cannot be addressed by software. With industries such as nuclear power this is impossible; with military systems, this can be achieved by hardwiring critical functions—such as missile launches.

Reduce integration. Integration increases cyber warfare risk because there are more avenues for cyber infiltration (and all system interconnections may not be known). To reduce cyber warfare vulnerability, integration should be limited as much as possible, and all system inputsand outputs must be fully defined. Critical cyber functions should be isolated physically so there are no inputs from outside. This type of compartmentalization should be considered when the use of cyber systems to control critical operations is necessary or desirable.

Keep the human element in the loop when integrating systems. Many software- controlled systems are integrated to reduce human workload. Although some systems require cyber integration to operate, many do not. When it is possible to keep a person in the loop or when a person can monitor or control a critical system, it is better to increase necessary monitoring and provide human interaction rather than automate the process. This is another way to isolate a system.

For instance, a request to shut down electrical power may generate a system message to tell a human operator to flip a switch. Only after the switch is moved can the automatic shutdown take place. An even safer setup would direct the operator through the shutdown sequence, instead of automating any of it. These methods may seem like we are turning back the technological clock, but protecting essential systems in this manner is necessary.

Inherent breach-points. Communication connections into the system are inherent, potential breaches of security. All connections into a system must be physically controlled and monitored to prevent cyber infiltration. The strongest breach-point occurs where the system is physically connected to an outside input. This part is also the most vulnerable to physical infiltration. Security must patrol, track, and control these inherent breachpoints to prevent physical infiltration.

Active Defense Methods

These methods make up the software programming that protects the system from unauthorized use.

Passwords and authentications. Passwords and authentications are necessary parts of system security to allow authorized human and other cyber system input. Because personal passwords are not usually very long (10 digits is the standard maximum), they are relatively easy to decode or predict. The longer the password, the better. Long passwords (32 characters or more) make code-breaking theoretically impossible, but codes that length are not commonly used and require other computers or hardware code devices such as tokens. Short passwords (eight characters or less) should be mixed into unpredictable, alphanumeric combinations and with other methods to provide an assured level of security. FIPS Publication 112, "Standard for Password Usage," provides specific information on the use of short passwords. Nicknames, popular words, and street names are easily predicted by some hacker programs.

Anthropomorphic measures. These measurements and data use a person's physical features—fingerprints, retinal scans, or face. These are better than passwords and can provide a much longer code, but are still relatively easy to break. Due to daily human physical changes, anthropomorphic measures cannot produce a large enough number to give a super-long password. For instance, if your face has swollen 0.001 of an inch during the night and the measure is to 0.0001 inch, you would not be able to log on your computer. However, anthropomorphic measures provide good security when combined with other methods such as passwords.

Tokens. These include magnetic cards or other code modules. They contain passwords and are read mechanically or electronically. Cards, modules, and other devices enable the use of very long codes and provide excellent security. Future encryption methods that use devices containing extremely long codes have the potential to make code-breaking almost impossible. A major drawback is that they must be kept physically secure because they can be lost or stolen. Tokens should be combined with anthropomorphic passwords to provide the best security.

Multiple authentications or log-ons. More than one interrogation is required to get into the system. For instance, logon may require a basic password followed by an anthropomorphic measure (fingerprint, for example), or a password followed by a token.

Multiple connection log-ons. More than one log-on over different addresses or lines is required for system entry. For instance, a log-on may be required at one phone number that activates a second, actual communication line. Another method is the call-back system. Using call-back, the user calls the computer and logs on, then the computer hangs up and calls back to the number authorized for the user. The user completes the sequence by logging on again with a second password. This method of log-on can also be used for Internet and LAN addresses.

Multiple log-on addresses. This requires either a call over two separate phone lines or two separate addresses at the same time. The signal is resolved in the user's computer only when both signals are received and the security authentication is passed on both lines. Multiple methods make it easy to detect cyber infiltration. Infiltrators who log-on in the initial layer, but whose second log-on fails, are instantly identified.

Monitoring software. At the lowest level, this software records the user's activities on the system. In many systems, this software limits the user's access based on a security level. More complex systems monitor activity and alert the system or people monitoring when a user attempts to access resources not authorized at the user's security level. These programs provide audit trails and system logs that are a primary means of tracking unauthorized access and operations. This kind of software also detects multiple attempts at system log-on.

Active Offense Methods

These methods include software programming and cyber operations that identify, attack, disable, tag, and capture I- and U-actors and their equipment. The chief problem to gaining the offensive is the detection of cyber infiltration. At least 75 percent or more cyber infiltrations are not detected. To an unsophisticated security system, cyber infiltration appears to be a normal connection.

The security itself needs a footprint that is unpredictable to the infiltrator —that separates authorized from unauthorized operators. Some active defense techniques are theoretical and based on extrapolations of current program capabilities. Simple active programs (e.g.,

Microsoft macro viruses) and passive programs can be used against unsophisticated computer security and systems with crippling results.

Commercially available system monitoring software can be used to accomplish cyber infiltration, assault, raid, and manipulation; to cyber infiltrate passwordsecured LANs requires only a rewrite of commercially available software. Highly proficient programmers can write machine code programs that can be sent across a data stream into a Web browser or other communications program. For example, "Back Orifice" is a Trojan horse program that surreptitiously sends information through the Internet back to its originator.

Most I-actors are not proficient enough to write these advanced programs, but simple offensive programs are available now on the Internet. Advanced programs can be written to do almost anything to a computer. They can tag a computer for identification (cookies), operate the different components of the computer, and rewrite programs in the computer.

Password-cracking programs. These were the first programs used for cyber infiltration. Password-cracking programs, at their simplest, repeatedly try different codes until they get a log-on. The main method of protecting against these simple programs is automatic monitoring that cuts off users who attempt multiple unsuccessful log-ons. Complex password cracking programs can potentially disable monitoring and other security methods. Super-long passwords and the defensive methods mentioned above protect against password cracking.

Identification, location, sniffer, spoofing, and watcher programs. Identification and location programs identify computers and users in a system. Sniffer and watcher programs glean passwords and other information from the system. Many of these programs are passive—that is, they are used by LANs to keep track of which computers and users are logged on. Some are active spoofers, actually asking for information from the user or the system.

The most widespread software-based method of obtaining passwords and other confidential information is through sniffer and watcher programs that monitor network traffic. These are commonly deployed using Trojan horse programs such as "Back Orifice." Defeat these programs by applying the password encryption methods delineated in FIPS Pub 112. Sophisticated identification programs can make undetectable queries to the user's computer and even allow the cyber raid of data. The main line of protection from these programs is active-defense methods. Cyber protection systems should use covert identification programs to discover information about an infiltrator.

Attack programs. An attack program is any program used to cripple or destroy a computer or computer system. These programs are complex and uncommon. They are like viruses, but are directed and singular, instead of random and replicating. Attack programs can be developed to impair the target's software, writable system basic input/output systems (BIOS), and disks. When employed in defense, these programs should be used by cyber forces to immediately stop any cyber attack-in-progress, to prevent the infiltrator from continuing operations from the attacking computer. Any cyber attack should tag the system for identification.

Protection against direct attacks is best accomplished by defensive methods. However, because all parts of a network or the Internet may not be secure, each individual computer must have some way of independently identifying attacks and rejecting them. Similar methods are used extensively now to protect against viruses and reject cookies.

Tagging programs. These programs insert data on a computer for later identification and cyber infiltration. These programs can be as simple as a "cookie"8 or as complex as a BIOS tag. Some versions write data to the boot sector on the hard drive; the drive must be low-level reformatted to remove it. Cyber forces should be able to tag a computer for later criminal investigation. Methods of defense from tagging are similar to those from attack programs.

Viruses. These are programs that replicate themselves by attaching their codes to other programs, disk boot sectors, and writable-system BIOSs. Viruses can be used both for malicious terrorism and cyber warfare. This capability can be added to any offensive program. It attacks computers in the opponent's system except for the primary infiltrator's computer. Virus capabilities can be added to tagging programs when there is a threat that the infiltrator will destroy the system or hard drives attacked, and thus attempt to prevent later identification. Because of their ability to get into nonopponent computer systems, viruses should be used cautiously by cyber forces. Viruses can be written with checks that only target specific systems.

Methods of defense from viruses are:

— programs that scan for identified viruses and virus-like code (virus scanners),

— inoculation of systems by identification of authorized programs and data (Cyclic Redundancy Code [CRC]

records; many virus checkers provide this capability), and

— personnel training.

Unfortunately, by 1997 as many as 15,500 viruses were identified and an estimated 400 new ones are reported each month. This makes absolute protection from viruses and viruslike programs impossible without the use of the defensive methods enumerated previously.

Trojan horses. These programs are the most common method of cyber infiltration. These are programs that perform like any other program a user may wish to run, but they execute unauthorized operations. A common example of a Trojan horse program is a Microsoft macro virus. Trojan horses can be defeated by the same methods used against viruses.

System overflows. One method of cyber infiltration and cyber assault is the use of large amounts of data to cause a system overflow or "crash." The typical e-mail pyramid letter is a crude example of e-mail overflow. This kind of letter can accumulate an address tail that will choke any e-mail system. A cyber attacker can also be attacked and infiltrated in this manner.

Overflows are most effective when the overflow is not detected immediately. This can be achieved when the infiltrator has a very fast connection or when there is a second signal input line to the attacking computer. Data overflows are also an excellent method to mask the transmission of offensive programs. Methods of defense from overflows are e-mail scanners that check for very large e-mail files, and personnel training. For instance, all personnel must be taught not to pass on dubious e-mail warnings, chain e-mails, and massive official e-mail. In addition, all employees should never open files from questionable sources or unofficial files.

Direct manipulation. When a computer is connected to another computer, current software makes it relatively easy to take control of many of the basic functions of the computer. Machine code and operating systems address codes can be used to turn on peer-to-peer sharing or to directly manipulate devices controlled through the operating system and BIOS. Cyber forces should develop programs that will allow this kind of manipulation of infiltrator computers. Cyber systems must lock out unauthorized system requests at all levels.

Logic bombs. Some code sequences in data files manipulate both the programs using the data files and the address codes of the BIOS and operating system. This is evident in macro viruses found in document files and files that result in program and operating system crashes. These kinds of programs can be written to achieve even more pointed results: for example, tagging or systems impairment. Logic bombs can also be used against infiltrators when they are attached to password data bases, classified data files, or to other files that might be downloaded following cyber infiltration.

Statutory action (legal actions). Cyber forces cannot be fully effective without capturing and prosecuting both U- and Iactors.

The primary goal of offensive cyber operations must be to identify and tag infiltrating systems. These actions allow prosecution as well as confirmation of the infiltration. Because it is relatively simple to back up systems and replace damaged computer components, the infiltrator will not be out of action for long unless legal action is taken. When it is not possible to extradite and prosecute U- or Iactors outside the United States, national policy must determine the extent of the cyber operations to be undertaken against the shielding foreign nation.

The effectiveness of cyber forces cannot be measured by a lack of detected cyber infiltration against targets This is because undetected cyber infiltration is certainly taking place, and most cyber infiltrations and attacks go undetected. The only reasonable measure of effectiveness is detecting cyber infiltration when it happens. This is why a multilayered approach to cyber system defenses is necessary. If the policy of the United States regarding CyW is wholly one of defense, the absolutely perfect measure of defense effectiveness is that every cyber infiltration is identified and the Uor I-actor neutralized. The success of cyber operations against and in support of the U.S. government must be classified.

As mentioned previously, when a cyber attack occurs, with due regard for active cyber operations, the detecting agency should immediately inform all possible targets. But, when an agent of the government is the victim of successful cyber infiltration or attack, that agency should not release the degree or effects of any cyber operation against it. Acknowledging the results would be similar to acknowledging the classification of publicly published materials. It would tell the enemy they are successful and provide information so the next attack might be even more effective. The best approach is for the agency to make no comment at all and provide immediate recovery and cleanup as part of its cyber operations.

4

Cyber Security

The phenomenal growth of the Internet has spawned the emergence of a global information society. Businesses possessing highly distributed information assets can function internationally with great efficiency, exchanging information quickly and seamlessly among their divisions, partners, suppliers, and customers. Governments use the Internet to provide information to their citizens and to the world at large, and they will increasingly use the Internet to replace manual methods of collecting information and providing government services. Governmental use of the Internet will increasingly extend to international information sharing and collaboration.

The scientific, engineering, and educational communities are all using the Internet as an indispensable tool for collaboration and rapid dissemination of information on advances in research and practice at all levels of scientific and engineering endeavor. Critical national infrastructures supporting such vital areas as power, transportation, communications, banking and finance, and defense are growing progressively more dependent upon Internetbased applications. The older, often manual, closed, and proprietary methods of providing the essential services that societies depend on are gradually disappearing as they are replaced by cheaper, open, more efficient, and highly distributed Internet applications.

All of the benefits that the Internet and the global information society can provide, including support for the most basic and essential services that nations depend on, are subject to disruption by Internet-based cyber-attacks that use the global computer network to cross international boundaries with ease.

Historically, attacks on a nation's essential services typically required a physical attack that crossed the nation's borders slowly enough that it was subject to recognition and interception by that nation's military. At the very least, some physical evidence would likely be left that would allow for the tracking, tracing, and identification of the perpetrators and the tools or weapons used in the attack. Today, cyber-attackers use the speed and global connectivity of the Internet to make national boundaries irrelevant, and sophisticated attackers leave little in the way of electronic evidence that can be used to track or trace them.

The domestic and international implications of an increasingly critical societal dependence on the Internet makes necessary the ability to deter, or otherwise minimize, the effects of cyber-attacks. The capability of a nation (or a cooperating group of nations) to track and trace the source of any attacks on its infrastructures or its citizens is central to the deterrence of such attacks and hence to a nation's long-term survival and prosperity.

An acknowledged ability to track and trace both domestic and international attackers can preempt future attacks through fear of reprisals such as criminal prosecution, military action, economic sanctions, and civil lawsuits. The process of trac-ing an attack back to its source may also help to uncover sufficient details of the attack techniques to allow for the development of defensive measures that could prevent similar attacks in the future.

Moreover, tracking and tracing an attack quickly could enable the interruption of an attack in progress. As the critical nature of Internet-based applications and services continues to increase, the ability to deter, prevent, or interrupt attacks in progress will be of greater value to society than assigning blame and collecting damages after a disaster has occurred.

In the cyber world, the current state of the practice regarding the technical ability to track and trace Internet-based attacks is primitive at best. Sophisticated attacks can be almost impossible to trace to their true source using current practices. The anonymity enjoyed by today's cyberattackers poses a grave threat to the global information society, the progress of an informationbased international economy, and the advancement of global collaboration and cooperation in all areas of human endeavor.

The Internet (originally known as ARPANET) began its life in 1969 as a research network sponsored by the Advanced Research Projects Agency (ARPA) of the Department of Defense (DoD). By the end of that year, the ARPANET consisted of four nodes, connecting four U.S. universities, and by 1973 the first international connections to the ARPANET were made.

In 1982, the earliest definitions of an internet as an interconnected network of networks began to appear, along with the establishment of a standard network protocol suite to support inter-networking communications. This protocol suite, comprised of an Internet Protocol (IP) and a Transmission Control Protocol (TCP), became widely known as "TCP/IP," which still forms the foundation of network communications on today's Internet. In December 1988, as a direct result of the first major computer security incident on the Internet (the Morris Worm in November 1988), DARPA founded the CERT® Coordination Center (then known as the "Computer Emergency Response Team") to provide a central place for coordinated responses to Internet cyber-attacks.

Today, the Internet is an interconnected network of networks comprised of approximately 150 million hosts worldwide. The number of computer security incidents handled by the CERT Coordination Center (CERT/CC) has grown from 6 in 1988, to 52,658 in 2001. By the end of September 2002, the CERT/CC had already seen over 73,000 incidents. And yet, despite serious security shortcomings, TCP/IP is still the standard protocol suite for network communications on the Internet, greatly limiting our ability to track and trace Internet cyber-attacks to their source.

At the highest level of abstraction, the Internet is a network of interconnected networks comprised of a myriad of host computer systems joined together by communications links (wired and wireless). Host computer systems communicate by sending messages to each other over the communication links, where a standard network protocol suite called TCP/IP specifies the data formats and transmission rules.

Looking at a greater level of detail, one sees that the Internet is a packet-switched network. Messages to be transmitted across the Internet are broken into manageable chunks called IP packets, which contain the data to be sent (such as part of an email message or web page content); the destination address (i.e., the "TO" field); the source address (i.e., the "FROM" field); a port number (which represents a specific type of service offered by a host, such as mail transfer, file transfer, or web browsing); and other miscellaneous header information that supports the reliable transmission of data.

A vast array of network devices called routers forward each packet, so that it moves from router to router until it arrives at its desired destination, or until the number of routers touched by the packet exceeds a maximum allowed value. The forwarding of a packet from one router to a second router is called a hop. Each router has a table of routing information (containing a snapshot of the network topology) that it builds and updates by communicating with other routers. The router uses this routing information in an attempt to choose the best path for sending a packet towards its desired destination. In simplest terms, a router looks at the destination address of a packet and sends the packet to another router that moves the packet closer to its final destination.

Typically, there are many alternative paths to a destination, which enables packets to be routed around communications links or routers that are out of service due to attack, accident, or even maintenance. Thus, this packet-switched design allows the Internet to be robust in the face of accidents or external physical attacks on the routing infrastructure. This, in fact, was one of the original design goals of the Internet.

TCP attempts to ensure that the packets are successfully delivered, in the proper order, and it will retransmit packets in the event of their loss. TCP allows two hosts to establish a connection or a session for a period of time to exchange streams of packets to support a service such as email, FTP, or web browsing.

Each host on the Internet has an IP address, which allows packets to be delivered to and received from a specific host. An IP address consists of four decimal numbers in the range 0–255, separated by periods. For example, the IP address of the CERT Coordination Center's web server is 192.88.209.14. However, it is clearly more mnemonic and convenient for a human to enter a name like "www.cert.org" in a web browser window than to enter a purely numeric address. An Internet-wide Domain Name System (DNS) supports the translations of IP addresses into hostnames, using a huge distributed database and a vast number of cooperating systems (DNS name servers) to provide the DNS name translation service.

Therats to the Cyberspace

Perhaps the greatest threat to the Internet today is the abysmal state of security of so many of the systems connected to it. There are many contributing factors, including commercial off-the-shelf (COTS) software, in which the number of features and rapid time to market outweigh a thoughtful security design. New vulnerabilities are continually being discovered in such software.

The widespread use of many COTS products means that once a vulnerability is discovered, it can be exploited by attackers who target many of the thousands or even millions of systems that have the vulnerable product installed. A lack of security expertise by most Internet users means that vendor security patches to remove the vulnerabilities will not be applied promptly, if at all. As a result, systems with unpatched vulnerabilities can be easily compromised, in large numbers, by motivated attackers, who will then use these systems as launching points to concentrate an attack against better-protected systems and to hide the tracks of the attacker.

Although the sophistication of Internet attacks has increased over time, the technical knowledge of the average attacker is declining, in the same manner that the technical knowledge of the average user has declined. Sophisticated attackers routinely build attack scripts and toolkits that the novice attacker can use with the click of mouse, with devastating effects. Hiding the tracks of the attacker and expunging or concealing any related evidence is an integral part of many attacker toolkits today.

A purely defensive "patch and pray" approach to computer security will never be sufficient to protect the extremely critical applications that are increasingly becoming a part of the Internet landscape. For such critical applications, a cyber-attack can mean significant economic loss and even the loss of human life. This means that the deterrent value of successfully tracking and tracing attackers will become increasingly vital to the survival of the Internet and the nations that depend on it.

Some of the major threats to internet is breifly discribed below.

The Internet was never designed for tracking and tracing user behavior. Unlike the telephone system, which has an effective tracking and billing capability based on the need to charge users of its services on a per-call basis, the

Internet has no standard provisions for tracking or tracing the behavior of its users. The original Internet model never envisioned billing on the basis of single host-to-host connection or some fine-grained unit of delivery of service (such as a small charge for each email message sent or received).

Originally, access to the Internet was sponsored by ARPA and was free to its end users. Current Internet charges are based on large-grained service provisions, such as monthly connectivity, connection speed, and storage capacity, all of which do not require Internet service providers (ISPs) to track the fine-grained behavior of their customers in order to bill them.

Moreover, the Internet was originally designed to link together a cooperative and collaborative community of researchers. It was designed to explore the many possible uses of networking, and in particular to facilitate research collaboration. Facilities for tracking and tracing the behavior of such benign users were never a consideration, and a tracking infrastructure was never designed or implemented. ARPA funds were instead focused on improving the functionality and performance of the Internet.

The Internet was not designed to resist highly untrustworthy users. One of the original design goals of the Internet was that the network be survivable in the face of external physical attack or accident that damaged some significant portion of the routing infrastructure. With its vast array of communications links and routers, the current Internet readily meets that design goal. The routing infrastructure has the inherent ability to route traffic along alternative paths that bypass damaged portions of the network.

Although the original design goals of the Internet recognized the need to be robust in the presence of external attack, there was no equivalent concern with regard to the possibility of internal cyber-attacks by the Internet's own users. After all, the original users of the Internet were university researchers, seeking to collaborate with their colleagues and openly share and exchange information for the benefit of all.

Thus, the Internet designers' view was that the user community was essentially benign and trustworthy, so simple security measures (such as passwords) would be sufficient to ensure the protection of the Internet community. Under this worldview, provisions to track and trace malicious user behavior were never designed or implemented.

A packet's source address is untrustworthy, which severely hinders tracking. One of the consequences of Internet protocols being designed under the assumption of a benign and trustworthy user community was the lack of any provision for cryptographic authentication of the information contained in IP packets. Therefore, an advanced user can readily modify any information in an IP packet and, in particular, can forge the source address of a packet, effectively hiding its true origin.

For a one-way communication, an attacker needs only to insert a false address in the source field, a relatively straightforward task. For a two-way communication, forging the source address is more complex, but the techniques are well known to the attacker community. Another way to obscure the true origin of an attack on a desired target host is to first compromise a number of intermediate hosts and to then use them as stepping stones on the way to the final target.

It's not uncommon for a large number of stepping stones to be used, and from the target's perspective, the attack will appear to have originated from the last stepping stone (i.e., the compromised host that transmitted the attack packets directly to the target). This "packet laundering" technique is quite effective at thwarting traceback attempts, particularly if there is a significant time delay between any attacker activities involving the stepping stones and the attack on the final target.

Moreover, an attacker may arrange things so that the packets transmitted from stepping stone A to stepping stone B may be quite different in nature from the packets transmitted from stepping stone B to stepping stone C on the way to the final target T, making traceback even more difficult because attempts to trace the attack by correlating similar packets will fail.

A specific type of stepping stone, often called a zombie, provides a "remote control" capability for an attacker and can severely obscure tracking. One common type of remote control attack is known as a distributed denial-of-service (DDoS) attack. During the preparation phase of a DDoS attack, the attacker compromises a large number of insecure machines (preferably having high bandwidth connections) and installs software on each of them that will later be used to target the ultimate victim during the attack phase.

During that attack phase, the attacker sends a command to each of the zombies, commanding them to flood the victim with packets, overwhelming the victim's system with a distributed coordinated attack and putting it out of service. Alternatively, the attack software on the compromised machines (i.e., the zombies) may have a timer that triggers a coordinated attack on the victim.

The small number of command packets used to trigger the attack are difficult to trace (and there are none to trace if the remote timer option is used), so if the attacker takes care not to arouse suspicion (or leave evidence, such as in log files) during the preparation phase, then determining the true source of the attack will be close to impossible. Forged source addresses are also the key to a new and very potent type of DDoS attack, called a reflector attack.

In the most potent version of this attack, packets containing the victim's IP address in the source address field are transmitted by the attacker to a huge number of servers and/or routers situated throughout the Internet. The servers or routers see the packets as a request for service, and send (or "reflect") replies directly to the source address of the packet (i.e., directly to the victim).

The overall effect is to overwhelm the victim's system with an enormous flood of packets, which are difficult to trace because the reflected packets are coming from so many different machines, each sending only a relatively small number of packets diffused throughout the Internet. An attacker that rotates the attack among some subset of a vast "inventory" of reflectors makes traceback even more difficult.

The current threat environment far exceeds the Internet's design parameters. The Internet's fundamental technology was developed to serve the needs of a benign community of researchers and educators. In the context of an environment that posed little or no threat, there was scant motivation for the development of significant security capabilities. Password protection was seen as sufficient to deter inappropriate behavior in a perceived threat environment consisting solely of occasional pranksters.

The Internet's original design goals never included the support of today's mission-critical and high-stakes applications in business, energy, transportation, communications, banking and finance, and national defense. These high-stakes Internet applications pose enormously tempting targets of opportunity for criminals, terrorists, and hostile nations, and they overly stress the technology designed for a more innocent time.

The migration of critical applications from expensive, closed, arcane, and proprietary technology to less costly, open, highly-distributed Internet applications, based on widely available COTS or public-domain software, makes these applications much more accessible and more easily attacked by malicious adversaries.

In this high-threat, target-rich environment, the technical ability to reliably track and trace intruders (supported by international agreements on monitoring and information sharing, and by international law proscribing attacks and specifying sanctions and punishment) is an indispensable element for enabling the continued use of the Internet to provide many of the essential services that societies depend on.

The expertise of the average system administrator continues to decline. In the early days of the Internet, a relatively small number of systems were attached to the network, and these machines were typically administered by individuals possessing a reasonable amount of skill in configuring and maintaining at least a basic level of system security.

A huge and growing percentage of the computer systems attached to the Internet today are operated by users with little or no security or system administration expertise (e.g., the vast majority of ordinary consumers who own a desktop PC or laptop). Such machines are easy prey for attackers, who can, in turn, use these machines as stepping stones to attack more lucrative and welldefended targets.

By moving from stepping stone to stepping stone on their way to the final target, attackers can obscure the true origin of the attack, making tracking and tracing the attacker an extremely difficult task. Just as a fire-safe building situated in a neighborhood of poorly maintained firetraps can be overwhelmed by a conflagration caused by its neighbors, the generally poor security of the majority of Internet systems makes even well-protected targets more vulnerable and severely hinders any attempt to track and trace an attack to its true origin.

Attacks often cross multiple administrative, jurisdictional, and national boundaries. Before the Internet, computer systems and networks were typically under full central administrative control. System administrators had complete control of all system and network hardware and software in the administrative domain of their organization, including full control of hosts, cabling, hardware add-ons, and the selection of system and application software that was loaded on their systems.

Other than dial-in lines that traversed the telephone company's domain, the administrative domain of the organization encompassed the entire computer system or network being managed. Moreover, all of the users of the system were typically members (e.g., employees) of the organization that administered it. Therefore, they could be expected to closely adhere to that organization's security policy, and they knew they could quickly be subject to sanctions or dismissal for misuse or abuse of the system.

Although most aspects of such centrally administered systems were not continuously monitored, the system administrator had both the technical ability and the organizational authority to monitor any part of the system at any time, should the need arise.

Today, the Internet interconnects an international collection of countless administrative domains, each controlled by an organization or an individual, but no single organization or entity is in charge of the Internet as a whole. There is no central administrative control of the Internet and no global visibility—no single organization or entity has a complete picture of any activity that crosses its administrative boundaries and, in the absence of cooperation, no single organization or entity can monitor, track, or trace packets outside of its administrative domain.

During the execution of Internet applications, IP packets often cross multiple administrative, jurisdictional, and national boundaries. There are no universal technical standards or agreements for performing the monitoring and record keeping necessary to track and trace attacks. Moreover, there are no universal laws or agreements as to what constitutes a cyber-attack, and what punishments, economic sanctions, or liability should ensue.

There are no universal international agreements for the monitoring, record keeping, and information sharing necessary to track and trace intruders. No existing privacy laws span the Internet as a whole. Existing international laws and agreements that might touch on these issues were not written for the Internet and need to be tested on cases involving Internet cyber-attacks.

High-speed traffic hinders tracking. Users demand, and are willing to pay for, high speed on the Internet.

Contemporary Internet applications, such as continuous digital video, require very high bandwidth, so routers are designed to push packets through as quickly as possible. Therefore, it is not considered practical for a router to do much in the way of processing packets other than routing them.

The analysis or marking of any significant number of packets to augment our ability to track and trace attackers would slow a router's throughput to below what is considered to be an acceptable level. Very high bandwidth also means that packet information that might assist tracking or tracing can't be stored for very long (e.g., minutes or hours, not days), because the large number of packets passing through the router per unit of time will quickly overwhelm a reasonably sized storage device.

As a result, information that might be useful for tracking is very ephemeral—if a traceback is not done quickly, the information needed to carry it out will be gone. This suggests that statistical approaches in which a sampling of packets is saved for a longer period of time might bear fruit. However, a subtle attack (using a small number of packets) would fall below the radar of statistical approaches.

Tunnels impede tracking. IP tunneling (also known as encapsulation) is the wrapping (or hiding) of IP packets within the data portion of new IP packets, often involving the encryption of the original packets. Encrypted IP tunneling is used to create virtual private networks.

Hackers destroy logs and other audit data. Hackers routinely attempt to hide their tracks by destroying or modifying system logs or other audit data, and seeding misinformation. Attacker toolkits often help to automate the process.

Anonymizers protect privacy by impeding tracking. A number of commercial and non-profit sites offer "anonymizer" services, functioning as an intermediary between a user and the sites the user wants to connect to. The anonymizer service hides identifying information, in particular the IP address of the user. Such sites typically state in their terms of service that they will reveal user information in response to a request by law enforcement.

Onion routing was a research project that produced a very sophisticated anonymizing technique, in which a large number of intermediate hosts cooperate to protect the anonymity of the user. In onion routing, packets are routed through multiple cooperating hosts, providing multiple layers of encapsulation and encryption to provide a very high level of protection against tracking and surveillance. The ultimate recipient of a packet sees only the IP address of the last intermediary. Onion routing can also defeat attempts by a small number of intermediate hosts to discover identifying information about the user.

The ability to link specific users to specific IP addresses is being lost. Tracking and tracing attack packets to the machine from which a sophisticated attack originated is indeed a daunting task. One primary purpose for tracking and tracing attacks is to deter future attacks by punishing or sanctioning the individuals or entities that originated them. To accomplish this, a direct link must be drawn between the IP address of the machine that originated the attack and the individual or entity that set the attack in motion.

However, several Internet trends are making it increasingly difficult to link IP addresses of machines to the entities or individuals who use them. In the early days of the Internet, every connected machine was assigned a static (or relatively permanent) IP address. However, the 32-bit address field of the current IP protocol limits the number of possible addresses, and the tremendous growth of the Internet threatens to eventually make IP addresses a scarce resource.

Already, organizations consider IP addresses to be a limited resource and are using schemes, such as the Dynamic Host Configuration Protocol (DHCP), to share a pool of IP addresses among their users' machines. For example, an ISP will typically assign a dynamic IP address to a dial-in user, from a pool of IP addresses owned by the ISP.

The dynamic IP address will remain valid until the user's modem connection to the ISP is terminated. Upon initiating a new dial-in session, the user will most likely be assigned a different dynamic IP address. An attack that is traced to one of an ISP's dynamically assigned IP addresses can only be linked to an individual through the ISP's logs and record keeping and is dependent on the ISP's willingness to collect, preserve, and divulge that information.

Many ISPs inform their customers (via "terms of use" agreements) that information about a customer's use of their service may be made available to law enforcement or other governmental authorities at the ISP's sole discretion. By and large, ISPs have a strong incentive to cooperate, at least domestically, with law enforcement and governmental authority.

Far more serious erosions in the ability to link an IP address to a particular user or entity are the appearance of "pay as you go" ISPs and the growth of (and ability to anonymously purchase) mobile wireless computing devices. "Pay as you go" ISPs, and in particular prepaid

Internet access cards, allow one to purchase Internet access time without a monthly commitment or long-term contract and, unlike the traditional ISP arrangement, require little or nothing in terms of identification.

A potential attacker who pays cash (or uses a stolen credit card) can achieve nearly complete anonymity in accessing the Internet. Consider a fast-growing mobile digital technology called Global System for Mobile Communications (GSM), which integrates voice, high-speed data, fax, paging, and messaging. GSM mobile devices incorporate a Subscriber Information Module (SIM) "smart" card, which provides the authorization to use the network. An individual can go into a store, put down cash, and anonymously buy a wireless phone/computing device with a prepaid subscriber agreement (Subscriber Information Module). One of the services available under GSM is the General Packet Radio Service (GPRS).

Purely defensive approaches will fail, so deterrence through tracking and tracing is crucial: On the Internet, attackers have the same advantages with respect to asymmetrical warfare as terrorists do in the physical world. They can choose the time and place of their attacks, having only to discover and exploit one vulnerability, or at most a limited number of vulnerabilities. Security personnel must cover all the bases (i.e., eliminate or block all the vulnerabilities), leading to a severe inequity in the technical and economic resources required for defense versus those required for offense.

Only the threat of retaliation, sanctions, or other punishment for the attacker can even the playing field and provide a deterrent effect. The ability to trace an attack and identify the attacker (or the sponsoring entity) is indispensable if the Internet is to be able to survive and thrive as the foundation for delivering the essential services needed to support a global information-based society.

Traceback Methods

This section examines the current best practices and the most promising research approaches in a search for near-term and long-term solutions to the traceback problem. However, it is clear that technical approaches alone can never offer a complete solution to the problem. Some of the basic approaches are descirbed below.

Hop-by-Hop IP Traceback

The most common and basic method in use today for tracking and tracing attacks is hop-by-hop traceback. This method is only suitable for tracing large, continuous packet flows that are currently in progress, such as those generated by ongoing denial-of-service (DoS) packet flood attacks. In a DoS flood attack, the source IP addresses are typically spoofed (i.e., they are forged addresses inserted into the source address field of a packet to disguise the true IP address of the machine that originated the packets), so tracing is required to find the true origin of the attack. For example, assume that the victim of a flood attack has just reported the attack to their ISP. First, an ISP administrator identifies the ISP's router that is closest to the victim's machine. Using the diagnostic, debugging, or logging features available on many routers, the administrator can characterize the nature of the traffic and determine the input (ingress) link on which the attack is arriving. The administrator then moves on to the upstream router.

The administrator repeats the diagnostic procedure on this upstream router, and continues to trace backwards, hop-by-hop, until the source of the attack is found inside the ISP's administrative domain of control (such as the IP address of a customer of the ISP) or, more likely, until the entry point of the attack into the ISP's network is identified. The entry point is typically an input link on a router that borders another provider's network.

Once the entry point into the ISP's network is identified, the bordering provider carrying the attack traffic must be notified and asked to continue the hop-by-hop traceback. Often there is little or no economic incentive for such cooperation. Traceback to the origin of an attack fails if cooperation is not provided at every hop, or if a router along the way lacks sufficient diagnostic capabilities or resources. If the attack stops before the trace is completed, the trace fails. Hop-by-hop traceback is a very labor-intensive, technical process, and since attack packets often cross administrative, jurisdictional, and national boundaries, cooperation can be difficult to obtain. Partial traceback is still of value, since packet filters can be put in place to limit the DoS flood. How anomalous the attack packets are and how well they can be characterized determines how restrictive the filters have to be. Overly restrictive filters can contribute to the negative effects of a DoS attack.

Hop-by-hop traceback can be considered to be the baseline from which all proposed improvements in tracking and tracing are judged. It is the most basic method for tracing large packet flows with spoofed source addresses, but has many limitations and drawbacks. For example, DDoS attacks are extremely difficult, if not impossible, to trace via this process, since there are multiple sources of attack packets, multiple paths through the Internet, and potentially a relatively small number of packets coming from each source.

Ingress Filtering

Much of the havoc inflicted on the Internet by attackers is accomplished using attack packets with spoofed source addresses. The occurrence of packets with spoofed source addresses, and their ability to transit the Internet, can be greatly limited through cooperative efforts by ISPs, using a basic packet filtering approach called network ingress filtering. For example, assume that an ISP provides Internet connectivity to a customer network and assigns the customer a fixed set of IP addresses. Assume that the connectivity is provided via the ISP's router R. To limit IP source address spoofing, the ISP places an ingress (input) filter on the input link of router R, which carries packets from the customer network into the ISP's network and onto the Internet. The ingress filter is set to forward along all packets with source addresses that belong to the known set of IP addresses assigned to the customer network by the ISP, but the filter discards (and optionally logs as suspicious) all packets that contain source IP addresses that do not match the valid range of the customer's known IP addresses. Hence, packets with source addresses that could not have legitimately originated from within the customer network will be dropped at the entry point to the ISP's network.

The widespread use of ingress filtering by all service providers would greatly limit the ability of an attacker to generate attack packets utilizing a broad range of spoofed source addresses, making tracking and tracing the attacker a much easier task. Any attacker located within the customer network, would either have to generate packets that carry the attacker's legitimate source address or (at worst) spoof a source address that lies within the set of IP addresses assigned to the customer network.

So, even in the worst case, an attack originating within the customer network in our example can be traced to some machine in that customer network, simply by reading the source address on the attack packet. With the help of the administrator of the customer network, the search for the attacker can then proceed in a greatly narrowed search space.

Ingress filtering is described in detail in an Internet Engineering Task Force (IETF) document [Ferguson 2000]. It is one of the IETF documents that specify "Internet Best Current Practices for the Internet Community." Ingress filtering can be supplemented by egress filtering (i.e., exit filtering) on the part of users, such as corporate network administrators, to ensure that packets exiting a network domain contain only valid source addresses that correspond to IP addresses contained within that domain.

Ingress filtering has yet to be implemented on a very widespread basis. There is a broad element of "citizenship" involved, since many of the attack victims protected by a particular ISP's ingress filters would likely not be the ISP's customers. Also, ingress filtering can break certain network services, and ISPs would have to expend extra effort to get those services to work despite ingress filtering.

Whether the liability for an attack extends to the ISP through which the attack originated is an open question, domestically and internationally. The existence of Internet best practices such as ingress filtering may eventually establish a level of "due care" that ISPs and other providers would be expected to fulfill.

Backscatter Traceback

Backscatter traceback is a technique for tracing a flood of packets that are targeting the victim of a DDoS attack. This tracking approach was developed by Chris Morrow and Brian Gemberling of UUNET, a major ISP. The UUNET backscatter traceback technique relies entirely on the standard characteristics of existing Internet routing protocols, and although some special router configurations are used, there is no custom modification of protocols or equipment that is outside of current Internet standards. In a typical DDoS attack, a victim's system is put out of service by a flood of malicious attack packets originating from a large number of zombie machines previously compromised by the attacker. The destination address field of each attack packet contains, of course, the IP address of the victim. The source IP address of each packet is typically spoofed.

In contemporary DDoS attacks, the spoofed source address is typically chosen at random (by an attacker support tool) from the universe of all possible IP addresses. However, large blocks of the Internet address space have not yet been allocated for global routing, so many of the randomly chosen spoofed addresses are not legitimate source addresses.

Hence, all attack packets in a typical DDoS attack contain fake source IP addresses, which give no clue as to the true addresses of the zombie machines that are participating in the DDoS flood. Moreover, a large number of the attack packets in a typical DDoS flood carry invalid source addresses, which could not correspond to any machine on the Internet.

The UUNET backscatter traceback technique makes clever use of the large number of invalid source address that are characteristic of contemporary DDoS attacks. Here is how the technique works:

1. *The attack is reported to an ISP*. The victim of a DDoS attack reports the problem to their ISP. The flood of attack packets has made the victim's Internet connection essentially unusable, putting the victim out of service.

2. *The ISP configures all of its routers to reject all packets destined for the victim*. The ISP uses a standard routing control protocol to quickly configure all of its routers to reject (i.e., filter) packets that are targeted to the victim. In essence, the router configuration is set so that the victim's machine is now unreachable through the routing infrastructure. Note that by rejecting all packets that have the source address of the victim, benign packets carrying legitimate traffic will also be lost; however, by and large, the overwhelming number of packets heading for the victim will be attack packets. If the technique is successful, the total blockade of packets destined for the victim will only be in place for a very short period of time (a matter of minutes).

3. *Rejected packets are "returned to sender*." Well, that's roughly what happens, but here is a more precise explanation: When a router rejects a packet with the destination address of the victim, it sends an Internet Control Message Protocol (ICMP) "destination unreachable" error message packet back to the source IP address contained in the rejected packet. Some of

the "return to sender" ICMP error messages will be sent to legitimate users at legitimate addresses whose benign packets have been rejected along with the malicious ones. However, most of the packets destined for the victim are malicious attack packets.

Each ICMP "return to sender" error message packet contains, in its source IP address field, the address of the router (controlled and configured by the ISP) that blocked and rejected the packet heading for the victim. The router is also the machine that is generating the ICMP message. In its destination IP address field, the ICMP "return-tosender" error message packet contains the source IP address found in the rejected packet that had been heading for the victim. These ICMP error packets are the "backscatter" or "noise" that enable the ISP to trace the attack packets back to their ingress point in the ISP's network.

4. *The ISP configures all of its routers to blackhole (that is, route for capture) many of the ICMP error packets (i.e., the "backscatter") with illegitimate destination IP addresses.* The Internet Address Naming Authority (IANA) has yet to allocate, for global routing, several very large blocks of IP addresses. One should never see any legitimate packet containing an IP source address from this unallocated address space entering a domain from an external network.

   However, network administrators can use these addresses for internal routing as long as the packet flow remains entirely within the administrative boundaries of their own network. The next step in backscatter traceback is for an ISP to select a large range of IP addresses unallocated by IANA and to configure all of the ISP's routers to send packets destined for these invalid addresses to a specific machine for analysis. Hence, the packets containing these invalid destination addresses have been "blackholed" by the ISP's routing infrastructure. The centermost region represents the fraction of the overall packets arriving at an ISP's router that are blackholed for analysis. Since packets with these invalid destination addresses cannot have been routed into the ISP's network from an external source, these packets can only be some of the ICMP "destination unreachable" error message packets generated internally by the ISP's routers, which have been configured to reject all packets destined for the victim.

5. *Analysis by the blackhole machine quickly traces the attack to one or more routers at the outermost boundary of the ISP's network.* A human or program at the blackhole machine need only look at the source address of each ICMP error packet to determine the address of the router that sent it. Typically only a single router, or a small number of routers, will be identified as the ingress (i.e., entry) point of the attack into the ISP's network.

6. *The ISP removes the filter blocking the victim's IP address from all routers except those serving as the entry points for the DDoS attack.* The ISP leaves the blocking filter in place at those routers that have been traced as the entry points of the attack into the ISP's network and removes the blocking filter at all other routers. The DDoS attack remains blocked, but most of the flow of legitimate traffic to the victim is thereby restored. The entire backscatter traceback process can typically be executed in under a minute. Only that portion of the

inbound legitimate traffic that passes through the same entry points as the DDoS attack and is intended for the victim's IP address will remain blocked. Further analysis can identify specific characteristics of the attack packets that would allow the blocking filter on the attack entry point router(s) to be refined to be more permissive of benign traffic that has followed the same path as the attack packets. This will restore an even higher level of service to the victim.

7. *The ISP asks neighboring ISPs, upstream of the attack, to continue the trace.* The ISP further identifies the specific router interface(s) through which the attack is entering the ISP's network and notifies the neighboring ISP(s) directly upstream of the entry points. The neighboring ISP(s) can continue to trace the attack closer to its ultimate source, using the backscatter traceback technique or any alternative tracking method.

The UUNET backscatter traceback technique is a fast and efficient method for countering contemporary DDoS flood attacks and for tracing such attacks to the boundaries of an administrative network domain. Tracking beyond an administrative domain depends on the trustworthiness, cooperation, and skill of upstream ISPs that lie between that domain and the source of the attack. This tracking technique is not a general-purpose traceback approach but rather depends heavily on the specific characteristics of the DDoS attacks it was designed to defeat.

Like many approaches designed to work against DDoS floods, it depends on a large number of attack packets being directed toward the victim. This is not an appropriate traceback mechanism for more subtle attacks. Eventual advances in the attack method can also defeat this approach, such as a DDoS attack tool that ensures that all of the randomly selected spoofed source addresses are valid IP addresses, allocated by IANA. DDoS attacks in which the zombie source addresses are not forged would also defeat this technique.

The backscatter traceback method is a very good example of a class of traceback and remediation techniques that can be used to track attack packets to their entry point at the boundary of an administrative domain. One may assume that within a typical domain of administrative control an adequate level of trustworthiness among personnel and systems exists.

Tracking beyond an administrative domain of control to the ultimate source of an attack depends on the trustworthiness, cooperation, and skill of upstream ISPs. Clearly, the traceback of a particular attack will likely cross multiple administrative, jurisdictional, and international boundaries. Having international agreements in place to facilitate the required cooperation will be an essential element of a traceback capability. This may include agreements to share traceback technology to raise the overall level of skill needed to complete a trace across multiple ISPs.

However, any lack of trust among the entities participating in a given trace can be a major stumbling block to its ef-fective execution. One or more of the entities involved in the traceback may even share responsibility, liability, or merely tacit approval for the attack being traced and may therefore have sufficient incentive to be deceptive. Nothing in the technology of backscatter traceback provides authentication or any other trust mechanism that would improve the trustworthiness of information provided by multiple organizations ostensibly cooperating in a traceback.

Overlay Network for IP Traceback

Routers are typically optimized for the high-speed forwarding of packets, not for analyzing the packets or tracing them back to their source. The most basic traceback capability of a router is the ability to report on which of the multiple inputs (i.e., interfaces) to the router a packet arrived, thereby identifying the neighboring router (from the previous hop) that delivered the current packet.

Routers on the highest speed links are often particularly lacking in the capabilities or resources to perform even the most basic traceback. This is a marketplace decision based on the desire for the greatest possible speed, and therefore the networks administered by ISPs are typically not well-suited for the effective tracking and tracing of cyber-attacks. Robert Stone has proposed an innovative approach that can improve traceability by adding an overlay network, optimized for hop-by-hop tracing and analysis, on top of an existing ISP network.

An overlay network is a supplemental or auxiliary network that is created when a collection of nodes from an existing network are joined together using new physical or logical connections to form a new physical or logical network on top of the existing one. New physical connections can be quite expensive, so new logical connections (such as IP tunnels) are more common.

The goal of Stone's approach, called CenterTrack, is to improve the traceability of the large packet flows associated with DoS flood attacks. The first step in the CenterTrack approach is to create an overlay network, using IP tunnels to connect the edge routers in an ISP's network to special-purpose tracking routers that are optimized for analysis and tracking.

The overlay network is also designed to further simplify hop-by-hop tracing by having only a small number of hops between edge routers. In the event of a DoS flood attack, the ISP diverts the flow of attack packets (destined for a victim's machine) from the existing ISP network onto the overlay tracking network containing the special-purpose tracking routers. The attack packets can now be easily traced back, hop-by-hop, through the overlay network, from the edge router closest to the victim, back to the entry point of the packet flood into the ISP's network.

The CenterTrack method is an interesting short-term research approach for tracing a large packet flow from the entry point in an administrative domain to its exit point. The approach requires no modification of existing Internet protocols. Stone states that probabilistic approaches to packet tracing are superior to CenterTrack, but since they require new protocol development, they are longer-term solutions. Stone outlines some of the advantages and disadvantages of the CenterTrack approach.

Advantages include the fact that special-purpose tracking and analysis features are only needed on the edge routers and the special-purpose tracking routers. The small number of hops between edge routers on the overlay-tracking network simplifies hop-by-hop tracking. Disadvantages include an increase in overall complexity, which can lead to operational errors (for example, in routing updates).

The overhead inherent in creating IP tunnels could amplify a DoS flood's negative effects on the network. The CenterTrack technique does not work with attacks that originate inside an ISP's network, and it is uncertain if this technique is highly scalable for distributed denial-of-service (DDoS) attacks with many entry points into the ISP's network. Stone notes that CenterTrack has been successfully tested in a lab setting, but the feasibility of this approach for real production environments needs further investigation.

The policy implications of this approach are identical to those of plain hop-by-hop traceback. Cooperation is needed at each backward hop for attacks with packet flows that cross administrative, jurisdictional, or national boundaries.

Probabilistic Approaches to Packet Tracing

For very practical reasons (the extremely high overhead), most of the promising research approaches to tracking and tracing attack packets do not attempt to audit all of the traffic passing through a given router. Instead, these research approaches use a probabilistic (i.e., statistical) scheme to sample the packet flow.

One such approach is called ICMP Traceback or simply iTrace. A significant amount of computational resources are required for iTrace, and these resources could best be provided by building iTrace support into the router hardware. The fundamental concept is that about once in every 20,000 packets, a router sends an ICMP traceback message (called an iTrace packet) to the same destination address as the sampled packet (or to an outboard monitor). The destination (or monitor) collects and correlates the tracking information, and for large packet flows (as in DDoS attacks) there will be sufficient information to successfully trace the attack.

However, an attacker can defeat or disrupt the trace by sending spoofed iTrace packets, so iTrace packets include an authentication field. Which authentication method to use is an open research issue, based on a trade-off between the need for good security (e.g., cryptographic strength) versus the need to minimize the computational resources required. There are also public key infrastructure (PKI) issues associated with who has the right to sign an iTrace packet (an open policy question) and how one validates that signature.

One disadvantage of the iTrace scheme is that if one wants to trace a higher percentage of the packet flow, one must increase the probability that an iTrace packet will be emitted, and then the increase in trace packets will unfortunately increase the overall traffic. Other probabilistic tracing approaches, such as those described in "Practical Network Support for IP Traceback"and "Advanced and Authenticated Marking Schemes for IP Traceback" also audit only a statistical sampling of the packet flow. However, instead of generating additional ICMP packets to carry tracking information, these schemes place tracking information into rarely used header fields inside the IP packets themselves.

This approach is known as probabilistic packet marking (PPM). The tracking information is collected and correlated at the destination of the packets, and, like the iTrace method, for a sufficiently large packet flow there will be enough tracking (path) information embedded in the packets to successfully complete the trace. As with the iTrace approach, there is the real danger of an attacker tampering with, or spoofing, the tracking information. In response to this threat, Song and Perrig enhanced the work of Savage by adding authentication to the embedded encodings of tracking information. However, it appears that the PKI issues raised by Bellovin for iTrace apply to the packet marking approaches as well.

All of the probabilistic traceback approaches depend on auditing very sparse samples of large packet flows and thus are well suited for attacks that generate massive packet flows, such as DDoS floods. These approaches are entirely infeasible for tracking attacks that employ only a small number of packets. In a recent paper, Marcel Waldvogel shows how an attacker can effectively generate packets containing false tracking information and thereby defeat the Savage et al. PPM approach. The attack depends on the fact that the PPM tracking information must be split over several packets because of the very limited space within IPv4 headers for encoding the tracking information.

The most significant policy implication of the probabilistic traceback approaches is the need for international agreements to formalize the necessary cooperation to make the techniques effective. The authentication of tracking information added by the Song and Perrig approach can enhance the trust necessary to make international cooperation effective. In some cases, technical and financial assistance to ISPs to support probabilistic traceback approaches will be required.

Single-Packet IP Traceback

All of the traceback methods discussed thus far have limited applicability because each of these techniques requires a large amount of attack traffic to support tracking. As devastating as DDoS flood attacks can be, Internet-based attacks that are equally or even more destructive can be far more subtle in terms of traffic flow. In the extreme case, an attack can be carried out with a single packet. Since a single IP packet is the smallest unit of Internet traffic, it has long been the aspiration of security researchers to be able to reliably track a single packet to its source. In theory, one can address the problem of tracking traffic as small as a single packet by keeping a log at each router in the Internet infrastructure of every packet that passes through it, in a tamperproof, fully-authenticated manner.

When the victim of an Internet-based attack discovers the attack, the victim could then examine their own system logs to determine which packets participated. The victim would then need only to query the routing infrastructure ("Have you seen this packet?") to fully trace the path of the attack.

While appealing in theory, this approach is, of course, impossible in practice. A major technical problem is the need for extremely fast, virtually unlimited storage at each router to record a log of all packets passing through and to maintain that rapidly growing log indefinitely so that attacks not immediately discovered by a victim can still be traced at a later date. High-speed Internet backbone connections operating at OC-192 can transmit on the order of 1.25 gigabytes per second per router interface (i.e., per link). At these speeds, each router can require 75 GB of storage per minute per interface, to record all the tracking information.

Hence, a router with 16 links would require up to a massive 1,200 GB (1.2 TB – Terabytes = thousand billion bytes) of storage to keep only a minute's worth of traffic. Even if each of the routers along an attack path had this much storage available, a victim would have to recognize the attack and complete the query in 60 seconds or less, before the relevant logs were overwritten by new traffic. In addition to the technical infeasibility of this approach, there are very serious policy issues with respect to privacy.

Privacy would be nearly impossible to maintain in an environment where complete traffic logs, including all packet contents, were kept at all routers in the Internet infrastructure. These logs would certainly be tempting targets for snooping attackers who could access massive amounts of stored Internet traffic by compromising a router's security and reading its logs. Trust would also be a primary issue—could you rely on the response to your query from routers outside your administrative domain or national boundaries? A very promising new research approach called Hash-Based IP Traceback, also known as Single-Packet IP Traceback, offers the possibility of making the traceback of single IP packets feasible. The fundamental idea is to store highly compact representations of each packet rather than the full packets themselves. These compact representations are called "packet digests" and are created using mathematical functions called hash functions. Note that the complete original packets cannot be restored from the packet digests, for all practical purposes.

Here's the definition of a hash function from the American National Standards Institute: hash function: A mathematical function that maps values from a large (or very large) domain into a smaller range, and that reduces a potentially long message into a "message digest" or "hash value" or that is sufficiently compact to be input into a digital signature algorithm. A "good" hash function is one that results from applying the function to a (large) set of values that are evenly (and randomly) distributed over the range. Hash functions play a significant role in cryptography. The only aspect of hash functions of importance for this traceback application, however, is the ability to create highly compact "digests" of long messages to greatly reduce the storage requirements at each router.

In addition to the use of hash functions, Snoeren and his colleagues make use of a special data structure called a Bloom filter, which provides an additional major reduction in the storage requirements needed to uniquely identify each packet. The hash functions and Bloom filter reduce the storage requirement to 0.5% of the link capacity per unit of time, making single IP traceback technically feasible with respect to storage requirements. Moreover, this approach addresses the privacy issues posed by the universal logging of Internet traffic, since only the packet digests are stored at each router and not the actual packet contents. Note that, in general, a victim submits a query by presenting the actual contents of the attack packet, and not the digest. However, for particularly sensitive cases, a victim will be able to submit a query without revealing the actual packet contents, at the cost of significant additional computational resources.

An additional problem in single-packet traceback remains. During its transit through the Internet, a packet can be transformed in a number of ways, making it difficult to match transformed instances of a packet with the original packet. Common transformations include address translation, fragmentation, and tunneling. Transformation information corresponding to the packet digests is stored in a transformation lookup table, which provides the information needed to track packets despite common transformations. The transformation information is retained by the router for the same amount of time as the packet digests are.

Hash-based IP traceback is accomplished using a system known as a Source Path Isolation Engine (SPIE), developed by Snoeren and his colleagues. Hardware enhancements are necessary to support the hash-based traceback approach for very high speed routers, but these enhancements appear to be quite practical for current- or next-generation routers. Extensive simulations of this method have been run by Snoeren and his colleagues, and the results appear to validate the overall approach.

This is arguably the most promising approach to packet tracking and tracing described in the research literature. It demonstrates the feasibility of tracking and tracing single packets, which has long been considered impractical. A major drawback of this method is that the storage interval at each router is very short, in the order of a minute or a few minutes at best for high-speed routers. The high bandwidth and high traffic levels of today's Internet mean that hashes based on new traffic quickly fill storage and push out the old. The problem is most severe for routers in or near the high-speed core of the Internet.

For routers in more "rural" lower speed locations, the traffic is significantly less, and packet hashes can be stored for a somewhat longer period of time. Snoeren and his colleagues have stated that probabilistic aging of packet digests (i.e., saving a sampling of packet digests for longer periods of time) can allow you a significantly longer window of time in which to trace attacks comprised of large packet flows. For example, if you decide to save every nth packet for an extended period of time, then some attacks (i.e., those involving large packet flows) will still be traceable long after the storage interval for the complete set of packet digests would have expired.

The short-lived nature of stored packet hashes places a severe burden on the capability of the victim to quickly detect subtle attacks. The speed with which an attack can be detected is a crucial element in making this technique effective. With DDoS attacks, not only is there high-traffic volume (which makes traceback easier), but the detection of the attack is a "no-brainer"—there is no attempt by the attacker to disguise the attack, and the flood of traffic is obvious to the victim. For more subtle attacks, the burden is on the victim's intrusion detection system to quickly identify (say, in under a minute) a possible attack and to isolate the corresponding small number of packets so the routing/tracking infrastructure can be immediately queried to determine the path of the attack packets.

In many cases, forensic analysis will reveal an attack long after the packet digest cache on most of the routers along the attack path has expired (i.e., the cache has been overwritten by new traffic). All this being said, the reduction of storage requirements by the hash-based traceback method to 0.5% of link capacity per unit of time is an impressive achievement that, combined with the SPIE architecture, demonstrates the feasibility of tracing single IP packets.

This method overcomes many of the privacy concerns associated with maintaining logs of Internet traffic, because it stores only packet digests and not the complete packet contents. Although communications among the components of a SPIE system can be authenticated, the query results produced by a SPIE component under the control of a malicious individual or organization could be falsified. Hence, one must rely on the trustworthiness of the ostensibly cooperating entities to reliably trace a packet to its source. A query result indicating an impossible or unlikely attack path can suggest the duplicity of one of the reporters.

Traceback is only possible within a single administrative domain of control, unless cooperation and collaboration in the legal, policy, and technical realms permit cross-domain traceback. The need for hardware enhancements and the significant amount of technical skill required to support this traceback technique suggest the value of providing financial and/or technical assistance as part of any international agreement involving cooperation and collaboration in establishing and using the traceback infrastructure.

Challenges of Forensic Computing

'Computer forensics' or 'forensic computing' is the process of identifying, preserving, analysing and presenting digital evidence in a manner that is legally acceptable or the application of computer science to the investigative legal processes. It is used to uncover the proverbial 'smoking gun' and to organise voluminous amounts of data.

Specialists also draw on an array of methods for discovering data that resides in a computer system or recovering deleted, encrypted or damaged file information. The process draws upon many disciplines and involves the application of information technology to the search for digital evidence. It comprises three primary activities:

- Media and electronic device analysis - the examination of various types of storage media;
- Data communications analysis - which encompasses the two main activities of network intrusion or misuse and data interception;
- Research and development.

While computer crime is the most obvious example of where forensic computing is required, any kind of crime may contain digital evidence, from a variety of electronic devices, that needs to be examined eg. email between victim and suspect in a sexual assault case, electronic spreadsheets with financial implications in a fraud or drug case, or a victim's email, calendar or to-do list in a murder case. In fact, evidence recovered from a computer may prove vital to an investigation despite the suspect computer being incidental to the actual offence.

The computer forensic professional is said to be a cross between technician, programmer and investigator. Perhaps the first high profile forensic computing practitioner could be said to be Clifford Stoll who tracked a spy through a maze of computer espionage, in what became the 'Cuckoo's Egg' case. The Case is as follows:

In 1986, an astronomer-turned-systems-manager at the University of California at Berkeley found a 75 cent accounting error in a computer's billing program, which led to the discovery that an unauthorised user had penetrated Berkeley's computer system. When the astronomer, Clifford Stoll, began to investigate further, he discovered that a hacker identified as 'Hunter' was using the university's computer system as a conduit to break into US government systems and steal sensitive military information. The hacker's objective seemed to be to attain US anti-ballistic missile technology.

As he began to pursue the hacker, Stoll encountered serious problems. To begin with, Stoll was unable to find computer-literate law enforcement personnel with an appreciation of the technical nature of the criminal activity. Local and federal agencies that Stoll contacted, including the FBI and CIA, initially expressed little interest in pursuing what at first looked like a computer prank. Moreover, until government investigators learned of the potential threat to national security, they had no interest in pursuing a case which appeared to have damages valued at less than one dollar. Because Hunter's trail vanished each time he ended a communication, he could only be traced when he was online. But because it was often after business hours (and, indeed, sometimes in the middle of the night) when Hunter attacked, there were few if any law enforcement personnel available during those sessions. Stoll cleverly resorted to generating phoney official-looking data to keep the hacker interested and online long enough for a trace to be completed. Eventually, the source of the attacks was identified as a German hacker, and he was successfully prosecuted in that country.

Stoll describes the analogy as follows:

> The hacker had sneaked through a hole in our system to become a super-user – he'd never even logged into the system manager's account. He was like a cuckoo bird. The cuckoo lays her eggs in other birds' nests. She is a nesting parasite: some other bird will raise her young cuckoos. The survival of cuckoo chicks depends on the ignorance of other species. Our mysterious visitor laid an egg-program into our computer, letting the system hatch it and feed it privileges.

Despite significant progress since the time of this case, it remains a useful illustration of some of the fundamental issues that continue to need further attention at the domestic and international level in order to eliminate any weak links in the chain of an investigation.

Forensic computing is a complex area which involves a range of disciplines such as software engineering, cryptography, electronic engineering and data communications. It is recognised that consideration of forensic computing issues also entails matters relating to telecommunications interception and technical surveillance.

There are a number of axiomatic principles governing the collection and examination of evidence intended for presentation in a Court of Law. These apply just as much to computer based information as they do for example, to such disciplines as DNA typing, fingerprint identification or explosives analysis. However, when attempting to apply such principles to the examination of computer based information, there are some areas where the special nature of computing requires additional considerations and some change of emphasis.

Computer stored information by its digital nature is 'media independent' and it follows that without taking external factors into account, any differentiation between original and copied information is impossible. This media independency gives computer forensic scientists the immense advantage of being able to conduct investigations on copies of the data rather than on the data itself. Other special considerations in relation to electronic evidence include the fragility or volatility of potential evidence and the need to be able to document all processes and to demonstrate persuasively to a court that the original material has not been changed or tampered with in any way. The international and cross-jurisdictional features of much cybercrime will also present unique and complex challenges for both investigators and forensic computing specialists.

Forensic computing is a fast developing area and there are a number of factors impacting on future directions, including:

— The reducing cost of technology;

— The reducing cost of the Internet;

— Rapidly increasing storage capacity;

— Rapidly expanding bandwidth (or the capacity of a communications channel);

— Enhanced awareness amongst offenders of the nature of electronic evidence and increasing use of techniques to hide evidence, such as encryption, digital compression, steganography, remote storage, and audit disabling etc., as well as the use of caches and booby traps;

— Increasing technical complexity; and

— Increased computer literacy within the general community.

Such factors indicate that a well developed forensic computing capability will be essential as information technology becomes more pervasive and complex. This is a particularly challenging area as it is said that the field of computer technology changes completely every 18 months. But on a more positive note, many offenders will leave their 'footprints' in cyberspace and, as Berwick states:

> It should not be overlooked that the rapid advances in information technology can also be used to benefit law enforcement in the evidence collection and analysis process. Law enforcement agencies need to exploit these technologies to automate and simplify the analysis process wherever possible. The use of advanced technologies such as expert and artificial intelligence systems; sophisticated utility software; advanced data communication technologies; and high-density storage media will enable sophisticated technologies to be within the reach of investigative and forensic specialists.

In following the cyber 'footprints', new techniques, and unprecedented international coordination and cooperation, will be required. Data retention by Internet Service

Providers (ISP's) and the ability for law enforcement to move quickly to preserve evidence will be essential. It will also be essential to develop and share law enforcement tools. These will be used to identify suspect behaviour, access and compile evidence, and present it in a form comprehensible to investigators, prosecutors, judges and juries.

Forensic computing and its technologies, methodologies, and conceptual frameworks need considerable attention if we are to successfully prevent, detect, investigate and prosecute electronic crime. The US Department of Justice in a recent report identified four major challenges in relation to forensic evidence collection and analysis:

— *Finding evidence in the 'information ocean'*: Finding important evidence can be nearly impossible. Separating valuable information from irrelevant information also requires extraordinary technical efforts. Determining the location where evidence is stored can also be quite difficult.

— *Anonymity:* Computer networks permit persons to easily maintain anonymity and most web surfers have a 'handle', a false name or identity.

— *Traceability:* Related to anonymity, traceability refers to how difficult it is to establish the source and destination of communications on computers and communication networks, such as the Internet. Traceability is becoming even more difficult because of the proliferation and easy availability of multiple communications providers. Communications on the Internet, for example, can easily pass through 10 different Internet Service Providers (ISP's), each of which must provide information (often in real time) to trace a communication.

— *Encryption:* Shortly, the vast majority of data and communications will be encrypted. Encryption can hinder law enforcement investigations and increase costs because of the problems associated with cracking the encryption.

Some other more specific forensic related challenges include:

— Training police and other investigators to:

  — deal with and preserve what amounts to a 'crime scene within a crime scene' or a 'virtual', possibly limitless (even booby-trapped), crime scene; and

  — secure, seize, transport and recover evidence in a safe and legally acceptable manner (for instance, just turning on a computer is the electronic equivalent of walking over the scene of a crime).

— Dealing successfully with the jurisdictional issue, including the searching of networked databases;

— Ensuring that appropriate legislative powers exist to enable required monitoring, searches etc;

— Understanding the social engineering dimension of hacking and some types of cybercrime;

— Dealing with new and emerging technologies such as 'Blue Tooth' and Wireless Application Protocol (WAP), which will, inter alia, allow mobile phones to access the Internet directly, making such communication harder to detect and intercept.

There is said to be as many as 25 separate forensic disciplines. However, forensic computing is still very much a developing and emerging area and has been referred to as 'largely ad hoc'. It will be necessary to eventually develop accredited training courses, to accredit forensic computing laboratories and certify practitioners and to also develop international best practice standards in relation to the retrieval, handling and presentation of digital evidence in the courts.

Forensic computing, while quite different to IT security, can be usefully linked in with practitioners in this area to provide even more effective measures to prevent, detect and reduce electronic crime. An important issue will be the need to develop a life cycle for using the results of investigations as input to the development of security and management technologies. Forensic computing must become more *proactive*, rather than being only a *post mortem* activity as at present, so that it can help prevent crimes recurring as knowledge about them spreads.

Policy Issues

Tracking and tracing attackers across a borderless cyber-world, and holding them accountable, requires multilateral actions that transcend jurisdictions and national boundaries. Tracking and tracing requires cooperation encompassing the legal, political, technical, and economic realms. Significant international efforts to achieve effective, cooperative, and collaborative approaches for dealing with cybercrime and cyber-terrorism are currently underway. For example, the G8 Recommendations on Transnational Crime and the Council of Europe Convention on Cybercrime provide high-level frameworks for international cooperation and collaboration in the legal, policy, and technical realms.

One of the most significant policy implications of the technical approaches to tracking and tracing is the need for intense international cooperation at a deeply technical level. This cooperation must go well beyond simple agreements in principle to share tracking data. The hacker community exchanges vulnerability information, detailed exploits, and attacker toolkits on a continual basis.

As a result, defenders will be completely outmatched unless they routinely and extensively share highly technical information and resources, such as vulnerability information, incident data, new tracking methodologies and techniques, recommendations on hardware and software tools to support tracking, recommendations on best practices, and intelligence on the latest hacker capabilities and trends, including means of evading attempts to track and trace malicious activities. The development of interoperation standards for track and trace technology is an essential part of the required technical cooperation.

A variety of organizational arrangements for exchanging highly technical information is possible. One of the most effective arrangements could be in the form of a shared multilateral technical organization, somewhat akin to the successful (domestic) Bellcore model. After the breakup of AT&T in 1984, the newly-formed regional Bell operating companies (also known as the "Baby Bells") created (and supplied ongoing funding for) a shared research organization called Bellcore. It was Bellcore's mission to research new telecommunications technologies for the benefit of all the regional Bells. Similarly, a shared multilateral technical organization would be far superior to ad-hoc arrangements for information exchange. In particular, due to the continual, rapid evolution of technology and attacker-defender capabilities, much of the technical information in the cyber realm has a very short "shelf life."

A technical team needs stability and continuity to develop and maintain world-class expertise in this highly volatile environment. Regardless of the precise organizational structure, a multilateral technical research, engineering, and advisory capability is essential to

(a) research and recommend the best tracking and tracing techniques and practices,

(b) provide ongoing support for a multilateral tracking and tracing capability,

(c) provide ongoing training and awareness for cooperating incident response and investigatory teams world-wide,

(d) make recommendations to international engineering bodies, such as the Internet Engineering Task Force (IETF), for protocol improvements and standards creation in support of member states' requirements for tracking and tracing attackers,

(e) interact with those creating cyber-law and policy to ensure that the technical and non-technical approaches complement and support each other,

(f) help assure that the tracking and tracing infrastructures and technologies of cooperating entities can interoperate, and

(g) assess the results of cooperation already undertaken by technical and law enforcement agencies, in order to provide feedback for continual improvement.

Although a multilateral technical organization could provide resources (such as tools, procedures, and expert advice) to support forensic analysis by incident response teams and investigatory groups, it is less likely that its services would be extended to provide global incident response. In contrast to providing technical advisory, engineering, and research services, a full-blown involvement in day-to-day incident response operations would be more likely to place the team at the focal point of conflicts of interest among member states.

Migrating Critical Applications to the Internet

Although promising, research on tracking and tracing cyber-attacks is in a nascent state. The lack of proven techniques for effectively and consistently tracking sophisticated cyber-attacks to their source severely diminishes any deterrent effect. Perpetrators feel free to act with nearly total anonymity. Moreover, the general state of computer security is arguably worse than it was thirty years ago. In their paper, "Thirty Years Later: Lessons from the Multics Security Evaluation", Karger and Schell argue that the decades-old Multics operating system is more secure than most operating systems of today, which must function in a wide-open Internet environment.

Given the understanding of system vulnerabilities that existed nearly thirty years ago, today's "security enhanced" or "trusted" systems would not be considered suitable for processing even in the benign closed environment. Also, considering the extent of network interconnectivity and the amount of commercial off-the-shelf (COTS) and other software without pedigree, today's military and commercial environments would be considered very much "open."

To make matters worse, everyone is now expected to be a system administrator of their own desktop system, but without any training! Thus, systems that are weaker than Multics are considered for use in environments in excess of what even Multics could deliver without restructuring around a security kernel.

The logical policy implication of poor security combined with an extremely limited track and trace capability is to move with extreme caution in migrating critical applications and infrastructures to the public Internet environment. This is particularly important in those cases where there are significant risks to public health and safety or risks of major economic loss or disruption of essential societal services.

Caution may be expressed in the form of delaying the migration of critical applications to the Internet, or by incorporating Internet technologies—but only for use on a private network. However, these approaches are often impractical, as the economic benefits of being on the Internet are typically essential for corporate survival.

A more general approach is to design systems for survivability to keep mission-critical services running despite attacks, accidents, or subsystem failures. This survivability engineering approach reduces risk by providing redundant and diverse means of delivering the essential services that support a system's mission despite the compromise of individual components by cyber-attack.

Privacy Issues

Privacy is a central issue in all tracking and tracing technology. An important policy consideration in choosing among alternative technologies is to select a technology that not only minimizes the disclosure of information under normal operation, but also does not create a target of opportunity for attackers. For example, technologies that concentrate lots of tracking information in a single location create the opportunity for massive disclosure (unless the information is highly sanitized).

Another critical part of the privacy equation is the period of retention for data that may be used for tracking evidence of a crime, evidence of a treaty violation, and so forth. International agreements on how long data must be retained and when it must be expunged are important components of a comprehensive policy of cooperation on tracking and tracing. Note that those formulating policy in this area must take into account the technical limitations on retaining large amounts of tracking data for very long, since the high bandwidth of the contemporary Internet can quickly overwhelm even large storage systems.

There has been considerable concern that the Council of Europe Convention on Cybercrime too broadly defines the tracking data to be collected and retained by ISPs, thereby threatening privacy. Here is a situation in which the multilateral technical team could help interact with policy and legal groups to implement a technical solution that collects, retains, and exchanges only data that is essential for tracking and tracing, thereby improving privacy.

The particular solution will vary or evolve over time, but the selection of tracking methodologies that seek to lessen the privacy impact (such as retaining hashes of content instead of the full packet), could be one of the contributions of the experts on the multilateral technical team.

Policies for Automated Tracking

The increasing criticality and time-sensitive nature of today's highly distributed applications is continually increasing the need for rapid tracking, response, and recovery. The Council of Europe's Convention on Cybercrime calls for each State to establish a 24/7 point of contact to provide assistance during an incident. However, due to the increasingly severe timeliness requirements of many mission-critical Internet applications, it will soon be essential for many aspects of tracking, response, and recovery to be automated. As a result, many policy decisions will have to be incorporated into the automated procedures.

For example, the amount of information to be shared in support of tracking may depend on the severity of the incident involved. Nations or other entities may agree to share a larger quantity of data, or more sensitive data, in the event of a severe incident. After an incident has occurred, it will be important to be able to audit the means by which the severity of the incident was determined, to verify that the sharing of additional data was justified.

Imprecise Jurisdictional Boundaries

The borderless cyber-world has created legal and political gray areas, where existing laws and agreements intended for the physical world (including the jurisdictional boundaries of law enforcement) are open to differing interpretations in the virtual world. For example, in a well-publicized "sting operation", the FBI lured two Russian hackers to Seattle in November 2000 by offering them consulting jobs in a firm that appeared to be genuine but had only been created to serve as bait for the hackers.

The FBI believed that the two Russians had stolen tens of thousands of credit card numbers through unauthorized computer accesses and had also attempted extortion by threatening businesses with the disclosure of sensitive information. As part of the "job interview," the Russians were asked to demonstrate their hacking talent. During the demonstration, the hackers accessed their machines in Russia, using workstations at the offices of the FBI's phony firm.

Unbeknownst to the hackers, the workstations had been set up with keystroke monitoring software, so that the hackers login IDs and passwords could be captured. The FBI later used the captured IDs and passwords to download information from the Russian computers to use as evidence. Both men were arrested and indicted. One has since been convicted and the other is awaiting trial.

The most recent and ironic twist to this story is that in August 2002, Russia's Federal Security Service charged one of the FBI agents with illegally accessing the hackers' computers, which were physically located in Chelyabinsk, Russia. However, it is more likely that this particular case will be resolved in a political forum, rather than a legal one.

From the FBI's perspective, immediate access to the evidence on the Russian hackers' computers was crucial, since the electronic evidence could quickly be destroyed at any time. The FBI called this the first case in their history to "utilize the technique of extra-territorial seizure." From the Russian perspective, traditional national boundaries and legal jurisdiction need to be respected, and this case sets a troublesome precedent for future actions.

The very ephemeral nature of evidence in the cyber-world means that time is of the essence, much more so than in the physical world. In the physical world, law-enforcement cooperation across international boundaries depends on treaties and other international agreements that are often arduously slow in practice.

One can envision international agreements that permit electronic "extra-territorial seizure" under explicitly specified circumstances, but with protections that help prevent misuse. Such protections may include placing the seized evidence in escrow, where it will remain locked away until permission (e.g., a search warrant) is granted for its use by the nation on whose territory the elec-tronic seizure took place. If permission is denied, the international agreement may specify that the seized data must be destroyed.

Thus, since cyber-attacks transcend our traditional notions of physical borders, our technical ability to track and trace attackers must be complemented by well-crafted international agreements that formalize the cooperation and collaboration necessary to track attacks (and collect evidence) across administrative, jurisdictional, and national boundaries.

General agreements regarding cooperation and collaboration should include specifics such as the degree of information sharing, the speed with which a request for tracking information will be granted (which could vary according to attack severity), the equipment and procedures to be used, who will be responsible for the day-to-day fixed costs, and who will be responsible for the variable costs associated with a big incident. What financial and technical assistance should be provided to make the international tracking infrastructure more effective? What issues will arise if an attack packet crosses multiple international boundaries and is considered a criminal act in one country but not others? International agreements may specify cooperation in tracking only in the case of a criminal act. Who decides, and how can agreement be reached to resolve this prior to a major event?

Additional issues arise when one considers extra-territorial actions that extend beyond the collection of evidence in response to a cyber-attack. Extra-territorial defensive or retaliatory actions by the victim of an electronic attack might be justified by Article 51 of the United Nations charter, which confirms a nation's inherent right of self-defense. One could defend the right of a nation to take extra-territorial actions that interrupt a serious cyber-attack in progress, but it is less clear what responses are justified when an attack appears to be over.

The appropriate response may depend on how severe the consequences of the cyber-attack were, the time scale over which multiple attacks occurred, and the severity of the threat of further attacks. Rather than leave extraterritorial action in response to a cyber-attack as a solely unilateral decision, international agreements are sorely needed to create a framework for acceptable behavior under a variety of complex circumstances.

Levels of Evidence

International agreements will be needed to specify what quality or level of forensic evidence (and the assurance that it was well preserved) will constitute an internationally recognized justification for sanctions, an information warfare response, or even a military response. Issues that come into play include the ability to demonstrate high assurance of the tamper-resistance of hardware and software systems that support tracking. A provable degree of certainty of correctness (i.e., accuracy, precision, and tamper-resistance) in tracking perpetrators is needed if serious responses to cyber-attack are to be justified.

Levels of Damage and Threat

Once tracking of attacks becomes highly effective, it will be more important than ever to establish international agreements on liability (such as for intermediate systems that inadvertently help to amplify an attack), on defining levels of damage or threat (such as what constitutes an act of war in cyber-space), and on the appropriate response to each level of damage. Agreements in these areas are crucial, since prosecution, retaliatory information war, or even military retaliation can occur. Level of damage must be combined with the level of evidence to provide an internationally recognized justification for a response to cyber-attack.

Liability Issues

Here are some liability issues that could become the subject of international agreements once tracking and tracing makes it easier to identify entities and individuals who may bear some responsibility for the results of a cyber-attack:

— What are the liability exposures for the following?

  — the perpetrators of the attack

  — vendors of software whose vulnerabilities made the attack possible

  - — owners and administrators of the intermediate (e.g., zombie or anonymizer) systems that participated in generating attack packets or obscuring the original source of the attack
  - — transmitting ISPs and networks that did not squelch the attack when notified or did not help trace in accordance with international policy agreements

— Would there be waivers of certain kinds of liability exposure for those who participate in tracking and tracing? For example, a corporation may share computer security incident data with other organizations to aid in tracking and tracing attackers. However, by sharing this information the corporation may reveal information involving their own system vulnerabilities, which may provide evidence of liability, thereby increasing their risk of being successfully sued. As another example, if the system vulnerabilities are exposed, can an insurer avoid paying a business interruption claim to the corporation?

— Should liability extend to the owners of systems that participated in an attack without the owners' knowledge or permission? What are the standards of "due care" that system owners must comply with to avoid responsibility for use of their systems by attackers?

— Are those who provide anonymizer services liable for providing anonymity to attackers, even inadvertently? On the other hand, the privacy protection provided by anonymizers is a valuable social function. Should anonymizers receive special protection from liability claims?

— Should liability extend to system designers or owners who participate in placing an overly critical system on the Internet, despite knowledge of the fragility and poor security of the system, and without taking adequate backup measures (e.g., employing appropriate survivability strategies) in the event of attack? Placing highly critical, yet fragile, systems on the Internet could be an international destabilizing factor, and could allow mischief-makers to force international confrontations.

Honeypots and Honeynets

Honeypots and honeynets are decoy hosts and networks used to observe and document attacker behavior. Honeypots and honeynets are controlled environments that employ deception to masquerade as vulnerable and valuable targets of interest. Unless an attacker goes beyond the confines of a honeynet or honeypot system, no real harm is done, although the actions taken by the attacker can be fully recorded for use as evidence of the attack.

Domestic laws and international agreements need to specify whether breaking into (or otherwise directing an attack against) a honeynet or honeypot would be sufficient cause for criminal prosecution (or a retaliatory response), or would instead be considered "entrapment."

At the very least, from the perspective of tracking and tracing attackers, international agreements should specify whether multilateral track and trace procedures should be triggered by attacks against decoy systems or whether they should be reserved solely for "real" attacks. It would be beneficial for such agreements to support multilateral cooperation for tracing attacks against decoy systems, even though many requests for assistance in tracking and tracing an attacker would likely be made without revealing that the victim of the attack was, in fact, a decoy system. The bottom line is that honeypots and honeynets can play a significant role in gaining early warning of, and thereby preempting, high-consequence cyber-attacks. Hence, there can be considerable justification for using a multilateral track and trace infrastructure to help identify perpetrators of attacks against decoy systems, and for having international agreements that support this.

Policy Requirements for Next-Generation

The standard Internet protocols in widespread use today were designed for a network environment in which the users of the network were considered to be trustworthy and the motivations and rewards for malicious activity were negligible. A high degree of anonymity for users was more the exception than the rule.

As late as the early 1990s the "whois" databases maintained by the various Regional Internet Registries around the world painted a reasonably accurate picture of who was responsible for any allocated range of IP addresses, and provided administrative and technical contact information. These contacts could often be expected to be able to trace misuse of a given IP address in their range to an individual user or group.

As the Internet population continued its exponential growth, anonymity increased. Moreover, the kinds of applications that were placed on the Internet grew more critical in nature and were more tempting targets for malicious attackers with financial, political, or terrorist motives. Early on, traditional security approaches, such as firewalls, were seen as the solution to the problem of malicious users. However, fortress models of security were largely ineffective in protecting highly distributed applications. Such applications typically have a diverse and highly distributed user community, with varying degrees of trustworthiness (e.g., employees, collaborators, customers, suppliers, the general public, etc.)

Fortress models are binary in nature: the attacker is outside and everything is fine, or the attacker is inside and all is lost. Highly distributed applications have indistinct physical and logical perimeters, so it difficult to distinguish inside from outside in a binary fashion. Rather, there are varying shades of gray, varying degrees of trust. In fact, in modern highly distributed systems, trust boundaries are essentially replacing the physical boundaries of earlier computer systems. Next-generation Internet protocols will be required to deal with trust not on a binary basis but at very fine levels of granularity.

On the Internet today, traditional computer security is being replaced by a new security paradigm called survivability. Survivability is the ability of a system to continue to fulfill its mission despite attacks, accidents, or subsystem failures. This approach is a blend of computer security and busi-ness risk management.

Trust management is a central part of survivability, and it is trust that has been gradually eroding throughout the Internet. Ultimately, trust is a human quality, based on individual and organizational attributes. It is particularly difficult to establish trust in an environment in which the users of a network have near-total anonymity, and where IP source addresses can be readily spoofed.

Entry-Point Anonymity Problem

Even the tracing pf attack packet to the IP address of its point of origin can be accomplished, it is becoming increasingly difficult, if not impossible, to link that IP address with the actual perpetrator of the attack. As an example, consider the emergence of prepaid Internet access cards, for which no personal identification of any kind is required by the ISP.

The ISP assigns a dynamic IP address from its pool of IP addresses whenever the user dials in to a local or toll-free access number. The only clues to the identity of the user might be the phone number used to access the ISP and the hardware (MAC) address of the computer that makes use of the dynamic IP address (if logged and retained).

However, prepaid cellular phones can be untraceable, and hardware addresses can be readily cloned. The existence of cyber-cafés (wired and wireless), as well as public Internet access in libraries, makes it possible for a user to be totally anonymous, and untraceable, at his or her point of entry to the Internet.The term entry-point anonymity is used to refer the inability to link an Internet IP address to any human actor or organization. In response to an Internet attack, it is often a human actor or organization one wishes to track or trace, not solely an IP address. Moreover, an IP address is a poor surrogate on which to establish a basis of trustworthiness.

Many denial-of-service attacks work by overwhelming the limited resources of a host or network device. In such attacks, the computational or other resource cost to the defender may be orders of magnitude higher than the cost to the attacker. Can next-generation protocols be designed so as to increase the cost to the attacker and decrease the cost to the defender? Over the past few years, researchers have been investigating protocol design from the perspective of relative costs to the attacker versus the defender.

The basic idea is to be very vigilant in the commitment of system resources to the processing of packets. One approach is to gradually ramp up the commitment of resources as trust in the validity of a packet is increasingly established. For example, if part of the processing of a packet involves the verification of the packet using cryptographically strong authentication, a protocol could be designed that first allows authentication using a weaker, less computationally expensive algorithm. If the packet fails this first step, then it can be rejected at a lower computational cost to the defender. If the packet succeeds, then authentication proceeds to the second step with a greater commitment of resources, but with a higher level of confidence that the resource allocation is justified. This is not a guaranteed defense against an intelligent adversary, but it would significantly increase the costs to an attacker who tried to overcome this defensive measure.

Supporting this kind of vigilant resource consumption would be a most desirable capability of next-generation Internet security protocols. This risk-mitigating approach is much more in line with the new survivability paradigm than it is with traditional computer security. The only policy implication of this technical approach might be an attempt to ensure that this technical issue is placed in front of an appropriate standards-making body, such as the IETF. Some very practical examples of vigilant resource consumption have been provided by D. J. Bernstein and Schuba et al., who describe techniques for preventing a host from over-committing resources in response to "session opening" requests by packets with spoofed IP addresses. Their techniques help to defeat the classic SYN Flooding denial-of-service attack, which attempts to drain the resources of a victim.

Another interesting aspect of the resource consumption issue relates to the amount of resources consumed by the track and trace infrastructure. Hackers can do more than just attempt to evade track and trace technology. Hackers can exploit an overly reactive track and trace infrastructure by taking actions that trigger the infrastructure to consume inordinate amounts of resources, thereby creating a denial-of-service scenario that could cripple not only the track and trace infrastructure, but also the systems that the infrastructure was designed to protect. This is analogous to the effects of diseases caused by an overly reactive immune system. Designers of the track and trace infrastructure must take measures to lessen the likelihood that such scenarios could occur.

Trust Management and Privacy

In any Internet transaction, trust ultimately depends not on IP addresses but on particular relationships among individuals and their roles within organizations and groups (which may be economic, political, educational, or social). Trust cannot be established while maintaining total anonymity of the actors involved. It goes without saying that there is a great need for privacy on the Internet, and it must be carefully guarded. For example, oppressive regimes may take draconian measures to stop activities that would be considered perfectly justified in a democratic society. However, trust and privacy trade-offs are a normal part of human social, political, and economic interactions, and such tradeoffs can be resolved in a number of venues, particularly in the marketplace. Consider the telephone system, in particular the caller ID feature, which displays the phone number and name associated with incoming calls.

Customers can pay extra to have additional privacy (for an unlisted number) and sometimes are given the option to be anonymous by default (i.e., have their phone number and their name blocked on the displays of customers who pay for caller ID). However, the caller ID customer can choose to block all incoming calls from anonymous callers.

The anonymous caller is notified of this fact by an automated message. The only way to complete the call is to enter a key sequence to remove the anonymity for this particular call and redial. This choice is a form of negotiation between the caller and the intended recipient of the call, and it is a trade-off between anonymity (privacy) and trust that is supported by the technology of caller ID and the marketplace.

There is no government mandate that all calls must be anonymous or that no calls are allowed to be anonymous. The individual caller chooses whether or not to relinquish anonymity (i.e., some degree of privacy) in exchange for the perceived value of completing the call by increasing the degree of trust as seen by the recipient.

One can envision next-generation Internet protocols supporting this kind of marketplace negotiation of trust versus privacy trade-offs. This would involve third-party certifying authorities, which would serve as brokers of trust. These "trust brokers" would be commercial, non-profit, or governmental (e.g., governmental certifying authorities may be required to establish the trust necessary for accessing national critical infrastructure and defense systems, but would not be involved in the vast majority of commercial, political, social, or educational activities).

These certifying authorities would provide mechanisms whereby packets would be cryptographically signed with very fine-grained authentication credentials of the sender, such as the fact that the sender works for a particular company, works in a certain industry, or lives in a certain zip code. This is not the same as having an individual digitally sign a message—a digitally signed message may be too coarsegrained for a particular scenario and may reveal too much.

As an example of the use of fine-grained authentication, the owners of a web site may decide to only allow visitors who are authenticated as residents of Pennsylvania. The individual accessing the web site may only wish to access web sites that permit full anonymity, or he or she may choose which personal credentials may be revealed to obtain whatever value the web site may provide.

A more controversial capability would be the escrowing, by these certifying authorities, of complete identifying information for a specified period of time, to be revealed in the event that one or more of a user's packets have been identified as participating in a confirmed attack. Note that there would be no centralized authority for fine-grained trust management. This trustmanagement approach would be based on a multitude of individual arrangements and marketplace concerns, though standards for implementing the approach would emerge over time. This approach allows for the individual, the marketplace, and policy negotiations to determine the trade-offs between trust and privacy. Protocols supporting this approach would not dictate the particular trade-offs to be made, which could vary over time according to the social, political, and legal climate. Privacy legislation would restrict the information that could be asked for and would set specific limits on retention and on how the information could be used.

Situation-Sensitive Security

Survivability demands the ability to gracefully degrade service and increase security in the event of attack or accident. Next-generation Internet protocols must allow for variable levels of trust under various attack states. Protocol elements that are not processed during ordinary conditions may be called into service during ongoing periods of attack or heightened threat of attack. It is essential that next-generation protocols support this capability.

Sufficient Header Space for Tracking Information

One of the most basic requirements for next-generation Internet protocols, in support of tracking and tracing, is to provide sufficient header space to hold authenticated tracking and other audit information that may be inserted into a packet by all cooperating routers along the packet's path. Under the current Internet protocol (IPv4), packet-marking schemes must squeeze tracking data into rarely-used header fields. Because of the severe space limitations, tracking data must be split across multiple packets. This provides the opportunity for attackers to insert false tracking information into a stream of packets.

There are, of course, serious policy implications associated with the technical capability to gather large amounts of tracking data. Use of the technology must be limited by international agreements on policy and law stating under what circumstances tracking data can be collected, retained, and used. Such policy and law may be situation-sensitive. For example, under severe circumstances, multilateral agreements may allow more data (or more sensitive data) to be collected and retained for a longer period of time.

Emerging Next-Generation Security Protocols

IPsec: IPsec is an emerging security standard for IP. It provides two new security protocols: an Authentication Header (AH) and an Encapsulating Security Payload (ESP). The goals of this security standard are described in Request for Comments (RFC) 2401: "IPsec is designed to provide interoperable, high quality, cryptographically-based security for IPv4 and IPv6. The set of security services offered includes access control, connectionless integrity, data origin authentication, protection against replays (a form of partial sequence integrity), confidentiality (encryption), and limited traffic flow confidentiality. These services are provided at the IP layer, offering protection for IP and/or upper layer protocols."

These objectives are met through the use of two traffic security protocols, the Authentication Header (AH) and the Encapsulating Security Payload (ESP), and through the use of cryptographic key management procedures and protocols. The set of IPsec protocols employed in any context, and the ways in which they are employed, will be determined by the security and system requirements of users, applications, and/or sites/organizations. IPsec provides for packet authentication and confidentiality, and in particular it can be used to authenticate the source address of a packet.

However, the overall approach is much more akin to traditional security than it is to the new survivability paradigm. As a result, it does not provide explicit support for vigilant resource consumption, fine-grained authentication of trust, and situation-sensitive processing, which are three of the requirements for nextgeneration Internet protocols. So there is much work to be done in designing and implementing protocols that effectively fulfill these requirements, thereby preempting many potential attacks and enhancing the technical ability to track and trace attacks to their point of origin and to the responsible individuals or organizations.

Internet Protocol Version 6 (IPv6): Internet Protocol Version 6 (IPv6) is the next generation IETF standard protocol that is slowly replacing the current IPv4. The new protocol's most salient feature is an enormously expanded address space compared to IPv4. An IP address is 128 bits long in IPv6, as compared to only 32 bits in IPv4. Another key feature is that this next generation protocol has IPsec security built in. In addition, the IPv6 header design is particularly flexible and efficient, providing for a sequence of extension headers to carry optional information.

In contrast to IPv4, the IPv6 header structure can provide ample space for recording tracking or other audit data. Recall that the packet marking techniques had to make use of very limited space in rarely used IPv4 header fields to store tracking data. The need to distribute the tracking data over several packets allows an attacker to defeat the packet marking schemes by generating packets containing false tracking information. The flexible header structure of IPv6 potentially offers considerable space in which to store tracking data along the path of the packet. However, if the tracking information causes the packet to grow beyond the maximum allowable packet size, packets would have to be fragmented and performance would suffer.

The growing shortage of IP addresses under IPv4 has resulted in an increased sharing of global IP addresses through the use of network address translation (NAT) and dynamic IP assignment. This sharing of IP addresses is a detriment to tracking and tracing, since there is no long-term correspondence between a computer and an IP address. The transient correspondence may be temporarily recorded in an ISP's logs or in a network administrator's configuration documents, but it is certainly ephemeral. In contrast to IPv4, the IPv6 the address space is enormous, making it possible for every network device to be assigned a static (fixed) IP address within a multi-level hierarchy of addresses.

5

Challenges of Cybercrime Prevention

The American Heritage Dictionary defines the term 'security' as "freedom from risk or danger; safety. " This definition is perhaps a little misleading when it comes to computer and networking security, because it implies a degree of protection that is inherently impossible in the modern connectivity-oriented computing environment. This is why the same dictionary provides another definition, specific to computer science: "The level to which a program or device is safe from unauthorized use". Implicit in this definition is the caveat that the objectives of security and accessibility are, by their very natures, diametrically opposed. The more accessible the data, the less secure it is.

Any security plan is an attempt to strike the proper balance between the two objectives. The first step is to determine what needs to be protected, and to what degree. Because not every asset is equally valuable, some assets need stronger protection than others. This determination leads to the concept of instituting multiple layers of security. An effective security plan does not rely on one technology or solution but instead takes a multilayered approach. Compare this approach to a business's physical security measures; most companies don't depend on just the locks on the buildings' doors to keep intruders and thieves out. Instead, they might also have perimeter security, perhaps additional external security such as a guard or guard dog, external and internal alarm systems, and to protect special valuables, further internal safeguards such as a vault. IT security should be similarly layered. For example:

— Firewalls at network entry points that function as perimeter protection

— Password protection at local computers, requiring user authentication to log on, to keep unauthorized persons out

— Access permissions set on individual network resources to restrict access of those who are "in".

— Encryption of data sent across the network or stored on disk to protect what is especially valuable, sensitive, or confidential

— Servers, routers, and hubs located in locked rooms to prevent people with physical access from hijacking data without authorization

The Intrusion Triangle Crime prevention specialists use a model called the Crime Triangle to explain that certain criteria must exist before a crime can occur. We can adapt this same familiar law enforcement concept to network security. The point on the triangle are:

i) *Motive:* An intruder must have a reason to want to breach the security of the network (even if the reason is "just for fun"); otherwise he or she won't bother.

ii) *Means:* An intruder must have the ability (either the programming knowledge or, in the case of script kiddies, the intrusion software written by others) or he or she won't be able to breach your security.

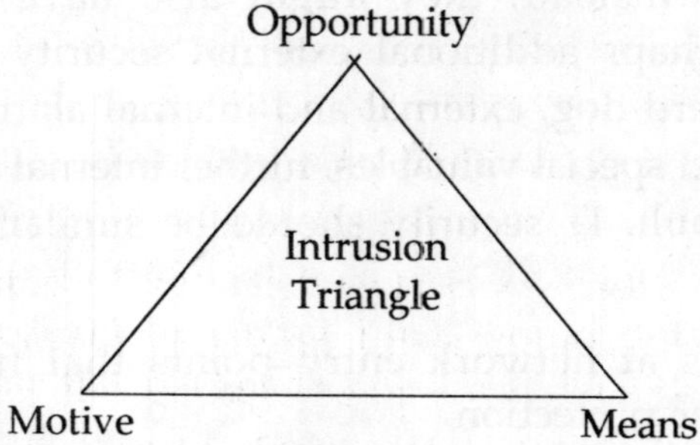

— *Opportunity:* An intruder must have the chance to enter the network because of flaws in the security plan, holes in a software program that open an avenue of access, or physical proximity to network components. If there is no opportunity to intrude, the would-be hacker will go elsewhere. If you think about the three-point intrusion criteria for a moment, you'll see that there is really only one leg of the triangle over which the network administrator or security specialist has any control. It is unlikely that anyone can do much to remove the intruder's motive. The motive is likely to be built into the type of data that's on the network or even the personality of the intruder him- or herself. It is also not often possible to prevent the intruder from having or obtaining the means to breach your security. Programming knowledge is freely available, and many experienced hackers are more than happy to help less sophisticated ones. The one thing that people who strive to prevent cybercrime *can* affect is the opportunity afforded the hacker.

Crime prevention officers tell members of the community that they probably can't keep a potential burglar from wanting to steal, and they certainly can't keep the potential burglar from obtaining burglary tools or learning the "tricks of the trade. "What they *can* do is take away, as much as possible, the opportunity for the burglar to target their own homes.

This means putting dead-bolt locks on house doors (and using them); getting a big, loud dog who is unfriendly to strangers; and installing an alarm system. In other words, the homeowner's goal is not to prevent the burglar from burglarizing but to make his or her own home a less desirable target. For network "owners," the objective is to "harden" the network, so that all those hackers out there who already have the motive and the means will look for an easier victim.

The best and most expensive locks in the world won't keep intruders out of your house if you don't use them. And if those locks are difficult to use and cause you inconvenience in your everyday comings and goings, you probably *won't* use them—at least, not all the time. A poorly implemented network security system that is difficult to administer or that unduly inconveniences network users might end up similarly; eventually the person burdened with maintaining it will throw his or her hands up in frustration and just turn the darn thing off. And that will leave the network wide open to intruders.

Every industry has its own "language," the jargon that describes ideas, items, concepts, and procedures that are unique to the field. Lawyers speak "legalese," rife with *wherefores* and *hereuntos;* doctors and nurses use terms like *crash cart* and *defib*, and police reports are sprinkled with references to *perps* and *vics* and *MVAs*. Computer networking is infamous for its "technotalk" and the proliferation of acronyms that often mystify outsiders. Specialty areas within an industry often have their own brands of jargon as well, and the computer security subfield is no exception.

It might not be absolutely necessary for the cybercrime investigator to understand all the technical aspects of how security measures work—but knowledge of the technical language used to describe security concepts and devices will serve a couple of important purposes:

— It will make you aware of what can and can't be accomplished by a hacker in particular network environment.

— If you are able to "talk the talk"—to converse intelligently about security issues and measures—you will be better able to win the trust of and communicate with the IT professionals who provide much of the information necessary to your investigation.

Let us define some of the more common words and phrases that you might encounter as you begin to explore the fascinating world of computer security:

— *Authentication:* Verification of identity of a user, computer, or process.

— *Authorization:* The actions that a user, computer, or process, once identified, is permitted to do.

— *Audit:* To track security-related events, such as logging onto the system or network, accessing objects, or exercising user/group rights or privileges.

— *Breach:* Successfully defeating security measures to gain access to data or resources without authorization, to make data or resources available to unauthorized persons, or to delete or alter computer files.

— *Cipher:* A method used to encrypt data.

— *Cipher text:* Data in encrypted form.

— *Confidentiality of data:* Ensuring that the contents of messages will be kept secret. See also integrity of data.

— *Cryptography:* The science of hiding information.

— *Encryption:* The process of converting data (plain text) into a format (cipher text) that cannot be read or understood by anyone except those authorized to receive it.

— *Encryption algorithm:* A formula or calculation that is applied to data to encrypt, or scramble, it.

— *Integrity of data:* Ensuring that data has not been modified or altered, that the data received is identical to the data that was sent.

— *Key:* A variable that is used in conjunction with an algorithm to encrypt or decrypt data.

— *Penetration testing:* Evaluating a system by attempting to circumvent the computer's or network's security measures.

— *Reliability:* The probability of a computer system or network continuing to perform in a satisfactory manner for a specific time period under normal operating conditions.

— *Risk:* The probability that a specific security threat will be able to exploit a system vulnerability, resulting in damage, loss of data, or other undesired results.

— *Risk management:* The process of identifying, controlling, and either minimizing or completely eliminating events that pose a threat to system reliability, data integrity, and data confidentiality.

— *TCSEC:* Trusted Computer System Evaluation Criteria, a system for evaluating a system's level of security.

— *Technical vulnerability:* A flaw or bug in the hardware or software components of a system that leave it vulnerable to security breach.

— *Vulnerability:* A weakness in the hardware, software, or security plan that leaves a system or network open to threat of unauthorized access or damage or destruction of data.

Physical Security

One of the most important aspects of a comprehensive network security plan is physical access control. This matter is often left up to facilities managers and plant security departments or outsourced to security guard companies.

Network administrators concern themselves with sophisticated software and hardware solutions that prevent intruders from accessing internal computers remotely while doing nothing to protect the servers, routers, cable, and other physical components of the network from direct access.

In far too many supposedly security-conscious organizations, computers are locked away from employees and visitors all day, only to be left open at night to the janitorial staff—who usually have keys to all offices. It is not at all uncommon for computer espionage experts to pose as members of a cleaning crew to gain physical access to machines that hold sensitive data. This is a favorite ploy for several reasons:

— Cleaning services are often contracted to outside firms; thus company management has minimal control over the screening of the individuals who are hired by the contractor and who are given access to the offices and other parts of the building.

— Workers in the cleaning industry are often transient, so company employees might not be easily aware of who is or isn't a legitimate member of the cleaning crew.

— Cleaning is usually done late at night, when all or most company employees are gone, making it easier to surreptitiously steal data.

— Cleaning-crew members are often paid little or no attention by company employees, who take their presence for granted and think nothing of cleaners being in areas where the presence of others would be questioned.

Physically breaking into the server room and stealing the hard disk on which sensitive data resides may be a crude method of committing cybercrime; nonetheless, it happens. In some organizations, it could be the easiest way to gain unauthorized access, especially for an intruder who has help "on the inside."

One of the first things an investigator will want to do in a network intrusion case is to review the physical security measures in place to determine whether access could have been gained this way. Knowledge that the intruder was physically on the site narrows your list of possible suspects from "all hackers, all over the world" to persons who are or have been in the immediate vicinity.

Ensuring physical access control means:

- — Controlling physical access to the servers
- — Controlling physical access to networked workstations
- — Controlling physical access to network devices
- — Controlling physical access to the cable
- — Being aware of security considerations with wireless media
- — Being aware of security considerations related to portable computers
- — Recognizing the security risk of allowing data to be printed
- — Recognizing the security risks involving diskettes, CDs, tapes, and other removable media.

Protecting File Servers

File servers on which sensitive data is stored, as well as infrastructure servers that provide mission-critical services such as logon authentication and access control, should be placed in a highly secure location. At the minimum, servers should be in a locked room to which only employees who need to work directly with the servers have access. Keys should be distributed sparingly, and records should be kept of keys' issuance and return.

If security needs are high due to the nature of the business or the data, access to the server room could be controlled by magnetic card, electronic locks requiring entry of a numerical code, or even biometric access control devices such as fingerprint or retinal scanners. Other security measures include monitor detectors or other alarm systems, activated during nonbusiness hours, and security cameras. A security guard or company should monitor these devices.

Protecting Workstations

Many network security plans focus on the servers but ignore the risk posed by workstations that have network access to those servers. It is not uncommon for employees to leave their computers unsecured when they leave for lunch or even when they leave for the evening. Often there will be a workstation in the receptionist area that is open to visitors who walk in off the street. If the receptionist manning the station must leave briefly, the computer—and the network to which it is connected—is vulnerable unless steps have been taken to ensure that it is secure. A good security plan includes protection of all unmanned workstations.

A secure client operating system such as Windows NT or Windows 2000 requires an interactive logon with a valid account name and password in order to access the operating system. These systems allow users to "lock" the workstation when they are going to be away from it, so someone else can't just step up and start using the computer. Organizations must not depend on access permissions and other software security methods alone to protect the network. If a potential intruder can gain physical access to a networked computer, he or she is that much closer to accessing valuable data or introducing a virus onto the network.

Many modern PC cases come with some type of locking mechanism that will help prevent an unauthorized person from opening the case and stealing the hard disk. Locks are also available to prevent use of the diskette drive, copying of data to diskette, or rebooting the computer with a diskette.

Protecting Network Devices

Hubs, routers, switches, and other network devices should be physically secured from unauthorized access. It is easy to forget that just because a device doesn't have a monitor on which you can *see* data, this does not mean the data can't be captured or destroyed at that access point. For example, a traditional Ethernet hub sends all data out every port on the hub. An intruder who has access to the hub can plug a packet-sniffing device that operates in "promiscuous mode" into a spare port and capture data sent to any computer on the segment.

Although switches and routers are somewhat more secure than hubs, any device through which the data passes is a point of vulnerability. Replacing hubs with switches and routers makes it more difficult for an intruder to "sniff" on your network. However, it is still possible to use techniques such as *router redirection* via ARP spoofing, in which nearby machines are redirected to forward traffic through an intruder's machine, by sending ARP packets that contain the router's IP address mapped to the intruder's machine's MAC address. This results in other machines believing the intruder's machine is the router, and so they send their traffic to it.

A similar method uses ICMP router advertisement messages. With certain switches, it is also possible to overflow the address tables with multiple false MAC addresses or send a continuous flow of random garbage through the switch to trigger it to change from bridging mode to repeating mode. This means all frames will be broadcast on all ports, giving the intruder the same opportunity to access the data that he would have with a regular hub. This activity is called *switch jamming*.

If the switch has a special monitor port designed to be used with a sniffer for legitimate purposes, an intruder who has physical access to the switch can simply plug into this port and capture network data. For these reasons, all network devices should be placed in a locked room or closet; administrators should protect these devices in the same manner as the servers.

Protecting the Cable: The next step in protecting the network and its data is to secure the cable across which that data travels. Twisted-pair and coaxial cable are both vulnerable to data capture; an intruder who has access to the cable can tap into it and eavesdrop on messages being sent across it. A number of companies make "tapping" devices.

Fiber optic cable is more difficult to tap into because it does not produce electrical pulses but instead uses pulses of light to represent the 0s and 1s of binary data. It is possible, however, for a sophisticated intruder to use an optical splitter and tap into the signal on fiber optic media.

Cable taps can sometimes be detected using a time domain reflectometer (TDR) or optical TDR to measure the strength of the signal and determine where the tap is located. Compromise of security at the physical level is a special threat when network cables are not contained in one facility but span a distance between buildings. There is even a name for this risk: manhole manipulation, referring to the easy access intruders often have to cabling that runs through underground conduits.

Protecting Laptops: Portable computers—laptops, notebooks, and new fully functional handheld computers such as the Pocket PC and Palm OS machines—present their own security problems based on the very features that make them popular: their small size and mobility. Physical security for portable computers is especially important because it is so easy to steal the entire machine, data and all.

A large number of companies make theft protection devices and security software for laptops. Locks and alarms are widely available, along with software programs that will disable the laptop's functionality if it is stolen or even help track it down by causing the computer to "phone home" the first time the portable computer is attached to a modem. In addition, data on portables can be encrypted to protect it from access if the devices are stolen. An example of theft recovery and tracking software for laptops is Cyber Angel from Computer Sentry Software. Another product, TrackIT, is a hardware antitheft device for computer cases and other baggage.

Some laptops come with removable hard disks. If users have highly sensitive data that must be accessed with a laptop, it's a good idea to store it on a removable disk and encrypt it. The user should also separate that disk from the computer when it is not in use.

Protecting the Paper Chase: Network security specialists and administrators tend to concentrate on protecting data in electronic form, but intruders can also steal confidential digital information by printing it or locating a hard copy that was printed by someone else. It does little good to implement strong password policies and network access controls if employees can print sensitive material and then leave it lying on desks, stored in unlocked file cabinets, or thrown into an easily accessed trash basket.

"Dumpster diving" (searching the trash for company secrets) is a common form of corporate espionage—and one that surprisingly often yields results. If confidential data must be printed, the paper copy should be kept as physically secure as the digital version. Disposal should require shredding, and in cases of particularly high-security information, the shredded paper can be mixed with water to create a pulp that is impossible to put back together again.

Removable Storage Risks: Yet another potential point of failure in the network security plan involves saving data to removable media. Diskettes, Zip and Jaz disks, tapes, PC cards, CDs, and DVDs containing sensitive data must be kept physically secured at all times. Although removable media can present a security threat to the network, it can also play an important part in the overall security plan, when used properly. Removable disks can be removed from the computer and locked in a safe or removed from the premises to protect the data that is stored there.

Cryptography

Cryptography is a word derived from the Greek *kryptos* ("hidden"), and the use of cryptography pre-dates the computer age by hundreds of years. Keeping secrets has long been a concern of human beings, and the purpose of cryptography is to hide information or change it so that it is incomprehensible to people for whom it is not intended. Cryptographic techniques include:

— *Encryption,* which involves applying a procedure called an *algorithm* to plain text to turn it into something that will appear to be gibberish to anyone who doesn't have the *key* to decrypt it.

— *Steganography,* which is a means of hiding the existence of the data, not just its contents. This is usually done by concealing it within other, innocuous data.

Cryptographic techniques are an important part of a multilayered security plan. Some security measures, such as implementation of a firewall and use of access permissions, attempt to keep intruders out of the network or computer altogether, much like fences and door locks attempt to keep burglars off the grounds or out of the house.

Cryptography provides an inner line of defense. Like a wall safe that is there in case the burglars *do* make it inside your house—and to protect valuables from people who are authorized to come into your house—cryptography protects data from intruders who are able to penetrate the outer network defenses and from those who are authorized to access the network but not *this* particular data.

Cryptographic techniques concern themselves with three basic purposes:

— *Authentication:* Verifying the identity of a user or computer.

— *Confidentiality:* Keeping the contents of the data secret.

— *Integrity:* Ensuring that data doesn't change between the time it leaves the source and the time it reaches its destination.

One or more of these goals may be a priority, depending upon the situation. For example, if an investigator receives a message from the Chief to fly to the West Coast to interview a witness in a case, the overriding concern might be knowing that it was, indeed, the Chief of Police who sent the message and not a fellow officer playing a practical joke. In this case, *authentication* of the message sender's identity is of utmost importance. If the case relates to an internal affairs investigation and it is important that no one else in the department know where the investigator is going, *confidentiality* of the data might be important as well. And if the message states that the investigator is authorized to spend $3000 on the trip, it might be important to ensure that the message has not been changed in transit—in other words, that the message's *integrity* has not been compromised.

Authentication

Many different methods can be used to authenticate a user's identity. In general, the user is asked to provide something that is associated with his or her user account that could not easily be provided by someone else. The requested credential is generally one (or more) of the following:

— *Something you know:* One way to determine that a person is really who he or she claims to be is to ask a question that only the "real McCoy" is likely to be able to answer. If you are engaging in online messaging with someone who purports to be your brother, before discussing personal or sensitive subjects, you might ask him what your mother's oldest sister's name is, or ask him to name the song that the two of you played in a piano duet as children. In information security, the "something you know" is usually a password or personal identification number (PIN).

— *Something you have*: Passwords can be compromised. For example, someone can discover passwords through a brute-force attack or by watching over a user's shoulder as he or she types the password. In many of these cases, the user doesn't know that someone else now knows the password. A better authentication method is to require that the user provide a physical object, such as a "smart card". If the card is lost or stolen, the user is likely to know about it. Smart cards are used to log onto computer networks and to access bank accounts and make purchases.

— *Something you are:* Although a card or other physical object that must be in the user's possession is a step up from password authentication, cards can be lost or stolen or perhaps even duplicated. An even more secure method of proving identity is via what you are, that is, biological data such as a fingerprint, voice print, or retinal or iris scan. Biometric methods are much more difficult to defeat than other identification methods.

Because none of these authentication methods (or any other) is absolutely foolproof, it makes sense in a high-security environment to use a multifactor authentication system (sometimes called *two-way* or *three-way authentication*, depending on the number of authentication methods used) by combining two or more of them. That is, a user is required to provide both something he has *and* something he knows, or he must both undergo a biometric scan and provide a password before being granted access. Another method of implementation is *layered authentication,* in which one form of authentication is accepted to provide a lower level of access, and additional authentication is required for a higher level of access.

There are a number of different circumstances in which authentication is necessary, and different authentication methods are used in different circumstances. For example:

— *Logon authentication:* When users initially access the computer or network (log on), a secure operating system will require that the user authenticate to a security accounts database. When logging onto the local computer, the user must enter an account name and password that are stored in a local security database on that machine's hard disk. When logging onto a server-based network, the user must enter an account name and password that is in the authentication server's database. Additionally, Windows domains require that NT/2000/XP Pro/. NET computers have a computer account in order to join the domain. However, a user with a domain account can log on from an insecure computer, such as a Windows 9*x*/ME/XP Home machine. Windows NT uses NTLM authentication, whereas Windows 2000—although it supports NTLM for backward compatibility—uses Kerberos authentication by default.

— *Remote access authentication:* When users access the network over a remote connection (dialup or VPN), security is especially important because the computer from which the user is logging on isn't physically wired to the local network. Different, additional protocols are used for remote access authentication.

When a remote logon is initiated, the remote client and the remote access server generally negotiate an authentication method and protocols that both are configured to support.

Authentication Protocols

The protocols used for authenticating identity depend on the authentication type. Some common protocols used for authentication include the following:

— *Kerberos* is a logon authentication protocol that is based on secret key (symmetric) cryptography. It usually uses the DES or Triple-DES (3DES) algorithm, although with the latest version, Kerberos v5, algorithms other than DES can be used. Kerberos uses a system of "tickets" to provide verification of identity to multiple servers throughout the network. This system works a little like the payment system at some amusement parks and fairs where, instead of paying to ride each individual ride, customers must buy tickets at a central location and then use those tickets to access the rides.

Similarly, with Kerberos, a client who wants to access resources on network servers is not authenticated by each server; instead, all the servers rely on "tickets" issued by a central server, called the Key Distribution Center (KDC). The client sends a request for a ticket (encrypted with the client's key) to the KDC. The KDC issues a ticket called a Ticket-Granting Ticket (TGT), which is encrypted and submitted to the Ticket-Granting Service (TGS). The TGS can be running on the same physical machine that is running the KDC. The TGS issues a session ticket to the client for accessing the particular network resource that was requested (which is usually on a different server). The session ticket is presented to the server that hosts the resource, and access is granted. The session key is valid only for that particular session and is set to expire after a specific amount of time. Kerberos allows mutual authentication; that is, the identities of both the client and the server can be verified.

— *NT LanMan, or NTLM,* is another Microsoft logon authentication method, used by Windows NT domains and supported by Windows 2000 in case "down-level" client computers want to log onto the network. NTLMv2, the current version, provides more security than NTLMv1. Version 2 is supported by Windows 2000 and NT 4. 0 with SP4 or higher. If the Directory Services client software is installed on Windows 9x computers, NTLMv2 can be used; however, it is necessary to edit the registry to enable it. Unlike Kerberos, with NTLM, when a client wants to access a server's resources, that server must contact the domain controller to have the client's identity verified. The client doesn't have credentials already issued that the file or application server knows it can trust.

— *Password Authentication Protocol (PAP)* is a remote access authentication protocol used for PPP (dialup) connections. Its distinguishing characteristic (and the reason it should not be used on secure networks) is the fact that it sends passwords in plain text. This means the passwords can be intercepted during transmission and used by an unauthorized person. The only good reason to use PAP is if you face a situation where the remote server doesn't support other, more secure authentication methods. Shiva PAP (S-PAP) addresses this problem by using a two-way reversible authentication method that encrypts passwords so they will not be subject to interception and misuse.

— *Challenge Handshake Authentication Protocol (CHAP)* uses a hashing algorithm and a shared secret to protect the password. CHAP provides more security than PAP. Microsoft developed its own version of the protocol, called MS-CHAP, which uses the DES encryption algorithm and LM/NTHASH.

— *The Remote Authentication Dial-In User Service (RADIUS)* is another means of authenticating remote connections that takes the authentication responsibility off each individual remote access server by providing a centralized server to authenticate clients securely. Exchanges are encrypted using a shared key, and multiple RADIUS servers can communicate with each other and exchange authentication information.

— *The AppleTalk Remote Access Protocol (ARAP)* is a two-way authentication protocol that uses DES encryption for remote access connections on AppleTalk networks.

— *Secure Shell (SSH)* allows users to log into UNIX systems remotely. Both ends of the connection (client and server) are authenticated, and data—as well as passwords—can be encrypted. 3DES, Blowfish, and Twofish are encryption algorithms that are supported by SSHv2, which also allows the use of smart cards.

A concept that is closely related to authentication is nonrepudiation. This is a means of ensuring that whoever sends a message cannot later claim that he or she didn't send it. Nonrepudiation is sometimes considered to be a fourth, separate purpose of cryptography, but we include it here in the discussion of authentication because the two concepts go together; nonrepudiation just goes a step further than authentication.

Confidentiality

Confidentiality refers to any method that keeps the contents of the data secret. Usually this means encrypting it to prevent unauthorized persons from understanding what the data says even if they intercept it. In a high-security environment, where network communications necessarily involve information that should not be shared with the world, it is important to use strong encryption to protect the confidentiality of sensitive data.

Integrity

Data integrity, in the context of cryptography, means that there is a way to verify that the data was not changed after it left the sender, that the data that was sent is exactly the same as the data that is received at the final destination. It is essential to be able to count on data integrity in network transactions such as e-commerce.

Implementation of Cryptographic Technologies

Cryptographic techniques such as encryption are the basis of digital certificates, digital signatures, and the public key infrastructure, or PKI. All of these technologies are important components of an enterprise-level security plan.

Now let us look at the mechanics of how these technologies are implemented.

Scrambling Text with Codes and Ciphers

There are many different ways to "scramble" text or hide its meaning in such a way that only authorized persons (at least in theory) are able to read it. This scrambled (encrypted) text is called cipher text. A method for encrypting text is called a cipher or a code.

Technically, a code uses substitution at the word or phrase level, whereas a cipher works at the level of individual letters or digits. The two words are often used interchangeably, but computerized cryptographic techniques generally rely on ciphers that operate on the binary form of the data by applying an algorithm (a mathematical calculation). Some common cipher/code types are:

— Substitution

— Transposition

— Obscure languages

Substitution Ciphers: Simple substitution is a method often used by children in their first experiments with secret code. A substitution cipher merely substitutes different letters, numbers, or other characters for each character in the original text.

Some types of substitution ciphers are:

— *Monoalphabetic substitution:* Each letter is represented by another letter or character in a one-to-one relationship.

— *Polyalphabetic substitution:* Different cipher-text characters can represent the same plain-text letter, making it more difficult to decrypt messages using the frequency analysis technique. Renaissance architect and art theorist Leon Battista Alberti is credited with developing this technique, earning him recognition as the "father of Western cryptography."

— *Polygraphic (block) cipher:* Several letters are encrypted at the same time, using a system that can handle all the possible combinations of a set number of characters.

— *Fractionation*: Multiple symbols are substituted for each plain-text letter, then the letters or digits are transposed.

Transposition Ciphers: Transposition ciphers use tables in which the plain text is entered one way, then read another way to create the encrypted text. For example, each character of text is entered into the table cells going across from left to right, then the cipher text is produced by reading the characters in columns. A variation uses a square grid with holes that is placed on top of a sheet of paper, then the message is written, rotating the grid at intervals.

Obscure Languages as Code: Obscure languages have been used as code by governments for military communications. Ancient languages have been used in this way. The U. S. military even used Navajo "code talkers" (speakers of the complex and little known Navajo language) in World War II to send secret communications. This language was chosen because it was hard to learn, and only a few people in the world knew it. The Navajo language had never been written, which made it even more obscure. Members of the Navajo tribe were recruited to develop a code based on the language.

Cipher devices such as cipher wheels and cylinders can be used to encrypt and decrypt text. An early example of this technique was the skytale cipher or staff cipher used by the Spartans. They wrapped a sheet of papyrus around a staff and wrote their message down the length of the staff. When the sheet was unwrapped, the message couldn't be easily read unless it was wrapped around a staff of the same diameter as the original one.

Leon Battista Alberti used a set of disks that both had the alphabet etched on them to employ his polyalphabetic ciphering system. He lined up the two disks to determine what cipher-text character would represent each plain-text letter. By rotating the disks at set intervals, he caused different cipher-text letters to represent the same plain-text letters at different places in the message.

Many different cipher machines have been developed by government and military entities. Most use multiple rotating disks to create letter substitutions, and they can be operated either mechanically or electrically. Thomas Jefferson invented a cipher wheel of this type. During World War II, the Japanese used cipher machines called RED and PURPLE, and the German Enigma machine (wired rotor machine that has equally spaced electrical contacts on each side of a disk, which are connected to one another in scrambled order) is perhaps the most famous—or infamous—of the cipher devices.

The availability of computer technology made it much easier to encrypt messages using very complex methods that would be difficult or impossible to use by hand or with mechanical and electrical devices.

One of the first well-known computer ciphering systems was LUCIFER, an IBM project that formed the foundation of the popular Data Encryption Standard (DES) cipher that is still widely used (along with its more secure version, 3DES). LUCIFER was a block cipher, as is DES. It used a 128-bit key to encrypt blocks of binary data that were 128 bits in length. The cipher was applied to each block several times. Even though LUCIFER uses a larger block and key than DES, it is less secure.

Encryption

Encryption is a form of cryptography that "scrambles" plain text into unintelligible cipher text. Encryption is the foundation of such security measures as digital signatures, digital certificates, and the public key infrastructure that uses these technologies to make computer transactions more secure. Computer-based encryption techniques use keys to encrypt and decrypt data. A *key* is a variable (sometimes represented as a password) that is a large binary number—the larger, the better. Key length is measured in bits, and the more bits in a key, the more difficult the key will be to "crack. "

The key is only one component in the encryption process. It must be used in conjunction with an encryption *algorithm* (a process or calculation) to produce the cipher text. Encryption methods are usually categorized as either symmetric or asymmetric, depending on the number of keys that are used.

The two basic types of encryption technology are:

— *Symmetric Encryption*: Symmetric encryption is also called secret key encryption, and it uses just one key, called a shared secret, for both encrypting and decrypting. This is a simple, easy-to use method of encryption, but there is one problem with it: the key must be shared between the sender and the recipient of the data, so a secure method of key exchange must be devised. Otherwise, if a third party intercepts the key during the exchange, an unauthorized person can easily decrypt the data.

— *Asymmetric Encryption*: To address the problem of key exchange, another type of encryption was developed. Asymmetric encryption is also called public key encryption, but it actually relies on a key pair. Two mathematically related keys, one called the public key and another called the private key, are generated to be used together. The private key is never shared; it is kept secret and used only by its owner. The public key is made available to anyone who wants it. Because of the time and amount of computer processing power required, it is considered "mathematically unfeasible" for anyone to be able to use the public key to recreate the private key, so this form of encryption is considered very secure. The primary advantage of asymmetric encryption is that there is no need to securely transmit a secret key. Instead, the public key is published openly, made available to the entire world. There is no need to keep it secret, because it can't be used alone. The encryption process works like this:

1. The sender of a message uses the intended recipient's public key, which is freely available, to encrypt a message.

2. The recipient decrypts the message using his or her private key. Only the private key associated with the public key that encrypted it can be used to decrypt the message.

This key pair can also be used to provide for authentication of a message sender's identity using the keys a little differently:This time the sender uses his or her own *private* key to encrypt the message. This system provides no confidentiality, because anyone can decrypt the message using the owner's public key. However, it does verify the sender's identity, because if the associated public key will decrypt the message, it could only have been encrypted with that person's private key.

Obviously, the most important issue in public key cryptography is the protection of the private keys. This concept is especially important because compromise of a private key not only allows the unauthorized person to read private messages sent to the owner, but it also allows the key thief to "sign" transactions emulating the owner, thus stealing the owner's identity. When the key pair is used for secure credit card or banking transactions, the result can be disastrous.

Cryptographic Algorithms

Literally thousands of different cryptographic algorithms have been developed over the years. Crytographic algorithms can be classified as follows:

— *Encryption algorithms* that are used to encrypt data and provide confidentiality

— *Signature algorithms* that are used to digitally "sign" data to provide authentication

— *Hashing algorithms* that are used to provide data integrity Algorithms (ciphers) are also categorized by the way they work at the technical level. This categorization refers to whether the algorithm is applied to a stream of data, operating on individual bits, or to an entire block of data. *Stream ciphers* are faster because they work on smaller units of data. The key is generated as a *keystream,* and this is combined with the plain text to be encrypted. RC4 is the most commonly used stream cipher.

— *Block ciphers* take a block of plain text and turn it into a block of cipher text. Common block ciphers include DES, CAST, Blowfish, IDEA, RC5/RC6, and SAFER. Most Advanced Encryption Standard (AES) candidates are block ciphers.

Encryption Algorithms

Some popular encryption algorithms are: Rijndael (AES standard); DES and 3DES; SAFER; IDEA; DEAL; CAST-256; MARS; Blowfish and Twofish. Other encryption algorithms include SERPENT, RC4/RC5/RC6, LOKI-97, FROG, and Hasty Pudding.

Signature Algorithms

Signature algorithms are used to create digital signatures. A digital signature is merely a means of "signing" data to authenticate that the message sender is really the person he or she claims to be. Digital signatures can also provide for data integrity along with authentication and nonrepudiation. Digital signatures have become important in a world where many business transactions, including contractual agreements, are conducted over the Internet. Digital signatures generally use both signature algorithms and hash algorithms.

When a message is encrypted with a user's private key, the hash value that is created becomes the signature for that message. Signing a different message will produce a different signature. Each signature is unique, and any attempt to move the signature from one message to another would result in a hash value that would not match the original; thus the signature would be invalidated.

Hashing Algorithms

Hashing is a technique in which an algorithm (also called a hash function) is applied to a portion of data to create a unique digital "fingerprint" that is a fixedsize variable. If anyone changes the data by so much as one binary digit, the hash function will produce a different output (called the hash value) and the recipient will know that the data has been changed. Hashing can ensure integrity and provide authentication as well.

The hash function cannot be "reverse-engineered"; that is, you can't use the hash value to discover the original data that was hashed. Thus hashing algorithms are referred to as one-way hashes. A good hash function will not return the same result from two different inputs (called a collision); each result should be unique. There are several different types of hashing, including division-remainder, digit rearrangement, folding, and radix transformation. These classifications refer to the mathematical process used to obtain the hash value. Standard hashing algorithms include:

— *MD2, MD4, and MD5:* These methods use a *message digest* (the hash value) that is 128 bits in length. They were created by Ron Rivest and are popularly used for digital signatures.

— *Secure Hash Algorithm (SHA):* There are several variations on this algorithm, including SHA-1, SHA-256, SHA-384, and SHA-512. The differences between them lie in the length of the hash value. SHA was created by a cooperative effort of two U. S. government agencies, NIST and the NSA.

Use of Encryption in Information Security

Encryption is used for a number of different purposes in organizations that deal in sensitive data of any type.

Encrypting Data Stored on Disk: Disk encryption refers to encrypting the entire contents of a hard disk, diskette, or removable disk. File encryption refers to encrypting data stored on disk on a fileby-file basis. In either case, the goal is to prevent unauthorized persons from opening and reading files that are stored on the disk. Support for disk/ file encryption can be built into an operating system or file system. NTFS v5, the native file system for Windows 2000/XP/. NET, includes the Encrypting File System (EFS), which can be used to protect data on a hard disk or large removable disk. (EFS can't be used to protect data on floppy diskettes because they cannot be formatted in NTFS format.) EFS allows encryption of individual files and/or folders.

Third-party programs—such as ScramDisk, PGPdisk, and SafeDisk for Windows operating systems and the Crypto File System and Transparent Cryptographic File System (TCFS) for UNIX/Linux—can be installed to provide encryption on file systems that don't natively support encryption or to provide partition-level or virtual drive encryption.

With partition-level and virtual drive encryption, a user does not have to explicitly set encryption properties on individual files and folders. Instead, an entire partition is marked as encrypted or an encrypted virtual drive is created, and all data that is stored there will be automatically encrypted. Many users choose these methods because performance is better than with file-level encryption. Some file/disk encryption methods use a password to protect encrypted data; when someone wants to access an encrypted file, he or she must enter a password. Other methods rely on the user account that is logged on to determine whether access will be granted.

EFS, for example, uses digital certificates that are associated with the user account. These later methods require less user interaction, but they have their drawbacks. It might not be possible to share encrypted files with others without decrypting them in cases where only one particular account is allowed access. In addition, there is a security risk if the user leaves the computer while logged on; then anyone who sits down at the machine can access the encrypted data.

Encrypting Data That Travels Across the Network: When sensitive data is transmitted across the network, users can protect against its decoding by ensuring that it is encrypted so that if unauthorized persons *do* intercept it, they won't be able to read it. The industry standard method for doing this on a TCP/IP network is to use the Internet Protocol Security (IPSec) encryption mechanism. Specifications for IPSec are laid out in RFC 2401. IPSec can be used with different operating systems and platforms. Windows 2000/XP/. NET include builtin support for IPSec. IPSec can provide machine-level authentication. It can be configured to work in one of two modes:

— *Transport mode:* This mode provides end-to-end security, from the source computer to the destination computer. It is also called host-to-host mode.

— *Tunnel mode:* This mode provides for encryption between two secure gateways.

Because it is capable of tunneling, IPSec can be used to create virtual private networks on its own, and it is also used in conjunction with the Layer 2 Tunneling Protocol (L2TP) to provide encryption in an L2TP VPN tunnel. Although often referred to as a protocol, IPSec is actually a security scheme that incorporates several different protocols. These include the following:

— *Authentication Header (AH) protocol:* This protocol is used for authentication and to ensure data integrity by signing each data packet. AH signs the entire packet but does not provide data confidentiality.

— *Encapsulating Security Payload (ESP) protocol:* This protocol is used to encrypt data for confidentiality. It also signs the data portion of the packet for authentication and integrity, but it doesn't sign the entire packet.

— *The Internet Security Association and Key Management Protocol (ISAKMP)*: This protocol creates security associations between two computers that communicate using IPSec, to define the process of exchanging information.

— *The Oakley Key Generation Protocol:* This protocol creates the keys used during the transaction. These are temporary keys that are discarded after the communication session is terminated.

Because IPSec uses shared keys (symmetric encryption), it is important that there be a way to exchange keys securely across the network. The *Diffie-Hellman Key Exchange algorithm* provides a way for the computers on both sides of the transaction to generate identical keys without ever actually sending the key itself across the network and exposing it to possible interception. The encryption algorithms used by IPSec are standard ciphers such as DES/3DES, IDEA, Blowfish, RC-5, and CAST-128.

Another important feature of IPSec is its ability to provide *antireplay*—protection against hackers who might try to capture transmissions and replay them to create a communication session, emulating one of the parties to the original transaction. IPSec is an important mechanism for protecting data during the vulnerable period when it is being sent across a network. The current version of the Internet Protocol, IPv4, allows the use of IPSec as an option; the next generation, IPv6, will require it.

Encrypting E-Mail Communications: More and more people are using e-mail for communications of all kinds, including messages that contain sensitive personal or business information. Several software programs encrypt e-mail; the most popular is Pretty Good Privacy (PGP), which was created by Phil Zimmermann in the early 1990s. Since then, PGP has become widely distributed, and versions are available for most common operating systems—even more outdated or obscure OSs such as OS/2 and Amiga. PGP first compresses and then encrypts the plain-text data using a one-time secret key (or *session key*), which is itself then encrypted with the public key of the intended recipient.

The encrypted session key is sent to the recipient along with the encrypted data, and the recipient uses his or her private key to decrypt the session key so it can be used to decrypt the message itself. Because both symmetric and asymmetric encryption are used in this process, PGP is called a *hybrid cryptosystem*. Different versions of PGP use different encryption algorithms.

Version 2. 6. *x* (sometimes called "classic PGP" and considered by some to be more secure than newer versions) uses a combination of the RSA asymmetric cipher and the IDEA symmetric cipher. The MD5 hash algorithm is also used to create a fixed-length replacement for very long text strings in digital signatures.

Public keys and private keys are stored in separate files called *keyrings* on the hard disk of the computer where PGP is installed. Both the sender and recipient must have PGP installed to use the program for secure communications. PGP's biggest vulnerability is related to the fact that users have to use a passphrase to perform actions such as signing documents and decrypting messages. Protecting this passphrase is a big security issue; good security practices require that the passphrase not be revealed to anyone else or stored on the system for "automatic" entry. Anyone who knows the passphrase can read the encrypted messages or send messages that purport to be from the legitimate user. If the passphrase does become compromised, a key revocation certificate can be generated and issued to render the associated public key null and void. PGP also includes a wipe option that can be used to overwrite the contents of an encrypted file when you delete it, so that it can't be easily recovered using data recovery utilities.

Steganography

Steganography (covered writing) refers to a method of hiding data—not just concealing its contents as encryption does, but concealing its very existence. Steganography is usually used in conjunction with encryption for added protection of sensitive data. This method ameliorates one of the biggest problems of encrypting data—the fact that it is encrypted draws the attention of people who are looking for confidential or sensitive information. The concept of steganography has been around for a long time.

The ancient Greeks are said to have sent secret messages by shaving the head of the messenger and writing the message on his scalp, then letting the hair grow back over it before sending him on his way to deliver the message. Early methods of steganography involved using "invisible ink" or concealing a message inside another message using a code whereby only every fifth word, for example, "counts" as part of the real, hidden message.

One of the earliest books on the subject, *Steganographica,* by Gaspari Schotti, was published in the 1600s. Steganography in the computer world also hides data inside other data, but the way it does so is a little more complex. Because of the way data is stored in files, there are often unused (empty) bits in a file such as a document or graphic. A message can be broken up and stored in these unused bits, and when the file is sent it will appear to be only the original file (called the container file). The hidden information inside is usually encrypted, and the recipient will need special software to retrieve it (and then decrypt it, if necessary).

Messages can be concealed inside all sorts of other files, including executables and graphic and audio files. Another form of steganography is the hidden watermark that is sometimes used to embed a trademark or other symbol in a document or file. A number of different software programs can be used for this purpose, including JP Hide and Seek, which conceals data inside . jpg files, and MP3Stego, which conceals data in . mp3 files. Steganos Security Suite is a package of software programs that provide steganography, encryption, and other services.

Other programs, such as StegDetect, are designed to look for hidden content in files. The process of detecting steganographic data is called *steganalysis*.

Decryption Methods

The use of cryptography naturally led to the science of *cryptanalysis*, the process of decrypting encrypted messages. One of the early methods for "cracking" polyalphabetic substitution ciphers was frequency analysis, which involved examining the encrypted text for repeated character strings and using the distance between the repeated strings to calculate the key length. Then statistical methods can be used to painstakingly determine which plain-text character each cipher-text character represents. Cryptanalysts throughout history have used a number of different methods to break encryption algorithms, including the following:

— *Known plain-text analysis:* If the analyst has a sample of decrypted text that was encrypted using a particular cipher, he or she can sometimes deduce the key by studying the cipher text.

— *Differential cryptanalysis:* If the analyst can obtain cipher text from plain text but is unable to analyze the key, it can be deduced by comparing the cipher text and the plain text.

— *Ciphertext-only analysis:* Used when only the cipher text is available and the analyst has no sample of plain text.

— *Timing/differential power analysis:* A means of measuring the differences in power consumption over a period during which a computer chip is encrypting information to analyze key computations.

— *Key interception (man in the middle):* The analyst tricks two parties to an encrypted exchange into sending their keys by making them think they're exchanging keys with each other.

Mathematician Claude Shannon put forth the theory of *workload.* This term refers to the fact that increasing the amount of work necessary to crack an encryption system increases the strength of the encryption and is an alternative to increasing the unicity distance. Computer encryption ciphers are difficult to crack, but it can be done. With enough time and patience, a brute-force attack that tries every possible key will be successful. The goal of cryptographers is to create ciphers for which this process will take such a long time—even using supercomputers or distributed processing methods—that the effort will not be worthwhile. Today's popular encryption algorithms rely on this deterrent effect.

We have been discussing the legitimate use of cryptographic techniques as part of an organization's security plan. There are many reasons to take steps to provide extra protection for data such as trade secrets, customer and client personal information, and so forth. However, these same technologies can be—and often are—also used by cybercriminals to conceal the self-incriminating information in messages they send to one another. Terrorists are believed to use steganography and encryption to communicate with one another and coordinate their financial activities and attacks. In cases of serious crimes, investigators might need to employ the services of a cryptanalyst to help decipher encrypted data that could contain information essential to identifying criminals or preventing future criminal activities.

Hardware and Software Security

A multilayer security plan will incorporate multiple security solutions. Security is not a "one size fits all" issue, so the options that work best for one organization are not necessarily the best choice for another. Security solutions can be generally broken down into two categories: hardware solutions and software solutions.

Hardware-Based Security

Hardware security solutions can come in the form of network devices: Firewalls, routers, even switches can function to provide a certain level of security. In general, these devices are dedicated computers themselves, running proprietary software.

Hardware-Based Firewalls

Many firewall vendors provide hardware-based solutions. Some of the most popular hardware firewalls include the Cisco PIX firewall, SonicWall, the Webramp 1700, the Firebox from WatchGuard Technologies, and the OfficeConnect firewalls from 3Com. Hardware solutions are available for networks of all sizes. For example, the 3Com products focus on small office/home office (SOHO) users, whereas the Cisco PIX comes in configurations that support up to 250,000 connections.

Hardware-based firewalls are often referred to as *firewall appliances.* A disadvantage of hardware-based firewalls is the proprietary nature of the software they run. Another disadvantage of many of these products, such as Cisco's highly respected PIX, is the high cost. Hardware-based firewalls perform basically the same functions as software-based firewalls.

Authentication Devices: Other hardware-based components of your network security plan may include devices that provide extra security for authentication, such as:

— Smart card readers

— Fingerprint scanners

— Retinal and iris scanners

— Voice analysis devices

These devices can be used in environments that require a high level of security for secure and reliable network authentication. Microsoft has acquired Biometric API (BAPI) technology from I/O Software and plans to incorporate support for biometric authentication devices into future versions of its operating systems. Windows 2000 already supports smart card authentication.

Smart Card Authentication: The term *smart card* has several different meanings. In a broad sense, it refers to any plastic credit-card-sized card that has a computer chip embedded in it to hold information that can be changed. A smart card *reader*—a hardware device—is needed to write to and read the information on the card. Smart cards can be used for different purposes, but one of the most popular is for authentication. Satellite television services use smart cards in the SATV receiver to identify the subscriber and that subscriber's service level. Banks use smart cards for conducting transactions. These cards are especially popular in Europe. Smart cards can also be used for network logon authentication. The cards are generally resistant to tampering and relatively difficult for a hacker to compromise, since they are self-contained. They're also inexpensive in comparison with biometric authentication devices.

Smart cards used for logon authentication generally store a *digital certificate* that contains user identification information, the user's public key, and the signature of the trusted third party that issued the certificate, as well as a time for which the certificate is valid. The certificates are stored on the cards by an authorized administrator. To log on with a smart card, a user must insert the card in the reader or swipe it through and enter a PIN that is associated with the card. If the PIN is compromised, an administrator can change it or issue a new card. To use smart cards for network logon, the computer must run an operating system that supports smart card authentication, such as Windows 2000 or XP, or use add-on software such as Sphinx. A number of companies manufacture smart cards and readers. Some vendors make keyboards that have built-in smart card readers, and there are combination fingerprint scanner/smart card readers for providing both card-based and biometric security.

Although smart cards provide for extra security, they are not foolproof. Many cryptographers have been able to "break" smart card encryption. In general, there are two methods for defeating smart cards: logical and physical. An example of the logical attack is erasing parts of the data on the embedded microchip by raising or dropping the voltage; in some cases, this activity "unlocks" the security without deleting the data. A physical attack might involve actually cutting the chip out of the card and using a laser-cutter microscope to examine it. Although a determined attacker might be able to crack the smart card in this way, these methods are not easy and they don't always work.

Biometric Authentication: Biometric authentication devices rely on physical characteristics such a fingerprint, facial patterns, or iris or retinal patterns to verify user identity. Biometric authentication is becoming popular for many purposes, including network logon. A biometric template or identifier must be stored in a database for the device to compare to a new sample given during the logon process. Biometrics are often used in conjunction with smart cards in high-security environments. The most popular types of biometric devices are the following:

— *Fingerprint scanners:* These are widely available for both desktop and portable computers from a variety of vendors, connecting via a USB or PC Card interface.

— *Facial pattern recognition devices:* These devices use facial geometry analysis to verify identity.

— *Hand geometry recognition devices:* These are similar to facial pattern devices but analyze hand geometry.

— *Iris scan identification devices:* Iris scanners analyze the trabecular meshwork tissue in the iris, which is permanently formed during the eighth month of human gestation.

— *Retinal scan identification devices:* Retina scanners analyze the patterns of blood vessels on the retina.

A large number of physiological characteristics can be used as identifiers, and devices have been developed that verify identity based on knee scans, ear geometry, vein pattern recognition, and even body odor recognition. In addition, some devices analyze and compare behavioral traits using methods such as voice pattern recognition, signature verification, keystroke pattern recognition, breathing pattern recognition, gait pattern recognition, and even brainwave pattern recognition, although many of these are only in experimental stages. Biometrics are considered to be among the most reliable authentication methods possible.

Software-Based Security

Software security solutions cover a much broader range than do hardware-based solutions. These solutions include the security features built into the network operating system as well as additional security software made by the operating system vendors or third-party vendors. Software security has its advantages: It is often less expensive than hardware-based solutions and integrates more easily into the system and network.

However, software security often suffers from decreased performance, compared to hardware-based security implementations, and security applications that run on popular operating systems can be easier to hack than the proprietary programs that run on dedicated hardware devices. Nonetheless, software security is popular and provides a full range of methods for protecting data and providing authentication, confidentiality, and integrity.

Cryptographic Software

Thousands of cryptographic products are available for different purposes: disk/file encryption, e-mail encryption, steganography, and more. In addition to the commercial products, many encryption and authentication software programs are available as freeware.

Digital Certificates

Public key encryption is more secure than secret key encryption because there is no need to transmit a key across unsecured channels, but public key cryptography is also more complex, and it's more difficult to implement on a large scale. There must be a system that ensures that public keys that are posted to the Internet are not forgeries posted by someone who purports to be another user. If this happens, the data that is encrypted with that public key could be intercepted by the unauthorized user who posted the key. That unauthorized person would then be able to decrypt the data and read the message.

We need a mechanism that will provide a way for a trusted third party to confirm that the user who publishes the public key is in fact who he or she claims to be. A digital certificate provides this assurance. To understand how a digital certificate works, think of the way a driver's license or state ID card is used for identity verification. If a store or bank requires that you prove your identity by producing a license or state ID card, that entity is relying on the word of a trusted third party that you are who you say you are. The store or bank presumes that the DMV has checked you out and would not have issued the official identification document unless your identity was confirmed.

Just as the store or bank accepts your driver's license as proof of your identity, another computer with which you want to exchange data or make transactions will accept the digital certificate issued by a trusted third party. In the case of digital certificates, the trusted third party is a *certification authority (CA)*. The CA verifies that a particular identity is bound to the public key that is included in the certificate.

Some public CAs, such as VeriSign, issue certificates to persons on the Internet. Private (internal) CAs are set up by organizations to issue certificates to users within the local network. The CA is a server that runs special software that allows it to issue, manage, and revoke digital certificates. The CA's role is to guarantee to other users, computers, and applications that a particular public key really belongs to the entity with whose name it is associated.

The Public Key Infrastructure

A public key infrastructure, or PKI, is a security framework based on digital certifi-cates. The PKI provides a system for users to request certificates and for CAs to issue, manage, and revoke certificates and disseminate certificate revocation lists CRLs) so that other entities will know when a particular entity's certificate is no longer valid. The PKI is based on the X. 509 standards established by the ISO.

An important component of the PKI is the set of security policies that govern it. These policies should define the rules for issuance and use of digital certificates and the keys that are associated with them. Public certification authorities like VeriSign are required to provide a certificate practice statement (CPS). This is a document that outlines in detail the procedures for implementing the PKI.

When there are multiple CAs in the same PKI, as is the case in most large organizations, they are arranged in a hierarchical manner. The *root CA* is the most trusted CA in the PKI. Its certificate is self-signed, and it is responsible for issuing certificates to all the other CAs in the PKI, which are called *subordinate CAs.* The subordinate CAs issue certificates to users and computers, whereas the root CA generally issues certificates only to subordinate CAs. Public CAs are published in the Global Trust Register, which acts like a root CA for public CAs (albeit in printed form).

Certificates can be issued by a CA for many different purposes, including file encryption, smart card authentication, e-mail, IP security, and network logon. Users can export or import certificates, moving them from one computer to another. The export function is also used to create a backup of a certificate, which can then be restored to the *certificate store,* the location on the hard disk where certificates are kept, if the original certificate is destroyed. Certificates are issued automatically in some cases; in other cases, they must be explicitly requested by the user.

It is very important that a PKI contain a mechanism for publishing certificate revocations so that other entities won't mistakenly rely on a certificate that is no longer valid. Certificates are revoked when the public key is compromised or when users leave the company or for some reason are no longer trusted. A CRL lists certificates that have been revoked and is updated regularly and distributed throughout the organization by the CA.

Software-Based Firewalls

In addition to the PKI software that provides for verification of identity, a vitally important type of software-based security is the *software firewall.* In reality, all firewalls are software-based. The hardware devices sold as firewalls run proprietary software that performs basically the same functions as a software program that can be installed on a regular PC. We use the term *software-based firewall* to describe firewall products such as Microsoft ISA Server or IBM SecureWay, as opposed to hardware/software (or firmware) combination appliances such as those produced by Cisco Systems. Some vendors, such as Check Point, market both types of product.

Firewalls

A firewall goes a bit further than just "standing in" for the local computers and hiding them from view on the global network, as a proxy server does. Firewalls are specifically designed to control inbound and outbound access, preventing unauthorized data from entering the network and restricting how and what type of data can be sent out. The firewall gets its name from the building industry. In commercial structures, it is common to build a barrier wall made of fireproof material between two areas of a building. This wall is designed to prevent fire from spreading from one part of the building to the other. Another example is the heat barrier between the engine of an automobile and the passenger compartment, also called a firewall. Likewise, a network firewall acts as a barrier to prevent "bad data"—whether that be virus code or simply messages to or from unauthorized systems — from spreading from the outside network to the internal network. It also prevents packets of a particular type or to or from a particular user or computer from spreading from the LAN to the outside network.

In choosing between different firewall solutions, organizations encounter two basic firewall design options:

— A firewall can be designed to *permit* all packets to pass through unless they are expressly denied.

— A firewall can be designed to *deny* all packets unless they are expressly permitted.

Obviously, the second method is more secure, but it can result in the denial of access that administrators actually want to allow. The first method is easier to implement but is also more easily penetrated or circumvented.

Firewall products support the filtering of messages to either allow data to pass through or prevent it from doing so, according to specified criteria. The best firewalls support *layered filtering*. This means they can perform filtering at the packet layer, the circuit layer, or the application layer; some firewalls support only one of these filtering types, but most advanced firewall products, such as Microsoft ISA Server or Check Point's Firewall-1 product, support all three types. Firewalls that combine packet filtering, circuit filtering, and application layer filtering provide the highest level of security. These types of firewall also tend to be the most expensive.

Packet Filtering

Packet filtering does most of its work at the network layer of the OSI networking model (equivalent to the internetwork layer of the DoD model), dealing with IP packets. Packet filters examine the information contained in the IP packet header of a message and then either permit the data to cross the firewall or reject the packet based on that information. When IP packet filtering is enabled, the firewall will intercept and evaluate packets before passing them on to a higher level in the firewall or to an application filter.

The information that the packet filter uses to make its decision includes the IP address of the source and/or destination computer(s) and the TCP or UDP port number. Packet filtering allows the data to proceed to the transport layer only if the packet-filtering rules allow for it to do so. Packet filtering lets administrators block packets that come from a particular Internet host or those that are destined for a particular service on the network.

Dynamic packet filtering provides higher security because it opens the necessary port(s) only when required for communication to take place, then closes the port(s) immediately after the communication ends.

Static packet filters are configured to allow inbound and outbound access to a predefined IP address (or group of IP addresses) and port number (or groups of ports).

It is important to note that packet filters cannot perform filtering based on anything that is contained in the data field of the packet, nor can they use the state of the communication channel to aid in making their decision to accept or reject the packet. If filtering decisions need to be made on the basis of either of these criteria, the firewall must be configured to use filtering that operates at a different layer (circuit or application filtering).

Circuit Filtering

Circuit filters operate at a higher layer of the OSI model, the transport layer (the host-to-host layer in the DoD model). Circuit filters restrict access on the basis of host machines (not users) by processing the information found in the TCP and UDP packet headers. This allows administrators to create filters that would, for example, prohibit anyone using Computer A from using FTP to access Computer B. When circuit filters are used, access control is based on TCP data streams or UDP datagrams.

Circuit filters can act based on TCP and UDP status flags and sequencing information, in addition to source and destination addresses and port numbers.

Circuit-level filtering allows administrators to inspect sessions rather than packets. A session is sometimes thought of as a connection, but actually a session can be made up of more than one connection. Sessions are established only in response to a user request, which adds to security. Circuit filters don't restrict access based on user information; they also cannot interpret the meanings of the packets. That is, they cannot distinguish between a GET command and a PUT command sent by an application program. To do this, application filtering must be used.

Application Filtering

At times, the best tactic is to filter packets based on the information contained in the data itself. Packet filters and circuit filters don't use the contents of the data stream in making filtering decisions, but this *can* be done with *application filtering*. An application filter operates at the top layer of the networking model, the appropriately named application layer. Application filters can use the packet header information but are also able to allow or reject packets on the basis of the data contents and the user information. Administrators can use application filtering to control access based on a user's identity and/or based on the particular task the user is attempting to perform. With application filters, criteria can be set based on commands issued by the application. This means that, for example, the administrator could restrict a particular user from downloading files to a specified computer using FTP. At the same time, the administrator could allow that user to upload files via FTP to that same computer. This is possible because different commands are issued depending on whether the user is retrieving files from the server or depositing them there.

Many firewall experts consider application gateways to be the most secure of the filtering technologies. This is because the criteria they use for filtering covers a broader span than the other methods. Sometimes hackers write malicious programs that use the port address of an authorized application, such as port 53, which is the DNS address. A packet or circuit filter would not be able to recognize that the packet is not a valid DNS request or response and would allow it to pass through. An application filter, however, is able to examine the contents of the packet and determine that it should *not* be allowed. There are drawbacks to this filtering type. The biggest problem is that there must be a separate application gateway for every Internet service that the firewall needs to support. This makes for more configuration work; however, this weakness is also a strength that adds to the security of the firewall.

Since a gateway for each service must be explicitly enabled, an administrator won't accidentally allow services that pose a threat to the network. Application filtering is the most sophisticated level of filtering performed by the firewall service and is especially useful in protecting the network against specific types of attacks, such as malicious SMTP commands or attempts to penetrate the local DNS servers.

Intrusion Detection

Many firewalls also incorporate an intrusion detection system that can actually recognize that an attack of a specific type is being attempted and can perform a predefined action when such an intrusion is identified, such as one of the following:

— Send an e-mail message to the administrator

— Send a network message to the administrator

— Page the administrator

— Write an event entry to the event log

— Run a previously specified program or script

— Stop the firewall service

Intrusion detection systems can recognize many different common forms of network intrusion, such as port scans, LAND attacks, Ping of Death, UDP bombs, out-of-band attacks, and others. Special detection filters may also be built in, such as a Post Office Protocol (POP) intrusion detection filter that analyzes POP mail traffic to guard against POP buffer overflows, or a DNS intrusion detection filter that can be configured to look for DNS hostname overflow or length overflow attacks.

An intrusion or attack can be scary, frustrating, maddening—as with a physical attack on one's person, the emotional reactions can make it difficult to exercise good judgment and make the correct decisions about how to respond. This situation is made easier if you have properly prepared for it.

Many companies, taking the proactive approach, form incident response teams—called *computer incident response teams*, or *CIRTs*—made up of individuals who train together (much like a military unit or police SWAT team) in how to handle anticipated incidents. The goal is to be able to swing into action when an actual incident occurs, with each team member covering a preassigned area of responsibility and thus decreasing the amount of damage and increasing the likelihood of apprehending the perpetrator of the incident.

In their book Incident Response: Investigating Computer Crime, Chris Prosise and Kevin Mandia define an incident as "an event that interrupts normal operating procedure and precipitates some level of crisis. "The CERT guidelines define specific incidents, including violation of security policy, attempts to gain unauthorized access, unwanted denial of service/resources, unauthorized use, and changes made to system or data without the owner's knowledge, instruction, or consent.

An incident can be anything from an attack that crashes all the servers and cuts off all network communications to an intrusion that causes no actual damage but demonstrates the vulnerability of the organization's systems. The response team should have its own hardware and software to use in conducting the investigation. It is important that the victim systems be preserved in the state they were in when the incident was discovered. Any changes made to these systems can compromise the integrity of the evidence and affect its admissibility in court.

Response team members may be called to testify in court if criminal charges or civil lawsuits are brought in relation to the incident. This is another reason to create extensive documentation that can be reviewed prior to giving testimony. Often, a case doesn't come to trial until months or even years after the incident, and the human memory often isn't reliable after so long a time without a little help. The team member who creates the documentation should be the one to testify to its authenticity if it is to be entered into evidence.

The steps involved in incident response include:

— *Training:* Once versed in the theory of incident response, the team should train together in realistic scenario-based drills until response actions become automatic. Training. should also address the law relating to privacy considerations and other issues that could affect or restrict team members' activities during the response.

— *Incident recognition:* Monitoring should be conducted to ensure that team members are alerted to the possibility that an incident is occurring in its earliest stages.

— *Incident verification:* This step involves examining logs, observing system/network behavior, interviewing witnesses, and so on to verify that an incident has in fact occurred.

— *Incident classification:* An assessment should be conducted to determine the nature of the incident and the threat level.

— *Incident containment:* Immediate steps should be taken to stop the incident and prevent any more damage.

— *Evidence preservation:* Immediate steps should be taken to preserve all evidence of the incident for the purposes of tracking the offender and possible prosecution or civil litigation.

— *Incident analysis:* A thorough investigation should be conducted to determine exactly what happened and how.

— *Restoration:* Systems should be brought back to a working state as soon as possible, to minimize loss of productivity.

— *Followup activities:* New security measures should be established to ensure that the same type of incident doesn't occur again.
— *Documentation:* Each step of the response process should be documented and preserved for later review and use.

It is not necessary for every member of the team to participate in every step of the response process. All team members should know their own roles and allow other team members to perform as assigned. Team member roles should be assigned according to each individual's area of expertise. Teams often include persons from the IT department, corporate security, management, legal department, and even the financial, human resources, and public relations departments. Response team members should be on call and able to respond to incidents at all hours and on any day of the week.

Security Policies

Security issues are at the forefront of organizational priorities today. Companies lose millions of dollars and untold hours of worker productivity due to lax security. Companies realize that protection of their assets—digital as well as physical—is no longer a luxury; in the twenty-first century, it has become a necessity.

An enormous amount of a company's most crucial information, including financial data, personnel records, customer information, and trade secrets, is concentrated in one virtual "place": the organization's network. This centralization renders this information vulnerable to unauthorized access and accidental or intentional destruction, both from within and (assuming the local network is connected to the Internet, as most today are) from outside intruders.

Implementation of security measures, to be effective, must be based on an organized plan that takes into account all aspects of the organization's security needs. There must be rules and guidelines governing how the plan is put into action. These are disseminated throughout the organization as *policies.*

A security policy, as the term is used here, refers to a written document that defines an organization's approach to security or a specific security area and lays down a set of rules to be followed in implementing the organization's security philosophy. Organizations may establish both written and unwritten rules pertaining to security matters and may issue a number of different types of documents dealing with these issues.

Generally, a security memorandum or freestanding security directive is issued in response to a particular incident and may be used as a way to establish a rule that is not covered in the policy. If the rule applies only to a specific one-time situation or will be in effect for only a limited time, a memorandum might be all that's needed. If the rule will be permanent or long-term and is applicable to a broader spectrum of situations, it should be incorporated into the organization's formal policy as soon as possible. A memorandum can also be informational only, its purpose to make users aware of security considerations without laying out specific rules or guidelines.

Standards and specifications are generally requirements that are to be met in implementing system-specific security procedures and may be used to measure or rate the overall reliability, compatibility, or other characteristics of the system. For example, the U. S. government has developed criteria, defined in the Department of Defense Trusted Computer System Evaluation Criteria handbook and the Trusted Network Interpretation of the TCSEC, for rating security implementations. Other countries have similar rating systems. The ISO has developed ISO 17799 as an internationally recognized set of "best practices" regarding IT security. The security policy might specify adherence to particular standards or specifications.

Procedural documents supplement the policy and may be incorporated into it as part of a policies and procedures manual. The procedural document gives stepby-step technical instructions for tasks that are required to implement the policies. For example, if the policy states that users must change their passwords every 30 days, you might have two associated procedural documents: one directed to network administrators that details how to set password requirements on the Windows domain controller to force users to change passwords at 30-day intervals, and another directed to users detailing how to change their passwords.

Investigators responding to cybercrimes that involve a corporate network need to have a thorough understanding of how security is implemented within the organization, just as an investigator responding to a home invasion needs to know the layout of the house, how and where commercial security devices are in place, what the family's security philosophy is, and so forth. Unlike most residential situations, corporations will often have formal, written documentation that lays out all the guidelines followed in implementing the security plan. However, these documents aren't always easy to understand—unless you also understand the process by which they're created, adopted, and implemented.

This background will make it easier for investigators to come into an organization and analyze its role as the victim or source of cybercrimes based on information contained in the policy document. For example, if an examination of the policies shows that the organization has an extremely strong password policy, and further investigative techniques such as interviewing employees reveal that the policies are universally enforced, this could indicate that intruders used techniques other than password cracking to gain access, or it could indicate that there is a "leak" inside the organization. In other words, understanding the policies can help to narrow the focus of the investigation. This is often one of the most difficult and most vital steps in the investigative process.

If we accept the stated definition of security policy, it becomes obvious that there is not and cannot be a one-size-fits-all IT security policy that will work equally well for all organizations. Security needs differ, based on:

— Risk factors

— The perceived and actual threat level

— Organizational vulnerabilities

— The organization's philosophy

— Legal factors

— Available funds

It is important to analyze all these factors carefully in developing a policy that offers both adequate protection and a desirable level of access. Security features are now built into operating system software;Windows NT, 2000, XP, and—coming soon to a server near you. NET include numerous security features. Microsoft recently announced that its developers will focus even more closely on security issues. UNIX and Linux distributions come with builtin security features. IT security products, both hardware and software, abound. Security training and numerous security certifications are available, and IT professionals are seeking them out. These are all important components of an organization's overall security plan, but they are not enough. Effective coordination and interaction of all these parts requires one more thing: a comprehensive security policy.

To assess security needs accurately, someone should review the company's infrastructure, processes, and procedures and involve personnel at all levels of the organization and from as many different departments as possible. Ideally, the following tasks will be performed by a carefully selected team that includes, at a minimum, members of management, IT personnel, and a company legal representative. Each team member should be assigned specific areas of responsibility, and deadlines for completion should be assigned.

The initial creation of a good security plan requires a great deal of thought and effort. The policy will impact those at all levels of the organization, and it is desirable to solicit input from as many representatives of different departments and job descriptions as is practical. An effective approach is to form a committee consisting of people from several areas of the organization to be involved in creating and reviewing the security plan and policies. A security planning committee of this type might include some or all of the following:

— The network administrator and one or more assistant administrators

— The site's security administrator

— Department heads of various company departments or their representatives

— Representatives of user groups that will be impacted by the security policies

— A member of the legal department who specializes in computer and technology law

— A member of the finance or budget department

— A member of upper management

Security policies will generally be implemented and enforced by network administrators and members of the IT staff. Job descriptions and policies should designate exactly who is responsible for the implementation of which parts of the plan. There should be a clear-cut chain of command that specifies whose decision prevails in case of conflict. In some cases—such as physical penetration of the network—the company security staff will become involved. Written, clearly formulated policies should be in place that stipulate which department has responsibility for which tasks in such situations. The security plan should also address the procedures for reporting security breaches, both internally and if the police or other outside agencies are to be brought in. In addition, it should be specified who is responsible for or has the authority to call in outside agents.

One of the most important factors in a good security policy is that it must be enforceable. If the policy can be enforced through security tools, this method is preferred. If the policies must be enforced through reprimand or other actions against employees who violate them, there should be clearly worded, universally distributed written documentation of what constitutes a violation and what sanctions will result, as well as who is responsible for imposing such sanctions.

Risk Analysis

Before the policy development team can set policies, they need to determine both the nature and the level of the security risks to the organization. Traditionally, risk analysis involves:

— Determining to what types of security breaches the organization is vulnerable

— For each type, determining the probability of such a breach occurring

— For each type, determining the extent of the loss that would be suffered if the breach did occur This process is known as quantitative risk analysis.

Another type of risk analysis, qualitative risk analysis, disregards the probability element and instead focuses on potential threats and the characteristics of the system or network that make it vulnerable to these threats. Then methods are developed for preventing or reducing the likelihood of breaches, detecting when breaches do occur, and decreasing and repairing the damage done if a breach does occur.

Risk analysis tools are available to help identify threats and vulnerabilities, rate the threat level, estimate the impact on the organization, and recommend solutions. An example is the COBRA Risk Consultant from C&A Systems Security Ltd.

COBRA methodology is used by major corporations and governmental entities. Why is a risk analysis necessary? There are several reasons, including the following:

— From the IT professional's point of view, a detailed risk analysis is the first and perhaps most important step in justifying to management the cost to implement needed security measures.

— From the business manager's point of view, the risk analysis document provides a solid, objective basis for making budgetary and personnelimpacting decisions.

— Data collected during the risk analysis process forces both IT and management to face and acknowledge threats and vulnerabilities of which they might not have been aware or which they previously might have been able to ignore.

— Risk analysis allows the organization to focus resources on the existing threats and vulnerabilities and avoid wasting time and funds on unnecessary measures.

Because the risk analysis process involves personnel throughout the organization, it can raise security awareness and help make appropriate security practices the responsibility of everyone who uses the computers and network. This is a basic tenet of crime prevention.

Assessing Threats

The dictionary defines a *threat* as "somebody or something likely to cause harm. " The threat assessment portion of the risk analysis should include:

— Sources of potential threats

— The nature of potential threats

— The likelihood of occurrence of each potential threat type

— The estimated impact of each potential threat type

Sources of potential threats can be divided into internal and external categories.

Although many security policies focus on the threat of a security breach from outside the network or organization, in actuality many organizations find that their biggest potential losses come from inside—the deliberate or unintentional actions of employees, contractors, and others who have legitimate access to the network. It is important to address both categories when performing a threat assessment. Further defining threat sources requires that the assessment team determine both *who* and *what* could pose a threat to the network. For example, people who could pose a threat include most of the cybercriminal types such as:

— Random hackers, motivated by fun, the personal challenge of breaking into the network, or competition with other hackers

— Data thieves who target the organization and information specifically; this type includes corporate espionage

— Emotionally motivated people, such as ex-employees out for revenge, business competitors who want to damage the company's ability to do business, or people with a grudge against the company, its personnel, or the industry to which it belongs

— People who accidentally or inadvertently cause damage or data loss

The nature of possible threats is the *what* in this equation. Any of these people could initiate threats of one or more of the following natures:

— Unauthorized access to data

— Unauthorized disclosure of information

— Destruction of data

— Modification or corruption of data

— Introduction of viruses, worms, or Trojans

— Denial or interruption of service or network congestion/slowdown

The next step in threat analysis consists of assigning a likelihood or probability to each type of threat event. A high probability indicates that the threat event is more likely than not to occur, as when there is a history of its occurrence in the past. A medium probability indicates that the threat event might or might not occur. A low probability indicates that the threat event is not likely to occur, although it is possible. Finally, the assessment team must evaluate the probable impact on the organization for each potential threat event. For example:

— If the company's customer database were destroyed, how would this affect such activities as sales, billing, and so on?

— If the company network were down for one day, what is the potential cost to the company in lost sales, lost employee productivity, and the like?

— If the company's client records were made public, what is the potential loss in terms of lawsuits, withdrawal of client business, or similar actions?

Once all these questions have been asked and answered, it is a relatively simple matter to construct a threat assessment matrix that will put this information into perspective and help the policy development team focus the company's security policies on the threat areas of highest likelihood and most significant impact.

Organizational and Network Vulnerabilities

Network vulnerabilities are often referred to as security holes. Security holes should be identified as part of the policy development process. These vulnerabilities can be caused by a programming characteristic or (mis)configuration of the operating system, a protocol or service, or an application. Examples might include:

— Operating system code that allows hackers to crash a computer by accessing a file whose path contains certain reserved words

— Unnecessarily open TCP/UDP ports that hackers can use to get into or obtain information about the system

— A Web browser's handling of JavaScript that allows malicious code to execute unwanted commands

The network's connections to the Internet and other networks obviously affect vulnerability. Data on a network that is connected 24/7 via a high-speed link is more vulnerable than on a network that is only intermittently connected to the outside.

A network that allows multiple outside connections increases vulnerability to outside attack. Dialup modem connections merit special consideration. Although a dialup connection is less open to intrusion than a full-time dedicated connection—both because it is connected to the outside for a shorter time period, reducing the window of opportunity for intrusion, and because it usually has a dynamic IP address, making it harder for an intruder to locate it on multiple occasions—allowing workstations on the network to have modems and phone lines can create a huge security risk.

If improperly configured, a computer with a dialup connection to the Internet that is also cabled to the internal network can act as a router, allowing outside intruders to access not just the workstation connected to the modem, but other computers on the LAN. One reason for allowing modems at individual workstations is to allow users to dialup connections to other private networks. A more secure way to do this is to remove the modems and have the users establish a VPN connection with the other private network through the LAN's Internet connection. The best security policy is to have as few connections from the internal network to the outside as possible and control access at those entry points.

Organizational vulnerabilities are those areas and data that are open to danger or harm if exposed to an attack. In order to determine these vulnerabilities, the policy team should first identify the assets that could be exposed to the types of threats previously identified. For example:

— The company's financial records

— Trade secrets

— Personnel information

— Customer/client information

— Private correspondence

— Intellectual property

— Marketing and business strategy documents

— Network integrity

— System and program files

A number of factors should be considered when the team is assessing vulnerabilities, including the nature of the data that goes through the organization's network. The vulnerability of data that is highly confidential or irreplaceable should be of highest priority. Vulnerability is also affected by the size of the organization and network. A larger number of people who have access to the network indicates a greater chance of exposure to someone who will want to do harm.

The next step in evaluating security needs is to determine the philosophy of the organization's management regarding security versus accessibility. It is important to remember that the two are conflicting characteristics; the more of one that a system has, the less of the other it will have. The organizational philosophy determines where on the security-access continuum a particular network falls.

Some companies institute a highly structured, formal management style. Employees are expected to respect a strict chain of command, and information is generally disseminated on a "need to know" basis. Governmental agencies, especially those related to law enforcement, such as police departments and investigative agencies, often follow this philosophy, sometimes referred to as the paramilitary model. Other companies, particularly those in "creative" industries and other fields that are subject to little state regulation, are built on the opposite premise: that all employees should have as much information and input as possible, that managers should function as "team leaders" rather than authoritarian supervisors, and that restrictions on employee actions should be imposed only when necessary for the efficiency and productivity of the organization. This is sometimes called the "one big happy family" model. Creativity is valued more than "going by the book," and job satisfaction is considered to be an important aspect of enhancing employee performance and productivity.

In business management circles, these two diametrically opposed models are called *Theory X* (traditional paramilitary style) and *Theory Y* (modern, teamoriented approach). Although numerous other management models have been popularized in recent years, such as management by objective (MBO) and total quality management (TQM), each company's management style falls somewhere on the continuum between Theory X and Theory Y.

The management model is based on the personal philosophies of the company's top decision makers regarding the relationship between management and employees. The management model can have a profound influence on what is or isn't acceptable in planning security for the network. A "deny all access"-based security policy that is viewed as appropriate in a Theory X organization could meet with so much resentment and employee dissatisfaction in a Theory Y company that it disrupts business operations.

Policy makers must always consider the company "atmosphere" as part of security planning. If there are good reasons to implement strict security in a Theory Y atmosphere, the restrictions will probably have to be justified to management and "sold" to employees, whereas those same restrictions might be accepted without question in a more traditional organization.

Security needs are dependent not only on the wishes of company managers, but they may also be dictated or at least guided by the criminal and civil law in a particular jurisdiction. If the company's industry is subject to government regulations, the information on its network falls under privacy protection acts, or company contracts prohibit disclosure of information on the company network, these are legal factors that must be considered in establishing security policies.

It is important to protect the company from liability that might be incurred if employees or others using the network violate laws. For this reason, it is essential that the security policy development team include one or more attorneys who are well versed in applicable laws and who are familiar with the terms of the company's contracts with partners, vendors, clients, and others.

Finally, but rarely of least concern, the needs evaluation must take into account the monetary cost of implementing heightened security. Determining the funds available for security upgrades will affect security policies by forcing the development team to differentiate the organization's security *needs* from security *wants*. Cost factors can also force the team to prioritize security needs so that those threats that are most likely or most imminent can be addressed, those assets that are most important can be protected, and those vulnerabilities that are most egregious can be closed first.

Security Solutions

Once the company has identified and documented its security needs and established a working budget for addressing those needs, it is possible to assess solutions and determine which one(s) meet those needs within that budget. Network security solutions can be generally divided into three broad categories: hardware, software, and policy-only solutions.

Hardware Solutions: Hardware-based security solutions involve adding some physical device such as a dedicated firewall to protect the network or a smart card reader for logon authentication. Removal of diskette and CD drives from desktop computers to prevent unauthorized copying of files to removable media or introduction of viruses is also a hardware-based solution. Other security hardware devices include:

— Keystroke capture devices for monitoring computer use
— Hardware tokens for storing security keys
— Cryptographic hardware devices for offloading the processing of crypto operations
— Biometric authentication devices such as fingerprint or retina scanners

Hardware solutions can be more costly than software-only solutions, but they offer several advantages. Hardware security is usually more secure because there is less exposure of security information such as private keys, and it is more difficult to tamper with hardware than software. Hardware solutions also often offer faster performance.

Software Solutions: Software solutions include intrusion detection systems, packet/circuit/application filtering software, and security auditing software, as well as software firewall packages such as Microsoft's Internet Security and Acceleration (ISA) Server, which combine these functions. Other software security solutions are antivirus programs such as those made by Symantec and McAfee,"spyware" used to monitor how computers are being used and network management packages that incorporate security features. Operating system and application "fixes" that patch security holes can also be placed in this category.

Policy Solutions: Most hardware and software security measures have accompanying policies that prescribe when and how they are to be deployed and used, but many security measures consist of policy only. For example:

— Policies that prohibit users from disclosing their passwords to anyone else

— Policies that require users to lock their workstations when they leave their desks

— Policies that require users to get permission before installing any software on their machines

— Policies that prohibit users from allowing anyone else to use the computer after they've logged in

Of course, in many cases policies will be enforced via software or hardware. For example, a policy that prohibits users from copying network files to their local disks can be enforced by permissions that allow read-only access. A policy that requires users to change their passwords every 30 days can be enforced by setting passwords to expire after that time period.

Complying with Security Standards: The security policy document should lay out standards regarding such issues as confidentiality and integrity of data, authorization and authentication, access, appropriate use of network resources, and employee privacy issues. If compliance with federal standards or industry-specific standards is required, then the specifications should be included and mandated in the policy document. Policies should be reviewed for compliance with international standards such as ISO 17799.

Government Security Ratings: Security ratings might be of interest in the development of a company's security policy, although they are not likely to be important unless the organization works under government contract requiring a specified level of security. The U. S. government provides specifications for the rating of network security implementations in a publication often referred to as the *orange book,* formally called the Department of Defense Trusted Computer System Evaluation Criteria, or TCSEC. The red book, or Trusted Network Interpretation of the TCSEC (TNI), explains how the TCSEC evaluation criteria are applied to computer networks. Other countries have security rating systems that work in a similar way. For example:

— CTPEC (Canada)

— AISEP (Australia)

— ITSEC (Western Europe)

To obtain a government contract in the United States, companies are often required to obtain a C2 rating. A C2 rating has several requirements:

1. That the operating system in use be capable of tracking access to data, including both who accessed it and when it was accessed
2. That users' access to objects be subject to control (access permissions)
3. That users are uniquely identified on the system (user account name and password)

4. That security-related events can be tracked and permanently recorded for auditing (audit log)

Utilizing Model Policies: Model security policies can be used to guide the policy development team in preparing a comprehensive policy document. Policy templates can be purchased from various sources, and sample policies are available for download from such organizations as the SANS Institute. An advantage is that purchased model policies may be guaranteed to be ISO 17799 compliant, HIPAA compliant, or the like. However, policy makers should beware of simply copying a sample policy without an extensive review to ensure that the policies fit the organization's philosophy, budget, and business model. Sample policies are usually "sanitized"—that is, organization-specific issues have been removed to provide a generic policy that is designed to serve as a starting point in creating customized policies.

Policy Areas

An important part of policy development involves defining the areas that will be addressed by the organization's security policies. This process will vary from one organization to another, but some common policy areas are always of concern. An example is the password policy.

Password Policies

In the networking world, passwords (in combination with user account names) are normally the "keys to the kingdom" that provide access to network resources and data. It might seem simplistic to say that a comprehensive security plan should include an effective password policy, but it is a basic component that is more difficult to implement than it might appear at first glance.

In order to be effective, a password policy must require users to select passwords that are difficult to "crack" yet easy for them to remember so they don't commit the common security breach of writing the password on a "sticky note" that will end up stuck to the monitor or sitting prominently in the top desk drawer.

A good password policy is the first line of defense in protecting the network from intruders. Careless password practices (choosing common passwords such as *god* or *love* or the user's spouse's name; choosing short, all-alpha, one-case passwords; writing passwords down or sending them across the network in plain text) are like leaving your car doors unlocked with the keys in the ignition. Although some intruders might target a specific system, many others are just "browsing" for a network that's easy to break into. Lack of a good password policy is an open invitation to them.

Policy developers must remember that expensive, sophisticated firewalls and other strict security measures (short of biometric scanning devices that recognize fingerprints or retinal images) will not protect the network if an intruder has knowledge of a valid username and password. It is particularly important to use strong passwords for administrative accounts.

Best practices for password creation require that you address the following:

- — Password length and complexity
- — Who creates the password?
- — Forced changing of passwords

Password Length and Complexity: It's easy to define a "bad" password—it's one that can be easily guessed by someone other than the authorized user. One way in which "crackers" do their work is via the *brute-force attack*. In this kind of attack, the cracker manually or, more often using a script or specially written software program, simply tries every possible combination of characters until he finally hits upon the right one. It goes without saying that using this method, it will be easier to guess a short password than a longer one because there are fewer possible combinations. For this reason, most security experts recommend that passwords have a minimum required length. Modern network operating systems such as Windows 2000 allow domain administrators to impose such rules so that if a user attempts to set a password that doesn't meet the minimum length requirement, the password change will be rejected.

Who Creates the Password?: Network administrators might be tempted to institute a policy whereby they create all passwords and issue them to the users. This policy has the advantage of ensuring that all passwords meet the administrator's criteria in regard to length and complexity. However, it has a few big disadvantages as well:

— It places a heavy burden on administrators, who must handle all password changes and be responsible for letting users know what their passwords are. Of course, an administrator would not want to notify a user of his or her password via e-mail or other insecure channels. In fact, the best way to do so is to personally deliver the password information. In a large organization, this becomes particularly taxing if there is a policy requiring that passwords be changed on a regular basis.

— Users will have more difficulty remembering passwords that they didn't choose themselves. This means they are more likely to write the passwords down, resulting in security compromises. Otherwise, they might have to contact the administrator frequently to be reminded of their passwords.

— If the administrator creates all passwords, this means the administrator *knows* everyone's password. This might or might not be acceptable under the overall security policy. Some users could be uncomfortable with the idea that the administrator knows their passwords.

Even though an administrator can generally access a user's account and/or files without knowing the password, it is less obvious to the users and thus less a concern. Allowing users to create their own passwords within set parameters is usually the best option. The user is less likely to forget the password because he can create a complex password that is meaningless to anyone else but has meaning to him.

Password Change Policy: Best practices dictate that users change their passwords at regular intervals and after any suspected security breach. Modern network operating systems such as Windows 2000 allow the administrator to set a maximum password age, forcing users to change their passwords at the end of the specified period (in days). Password expiration periods can be set from 1 to 999 days. Individual user accounts that need to keep the same passwords can be configured so that their passwords never expire. This overrides the general password expiration setting. Because it is the nature of most users to make their passwords as easy to remember as possible, policies should strive to prevent the following practices, all of which can present security risks:

— Changing the password to a variation of the same password

— Changing the password back and forth between two favored passwords each time a change is required

— "Changing" the password to the same password.

Administrators can use operating system features to prevent these practices. For example, in Windows 2000, you can configure the operating system to remember the user's password history so that up to a maximum of the last 24 passwords will be recorded and the user will not be able to change the password to one that has been used during that time.

Here is a short overview of the best password practices:

— Passwords should have a minimum of eight characters.

— Passwords should not be "dictionary" words.

— Passwords should consist of a mixture of alpha, numeric, and symbol characters.

— Passwords should be created by their users.

— Passwords should be easy for users to remember.

— Passwords should never be written down.

— Passwords should be changed on a regular basis.

— Passwords should be changed anytime compromise is suspected.

— Password change policies should prevent users from making only slight changes.

Other Policy Areas

Password policies are important to almost every organization, but other policy areas that often need to be addressed include the following:

— *Server and workstation security policies* define rules governing physical security of network-connected computers, mandating logoff or password-protected screensavers when leaving a station unattended, system shutdown policies, sharing of workstations, and so forth.

— *Encryption policies* define when encryption should or shouldn't be used and the encryption technologies or algorithms that are acceptable.

— *E-mail policies* govern such matters as opening e-mail attachments, using e-mail clients configured to display HTML mail, forwarding internal e-mail to people outside the organization, and so forth.

— *Remote access policies* define rules for connecting to the company network from outside using dialin or VPN connections, specify what remote authentication methods can be used, prohibiting "dual homing", and so forth.

— *Wireless access policies* set forth standards for connecting to the corporate network using wireless equipment, requiring use of WEP or other encryption technologies, prohibiting connection of unauthorized wireless access points to the network, and so forth.

— *Acceptable use policies* define what users are allowed to do or are prohibited from doing on the network, governing personal use, downloading files, posting to newsgroups, prohibiting installation of unauthorized software applications, and so forth.

Many other policy areas could be applicable to specific organizations; defining policy areas to be addressed is an important task for the policy development team.

Policy Document

The policy development team should ideally be chosen prior to and involved in the needs evaluation process. The team should comprise management and IT personnel, along with someone from each department within the organization. The team should include a legal advisor. As they begin to solidify and codify your policies, the team members must work closely together to:

— Establish security priorities based on the threat assessment matrix.

— Consider and incorporate security standards as needed.

— Determine the practices and procedures that are necessary to achieve the desired level of security at both the administrative and user levels.

— Clearly define both required and prohibited behaviors.

— Determine and define consequences for violations.

— Determine that policies are enforceable and methods for enforcement.

Policies should represent a consensus as to what is and is not appropriate computer-related behavior.

The policy development team should determine the scope of the policy document. For example, will policies regarding telephone, mobile phone, and fax use be included in the IT security policy or be part of a separate policy document? Will procedures for purchasing hardware and software be covered, or will this area be addressed in an overall organizational purchasing policy document? The easiest way to create a policy nightmare is to have two policy documents with conflicting directives. There might not be funds available to address all security needs. Even if enough funds are allocated, most organizations will not be able to implement all security measures simultaneously. Thus the team must establish priorities to determine which policies will be implemented first. Prioritization will be based on such factors as:

— Immediacy of the threat

— Potential loss

— Ease of implementation

— Available funding

Policies that can easily and quickly be implemented can be put in place first, while work begins on those that require more time and effort. Policies generally mandate one or more of the following: physical safeguards, technical security mechanisms, or administrative procedures. Changing administrative procedures can often be done more quickly and easily than implementing physical safeguards or technical mechanisms.

Policies can be divided into different policy types: *regulatory policies,* which must be implemented to comply with the law or regulatory agency requirements; *advisory policies,* which are strongly recommended though not mandated, and *information policies,* which provide information but do not prescribe or proscribe any action. Security policies canserve a number of secondary purposes in addition to the primary purpose of preventing unauthorized use of the network. For example, the policies can be the basis for personnel action (discipline or termination), can be used in the company's defense (or against it) in a civil lawsuit, and can even be instrumental in building a criminal case for prosecution. Thus it is imperative that the policies that are finally published be well thought out, reasonable, and clearly articulated.

Policy writers should avoid technical jargon insofar as is possible; the security policies must be understandable to and usable by company managers, human resources personnel, and the users to whom they apply, as well as IT personnel. It's a good idea to include a glossary to define the technical terminology that is unavoidable. It is also important to create accountability; the person(s) responsible for each area of network/computer security and that person's scope of responsibility should be identified in the policy document.

Policies should state what actions are required, recommended, or prohibited. In addition to defining the action, they should give an example of behavior that would constitute that action, or a violation. For example, if the policy states, "Each user is required to protect the secrecy of his or her network logon password," it should give concrete examples such as,"Users are required to memorize their passwords. Users are prohibited from possessing any written record of their passwords anywhere on company property and are prohibited from divulging their passwords to any other person. If any person asks a user to divulge his or her password, the user is required to report the request to the network administrator immediately. "

Policies should clearly state the consequences for violation. Consequences should be based on the severity of the violation, damage/loss caused, intent or lack thereof, and history of past violations. It's always important to ensure that the policies are consistent—not just with one another within the IT security policy document, but with other company and departmental policies. Finally, it's imperative to make sure that policies don't conflict with any local, state, or federal laws.

The policy document should not be a hodgepodge collection of security directives. It should be logically organized so that related policies are brought together under broadly defined areas. For example, sections might include:

- Physical security (e.g., placement of servers, installation of hardware, securing cabling, securing printers, location of backup tapes, access to rooms/ buildings where computer equipment is located)
- Local system security (e.g., users' responsibilities in regard to securing their own workstations, installation of software, copying files)
- Password security (e.g., policies governing length of passwords, complexity of passwords, changing passwords, and protection of passwords)
- Network security (e.g., policies governing use of firewalls, downloading/ uploading of files,Web access, using instant messaging software)
- Server security (e.g., access to servers, protection of Web servers, file servers, DNS servers, authentication servers)
- Remote access security (e.g., policies governing telecommuters, on-theroad executives, after hours access from home, designated VPN software and configurations)

— Data management and document-handling policies (e.g., policies that govern transferring and exchanging data, securing databases, modifying directory structures, creating/deleting files, filename policies, classification of data sensitivity)

— E-mail security (e.g., policies governing sending/receiving attachments, use of HTML mail, e-mail client configuration settings)

— Software development policies (e.g., governing security and control over in-house software code)

— E-commerce security (e.g., governing online sales and purchases)

— Wireless communication security (e.g., policies governing standards for use of wireless devices on the network)

— Intranet and extranet policies (e.g. , governing terms of access, acceptable use)

— Backup policies (e.g., scheduling, responsibility, retention, storage)

— Disaster prevention and recovery policies (e.g., continuity of service, power backup)

— Policies governing security violations (e.g., responsibility to report, response handling)

— Policies governing employees who leave the company, both on friendly and hostile terms (e.g., turning over equipment and access cards, deactivation of network accounts)

The policy document should contain a detailed table of contents. Each individual policy should have the following components:

— A title that describes clearly what the policy pertains to and a notation of any policy that it supercedes or replaces

— The effective date of the policy

— Reference to related policies

— A section stating the purpose or objective of the policy

— A section identifying the threat or vulnerability being addressed

— A brief summary of the policy

— A section that lays out in detail the policy itself—that is, defining the act or acts that are required or prohibited; this should include identification of people responsible for implementing the policy, to whom the policy applies, and any exceptions to the policy

— Signature of the authority issuing the policy.

Promoting Security Concerns

The best security policies in the world will be ineffective if the network users are not aware of them or if the policies are so restrictive and place so many inconveniences on users that they go out of their way to attempt to circumvent them. The security plan itself should contain a program for educating network users—not just as to what the policies are, but *why* they are important and how the users benefit from them. Users should also be instructed in the best ways to comply with the policies and what to do if they are unable to comply or if they observe other users deliberately violating the policies. If users are involved in the planning and policy-making stages, it will be much easier to educate them and gain their support for the policies at the implementation and enforcement stages.

In order to be effective, policies must be enforceable, and they must be enforced consistently. Policies that are unenforceable or that you are not willing to enforce are worse than useless; their existence undermines the credibility of the rest of the policies. Enforcement must not be selective; if exceptions to the policies are necessary for certain people or in certain circumstances, those exceptions should be laid out in the policy itself. Enforcement authority should be divided among a number of people to provide a system of checks and balances. Employees should be made aware of whom is responsible for policy enforcement, and the enforcement team must be given the authority to carry out the job. Employees should be informed, within the policy document, that they may be subject to such monitoring.

Copies of the IT security policy should be distributed to all personnel to whom the policies apply. All employees should be required to sign a statement acknowledging that they have received, have read, and agree to abide by the terms of the policy. Amendments to the policy should be distributed, and the distribution documented in the same way. This is important in the event that disciplinary action is taken against an employee for violation of the policy. Copies of the policy can also be made available to organizational personnel in electronic format.

6

Cybercrime Convention

Information technology has developed rapidly throughout the past decade. Such rapid progress has achieved significant advances in processing and transmitting data through use of computers and computer networks. Some refer to this era as the "Information Revolution," in effect a second "Industrial Revolution." Today, computers affect all aspects of our lives, from medical treatment to air traffic control, online banking and electronic messages.

The Internet provides substantial benefits to society, including the ability to communicate with others real-time, access a library of information and transmit data instantly without leaving home. In addition to these benefits, Internet expansion has fostered new kinds of crimes, additional means to commit existing crimes and increased complexities of prosecuting crimes. It seems that today, computer crimes affect everyone. A common example is credit card theft whereby a perpetrator illegally obtains the victim's personal information by "hacking" into a website where the victim maintains an account or makes purchases. The perpetrator may steal or charge thousands of dollars to the victim's credit card before he is apprehended, if ever. The problem persists because a perpetrator can easily remain anonymous by instantaneously manipulating or deleting data.

The consequences of crimes committed over the Internet reach farther than traditional methods of committing crimes because there are no geographical border restrictions. Current criminal laws are unable to respond quickly to the rapid changes in Internet technology. When Congress enacts a statute, perpetrators of cyber crimes find new technology to bypass an essential element of the crime or impede investigations. For example, prior to enacting the *No Electronic Theft Act of 1997* (NET), the United States could not prosecute an individual who hosted a computer bulletin board that enabled anyone to download software at no cost.

Authorities were unable to show that the perpetrator received a financial gain from illegal copying, which the law required for criminal wire fraud liability. Similarly, the Philippines Department of Justice dropped charges against the creator of the "ILOVEYOU" virus because existing criminal laws in the Philippines did not apply to computer hacking.

Internet investigations are inherently difficult to conduct because a maze of interconnected computer networks can transmit information instantaneously. Criminals can delete or alter data as quickly as they create it. The ability to destroy or alter data quickly makes it difficult to obtain evidence and perform investigative procedures. For example, perpetrators of crimes can easily change the sender of an e-mail so the receiver cannot identify the e-mail's origin. Likewise, a criminal could use a computer system to erase data subject to criminal investigations, thus, destroying valuable evidence. These factors make it difficult to prosecute cyber criminals and create an exigent need for international cooperation. The Council of Europe (CoE) attempted to address these concerns in the Cybercrime Convention. The Cybercrime Convention is an international treaty designed to police cyber crime through international cooperation.

The Convention requires additional substantive guidance because it requires parties to prohibit the crimes contained therein, but does not explain how to do so. The primary purpose of the Convention is to harmonize domestic substantive criminal law offenses and investigative procedures. The Convention drafters' principal concerns were two-fold. First, they wanted to ensure crime definitions were flexible enough to adapt to new crimes and methods of committing existing crimes as they evolve. Second, the drafters wanted the Convention to remain sensitive to the legal regimes of domestic states.

These concerns were especially challenging in the human rights area because states have different moral and cultural values. For example, European nations have a much higher degree of privacy protection than the United States. The United States, on the other hand, has stronger speech protection than other nations. To further its purpose, the Convention also empowers parties to restrict or eliminate criminalization of certain offenses and limit investigative procedures by reservation. The Convention's drafters, thus, attempted to balance crime definitions and the investigative needs of law enforcement with individual rights.

There are three multilateral organizations that focused on international cyber crime policy: the CoE, the European Union (EU) and the G-8. The Organization for Economic

Cooperation and Development (OECD) and the United Nations (UN) also participated, but to a lesser extent. In response to the increase in cyber crime the CoE's Committee of Ministers adopted Recommendation No. R. (89) 9 ("R89") in 1989, which required that member states consider computer crimes when reviewing old and enacting new legislation.

In 1995, the CoE adopted Recommendation No. (95) 13 ("R95") establishing procedures for applying R89. Investigations were still slow and difficult to coordinate, resulting in the untimely information retrieval necessary to combat cyber attacks. Moreover, many countries lacked criminal cyber law statutes. Countries with such laws found their laws were outdated.

In 1997, the CoE formed a Committee of Experts on Crime in Cyber-space ("PC-CY") in response to prior failed efforts to prevent and deter cyber attacks or address the damaging consequences of such acts. The United States Department of Justice (DOJ) also significantly participated in this effort. The CoE finalized the Convention on November 8, 2001 and opened it for signature on November 23, 2001. Twenty-six of the forty-three European member states signed the Convention, along with four non-members states, Canada, Japan, South Africa and the United States. The Convention will become effective when at least five states ratify it, three of which must be European member states.

Financial gain motivates many cyber criminals. Financial experts agree that cybercrime is most prevalent in the United States because of its financial wealth and the volume of commercial transactions occurring within its borders. Criminals also target the U.S. because of its strong First Amendment protections. Indeed, the U.S. is known amongst the western world as a "haven" for racial and hate speech.

Globally, cyber crimes constitute more than $15 billion in damages every year. Most organizations do not report cyber crimes because they fear exposure would make them vulnerable to future attacks by copycats or cause a loss of public confidence. The cost and difficulty associated with investigations also hinders a company's willingness to report crimes.

Experts predict that developing nations will need to experience significant technological growth over the next decade to be "self-sufficient and more competitive" in an international economy. Developing countries could thus eventually direct more cyber crimes to the United States, although financial constraints will most likely hinder such growth.

Cyber criminals range in both age and skill level. Studies show, however, that employees are the largest threat. Ostensibly, ex-employees, as corporate insiders, can easily exploit their knowledge of a company's computer network. For example, an employee may steal a company's source code by entering the corporate network remotely through unauthorized access using confidential passwords. Companies could prevent or at least mitigate computer fraud if they focus more on security through password controls, employee training and background checks.

Many states have enacted cyber crime laws. Those laws, however, were confined to a specific territory and were frequently outdated. Perpetrators of crimes have thus gone unpunished. Until we are able to cope with the fastpaced changes of the Internet, new kinds of crimes may continue to go unpunished. Those countries that actually have computer crime legislation will continue to operate under a conglomeration of varied and often disjointed laws. The CoE adopted the Convention in response to the need for harmonization.

The Convention is a welcome and necessary advance to international criminal laws. It is, however, largely "aspirational" and fails to provide substantive guidance for defining precisely what conduct constitutes a cyber crime. The Convention also does not identify what specific legal procedures states should apply when investigating and prosecuting cyber crimes.

The CoE was the first organization to develop an international cyber crime Convention. Although seemingly aspirational, the Convention presents a noble effort towards the harmonization of international law and procedure. Its provisions are not detailed enough to provide substantive rules and procedures for combating cyber crime.

Chapter One of the Convention identifies key definitions critical to interpreting the Convention's provisions. The definitions are overly broad and unclear about what conduct falls within the definitions. The Convention definitions should not, however, be so narrow that they disable the Convention's ability to adapt with technological changes. Instead, these Convention definitions should include only computer and Internet related transactions. For example, the Convention defines a computer as "any device or a group of interconnected or related devices one or more of which, pursuant to a program, performs automatic processing of data." The definition is problematic because it does not define or limit what constitutes a device, thus, potentially including devices such as children's toys, Palm Pilots or cable TV boxes. Moreover, it is difficult to tell whether the definition of computer data includes items such as bar codes used to scan groceries at the supermarket.

The Convention's broad definition of a service provider could conceivably encompass any Internet user who maintains a website, thus potentially imposing a huge cost and labor burden on a large user group. Furthermore, it is not clear whether the Convention's ambiguous definition of traffic data includes things such as hyperlinks and http requests. If the definition of traffic data does include hyperlinks and http requests, the definition may be far more invasive on communication than the drafters intended. Finally, it is unclear whether the term communication used in defining traffic data includes surfing the Internet, which is traditionally both a communication and a transaction. Arguably, the act of reading e-mail by connecting through an ISP to a web mail provider is a transaction rather than communication. Finally, denial of service attacks ("DDOS") could be construed as a communication even though they also include a transactional aspect.

The Convention encompasses a finite list of crimes, some of which currently are crimes in one signatory country but are not in another. Convention signatories agree to criminalize offenses included therein, in their domestic laws. The Convention does not, however, include guidance detailing the elements required for those offenses. In the case of countries that do have legislation, lack of guidance will still likely result in different conduct establishing guilt for the same crimes. For example, the U.S. may want to prosecute a citizen from France for the crime of illegal access. France's criminal cyber statute may not include access to a computer system connected to another computer system within the definition of illegal access. Thus, the U.S. could not prosecute a French citizen who accessed a computer connected to another computer. In contrast, if the U.S. and France were both signatories to a Convention codifying the elements of the crime, the U.S. could prosecute a French citizen because both countries would recognize the requisite criminal elements.

Furthermore, if signatories do not agree upon the elements of each crime, we could face a similar debacle as was confronted in *Yahoo, Inc. v. La Ligue* Contre Le Racism Et L'Antisemitisme recently. In the Yahoo debacle, the French Government found *Yahoo* violated French law because *Yahoo*'s auction website permitted the sale of Nazi memorabilia. The Convention would not require the U.S. to cooperate with French authorities if the crime is political. Authorities found this problematic because the U.S. considered the sale of Nazi memorabilia a political offense but France considered it a crime against humanity.

Crime standardization could, however, pose some difficulties for regulators because countries may be reluctant to sign the Convention if it infringes upon domestic legal regimes and cultures. Specifically, the CoE may face resistance in attempting to harmonize content related crimes, such as hate speech, because states established these types of crimes according to their own cultural values. For example, the CoE has recently approved a hate speech provision banning hate speech on the Internet. This ban includes hyperlinks to other web cite pages containing offensive content. The United States vehemently opposes the hate speech provision because it abridges the First Amendment. Accordingly, the U.S. is unlikely to ratify the Convention. Critics believe a ban on hate speech in the Convention would encourage hate groups to solely target the U.S.

The Convention drafters purposely empowered signatories to enact crime legislation out of concern that if the Convention retained too much power, members would be reluctant to ratify it. The drafters believed this was a better solution than if only a few countries ratified the Convention. Based on these examples, however, the Convention would be more valuable if it also included the elements of the crimes rather than leaving this decision to the signatories.

The Convention requires signatories to enact procedures domestically for evidence gathering, including expedited searches, seizures and data collection. Again, the Convention requires the parties to determine how to implement those procedures. In doing so, the drafters intended to respect distinctions in cultures and legal systems by recognizing, for example, disparities amongst parties in levels of privacy protection or speech protection.

Specifically, the Convention requires that the country from where the crime originates, must, at the request of the harmed country, preserve and disclose data to the requesting party. The provision does not, however, specify what law enforcement must demonstrate before accessing potentially private information. Parties with different human rights protections could thus encounter conflicts pertaining to what data must be disclosed. For example, many states do not consider the interception of content data and the collection of traffic data equivalent privacy interests because data collection, without more, does not disclose the communication's actual content. Consequently, the Convention allows parties to limit certain procedures through reservation to enable broader applications of powers and procedures for collection of realtime and traffic data.

Another conflict arises when a requested party's domestic laws permit the requesting party to gather more information from the requested party than the requesting party's own laws would permit. A dilemma exists over whether or not the requested party should supply only as much information as the requesting party is willing to provide. A third conflict arises because parties can decide whether or not to require notice before permitting a search rather than require such notice by law. Moreover, the Convention allows party's to individually determine the degree of severity required before they require interception or collection of content data. These procedures, however, could be crucial in investigating criminal offenses.

Nevertheless, in recognizing the sensitivities surrounding the collection of data, the Convention permits the states themselves to determine the scope of these procedures. Additionally, the Convention does not address payment of costs associated with data interception, storage and surveillance. Conceivably, such costs could be enormous and impose significant burdens on those required to comply. Critics believe that this could place a heavy burden on service providers to retain data and perform additional record-keeping functions. Furthermore, this provision may inundate ISPs with data requests from law enforcement, thereby disrupting core business operations. The Convention should include a provision to apportion payment of investigative costs. Furthermore, the Convention also requires that each signatory provide for conditions and safeguards to balance investigative procedures with the need to protect human rights, but does not articulate those safeguards.

The Convention does not clearly define those safeguards or require that signatories harmonize these safeguards with other international instruments, such as the United Nations Convention on Civil Rights. Even if the Convention required harmonization, existing directives such as the European Convention for the Protection of Human Rights and Fundamental Freedoms are outdated. For example, the United Nations Convention on Civil Rights, adopted in 1950, does not adequately respond to communication privacy issues in the digital age. Although countries currently have different procedures to investigate crimes, and admittedly will continue to after parties ratify the Convention, unless lawmakers harmonize these procedures, they will find it difficult to achieve the Convention's goals.

The Internet has changed the way law enforcement is able to prosecute crimes due to the lack of geographical boundaries. Jurisdictional issues are as critical as the substantive law itself because countries must share information quickly before it disappears. The Convention drafters included broad jurisdictional provisions to provide flexibility for states to decide jurisdictional issues in the event of a dispute. Investigators would lose valuable time needed to gather information and identify the perpetrator if the Convention required law enforcement to obtain a search warrant from each jurisdiction through which an electronic signal passes.

Under traditional common law jurisprudence, a court may exercise jurisdiction if it has both the authority over the area of law in controversy (e.g. subject matter jurisdiction) and personal jurisdiction over the defendant.

The Convention requires states to adopt legislation establishing jurisdiction over offenses committed within its territory, on board a ship flying that state's flag, on board an aircraft registered under the laws of that state or by one of its nationals if punishable by criminal law where committed. In addition, the Convention requires that parties declining to extradite a national have laws in place to enable investigation and prosecution of that individual domestically. Lastly, the Convention requires the parties to a jurisdictional dispute to determine amongst themselves the most appropriate forum.

As drafted, the Convention does not contain a mechanism to deal with conflicts in jurisdiction, further supporting the necessity of clear jurisdictional guidelines. For example, in a recent case, jurisdiction issues existed where a company incorporated in Vanuatu, operated its business from Australia, maintained its computer server in Denmark, maintained its source code in Estonia and the original developers resided in the Netherlands. In that situation, the court had to determine whether jurisdiction was properly in the home state, in each state through which the Internet traffic traveled or where the harm occurred.

A possible solution would establish a priority of jurisdiction. For example, the Convention could establish a hierarchy where the nation that incurred the harm has jurisdictional priority over the nation where the crime was initiated. Without clear jurisdictional guidelines in place, the Convention may yield unwieldy conflicts and inconsistent decisions.

The Convention requires signatories to provide mutual assistance to one another in cooperating with criminal investigations "to the widest extent possible." The drafters recognized the need for a mechanism allowing law enforcement to investigate offenses and obtain evidence quickly and efficiently, while remaining cognizant of each nation's sovereignty and constitutional and human rights.

As drafted, the Convention does not require "dual criminality" as a condition for mutual assistance consistently throughout the treaty. Dual criminality exists if the offense is a crime under both the requestor and requesting party's laws. If countries do not agree on what elements constitute a given crime, the perpetrator may go unpunished. For example, if Country A requires elements one through four to constitute a given crime but Country B only requires elements one through three, Company A may not receive cooperation from Company B and a perpetrator who commits element number four may go free in Country B.

Critics expressed similar concerns because they believe a country does not have the right to interfere with the privacy of another country's citizens or impose "onerous requirements" to investigate crimes. Furthermore, the Convention does not require that parties implement investigative restraints to prohibit the requested party from using techniques or procedures that go beyond the power of the requesting party. The language, as drafted, does not provide specific guidelines limiting a party's ability to avoid assisting in an investigation.

Opponents believe that signatories might use this open-ended language to justify a refusal to cooperate with crime investigations. If countries refuse to cooperate, law enforcement may resort to methods of self-help and take matters into their own hands. For example, a federal court recently sentenced a Russian hacker, Vasiliy Gorshbikov to thirty-six months in prison for crimes resulting from illegal hacking. Gorshbikov committed numerous computer crimes as well as fraud against various service providers, on-line banks and e-commerce networks in the United States. In an undercover investigation to stop the hackers, the F.B.I. tricked Gorshbikov, and his accomplice Ivanov into entering U.S. territory. The FBI used information obtained from Gorshbikov and Ivanov to hack into their computers located in Russia. The FBI then copied data from their accounts, pursuant to a warrant issued by a U.S. Magistrate Judge and obtained sufficient evidence to convict the hackers. Lastly, Article twenty-seven of the Convention specifically allows a party to refuse extradition under certain circumstances, such as crimes constituting political offenses or those that may prejudice a nation's interests. The provision, however, does not clarify what types of offenses qualify as "political" in nature or which they will consider prejudicial.

The Convention needs to provide more detailed guidance as to what types of political offenses or prejudices will legitimately justify a refusal to cooperate and who will render that decision. The Convention should also either provide additional guidance to signatories or set the standards itself to ensure timely and efficient criminal investigations through international cooperation.

The Convention is a welcome and long-overdue start towards addressing the exigent circumstances evolving from the Internet revolution. The CoE deserves much credit in accepting such a significant and valuable task. Computer crimes are difficult to solve due to the absence of geographical borders and the inherent ability to swiftly transfer and manipulate information instantly. Nevertheless, technological advances will continue to challenge law enforcement officials. As long as long signatories are permitted to codify cyber criminal laws domestically and countries remain unsubscribed to the Convention, authorities may be unable to obtain sufficient evidence to prosecute crimes.

Bibliography

Adams, James. *Next World War: Computers Are the Weapons and the Front Line is Everywhere*. New York: Simon & Schuster, 1998.

Alexander, Yonah. *Cyber Terrorism and Information Warfare: Threats and Responses:Terrorism Documents of International Local Control*. Ardsley, NY: Transnational Publishers, 2001.

Anthony, Keith D., "Information Warfare: Good News and Bad News", *Military Intelligence* 23, January-March 1997, pp. 31-34.

Bacard, Andr, *The Computer Privacy Handbook*, Berkeley: Peachpit Press, 1995.

Barac, Gregory G., "Interoperability: The Cornerstone of Information Warfare", *Strategy Research Project*, Carlisle Barracks: US Army War College, 12 April 1996.

Chris Prosise, Kevin Mandia, *Incident Response: Investigating Computer Crime*, McGraw Hill Professional Book Group, July 2001.

Denning, Dorothy. *Information Warfare and Security*. Reading, MA: Addison-Wesley, 1999.

El Mahdy, Galal. *Disaster Management in Telecommunications, Broadcasting, and Computer Systems*. New York: John Wiley, 2001.

Eoghan, Casey, *Digital Evidence and Computer Crime: Forensic Science, Computers, and the Internet with CD-ROM*, Academic Press, Incorporated, January 2000.

Franklin Clark,Vernon J. Geberth (ed.), *Investigating Computer Crime*, CRC Press, LLC, June 1996.

Herman, Michael. *Intelligence Services in the Information Age*. Portland, OR: Frank Cass, 2001.

Krause, Micki. *Information Security Management Handbook*. Boca Raton, FL: Auerbach, 2000.

Nichols, Randall. *Defending Your Digital Assets Against Hackers*, Crackers, and Spies. New York: McGraw Hill, 2000.

Rattray, Gregory J. *Strategic Warfare in Cyberspace*. Cambridge, MA: MIT Press, 2001.

Schwartau, William. *Information Warfare Cyberterrorism: Protecting Your Personal Security in the Electronic Age*. Emeryville, CA: Thunder's Mouth Press, 1996.

Schwartau, William. *Cybershock: Hackers, Phreakers, Identity Thieves, Internet Terrorists*. New York: Thunder's Mouth Press, 2000.

Sofaer, Abraham D. *The Transnational Dimension of Cyber Terrorism*. Stanford, CA: Hoover Institution Press, 2001.

Sterling, Bruce. *Hacker Crackdown: Law and Disorder on the Electronic Frontier*. New York: Bantam Books, 1992.

Stephen Northcutt, Judy Novak, Donald McLachlan, *Network Intrusion Detection: An Analyst's Handbook*, New Riders Publishing, September 2000.

Weible, Jack, "Vulnerable to Attack? Subcommittees Get an Earful on Threats to Information Systems", *Air Force Times* 57, 14 April 1997, pp.28.

Whitehead, YuLin, "Information as a Weapon: Reality versus Promises", *Airpower Journal* 11, 1997, pp.40-54.

Williams, Robert H, "Info Warfare Attacks Score in Military's Risk Pantheon, *National Defense* 81, September 1996, pp.16-17.

Winn Schwartau, *Cybershock: Surviving Hackers, Phreakers, Identity Thieves, Internet Terrorists, and Weapons of Mass Disruption*, Avalon, New York, April 2000.

Index

What are the Areas of Conflict in Cyberlaws?

Multiple cases have arisen where Internet activities considered to be legitimate in one country violate the laws of another. Additionally, one country may not have the procedural laws to enable it to respond effectively to requests for assistance from another country, or its law enforcement may not have the authority to assist in the search and seizure of electronic evidence. Examples of areas of conflict include jurisdictional issues, extradition, extra-territorial searches, violations of content laws, and inconsistent hacking laws. These inconsistencies underscore the important role the UN could play in acting as a coordinator on these issues.

Goldstein and Kamal note that:

Civil liberties groups have also expressed concern that the Council of Europe convention undermines individual rights to privacy and extends the surveillance powers of the signatory governments. Critics in the United States also note that the provisions of the convention are incompatible with current U.S. law. For example, by defining the sending of unsolicited e-mails as a criminal activity, the Convention is claimed to criminalize behavior which until now has been seen as lawful civil disobedience. In "How Might Harmonization of Cybercrime Laws Proceed Through Model Precedents" The UN Model Laws on Electronic Commerce and Electronic Signatures are considered to be the global "standard" for legislation in these areas. They have been looked to and followed by industrialized and developing countries around the globe. UN action that would provide a global model law and an accompanying explanatory memorandum that nation states could use as a guide, along with an international agreement on procedural, jurisdictional and cooperative aspects, would make the global harmonization of cybercrime laws an achievable goal.

CYBER CRIME
Issues Threats and management

CYBER CRIME
Issues Threats and Management
(In 2 Volumes)

Managing Cyber Crime to Cyber Warfare
(Volume-1)

Editor
Atul Jain

ISHA BOOKS
DELHI-110 033

Cyber Crime: Issues and Threats

ISBN: 978-81-8205-106-5 (Set)
ISBN: 978-81-8205-107-2(Vol. 1)

Reprint 2015 in India by
Isha Publications
B-69, New Gupta Colony
Near DDA Market
New Delhi-110009

Printed at: Chawla Offset, Delhi

Contents

Preface

The stability of modern society has been heightened by the ubiquitous nature of information and communication technologies (ICTs), which pervades all aspects of human activity. Indeed the utilization of ICTs is a recognized prerequisite to improved corporate competitiveness, government efficiency, human development, and the development of knowledge societies and economies.

The benefits of ICTs, however, can be undercut by negative uses of these technologies in the form of cyber attacks, viruses and other malware, economic espionage, sabotage of data and systems, exploitation of networks, etc. Individuals and small groups can use ICTs against the interests of nation states. These criminal acts can affect not only individual systems, but can also impact world peace and security and undermine development efforts. The resulting damage can ignite panic, cause a loss of confidence, create uncertainty, and destroy trust in modern society.

Since cybercrime was first identified and its dangerous potential recognized, the problem has shown rapid growth such that it challenges all ICT users—whether individuals, small businesses, multinational corporations, public sector entities, or nation states—and imposes responsibilities for cyber security upon them. The vulnerability of global and national information infrastructures gives birth to new challenges to national and international security, business activity, and human rights. The problem of cyber security will not be resolved by the efforts of just one state or a group of states or on a regional basis. The solution of this problem demands a unified effort of the entire international community.

This book offers a convincing analysis of the damaging potential of cyber attacks on almost all aspects of human endeavour. It also describes the actions need to be taken to control the threats from cyber attacks. This work will be a highly informative reference tool for decision-makers, academics, students, researchers and investigators.

Editor

1

Nature and Consequences of Cyber Crime

Until the last century, 'crime' was small-scale, consisting of unlawful acts committed by one person or a few loosely-associated persons that were directed against a single victim. Some offenders, of course, made crime their profession, but their activities remained small-scale, limited to the repetitive commission of certain single-victim offenses.

The "crimes," which were generally consistent across societies, fell into standard, clearly-defined categories that reflected the basic categories of anti-social motivations: crime was murder, robbery and rape. Crime also tended to be personal; if the offenders and victim did not actually know each other, they were likely to share community ties that put offenses into a manageable, knowable context. This not only facilitated the process of apprehending offenders but also gave citizens at least the illusion of security, the conceit that they could avoid being victimized if they avoided certain activities or certain associations.

Local law enforcement dealt effectively with this type of crime because its parochial character meant investigations were limited in scope and because the incidence of crime stood in relatively modest proportion to the size of the local populace. Law enforcement's effectiveness in this regard contributed to a popular perception that social order was being maintained and that crime did not go unsolved or unpunished.

The twentieth century's increased urbanization, geographical mobility and use of technology undermined this model to some extent, but it persisted and still functioned effectively for the most part. Legal systems quickly adapted to the fact that telephones could be used to commit fraud and to harass others; that motor vehicles introduced a dimension of mobility into robbery, kidnapping and other crimes; and that radio and television could be used to perpetrate crimes. Because legal systems modified their substantive criminal law to encompass these activities, the old model still functions effectively for traditional, "real world" crime.

Cybercrime is a different story: computers and the internet have created phenomenal possibilities for addressing a variety of human problems, but these technologies also have a dark side. What differentiates the criminal threats posed by the Internet is that it is based on a vastly more complex technology than the automobile. It spans the globe and moves information and potential criminal activity with a speed and efficiency heretofore unknown in human history. Not only does this give the police less time to react to any potential criminal threat, but it raises issues of jurisdiction, privacy, and anonymity.

Some cybercrimes such as stalking tend to be small-scale, single-offender/single-victim crimes. Although our experience with cybercrime is still in its infancy, large-scale offenses targeting multiple, geographically dispersed victims have already been committed. The February, 2000 denial of service attacks that targeted eBay, Yahoo and CNN, among others are just one notorious example. These attacks effectively shut down web sites for hours and were estimated to have caused $1.2 billion in damage.

To understand the sea change computer technology has introduced to criminal activity, consider a hypothetical: One can analogize a denial of service attack to using the telephone to shut down a pizza delivery business by calling the business' telephone number repeatedly, persistently and without remorse, thereby preventing any other callers from getting through to place their orders. While it may be possible for someone to execute this scheme, it would be very onerous to do so because it would require a great deal of physical effort and concentration on the perpetrator's part; he would have to be constantly dialing, maintaining the connection until it was broken and then redialing quickly to prevent any other calls from coming in. It would also involve a significant risk of apprehension because the victim could contact the authorities, who would presumably have no difficulty tracing the calls to the perpetrator, since he would presumably be using his personal or business telephone.

Cyberspace allows this attack to easily carry out such an attack with very little risk of apprehension. In addition to the increased scale it offers to criminal activity, cybercrime also has a tendency to evade traditional offense categories. While some cybercrime consists of using computer technology to commit traditional crimes such as fraud and theft, it also manifests itself as new varieties of anti-social activity that cannot be prosecuted using traditional offense categories.

Cybercrime's ability to morph into new and different forms of antisocial activity evading the reach of existing penal law creates challenges for law enforcement around the world. Cybercriminals can exploit gaps in their own country's criminal law to victimize their fellow citizens with impunity. They can also exploit gaps in the criminal laws of other countries to victimize the citizens of those and other nations.

Cybercrime presents the nations of the world with a problem they have never before had to address, i.e., the permeability of national borders. Technology gives the ability to loot and inflict harm upon the entire world with little risk of apprehension and allows for experimenting with new varieties of criminal endeavors.

The terms "cybercrime," "computer crime", "Information Technology crime," and "high-tech crime" are often used inter-changeably to refer to two major categories of offenses: in the first, the computer is the target of the offense; attacks on network confidentiality, integrity and/or availability—i.e. unauthorized access to and illicit tampering with systems, programs or data – all fall into this category; the other category consists of traditional offenses—such as theft, fraud, and forgery – that are committed with the assistance of or by means of computers, computer networks and related information and communications technology.

Cybercrimes range from economic offenses (fraud, theft, industrial espionage, sabotage and extortion, product piracy, etc.) to infringements on privacy, propagation of illegal and harmful content, facilitation of prostitution and other moral offenses, and organized crime. At its most severe, cybercrime borders on terrorism, encompassing attacks against human life and against national security establishments, critical infrastructure, and other vital veins of society.

Terrorism encompasses actions intended to provoke a state of terror in the general public, a group of persons or particular persons. Terrorist acts cause grave harm to society by disrupting civil order and/or causing mass terror, loss of life, physical destruction or economic hardship. In cyberterrorism, as in cybercrime, the "cyber" component usually refers to perpetrating qualitatively new offenses enabled by information technology or integrating cyberspace into more traditional activities (such as planning, intelligence, logistical capabilities, finance, etc.). The categories may also overlap, as they frequently do in the cases of capable, computer-savvy offenders.

Nations around the world are very concerned about cybercrime, a concern shared by many international organizations, including the United Nations, the G-8, the European Union and the Council of Europe. There are a number of reasons to be concerned, perhaps the most important being the problems law enforcement officials and prosecutors encounter in trying to apply existing law cyberspace crime.

Many legal challenges faced by police and prosecutors in pursuit of cybercriminals can be illustrated by the brief yet destructive career of the "Love Bug" virus. The virus destroyed files and stole passwords; it appeared in Hong Kong on May 11, 2000 and spread rapidly throughout the world. The virus affected NASA and the CIA on its two-hour race around the world, three times faster than its predecessor Melissa. The virus is estimated to have ultimately affected over forty-five million users in more than twenty countries. The various estimates of the damage caused, ranging from two billion dollars up to ten billion, reflect on the inherent difficulty of assessing the harm inflicted by cybercrime. Virus experts quickly traced the "Love Bug" to the Philippines. Philippines' National Bureau of Investigation and United States FBI agents identified individuals suspected of creating and disseminating the "Love Bug" using information supplied by an Internet Service Provider but ran into problems with their investigation.

Since the Philippines had no cybercrime laws, creating and disseminating the virus was not a crime; since there was no crime, the agents had a hard time convincing a magistrate to issue a warrant to search the suspects' apartment. Getting the warrant took days, ample time to destroy evidence. After finally executing the warrant authorities seized evidence indicating that Onel de Guzman, a former computer science student, was responsible for creating and disseminating the "Love Bug."

As hacking and the distribution of viruses had not been criminalized, officials struggled with whether de Guzman could be prosecuted. After finally charging him with theft and credit card fraud, the watched the charges be dismissed as inapplicable and unfounded. Because extradition treaties require "double criminality," that the act for which extradition is sought be a crime by the laws of each involved nation, de Guzman could not extradited for prosecution by other countries that do have cybercrime laws, such as the United States. Despite having caused billions of dollars in damage to thousands of victims in numerous nations, de Guzman could not be brought to trial in the matter. So, no one was ever prosecuted for the damage the "Love Bug" caused.

Law enforcement officials cannot take action against cybercriminals unless countries first enact laws which criminalize the activities in which these offenders engage. As the "Love Bug" investigators learned, the existence of such laws is a fundamental prerequisite for investigation as well as for prosecution. It would therefore seem obvious that all nations would have or at least desire to have cybercrime laws on the books.

The difficulty lies in properly defining the laws needed to allow for cybercriminals' apprehension and prosecution. While seemingly a straightforward task, difficult issues are raised. One is whether the definitional scope of cybercrimes should include only laws that prohibit activities *targeting* computers or should outlaw crimes against individuals affected through the computer as well, such as cyberstalking and cyberterrorism. Another is whether these laws should be cybercrime-specific, targeting only crimes committed by exploiting computer technology. Is it, for example, necessary for a country to add a "computer fraud" offense if it has already outlawed fraud? Both these issues are national in scope and go only to the nature of legislation a nation should adopt.

Other issues are international in scope, pertaining to the impact a country's cybercrime laws, or lack thereof, have on other countries. The Philippines' failure to have cybercrime legislation meant that a Philippine national could not be tried in any of the twenty countries to which he inflicted damage and thus suffered no consequences for his acts; the failure to have legislation was inadvertent, but it's impact was felt around the globe.

Effective law enforcement is complicated by the transnational nature of cyberspace. Mechanisms of cooperation across national borders to solve and prosecute crimes are complex and slow. Cyber criminals can defy the conventional jurisdictional realms of sovereign nations, originating an attack from almost any computer in the world, passing it across multiple national boundaries, or designing attacks that appear to be originating from foreign sources.

Such techniques dramatically increase both the technical and legal complexities of investigating and prosecuting cyber crimes.Nations must modernize their procedural law as well as their substantive law, their law of crimes. While an adequate framework of cybercrime penal law is an absolute prerequisite for effective action against cybercriminals, such action can be frustrated by antiquated procedural law which, for example, authorizes warrants only for search for and seizure of tangible evidence.

Since the prosecution of cybercrimes usually requires collecting and analyzing intangible evidence, this omission can be a serious problem for investigators. Countries must, therefore, also evaluate their procedural law governing evidence collection and analysis, and amend existing legislation as necessary so as to not suffer from such limitations.

Range of Cybercrime Activities

Cybercrimes are complex and sometimes elusive phenomena; there is no comprehensive, globally accepted definition that separates the sensational from the sensible and scientific. The following scenarios illustrate the range of activities that can be considered cybercrimes.

Hacking and Related Activities

Hacking, or gaining unauthorized access to a computer system, programs or data, opens a broad playing field for inflicting damage. A snooper might read the victim's personal information and even take over his computer, or a vandal might alter the victim's webpage. A saboteur could erase R&D data or paralyze a network, and an industrial spy might steal trade secrets. A blackmailer might plant a digital time/logic bomb and threaten to trash a system unless the victim pays up.

Virus and Malicious Programmes

Viruses and other types of malicious code can be even more destructive: A calamitous virus may delete files or permanently damage systems. A Trojan horse, masquerading as a utility (e.g. anti-virus software) or animation, may copy user-IDs and passwords, erase files, or release viruses. The program may be used for blackmail, with activation of a virus or 'detonation' of a digital bomb threatened unless demands are met. A virus might cause a minor annoyance, or tremendous losses in money and productivity, or even human lives, if it changes or destroys crucial data such as hospital medical records.

Fraud and Theft

Fraud is probably the largest category of cybercrime. The Internet has created what so far appears to be the perfect cybercrime—borderless fraud. So many different types of fraud are committed over computer networks that they have become almost impossible to police effectively. In computer chat-rooms, message boards, unsolicited email, and on web sites themselves, fraudsters lose no opportunity to trick and deceive others for the purpose of financial gain. Those who engage in fraud operate globally on 'Internet time,' 24 hours a day, 7 days a week. Although many of the schemes perpetrated online today are nothing more than repackaged versions of their 'real world' counterparts, the efficiency and speed of the network create new opportunities for criminals while simultaneously positing serious criminal threats to ecommerce.

One of the most common types of cyberfraud is online auction fraud: You are buying something you saw advertised on eBay, for example. Is the person you are dealing with trustworthy? Often not: the vendor may be describing products or services in a false or misleading manner, or may take orders and money, but fail to deliver goods. Counterfeit goods might be supplied. Investment fraud has been seen, whereby the Internet is used to fraudulently manipulate stock prices or facilitate illegal insider trading.

Using computers, thieves can steal credit card details and siphon funds from banks. A twentyfive year old Moscow hacker stole credit card information that was put onto blank cards and used at ATMs all over Europe; the fifty people involved in the scam managed to steal several million dollars before they were caught.

Gambling

Online casinos have proliferated widely, despite that fact that gambling is illegal in many jurisdictions. The Internet is also being used to distribute drugs, tobacco and liquor, again regardless of jurisdictional prohibitions.

Child Pornography

Many types of pedophilic activity - viewing images, discussing activities, arranging tourism, enticing a child to a meeting - are carried out over the Internet. Child sexual abusers are rapidly turning the Internet and commercial online services into red-light districts, where they can distribute vast quantities of pornography and organize with like-minded individuals. The Internet gives child molesters and pornographers unprecedented opportunities to target and recruit new victims. It allows sexual predators to stalk juvenile victims anonymously from the comfort of their homes.

The Internet gives the pedophile the advantages of a wider scope of communications and the likelihood of eluding the law, given the jurisdictional problems which arise in prosecuting cases that transcend borders, as is the nature of the Internet.

Stalking Harassment, Hate Speech

Stalking and harassment are malicious activities directed at a particular person. A case occured in California is as folows: A 50-year-old former security guard used the Internet to solicit the rape of a woman who rejected his romantic advances. He terrorized his 28-year-old victim by impersonating her in various Internet chat rooms and online bulletin boards, where he posted, along with her telephone number and address, messages that she fantasized of being raped. On at least six occasions, sometimes in the middle of the night, men knocked on the woman's door saying they wanted to rape her.

The dissemination of hate and racist speech has a more general focus, but can be equally traumatic for those it targets, and is becoming more widespread. Stalking, harassment, hate-filled and racist speech perpetrated over computer networks may or may not be criminal activities, depending on the jurisdiction.

Cyberhomicide

Cyberhomicide—using computer technology to kill someone—has not yet been reported, but it no doubt will. An aspiring mass murderer could, for example, hack into a hospital's computer system, learn about the medication prescribed for patients and alter the dosages, causing them to die.

Cyber Terrorism

Cyberterrorism has been defined as a "premeditated, politically motivated attack against information, computer systems, computer programs, and data which result in violence against noncombatant targets by subnational groups or clandestine agents." Such an attack can take many forms: a cyberterrorist might hack into computer systems and disrupt domestic banking, the stock exchanges and international financial transactions, leading to a loss of confidence in the economy. Or he might break into an air traffic control system and manipulate it, causing planes to crash or collide.A terrorist could hack into a pharmaceutical company's computers, changing the formula of some essential medication and causing thousands to die. Or a terrorist could break into a utility company's computers, changing pressure in gas lines, tinkering with valves and causing a suburb to detonate and burn.

2

Tactics of Cyber Offenders

Today's cyber attacks have many similarities with Medieval sieges and battles. There are many different forms of attack – just as there were many forms of weapons. The difference lies in the fact that today's weapons become more sophisticated very quickly. There are many kinds of warriors – from the leader and the professional soldier to the mercenaries and peasants conscripted against their will. Today's players also include professionals such as mercenaries who hack for personal gain or satisfaction; and those who hijack computers and turn them into zombies by planting them with malicious software. On the side of the defenders we may find reformed hackers who become security advisors and consultants.

As the various components of information technology such as computers, networks and software became tools, they took three roles in information security:

— Tools to perpetrate information offences

— Weapons

— Target for attack

Typical offences against a computer system include fraud, extortion, denial of service and the theft of proprietary information, either as the result of espionage or with intent to misuse it as for example credit cards details. The use of information technology as a tool or accessory also has a long history, which begins in World War II when early computers were used to break down codes used to encrypt military communications.

The use of information technology as a weapon is most evident when combined with other kind of weapons such as missiles, to provide them with additional capabilities such as the identification of targets and enhanced navigation. Malicious code, software designed to perform functions which will interfere with the operation of a computer or network, such as virus and worm software, are the latest manifestation of "weapons" of considerable economic impact.

Here are some numbers that illustrate the potential cost of information insecurity:

In the year 2000, the U.S. Association of Certified Fraud Examiners reported that the average sum of money robbed in a bank holdup was 14,000 dollars whereas the average computer theft was 2 million dollars.

Early in 2002, Computer Economics Inc., a U.S. company reported that their estimate for the total cost of computer virus and worm attacks to the U.S. economy amounted to 17 billion dollars. This estimate assumes that the average cost of an employee doing computer work in the U.S.A. is one dollar per minute and that the economic impact from malicious code includes the cost of:

— Removing all malicious code from computers and servers

— Restoring lost and corrupted data

— Returning all systems to normal operations

— Providing support to end-users, customers and other parties involved

— Lost productivity while the above processes took place

This economic impact needs to be seen in the context that:

— Computer systems are becoming more complex and, as a result, have greater vulnerabilities than previous generations - effectively doubling every year

— The trend for malicious code attacks shows a similar increase also doubling every year

Today's threats differs from that of medieval times for three main reasons:

— The timeframe has changed. Everything happens very quickly. In the middle ages, a good catapult team could shoot no more than two stones an hour.

— Physical security has become less dominant than logical security - data thugs, cyber-vandals and other players do not need physical contact with the victim.

— There is no need any longer to physically manufacture and transport weapons.

Types of Cyber Offenders

Cyber offenders can be categorised into two groups: cyber offenders by nature and cyber offenders by organisation.

Offenders by Nature

Information security players by nature can be categorised as follows:

1. *Good Guys:*
   - Responsible end-users
   - Security administrators
   - Security managers
   - Internal auditors
   - Security coordinators
   - Providers of security alerts
   - Ethical hackers, etc.
2. *Bad Guys:*
   - Malicious insiders
   - Script kiddies
   - Hackers, crackers, phreakers
   - Hacktivists
   - Spies (industrial and other)
   - Organised crimminals
   - Cyber-terrorists
3. *Very Special Guys:*
   - Vendors
   - Security auditors
   - Security consultants
   - Legislators

Good Guys

Good Guys can be described in just a few lines: these are the people whose role is to protect themselves and their employers from all forms of cyber-attack. How they actually do this is the subject of Information Security Management, a topic covered by extensive, largely technical bibliography and several professional journals and websites. These players are motivated by their work ethics to behave ethically, in the best interest of their employers and by deriving a high degree of job satisfaction.

Ethical hackers deserve a special mention: these are people with good technical knowledge and an understanding of how to identify vulnerabilities in products and procedures, and how to do so with the purpose of alerting their employer, vendors and bodies that monitor product vulnerabilities. The best ethical hackers often become professional security consultants and conduct controlled tests for organisations.

Very Special Guys

Very Special Guys are those external people who play key roles in defining security. Among them, vendors have the responsibility of providing products with the least possible number of vulnerabilities. This may be incompatible with the commercial pressures to bring products to market ahead of potential competitors and to generate new revenues. It is important to note that many software vendors disclaim liabilities for weaknesses, vulnerabilities or errors in their products whatever consequences these may cause to the end-user. When engaging security auditors there needs to be a very strong measure of trust as they will examine in detail and test security arrangements. Through this process they will acquire highly sensitive knowledge.

Bad Guys

Bad Guys are those players whose intent is to interfere with someone else's computer systems and data.

Malicious insiders: Any review of the Bad Guys must start with them. They are the most likely to combine access, knowledge and motivation to act against computer data, systems and networks. Motivation usually falls into two categories:

1. Those who seek financial gain for themselves and/or close associates by defrauding or extorting their employer. Computer fraud involves large sums of money, no physical violence and when done subtly, a good chance to remain undetected. Even when detected, it is difficult to produce evidence that will satisfy a court of law. Computer crimes leave few or no traces, there are unlikely to be witnesses and, given the risk to an organisation's reputation, such crimes are usually unreported.

2. Those driven to cause damage as a result of grudges against their employers or their colleagues, being coerced by a third party or in support of a political cause. These are, by far the most dangerous. Insiders know the vulnerabilities of systems and can corrupt data and software, plant malicious code, or sabotage their employers' systems in many other ways. The situation where a malicious insider who works for a country's critical infrastructures behaves as a cyber-terrorist, represents the most serious risk. It also

presents an ethical dilemma for employers, that of closely monitoring the activities of their employees and ensuring compliance with security policies.

Script-kiddies: These are usually young people who like computers but are not particularly knowledgeable. By visiting hacker club websites, chat-rooms and exchanging readily available tools with their peers, they can emulate more knowledgeable players.

Hackers, crackers and others: Hackers are technically knowledgeable people who understand and write software, and know how to identify security weaknesses in products. This enables them to make other peoples' software perform undesired functions, as well as to create tools to facilitate their exploits.

Hacker groups are well organised to share knowledge, certainly better than security managers: They convene conferences, run good websites, exchange tools and information on product weaknesses. The annual DEFCON conference describes itself as the "largest underground internet security gathering on the planet" and is a public event. The first DEFCON conference took place in 1993. Ethical hackers appear to be happy being able to prove they can overcome someone else's security defences. In a way they can be thought of as "explorers" trying to map a new, uncharted territory. Unethical hackers do so with intent to causing damage, or at the very least, embarrassment. Instead of explorers, they are like pirates and mercenaries and equally outside the law.

International Organisations and commercial companies have been the subject of synchronised Distributed Denial of Service attacks, in which their web servers and e-mail servers are bombarded by transactions to the point that they become unable to operate. These attacks make use of computers hijacked without their owners' knowledge by planting software in them that turns them into "zombies" whenever the hackers need them. Whenever hackers give interviews or write articles, they say little about their motivation. The reasons most frequently given by non-ethical hackers are:

— "Just because it's there and I know how to"

— "To cause maximum inconvenience and embarrassment"

— "To have access to data which allows fraudulent transactions to take place"

Writers of malicious code: "Malicious code" is an umbrella term for any computer software designed to make computers perform unwanted actions. Two best known forms of malicious code are viruses and worms. (Viruses use software in the affected machine to replicate. Worms are selfreplicating). Other forms of malicious code include:

— *Macros written for Microsoft Office applications* (file extension .vbs). This was used in the Melissa virus,

— *Executable files* (file extension .exe). A recent virus was hidden in a digital picture file (file extension .jpeg). This technique is called steganography.

— *Trojan Horse* – software which performs legitimate functions but which includes within it malicious code The skills and tools needed to write and/or modify viruses and worms are within the grasp of anyone with reasonable programming skills. Most of them are short programs and many are variants of a previous one. The producers of Anti-Virus software to develop the tools to detect and eliminate them use their "signature", like the DNA of biological viruses.

> Usually the detection software becomes available only after the code has infected a large number of machines.

It is not clear what motivates writers of malicious code. Some have no more than a perverse desire to indulge in a "practical joke". Others may be sponsored by other parties to research and develop mechanisms to access computers that evade detection for long enough to cause damage. The emergence of a militarystrength virus with a destructive payload that can corrupt or delete data and programs is inevitable and simply a matter of time.

Other forms of malicious code have been in existence since early computer applications, in this case designed and introduced by expert programmers. Examples of such code include:

— Logic bomb

— Back door and/or unauthorised Super-user rights

— Fraudulent transactions

A logical bomb is a piece of software which is concealed within an application, and which can be activated by its designer. An example is when the person has a grudge against the company where the software has been planted. Alternatively, the objective may be extortion or blackmail. Once activated, the usual script is as follows:

— Your payroll system will grind to a halt.

— I'm the only person who knows how to prevent it.

— If you wanted fixed, it will cost you.

A logical bomb is, in reality, "extra code", software that was never part of a system's specification. Finding and removing such code is easier said than done as some software consists of millions of line of code and the quality of source-code documentation is variable.

In the case of packaged software, the source code is not available for inspection and it is known that the practice of including extra code is regularly practiced. Non-malicious extra code, referred to as "Easter Eggs" is usually well hidden and may consist of games, the list of names of the software design team, utilities, etc. Disabling all extra code and software features, which are not specifically needed, is always a good security practice. This is easier said than done.

Back door and/or Super-user access rights are hidden in a system by designers to bypass security features and access data and the programs without having the authority to do so. Even with extensive auditing of computer systems, such back doors usually remain undiscovered given the size and complexity of such applications. The people who introduce such features have malicious intent against their employer, a target organization. This could be used for sabotage, extortion or to financially benefit the writer.

Hacktivists: The World Wide Web and Internet mail have enabled political activism to take new forms, such as Electronic Sit-Ins, the defacement of websites, or the hijacking of websites by redirecting traffic to a spoof website. The hacktivists' targets are usually government websites, international and multinational organizations, financial institutions. Hacktivists claim that this is a form of civil disobedience. The legal status of these actions is unclear in existing legislation.

Hacktivists have been highly successful in some recent civil disobedience actions. They claim that cyberspace gives them opportunity to make themselves heard on a global scale and gain publicity for the causes they support. A different form of hacktivism is the use of cyberspace to disseminate propaganda, disinformation, and incitation to violence and hate.

Spies: Espionage has a long history. Ever since the industrial revolution, industrial espionage has been big business, particularly where achieving and maintaining a position of leadership in a competitive market requires sophisticated research. Industrial espionage is on the increase because of the extensive reliance on computer systems and networks to document experiments and research. It is motivated by money – it is a well paid activity and the sponsor stands to gain knowledge worth millions of dollars at minimal expense and minimal risk.

The gathering of military and other intelligence is no longer exclusive to governments: it is also practiced by organised crime, guerrillas and terrorists. Electronic surveillance is practiced worldwide and the degree to which the existence of surveillance systems is reported in the press varies. Some systems are acknowledged: FBI's "Carnivore" is now called DCS1000. Others, despite rumours, may or may not exist such as "Echelon", the surveillance network supposed to have been set up by a number of governments to monitor global information flows.

An e-mail message is no more than a machine-readable unsealed postcard. Whilst the use of foreign languages and/or encryption for such messages provides a measure of assurance of confidentiality, it also signals to scanning systems (likely to exist despite denials) that the writer wants to keep something hidden. Encrypted messages become the focus of even greater attention.

Organised criminals: Technological innovations are quickly exploited by organized criminals for personal gain. Information and communication technologies are no different, and new forms of fraudulent and anti-social activities continue to emerge. It is invariably motivated by money, in most cases tax-free. Current examples include the use of cyberspace for money laundering, credit card fraud, blackmail, extortion, pornography, pedophilia, and offshore gambling. Most of these activities are aided by the ease of hiding in cyberspace, the lack of jurisdiction over cyberspace and the number of countries that do not have adequate legislation to address such activities. Even when the legislation exists, enforcing it may be a very complex matter.

Cyber-terrorists and cyber-warriors: There appears to be no agreed definition of a cyber-terrorist or of what constitutes "violence" in cyber-space. The latter is likely to become a subject of some concern in future as the gap between levels of technology advances further. Some of the recent manifestations of worms such as CODE RED in the Summer of 2001 and the NIMDA worm, may be a proof of concept for software that could paralyse the Internet and organisations that rely on it for their operations. The potential impact of a well-conducted cyber-attack in which the most likely targets would be critical infrastructures could be the equivalent of a full scale cyber-war.

Offenders by organisation

Critical Infrastructures

In the developed world, there are a large number of services and facilities that have become essential to what is thought of as "normal life". Most of them are obvious, such as utilities, financial and emergency services and public transport. Some are less so, such as is the case of Internet Exchange Points – a hundred or so places around the world where Internet Service Providers interconnect.

Wherever society has a culture of openness and transparency, much information about these critical infrastructures is readily available often online. The exact physical location of many Internet Exchange Points is in the public domain and this makes the work of security personnel that much more difficult. Because of their important role in the functioning of an orderly society, security managers working in critical infrastructures have to accept many special responsibilities:

— Their computing, networking, systems and facilities must be highly secure

— They must continually monitor for vulnerabilities and attacks

— They must have in place an Emergency Response Team and well developed and tested procedures to deal with security incidents

— They must have proven and tested disaster recovery, business continuity and crisis management plans and processes

— They must have an adequate number of trusted, qualified and trained security personnel

— Their interfaces with the public Internet must be sufficiently secure

— They should seek, achieve and maintain security certification

— They must maintain effective co-ordination with other critical infrastructures and exchange information on a regular basis The work of providing information security for critical infrastructures requires an appropriate government framework.

Legislation

Regardless of the ownership of the critical infrastructures, governments should implement national information security programs and ensure that regular information security audits are conducted for critical infrastructures and key functions of government agencies. It is also important that national governments should promote and adopt international standards and promote best practices for information security. All of the responsibilities listed above for critical infrastructures should also apply, to the appropriate degree, to government agencies and these should also conduct information security awareness training for all personnel.

International Organisations

There is much to be done by International Organisations to strengthen information security worldwide. In particular:

— Encourage the development and adoption of international standards, regardless if these are de-jure or de-facto

— Develop appropriate mechanism for international cooperation including a framework that avoids the possibility of "islands" in cyberspace where organised crime and cyber-terrorists can legally exist

— Establish effective cyberspace governance mechanisms

— Create effective fora for the sharing of information on information security The value of such cooperation was already proven by the two meetings of National Y2K Coordinators that took place in New York in 1998 and 1999 under the auspices of the United Nations.

Vendors and service providers

In the perfect world, vendors and service providers would exercise a higher level of quality assurance and security validation than appears to be the case at present. Many vendors product release policies appear to be driven by an urgency to be first in the marketplace and/or to release "fatware" loaded with functionality, with new versions succeeding each other at frequent short intervals.

The commercial incentives for doing so are understandable, but this results in buggy software and endless stream of "patches", "service packs", vulnerability alerts and downloads which present a major challenge to network administrators and to individuals.

A detailed examination of the terms and conditions of many software licenses reveals that vendors do not accept liability for any defects that the software may have. Service providers, particularly ISPs, have a major role to play in tracking bad guys as their logs will enable the identification of sources and flows as well as access to copies of transactions. However, other service providers, such as the anonymous remailers, work against such practices and instead provide useful tools for organised crime and cyber-terrorists. The international community faces the challenge that one or more countries may choose to stay outside agreements on the types of services and facilities that should be available in cyberspace. This can provide a valuable hiding place for uncivil society.

Academic Institutions

Characterised by a tradition of academic freedom, many attacks and malicious software designs have been traced as having originated in academic institutions. Their governing bodies have a responsibility to ensure that the ethical aspects of cyberspace are understood and respected.

Businesses, organisations and individual users

Their responsibilities are essentially internal and require that information security be managed in a manner consistent with the value of their information assets.

Unaware insiders

These are the employees, temporary staff, contractors, consultants and others working in an organization and granted various levels of system and network access rights who are unaware of the organization's security policies and practices and possibly genuinely not knowledgeable about information security issues. Under these circumstances, they may leave their passwords prominently displayed on a computer screen, open attachments containing malicious software which managed to get through the organization's defences, download shareware and freeware from websites, bring infected floppy disks or CD-ROMs into the organization, etc.

Security managers and administrators

These are the individuals whose responsibility it is to define, maintain and monitor an organizations defences against malicious code and the misuse of computer systems and networks. By 2001, this has become a major job, with considerable responsibilities, requiring close contact with all parts of an organization.

Security Consultants

The growing complexity of this field has led to the development of a major new service: consultancy in information systems security. Such consultancy services can include the development of security policies, conducting security awareness seminars, highly detailed technical reviews of products and how these are configured and applied, the development of best practices in the monitoring and resolution of security incidents, etc.

Auditors

Two distinct types of security audits need to be considered: Compliance and Penetration audits. Compliance audits focus on the way in which security policies and practices are applied in an organization, how they are monitored, how incidents are dealt with and how effective they are. Penetration audits involve creating a controlled attack on the organization's security arrangements, with or without prior warning. The purpose of these tests is to identify weaknesses in the defences and the subsequent development of recommendations for corrective action. Whenever an external company is used for such security audits, reliable references are essential as you will be revealing to them all the details of your security arrangements, technologies, organization, etc.

Hiding in Cyberpsace

There are two complementary ways of hiding in cyberspace: hiding information and becoming anonymous. The discipline of Digital Forensics deals with finding information hidden in cyberspace and turning it into evidence acceptable to a court of law.

Hiding information

There are many ways to hide information in digital form. The five most common are:

- hidden files,
- file compression,
- steganography,
- password protection of files,
- directories and computers and
- encryption.

Hidden files can be easily placed in a personal computer in different ways. Windows has a category of files – "hidden files" which are not displayed when examining a directory. Other ways to hide files include renaming it as a "temporary file" and placing it in a temporary folder. The owner of the file can easily retrieve it but a forensic investigator would need to examine all temporary files, which could be in the hundreds.

Compression involves reducing the size file by using an algorithm that allows this function and its subsequent simple reversal (WinZip is a product that performs this function). Custom designed compression algorithms can be hard to break without knowing what approach the designer took. The file is visible in the directory but, having been compressed it may be impossible to determine what program was used to create it or how to decompress it.

Steganography is one of many techniques for embedding information into another file so that it is hidden. The Anna Kournikova virus consisted of code embedded in a .jpeg file with an image of the tennis player. Steganography software is easily obtained or written.

Passwords are one of the oldest methods for preventing third parties from opening a file, directory or computer. There are several password breaking tools available from the hacker community that will break even a well designed password that contains mixed capitals and lower case characters, as well as a mixture of alpha and numeric characters. Given enough effort and time no passwords are break-proof.

Encryption transforms intelligible information into a format that can only be recovered if the key to the code is available. This technique has been used since the invention of writing. While it is theoretically possible to break a code that is based on mathematical processes, this usually requires considerable computing power and time. Should the code be based on a different approach, such as a one time code based on a particular book, it cannot be easily broken without the full knowledge of the code.

Anonymity

Anonymous remailers are mechanisms that allow e-mail to be sent in a way that does not identify the sender who cannot then be traced or identified. Anonymous remailer services can be linked in a chain to make it even harder to trace a message. Messages are typically encrypted.

Type-II or Mixmaster remailers, now the most commonly used, fragments messages into fixed-size packets that makes traffic analysis hard. This type of remailer requires the user to have special client software (typically Mixmaster or JBN).

Anonymous browsing is a facility available for a small fee from several sources. It masks the user's IP address and provides additional facilities such as cookie management, which allows a person to surf the Internet without leaving a trace of physical location, identity or Internet Service Provider.

Computer penetration and looping are techniques used by hackers to penetrate a network and gain control of an end-user's computer. Sophisticated hackers have developed techniques such as "distributed metastasis" that use agents to increase the depth of network penetration.

Cell-phone cloning occurs when hackers have made a copy of a valid SIM card and create a clone of a legitimate account to intercept phone calls, to listen to conversations and acquire personal information such as credit card details. It can also be used to make calls anonymously as they are registered and charged to a proper account without the possibility of locating the cloned copy.

Cell-phone prepaid cards are the mobile equivalent of the coin operated public telephone. This allows an individual to make call totally anonymously from a rented cell-phone with minimal or zero possibility of tracking, tapping or subsequent tracing of the call.

Digital Forensics

Digital forensics is the extension of the techniques used in audit and police investigations to the world of bits. It will gain in importance as information security is recognised as a threat to commercial companies, government departments and individuals. The essence of digital forensics is the acquisition, safeguarding and analysis of computer data in such a way that the findings can be used in a court of law as evidence. "e-Evidence" presents three distinct headaches:

— It is difficult to acquire and preserve, particularly when the attack originated in another country.

— Losses are hard to quantify.

— It is unclear what may or may not be admissible in a court of law.

The nature of the offence will determine whether any prosecution will take place in a civil court or in a criminal court. It needs to be noted however, that many organizations will not publicise information security breaches as this may have a serious impact on their reputation and stock market valuation. Financial fraud offences are usually settled out of court. Another potential legal scenario is when the IT Manager or Chief Information Officer is taken to court to determine whether there was due diligence on her/his part, negligence, dereliction of duty, misconduct, sabotage or aiding and abetting organized crime or terrorism. In many of these cases, the minimum penalty is dismissal.

Digital Forensics deal with the preservation, identification, extraction and documentation of computer evidence. In practice anyone who needs to handle a case of fraud, sabotage, industrial espionage or other offences needs to use digital forensics.

Executives and managers, criminal and civil lawyers, insurance companies, law enforcement officials and individuals need evidence. Such evidence must be obtained and secured in such a way as to retain its legal value. Evidence can be visible – in the form of unencrypted stored data in a computer or data intercepted as it flows through a network and which is not hidden. There are other more complex forms of evidence:

Visible-Invisible evidence: information that is deliberately hidden through the use of passwords or encryption or information hidden in another file. Steganography is an example of the tools used to hide data. In an investigation, logs, also part of the Visible Invisible evidence, may additionally show activity at unusual times or missing sequential numbers.

Invisible-Invisible evidence falls in to two categories:

— That which has not been hidden by an individual but hidden by the system itself, as is the case with Windows temporary files, swap files, Internet temporary files, etc

— That which has been hidden deliberately, which includes files erased (as opposed to deleted) by a person as deleted files can usually be recovered.

Securing the evidence requires a good knowledge of all applicable legislation. Invariably, there are several common elements in such legislation including:

- The documentation of the time, date and circumstances of the seizure
- The collection of all physical evidence associated with the event
- Labeling all evidence in a clear manner
- Discovering all files
- Recording all serial numbers, documentation of system layout, etc
- Transferring all items under investigation to a secure location taking particular care not to expose them to electromagnetic interference, and restricting access to this location
- Creating a secure set of no less than two copies of everything using disk imaging techniques, keeping one copy in an evidence container and many more such activities. The key point is that unless evidence has been collected, kept, analyzed, disclosed, etc., in full compliance with the applicable legislation, it risks being dismissed by a court of law.

It is strongly recommended that both the internal auditors of the organization as well as legal counsel be closely involved with these processes.

The following observations are presented in an effort to help establish a partial checklist of essential actions in cases of security breaches.

Liability

The possibility of legal liability after a security breach should be a major concern for any person responsible for managing information security in an organisation.A review or post-mortem should always take place after a security incident. This could be carried out by the security team itself but, in serious cases, auditors and external investigators may need be involved. However, should the review find that the responsible manager failed to exercise due diligence, this opens the possibility of being sued in a court of law for damages. Worse still, should the review indicate that the manager acted negligently, or that there are grounds to suspect fraud, sabotage or aiding and abetting crime, and should the organisation decide to pursue this matter through the law, the case could be referred to a civil or a criminal court.

Monitoring and searches

The legal situation concerning the right of an employer to monitor the work of an employee through, for example, scanning e-mail for offensive language or inappropriate attachments, and tracking the employee's mailing routes through the World Wide Web, differs from country to country. This raises complex issues when there is no indication of malicious intent as the rights of the employer are counterbalanced by the right to privacy of an individual while working for an employer. When there is adequate reason to believe that the employee's behaviour may be detrimental to the interests of the employer, monitoring and searches may be conducted and it is recommended that the organisation's legal counsel be consulted first.

Theft or misuse of personal information

In most countries, an individual has little recourse, other than insurance, if someone in cyberspace steals and misuses personal information. Such an offence may range from a simple theft of credit card information to a full identity theft. Should somebody steal an e-mail account and use it inappropriately, the legitimate owner would have great difficulty proving that this was somebody else's initiative unless a detailed forensic examination is conducted which, in turn, would require the evidence to be available.

Trust vis-a-vis security auditors

Whenever security auditors are brought in from outside an organisation, there is a major issue of trust to consider as by the time the audit is completed, the auditors will have an in-depth knowledge of the security arrangements and practices of an organisation, its vulnerabilities and shortcomings and, in particular, detailed information about the technologies used, how these are configured and how their audit succeeded in penetrating these defences. However reputable a security audit company, or a security consultant, the issue remains that the best security auditors are in fact ethical hackers.

Social engineering as an aid to cyber-crime

Openness and assumed trust characterise many organisations. It is therefore not all that difficult for a person with malicious intent to acquire privileged information just by asking for it. Example: a visitor to an organisation may have unsupervised access to a telephone. Calling an employee, particularly a new recruit, from an internal extension number and pretending to be the Help Desk, the visitor may be able to acquire a valid user ID and password by saying that it is necessary to confirm the setup. Similarly, a person can impersonate a maintenance technician and plug in a notebook computer into the corporate network. This is easier to do than it seems, due to the fact that, in large organisations the supposed practice that all visitors should be escorted at all times is often relaxed. At this point, all firewalls and security arrangements have become worthless.

National and international legislation

Effective legislation to cover cyber-crime in its many forms is considered to cover three main areas:

— The protection of intellectual property, including software

— The protection of individual privacy in cyberspace

— The definition of deterrents and the possibility of prosecution for cyber-crime offences.

Types of Cyber Offences

This section merely describes the nature of the most common form of attacks on information systems grouped in four categories of offences:

— Network-related

— Data-related

— Access-related

— Computer-related

All four forms impact deeply on the objectives of the organisation owning the information system.

Network related offences

These can be subdivided into three categories: interference, sabotage and anonymity.

Interference

The most common techniques for interfering with a network are Denial of Service Attacks, using a trusted network to gain access to another computer or network, "sniffing" traffic and hoaxes and brute force entry into a network.

Denial of Service and Distributed Denial of Service: The techniques used to overwhelm the corporate systems – until now websites and e-mail servers – by arranging to deliver massive pings, requests for web pages or thousands of e-mail messages in a very short period of time. These can be driven by a group of people acting in concert, as was the case when in 1999 cyber-hippies who organised a Distributed Denial of Service attack on the website of the World Trade Organization relied on cooperation amongst like-minded individuals to share software that could launch such an attack. More recently, these attacks have been automated by using someone else's computer without their knowledge.

Hijacking of an end-user's personal computer: Recent developments have automated the process of infiltrating an end-user's computer, to turn it on demand into a Zombie or a slave computer that will then perform whatever tasks the worm is designed to make it perform. Such a Zombie could also be programmed to provide a back door into a corporate network thus bypassing all security measures designed to keep outsiders out. Recent

Internet worms such as Code Red and Nimda could be used for this purpose and/or carry a destructive payload that could affect data and programs.

Spoofing and redirection of traffic: This is done either to impersonate a legitimate user or to redirect traffic to another location that contains content that has been modified without the knowledge of the original owner of the site. This modified content may be used to steal credit card details, to discredit the original owner or to provide disinformation or propaganda. Current legislation does not usually allow for the prosecution of a person impersonating someone else onlineHoaxes A fake attack that causes network and systems administrators considerable waste of time and can, when done properly, demand an in-depth investigation of a network and all the devices connected to it. It is the equivalent of a false alarm that then creates the need for a voluntary stoppage of the system.

Computer network break-in (brute force access): Hackers can break into computer systems using tools they have developed, procured or downloaded free from the Internet. Once inside someone else's computer or network, hackers can steal data, including legitimate passwords, plant malicious code or simply cause chaos by modifying corporate data, website pages, etc. Network intrusions of this kind are, when carried out by a serious hacker, difficult to detect. Even when detected, the identification of the culprit, who is often in another location, and possibly in another country, is very hard. If a successful identification is achieved, the current legal framework for seeking damages and other penalties is not particularly effective.

Sabotage

Sabotage involves the disconnection, unauthorised modification or damage to equipment, facilities or data. A certain degree of sabotage can be done without a physical presence. A hacker with malicious intent can disrupt the operation of critical items by, for example, corrupting password files, modifying parameters or injecting malicious code.

The most serious sabotage occurs when an individual obtains access to a computer room by, for example, pretending to be a maintenance engineer. If security is lax and the person is not accompanied and monitored, massive damage can be carried out in a very short time in such a way that it will not be discovered for several hours. Any attack on a critical infrastructure should, by its very nature, be considered as an act of sabotage.

Anonymity

Anonymous remailers are mechanisms that allow e-mail to be sent in a way that does not identify the sender who cannot then be traced or identified. Other methods to ensure anonymity include the theft and/or cloning of cell-phones and the hijacking of a legitimate user's identity and password.

Data related offences

These can be divided in three main groups: interception and monitoring of data traffic, modification of data and data theft.

Interception of data

These offences involve the interception (tapping) of voice and fax messages, e-mail and data transfers.Similarly, password sniffers are programs that monitor and record the names and passwords of network users as they log on. The security of the site is thus weakened as the recipient of this information can then impersonate the legitimate user and access restricted documents and perform transactions.

Monitoring of data traffic

There are many techniques that can be used to intercept data travelling between authorised origin and destination sources. These include:

— *The theft of a physical medium in transit* (for example backup tapes being taken to the off-site location where they are stored)

— *Wiretapping* – where an unauthorised entity monitors and records the data flowing between two points

— *Intrusion* – when access to the system or data flow circumvents a system's security features There are many other forms of monitoring of data traffic that can include:

  — Keystroke logging

  — The scanning and filtering of e-mail traffic by organizations other than those of the sender and recipient (such as Internet Service Providers, governments and/or their intelligence services) The tracking of the websites visited by an individual, including pages consulted, how much time is spent on them, etc. This can be done by an employer as well as by the owner of a website interested in learning about the usage patterns of individuals.

Modification of data

The most common situation arises when a computer system is used to commit fraud by creating false transactions or modifying data to benefit one or more individuals.

Industrial espionage

It would seem that many people just love to spy... The emergence of a global network of networks, like the Internet, has created a totally new environment where professional hackers-for-money can search for, find and remove information about, product development, commercial strategies, staff salaries, and other confidential matters. Professional hackers can do this leaving little or no evidence of theft and, as above, in the unlikely event of identifying the guilty party, legislation has not yet been written to cope with issues of electronic theft.

Software piracy and other copyright infringement : It is remarkably easy to make a copy of software and distribute it to others. This has been common since the early 1980s and the introduction of the personal computer, and continues to be practiced in many countries. The pirating of high value software represents a substantial loss to the companies developing and marketing such applications. Copied software works as well as the original and can be purchased for a fraction of the price. The chances of being found and prosecuted are relatively small. Pirated software is sold in many countries and while the authorities have taken action against this, the business continues to flourish.

Tracking code: The World Wide Web Consortium has defined a standard for "cookies", a mechanism that allows the server to store information about a user on the user's own computer. Cookies are simple text files stored on the end user's hard disk and they have many legitimate and beneficial uses, such as customising the content of a web page for an individual. A cookie tells the website that it's you who is looking at it. Undeleted cookies build a complete history of where you have been on the web – and many of these cookies are placed by companies who advertise on the web, and keep enormous databases of who looks at what.

Browsers can also be exploited as a surveillance tool: your browser can tell others how you access the web, what software and hardware you are using, details of the link you have clicked on and possibly even your e-mail address. In addition to browsers and cookies, there is extensive use of software such as "Web Bugs" (a one pixel by one pixel transparent graphic in GIF format) placed on a website or an e-mail. This is invisible to the user because it is transparent and very small.

Web-Bugs can be used to gather the following information:

— The IP address of the computer that "caught" the bug

— The URL of the page that the Web Bug is located on

— The time the Web Bug was viewed

— The type of browser that fetched the Web Bug image

— A previously set cookie value was caught Proponents of privacy on the Internet object to the use of Web Bugs. On the other hand, these bugs can also be used to track copyright violations on the Web.

E-mail related offences

Mail Spamming

It is relatively easy to write software that automates the process of repeatedly sending e-mail to a large number of recipients, usually unsolicited commercial e-mail. It is also possible to use, without permission, other peoples' computers to send large amounts of mail to an individual.

Snooping of e-mail messages

An ordinary e-mail message is today's equivalent to a machinereadable postcard. The machines that read them are either known to exist (Carnivore) or suspected (Echelon and similar in other parts of the world). At this time, the dividing line between the legality of a government owned machine and a privately owned one is unclear. It does not require much knowledge to identify from the e-mail header the IP address from which it originated, and the route it took to reach the recipient.

Faked e-mail

The 'From" line in an e-mail message can be faked in several ways:

— Spoofing

— Remailing

— Relaying

— Stealing accounts

— Bogus accounts

Spoofing of e-mail messages consists of making a message appear to have come from somewhere or someone else. Spoofing is easy. The sender uses a software tool that is readily available on the Web to cut out the original IP address and replace it with someone else's address. The good news is that spoofing is also relatively easy to deal with: the first server to receive the spoofed message records the real IP address of the sender, and this can be used to trace the original sender.

A remailer is a computer that strips the sender's IP address and then remails the message with the IP address of the remailer. The only way to find out who sent the message is to get access to the logs of the remailer – except that, designed to be anonymous, they don't log e-mail that has passed through that source. Anonymous remailers are used extensively by organised crime and terrorists as a means to hide in cyberspace.

Relaying consists of misusing someone else's e-mail server, something often done by spammers. A correctly configured e-mail server will not accept e-mail from IP addresses originating from outside its network. Unfortunately, not all e-mail servers are correctly configured to do so.

Stealing accounts requires the offender to gain access to someone else's e-mail account and password details, either by looking over someone's shoulder, or more technically, by sniffing a network to intercept such details. Once someone has a legitimate user ID and password, the whole e-mail system is compromised and all tracking will lead to the more than likely innocent victim whose account has been hijacked.

Bogus e-mail accounts are opened from, for example, free e-mail services such as Hotmail by giving a false identity and address. As these accounts can be accessed from any computer with access to the World Wide Web, it is difficult to catch someone who has done this since the e-mail provider never knows who opened the false account.

Other activities of doubtful legality

There are numerous other activities that take place on the World Wide Web which do not appear to fall under the above categories and about which1 the law is not always clear. Concerning what constitutes an offence or a crime and under what jurisdiction.

The debate continues on the following activities:

— Distasteful and/or controversial content (hate, pornography, etc)

— Arms and drugs trading

— Trading in antiquities and stolen goods

— Money laundering

— Political propaganda

— Disinformation.

Undeterred by the prospect of arrest or prosecution, cyber criminals around the world lurk on the Net as an omnipresent menace to the financial health of businesses, to the trust of their customers, and as an emerging threat to nations' security. According to the Computer Emergency Response Team Coordination Center the number of reported incidences of security breaches in the first three quarters of 2000 rose by 54 percent over the total number of reported incidences in 1999. Moreover, countless instances of illegal access and damage around the world remain unreported, as victims fear the exposure of vulnerabilities, the potential for copycat crimes, and the loss of public confidence.

There are, unfortunately, no surveys documenting the incidence of cybercrime at the global level. The results of national surveys, however, bear out the picture given in the quotation above: cybercrime is consistently and dramatically increasing. The most-often cited national survey for the United States is the "Computer Crime and Security Survey," which was conducted by the Computer Security Institute with participation by the FBI's Computer Intrusion Squad, San Francisco branch. The CSI/FBI survey, conducted annually since 1996, reports results of data obtained from several thousand information security professionals employed by corporations, financial institutions, government agencies and universities.

One area the survey explores is security breaches: whether respondents have experienced breaches of information security in the last year. The number responding in the affirmative has grown over the years: in the 2001 survey, 85% of respondents said they had detected breaches over the last year; only 42% of 1996 survey respondents reported detection of such breaches.Among other things, the survey shows (a) that the Internet continues to become an increased point of attack, (b) that denial of service attacks are increasing and (c) hat viruses are becoming increasingly common.

Those responding to the CSI/FBI survey are also asked to quantify the losses they attribute to cybercrime. The figure reported rose from $100,119,555 in the 1997 survey to $377,828,700 in the 2001 survey. Data from other countries reveal similar trends. "Cybercrime accounted for half of all fraud committed in the UK in the first six months" of 2000, and there was "a 56 per cent increase in hacking in the UK over the past 12 months, with most hackers seeking financial gain, for example by using their hack to demand money, or for political reasons such as posting messages for a certain cause on a company's website."

Statistics from China and Japan also showed dramatic increases in cybercrime, and the Australian version of the CSI/FBI survey found that "one third . . . of the companies surveyed reported an attack in the last 12 months." When those responding to this survey were asked about the future, the number "who indicated that increased virtual crime is a concern almost doubled," and those reporting "concern about the shift from conventional crimes against property to computer related crimes more than doubled."

As almost everyone concedes, it is difficult to gather accurate cybercrime statistics. One problem in gathering data about the commission of cybercrimes is that: an unknown number of crimes of all kinds are undetected. For example, even outside the computer crime field, we don't know how many financial frauds are being perpetrated. We don't know because some of them are not detected. How do we know they're not detected? Because some frauds are discovered long after they have occurred. Similarly, computer crimes may not be detected by their victims.

A commonly-held view within the information security community is that only one-tenth or so of all the crimes committed against and using computer systems are detected. Even if attacks are detected, it seems that few are reported in a way that allows systematic data collection. This belief is based in part on the unquantified experience of information security professionals who have conducted interviews of their clients; it turns out that only about ten percent of the attacks against computer systems revealed in such interviews were ever reported to any kind of authority.

Some of the reasons for the under-reporting of cybercrime are that victims may not realize that the conduct involved is a crime, or may decide not to complain for reasons of embarrassment or corporate credibility. Further problems arise with the mass victimization caused by offences such as virus propagation, because the numbers of victims are simply too large to identify and count, and because such programs can continue creating new victims long after the offenders have been caught and punished. A further factor complicating the gathering and comparison of national crime statistics will be the fact that transnational computer-related crimes are, by definition, committed in or have effects in at least two States, and, in some cases, in many States, risking multiple reporting or no reporting at all.

Methodological problems with the compilation of cybercrime statistics lie in certain of the techniques used to gather information, but do not cut clearly in favor of either under- or overestimating the incidence of cybercrime. So far, much of the information we have on cybercrime is the product of surveys directed toward individuals working in the field of information security.

Actual losses of cybercrime are difficult to quantify, but include direct costs of repairing systems and software, the loss of access or services to users and consequent damage, the loss of valuable data and the loss of revenue from site operations. Such crimes also necessitate the development and maintenance of security and other preventive measures, an added cost factor. The overall increases in such crime and the spectacular nature of some of the offences involved also generate substantial but unpredictable political pressures for the enhancement of criminal law controls, more severe punishments and technical precautions on the part of the producers of software and hardware and of companies that provide network access to customers. A further hidden cost of such incidents is the fear of cybercrime, which may erode usage of the technologies or deter Governments and populations in developing countries from making the most effective use of them.

3

Chronology of Cyber Crimes

The desire to make computer systems do things other than those for which they were designed has been around as long as computers. This chapter presents a short summary of this history in a chronological order.

1960s

The first computer hackers emerge at MIT. They borrow their name from a term to describe members of a model train group at the school who "hack" the electric trains, tracks, and switches to make them perform faster and differently. A few of the members transfer their curiosity and rigging skills to the new mainframe computing systems being studied and developed on campus.

The malicious code of this time fell into two distinct categories: that designed to defraud the employer (back door, trap door, Trojan Horse) and that designed to blackmail or damage (Logic bomb).

1970s

Phone hackers (phreaks or phreakers) break into regional and international phone networks to make free calls. One phreak, John Draper (aka Cap'n Crunch), learns that a toy whistle given away inside Cap'n Crunch cereal generates a 2600-hertz signal, the same high-pitched tone that accesses AT&T's long-distance switching system.

Draper builds a "blue box" that, when used in conjunction with the whistle and sounded into a phone receiver, allows phreaks to make free calls. Shortly thereafter, Esquire magazine publishes "Secrets of the Little Blue Box" with instructions for making a blue box, and wire fraud in the United States escalates. Among the perpetrators are two college kids (Steve Wozniak and Steve Jobs) later founders of Apple Computer, who launch a home industry making and selling blue boxes. Malicious code in computing remained generally the same as in the 1960s.

1980s

Phone phreaks begin to move into the realm of computer hacking, and the first electronic bulletin board systems (BBSs) spring up. The 8 bit personal computers had been around since the late 1970s and were popular with young technically minded people. electronic mail had also been around for some time and, in 1981, IBM introduced the 16 bit Personal Computer (PC) and allowed it to become an "open system," i.e. one that could be produced by other companies.

The precursor to Usenet newsgroups and e-mail, the boards—with names such as Sherwood Forest and Catch-

22--become the venue of choice for phreaks and hackers to gossip, trade tips, and share stolen computer passwords and credit card numbers. Hacking groups begin to form. Among the first are the "Legion of Doom" in the United States, and the "Chaos Computer Club" in Germany.

Worms are first used as a legitimate mechanism for performing tasks in a distributed environment. Network worms are considered promising for the performance of network management tasks in a series of experiments at the Xerox Palo Alto Research Center in 1982. The key problem is that of "worm management," controlling the number of copies executing at a single time. This would be taken advantage of later by authors of malicious worms.

1983

The movie War Games introduces the public to hacking, and the legend of hackers as cyber-heroes (and anti-heroes) is born. The film's main character, played by Matthew Broderick, attempts to crack into a video game manufacturer's computer to play a game, but instead breaks into the military's nuclear combat simulator computer.

The computer (codenamed WOPR, a pun on the military's real system called BURGR) misinterprets the hacker's request to play Global Thermonuclear War as an actual enemy missile launch. The break-in throws the military into high alert, or Def Con 1 Defense Condition 1.

The same year, authorities arrest six teenagers known as the 414 gang (after the area code to which they are traced). During a nineday spree, the gang breaks into some

60 computers, among them computers at the Los Alamos National Laboratory, which helps develop nuclear weapons. This was a very interesting time. The term "computer virus" is formally defined by Fred Cohen in 1983, while performing academic experiments on a Digital Equipment Corporation VAX system.

Viruses are classified as being one of two types: research or "in the wild. " A research virus is one that has been written for research or study purposes and has received almost no distribution to the public. On the other hand, viruses which have been seen with any regularity are termed "in the wild." The first computer viruses were developed in the early 1980s. The first viruses found in the wild were Apple II viruses, such as Elk Cloner, which was reported in 1981. Viruses have now been found on the following platforms: the Apple II, the Apple Mackintosh, the Atari, the Amiga and the IBM (and compatible) PCs.

1984

The hacker magazine 2600 begins regular publication, followed a year later by the online 'zine Phrack. The editor of 2600, "Emmanuel Goldstein" (whose real name is Eric Corley), takes his handle from the main character in George Orwell's 1984. Both publications provide tips for would-be hackers and phone phreaks, as well as commentary on the hacker issues of the day. Today, copies of 2600 are sold at most large retail bookstores.

1986

In the wake of an increasing number of break-ins to government and corporate computers, Congress passes the

Computer Fraud and Abuse Act, which makes it a crime to break into computer systems. The law, however, does not cover juveniles. The first IBM-PC virus – the Brain virus - appeared in 1986. Brain was a boot sector virus and remained resident. In 1987, Brain was followed by Alameda (Yale), Cascade, Jerusalem, Lehigh, and Miami (South African Friday the 13th). These viruses expanded the target executables to include .COM and .EXE files. Cascade was encrypted to deter disassembly and detection.

1987

Worms were first noticed as a potential computer security threat when the Christmas Tree Exec attacked IBM mainframes in December 1987. It brought down both the world-wide IBM network and BITNET. The Christmas Tree Exec wasn't a true worm. It was a trojan horse with a replicating mechanism. A user would receive an e-mail Christmas card that included executable (REXX) code. If executed the program claimed to draw a Xmas tree on the display. That much was true, but it also sent a copy to everyone on the user's address lists.

1988

Robert T. Morris, Jr., a graduate student at Cornell University and son of a chief scientist at a division of the National Security Agency, launches a self-replicating worm on the government's DARPAnet (the Defense Advanced Research Projects Agency network, the precursor to the Internet) to test its effect on UNIX systems.

The worm got out of hand and spread to some 6000 networked computers, clogging government and university systems. Morris was dismissed from Cornell, sentenced to three years' probation and fined $10,000.

The Father Christmas worm of December of 1988 was also a true worm. It was first released onto the worldwide DECnet Internet. This worm attacked VAX/VMS systems on SPAN and HEPNET. It utilized the DECnet protocols and a variety of system administration flaws to propagate. The worm exploited TASK0, which allows outsiders to perform tasks on the system. This worm added an additional feature: it reported successful system penetration to a specific site.

This worm made no attempt at secrecy; it was not encrypted and sent mail to every user on the system. About a month later another worm, apparently a variant of Father Christmas, was released on a private network. This variant searched for accounts with "industry standard" or easily guessed passwords.

1989

In the first cyber-espionage case to make international headlines, hackers in West Germany (loosely affiliated with the Chaos Computer Club) are arrested for breaking into U.S. government and corporate computers and selling operating-system source code to the Soviet KGB. Three of them are turned in by two fellow hacker spies, and a fourth suspected hacker commits suicide when his possible role in the plan is publicized. Because the information stolen is not classified, the hackers are fined and sentenced to probation. In a separate incident, a hacker is arrested who calls himself The Mentor. He publishes a now-famous treatise that comes to be known as the Hacker's Manifesto. The piece, a defense of hacker antics, begins, "My crime is that of curiosity ... I am a hacker, and this is my manifesto. You may stop this individual, but you can't stop us all."

With regard to malicious code, variable encryption also first appears in 1989 with the 1260 virus. Stealth viruses, which employ various techniques to avoid detection, also first appears in 1989, such as Zero Bug, Dark Avenger and Frodo.

1990

After a prolonged sting investigation, Secret Service agents swoop down on hackers in 14 U.S. cities, conducting early-morning raids and arrests. The arrests involve organizers and prominent members of BBSs and are aimed at cracking down on credit-card theft and telephone and wire fraud. The result is a breakdown in the hacking community, with members informing on each other in exchange for immunity. In 1990, self-modifying viruses such as Whale are introduced. The year 1991 brought the GP1 virus, which is "networksensitive" and attempts to steal Novell NetWare passwords. Since their inception, viruses have become increasingly complex.

1993

During radio station call-in contests, hacker-fugitive Kevin Poulsen and two friends rig the stations' phone systems to let only their calls through, and "win" two Porsches, vacation trips, and $20,000. Poulsen, already wanted for breaking into phone- company systems, serves five years in prison for computer and wire fraud. (Since his release in 1996 he has worked as a freelance journalist covering computer crime.) The first Def Con hacking conference takes place in Las Vegas. The conference is meant to be a one-time party to say good-bye to BBSs (now replaced by the Web), but the gathering is so popular it becomes an annual event.

1994

The Internet begins to take off as a new browser, Netscape Navigator, makes information on the Web more accessible. Hackers take to the new venue quickly, moving all their how-to information and hacking programs from the old BBSs to new hacker Web sites. As information and easy-to-use tools become available to anyone with Net access, the face of hacking begins to change.

1995

Serial cyber-trespasser Kevin Mitnick is captured by federal agents and charged with stealing 20,000 credit card numbers. He's kept in prison for four years without a trial and becomes a cause célèbre in the hacking underground. After pleading guilty to seven charges at his trial in March 1999, he's eventually sentenced to little more than the time he has already served while awaiting trial and fined just over 4,000 dollars. Not everyone is in agreement with his imprisonment. Russian crackers siphon $10 million from Citibank and transfer the money to bank accounts around the world. Vladimir Levin, the 30-year-old ringleader, uses his work laptop after hours to transfer the funds to accounts in Finland and Israel. Levin stands trial in the United States and is sentenced to three years in prison. Authorities recover all but $400,000 of the stolen money.

1997

AOHell is released, a freeware application that allows a burgeoning community of unskilled hackers—or script kiddies—to wreak havoc on America Online. For days, hundreds of thousands of AOL users find their mailboxes flooded with multimegabyte mail bombs and their chat rooms disrupted with spam messages.

1998

The hacking group Cult of the Dead Cow releases its Trojan Horse program, Back Orifice - a powerful hacking tool - at Def Con. Once a hacker installs the Trojan horse on a machine running Windows 95 or Windows 98, the program allows unauthorized remote access of the machine. During heightened tensions in the Persian Gulf, hackers touch off a string of break-ins to unclassified Pentagon computers and steal software programs. Then-U.S. Deputy Defense Secretary John Hamre calls it "the most organized and systematic attack" on U.S. military systems to date. An investigation points to two American teens. A 19-year-old Israeli hacker who calls himself The Analyzer (aka Ehud Tenebaum) is eventually identified as their ringleader and arrested. Today Tenebaum is chief technology officer of a computer consulting firm.

1999

In the wake of Microsoft's Windows 98 release, 1999 becomes a banner year for security (and hacking). Hundreds of advisories and patches are released in response to newfound (and widely publicized) bugs in

Windows and other commercial software products. A host of security software vendors release anti-hacking products for use on home computers. At the same time, computer systems are increasingly becoming homogeneous, and the exchange of executable programs through floppy disks is much less dominant than hitherto, with users being connected through networks and tighter control of software licensing and central software distribution. Viruses continue to appear.

Examples from the IBM-PC family of viruses indicate that the most commonly detected viruses vary according to continent. Stoned, Brain, Cascade, and members of the Jerusalem family, have spread widely and continue to appear. These are reasonably well dealt with by Anti-Virus software.

On March 26, 1999, a new type of infection emerged: An e-mail containing as an attachment an "infected" Microsoft Word document. This infection took advantage of a known design flaw in Microsoft Word and it required human action, i.e. the opening of the infected document for the virus to propagate. This became known as the Melissa (macro) Virus, and it spread itself to the first 50 addresses in the recipients' Microsoft Outlook directory. Melissa takes four days to become prevalent and causes an estimated US $385 million worth of damage. David L. Smith, arrested after an investigation into the release of this virus, confessed to being its author and was released on bail of US $ 100,000 in December 1999.

By August 2001, he was still free on bail and the date for sentencing remains undefined. In early December 2001, the World Trade Organization's Seattle Conference is subject to disruptions, involving demonstrations, violent at times in an attempt to disrupt the conference. In addition to these physical interventions, one website urged WTO protesters to help tie up the WTO's Web servers. The site, set up by a group calling themselves the Electrohippies, called it a virtual sit-in. By clicking on the sit-in link, a user's computer would be used to request information continually from WTO servers, tying up the user's Internet connection. This was essentially the use of hacker's denial-of-service techniques to perform an act of (in their words) civil disobedience in the shape of an electronic sit-in.

2000

In February 2000 hackers launch one of the biggest distributed denial-of-service attacks to date against eBay, Yahoo, Amazon, and others causing major business disruption to the owners of these websites. Whilst this was seen by most as an act of vandalism, there were a number of different views as to why these specific companies were targetted. One anarchist point of view is that they were attacked because the Internet has become the new tool for exploiting mankind and that the emergence of e-commerce is killing the hopes that others had for the Internet.

In May 2000 a new virus, called "I Love You", also affects thousands of corporate websites, and many companies have to shut down their e-mail systems in an effort to stop its spread. A leading vendor of Anti-Virus software, Symantec, states that in terms of spreadability, the "I Love You" virus outranked anything seen so far. Unlike Melissa, this virus has the ability to destroy data, in particular pictures and music files. Onel de Guzman, a computer programming student in the Philippines was identified as the author of the virus and later arrested.

Because of the lack of computer crime legislation in the Philippines, he was released shortly afterwards without charges. Although there is speculation that authorities in other countries would raise charges against de Guzman, this is not the case. In the year 2000, Activists in Pakistan and the Middle East deface Web sites belonging to the Indian and Israeli governments to protest oppression in Kashmir and Palestine. In October 2000, hackers break into Microsoft's corporate network and access source code for the latest versions of Windows and Office. This attack goes unnoticed for several weeks before Microsoft discovers it.

2001

In February 2001, a virus, encrypted and embedded in a photograph of Russian tennis player Anna Kournikova, spreads aggressively through e-mail – twice as fast as the "I Love You" virus. This virus uses a Visual Basic script to infect Windows based systems, and whenever the Microsoft Outlook e-mail program is used, it remails itself to the entire address book. This virus did not damage the systems it infected. At the time, it was believed that the Kournikova virus had been manufactured using a "Virus creation kit" – a set of programs that let any on-line vandal with rudimentary computer skills to create malicious code. It was in fact produced by the 20-year-old Jan de Wit in the Netherlands who was sentenced to 150 hours of community service. He is appealing against this sentence. In July 19, 2001, the Code Red self-replicating worm is released. This exploits a known vulnerability in Microsoft IIS servers, a product commonly used for websites. Code Red infiltrates 300,000 servers in only 14 hours, an unprecedented speed and slows the whole Internet.

The company Information Extraction and Transport, which conducts Internet epidemiology research for the Defense Advanced Research Projects Agency (DARPA), said about Code Red:

> "Imagine a cold that kills. It spreads rapidly and indiscriminately through droplets in the air and you think you're absolutely healthy until you start to sneeze. Your only protection is complete, impossible, isolation."

Although the effects of Code Red did not last, some 6 million IIS servers worldwide had to be checked and upgraded to plug the security hole exploited by Code Red at an estimated cost of some 10 billion US dollars.

On 18 September 2001, a new infection emerges: the NIMDA worm. What was new about NIMDA was that

— It can spread through multiple mechanisms: via e-mail, by being connected through a common network, such as a Local Area Network and by browsing a compromised website.

— It is fully automated and does not require human intervention (such as opening an attachment) to spread itself.

NIMDA contains a sophisticated mechanism for collecting e-mail addresses from the infected computer but does not destroy data in the infected computer. It spreads more quickly than Code Red as it generates an avalanche of Internet traffic affecting both servers and clients. The sources of Code Red and NIMDA are still unknown.

There are serious concerns being expressed that Code Red and NIMDA were no more than test runs for new concepts in worm design. In such a scenario, we need to consider the possible (expected?) arrival of professionally designed, automatic attack worms that could not only paralyse the Internet but also carry a destructive payload that could affect a substantial part of the data accessible through the Internet.

Today Hacktivism represents a whole new level of activity on the World Wide Web. It is motivated by a political cause. This is electronic civil disobedience. If we had widespread use of computers and the Internet in the 60's, the anti war movement would have been carried out in cyberspace, not on America's college campuses. There are many topics today – globalisation, human rights, the environment, and for each one of them there have been acts of electronic disobedience against it.

Hacktivism is more oriented towards political causes throughout the world rather than protesting the alleged injustice of individuals and is truly global in character with examples such as The Anonymous Digital Coalition, consisting of The Hong Kong Blondes, X-ploit, The Cult of the Dead Cow, The Electric Disturbance Theatre, and many others. It is likely that the medium of the Internet will continue to be exploited for the purposes of civil disobedience and propaganda.

4

Cyber Security: Principles and Practises

Despite the understandable current emphasis on cyber-terrorism, the impact of these cyber-threats and cyber-attacks goes far deeper into the economic and social fabric of life around the world, and can affect not just peace and security, but also the success of failure of all our developmental efforts. Enormous damage can be caused not just by an act, but also by the panic, the loss of confidence, the injection of doubts and hesitations, and the destruction of trust, all of which are the primary factors on which modern society is constructed.

A major aspect of this new threat arises from the nature and pervasive spread of criminal motivation. As we know all too well, it is virtually impossible to monitor motivations. The latter are universal and invisible, and largely undetectable. A problem lies of course in the fact that motivated individuals are highly creative. That creativity remains visible even in their warped motivations. That is why the motivation of the thief is always greater than the motivation of the detective. The criminal is always a couple of jumps ahead of the policeman. As and when the law plugs any of its numerous loopholes, the motivated criminal will always discover new cracks in the armor. The most important defense in cyber-space is thus twofold. First, to begin with a correct analysis of one's own vulnerabilities. Second, to try to determine the opponent's motivations. Vulnerability and motivation are then the two keys to a correct understanding of and reaction to the dangers of cyber-threats and cyber-attack.

The wide and pervasive integration of computers and embedded chips into modern society is what makes it vulnerable to cyberattacks. Computers are now integrated into the management and processing of our daily actions, and embedded chips are so omnipresent today that it is virtually impossible to determine even their actual numbers and locations. This profound integration of computers and information technology is obviously the strength of modern life, but it is also its vulnerability.

The motivation to commit cyber-crime is also increasing exponentially. The number of malicious code attacks reported by the CERT has gone up from just 8 in 1988 to almost 53,000 in 2001, and the graph shows a constantly steepening increase. The first half of the year 2002 shows a 26 percent increase over the same period of the previous year. Add to that the simple fact of its tempting results. Where the average bank hold-up brings in no more than $ 14,000, the average computer technology theft is of the order of magnitude of no less than $ 2 million. The temptation is just too great. The status of how much is lost annually as the result of cybercrime is unclear. Only a minute portion of computer crime gets reported. Most corporations have a well-defined tendency to conceal the manner and depth of the attacks on their facilities, for fear of the panic effect that this information would create on their stock prices. In short, reported incidents are just the tip of the iceberg. On the one hand, the true cyber-criminal has no interest in advertising his successes, while on the other hand, the victims are afraid of reporting them also. So the environment is entirely propitious for further damage.

A distinguishing feature of cyber-crime lies in the fact that the single unattached criminal – the hacker, or the virus spreader – is really not the main danger. That is of course what hits the tabloids, partly because of the Robin Hood syndrome, and partly because it is considered "fun" among the software-literate youth. The actual minefield lies, however, in "organized" cyber-crime and cyber-terrorism, where the technical competence of youth is exploited and channeled by organised elements towards criminal and politically motivated ends. Whereas the single hacker can work alone, organised crime requires proper networking through lines of communication between component elements. The need for those lines of communication is its vulnerability, so that is where the counterterrorism efforts will have to concentrate.

The cyber world is ethereal in its nature, and largely uncontrollable in its anarchy. The Internet was after all designed initially as a nonlinear means of communication that would survive any nuclear attack. That is what makes it indestructible. By the same token, it also becomes uncontrollable, a characteristic which makes it an asset for criminal behavior. Although many nations have written legislation against crimes committed over the Internet, such as hacking, illegal transfers of funds, identity theft, etc., the laws just cannot keep up with the technological advancements. The lure of the criminal mind and the opportunities are just too great. Add the fact that in many recent cases, the sentences have been minimal. This is virgin territory for the individual criminal, and even more attractive territory for the organized criminal.

Cyber-crime and cyber-terrorism, and possibly cyberwar, will be an inevitable part of our future landscape. We will of course continue to enjoy the benefits of the Information Age, but we must also remain constantly aware of the dangers and pervasive pitfalls of cyber-theft, cyber-threats, cyber-crime, and of course of cyber-terrorism and cyber-war. Any or all of these can hit each one of us at any time. So, read and be warned, and prepare for the inevitable negotiations that must soon start on developing, drafting, and adopting, a comprehensive Law of Cyber-Space.

History of Cyber Security

Humanity has defined itself as different from the rest of the animal kingdom. Scientists state that human DNA differs by less than 2 percent from that of the chimpanzee, the primate whose DNA resembles most closely that of a human. This small percentage accounts for some very important differences:

— Complex speech, language

— The ability to create tools

— Music, poetry, graphical arts and writing

Another difference, perhaps the most important from the perspective of security is in the use of tools: they can also be used as weapons.

Even before the invention of writing, the oral tradition passed stories from one generation to the next. Some became part of literature, such as the Iliad, describing the

Trojan War; some became part of religious texts, such as the Book of Genesis, which includes the killing of Abel by his brother Cain.

Reading the history of humanity reveals that the "ascent of man" through the exploration of the world and the skies through science and technology has many believe that this knowledge and tools are for the benefit of mankind as a whole. Many others see science and technology as the source of improved weapons. Sometimes, the use of tools and weapons was officially sanctioned as a "good thing" and led to many military campaigns, the birth and collapse of empires and many successive civilizations. Societies also adopted civil and religious practices to enable reasonably stable coexistence. These laws became the norm and breaking them became a crime. If found, criminals were judged by their peers and punished.

In the mid 1600s, Francis Bacon stated that "Information itself, is power" something which holds true today. The Information Age started – perhaps with the invention of the electric telegraph in 1840. Global networks, such as the telephone and the fax now connect well over one billion people, and the Internet some 400 million.

The insecurity of computer systems and networks goes much further than the well-known computer viruses, and has now become a priority.

Research from the firm Computer Economics estimates that the cost of computer viruses to the U.S. economy in the period January – August 2001 amounts to 10.7 billion dollars, of which 2.6 billion alone can be attributed to the Code Red worm. In this scenario, what would be the impact on the world economy and stability if banks, utilities and air traffic control were to be specifically targeted? Do we need a full-scale cyber security disaster for this subject to be given the attention it requires?

The need to protect information from being seen by people for whom it was not intended, is as old as the history of writing, going back five thousand years or more. Codes and cyphers have been developed over the centuries as a way to protect information from those not authorised to see it. However ingenious and sophisticated as these methods were, history has shown that sooner or later, all such protection methods were infiltrated and overcome. In addition, since the beginning of history, crime has been deterred by the prospect of punishment. In the "good old days", such punishment could be dramatic.

Often delegated to the IT department, the protection of information is much more than a technical matter. Human behaviour is just as important and a much more complex topic to manage. Examples include:

— the indiscriminate forwarding of confidential e-mail messages

— the practice of displaying passwords on Post-It™ notes stuck on a computer screen

— parents allowing their children access to their employer's corporate networks from home

— the opening of e-mail attachments known to contain a virus "just to see what they do"

In the networked world, the new generation of vandals and data thugs do not need to have physical contact with the victim. Data is easily copied, transmitted, modified or destroyed. As a result, the scene of crime is a particularly difficult one: there are no fingerprints or traces, identification of the culprits is nearly impossible, apprehension even more so and the legal framework does not make adequate provision for justice in this kind of crime.

The real-time nature of the Internet adds a further dimension to crime: it's instantaneous. If a thief steals a wallet containing credit cards, the thief needs time to use these cards, and the owner has at least a chance to stop the cards before they are used. When the details of credit cards are stolen from the Internet, the owner does not even know this and the thief, who effectively has stolen a person's electronic identification can, and does, use them immediately.

What is also known about the Internet world is that at the end of 2001 it has some 400 million users and that the number of users, volume of data and volume of traffic continue to increase at a very high rate. It is projected that by 2004 there will be over 1 billion users on the Internet using fixed and mobile access facilities. Clearly, even a minute percentage of people with malicious intent, constitute a substantial threat. Many publications suggest that 80% of companies worldwide have suffered malicious software attacks.

Cyber-crime, including fraud, is often not reported, but in some countries it has reached the same magnitude as arms and drug trading. The vulnerability of end users at work, at home and on the move has grown relentlessly. At the same time, dealing with the offenders can no longer be described as looking for a needle in a haystack. We are now looking for a particular needle in a stack of needles, anywhere in the world, often without jurisdiction and without adequate legislation.

In cyber security, cyberspace includes the domain of all computer systems connected to networks. This definition makes cyber-space into a vast domain that, in one way or another, extends into most human activities, only a few of which are shown. Every component part of cyberspace (communications links, satellites, computers, storage devices, data centres, telephone exchanges, etc) has an identifiable owner. The same is true for the data that flows around cyberspace. This is no different from marine transportation: all ports and their facilities have owners, and so do all ships. Each item of cargo on a ship also has an owner. There is one difference however: the international community developed and adopted the Law of the Seas. The Law of the Seas defines all aspects of the uses of the seas, including civilian, commercial and military navigation, continental shelves, island and archipelago states, the concept of the "high seas", conservation and management of species living in the seas, the common heritage of mankind, governance and many other topics. There is no equivalent for cyberspace.

The current governance of cyberspace is divided among many groups, some composed of volunteers such as the Internet Engineering Task Force (IETF), some like the World Wide Web Consortium (W3C) or the ICANN, composed and funded by 500 private and public sector entities, others run by the private sector, as are many domain name registration bodies. In 2002, International Organisations play a relatively peripheral role in cyberspace dealing with certain aspects of e-commerce (UNCTAD and WTO), intellectual property (WIPO), and technical standards (ITU, ISO and IEC). Other efforts to put into place appropriate governance and legislative mechanisms for cyber-space remain fragmented and include initiatives such as the Council of Europe's

Convention on Cyber-crime issued in 2001 and various national and regional Data Protection laws, but not yet at the truly global level.

As we learned to work with binary logic and data, this allowed the automation of repetitive processes, initially in payroll and accounting offices, financial services and other "information rich" activities. Binary formats started to be used in networks and other telecommunications links (such as satellites) many years ago. The technologies for photocopying, imaging and digitalising music were developed in the 1960s and matured quickly.

Personal computers (PC) have been around since the mid 1970s and the adoption of the 16-bit PC as a "personal productivity" tool in the early 1980s caused a revolution. The Internet has also existed for more than 30 years and the World Wide Web for more than 10 years but they became visible to the world at large around 1994 when the MOSAIC browser with its easy to use interface to access information became available. Today, there are few activities in the developed world that do not use information technologies and are not connected to some kind of network. This is why security has become an issue.

Computer crime has existed at least as long as computers. In the early days knowledgeable insiders carried out computer crime, as the expertise required was limited to "mathematical geniuses". Those smart enough not to draw attention to themselves performed fraudulent transactions for a long time, often without being discovered. Others, not worried about identifying themselves, planted malicious code such as a logical bomb to extort payment.

This kind of insider attacks continues. As the workforce has growing computer skills, having knowledge, legitimate access and motive makes it easier for insiders to commit computer crime. The situation is made worse by the unwillingness of organizations to disclose that they have been targeted. Even when offenders are identified and evidence acceptable to a court of law is available, prosecution is rare.

The emergence of the Internet with its outreach to some 400 million plus cybernauts has widened the potential for mischief. Whenever a hacker is traced, it is as a result of a massive, long and complex coordinated search. Many countries do not have the legislation to prosecute cyber-offenders. There have been several instances of people being arrested and subsequently released without charge (the author of the "I Love You" virus in the Philippines) or with minimal penalties (the author of the "Anna Kournikova" virus in the Netherlands).

Parameters of Cyber Security

Basically, cyber security is the discipline that addresses all the issues involving the protection of data and information in all forms, the related technologies used for information processing, storage and communications, and the computer resources of an individual or an organization.

Information has three characteristics: it has substance, it can be recorded and retrieved and it has value. It can exist in many forms, e.g. written, printed, spoken, electronically stored, physically transmitted or transmitted in electronic form. It can be created, processed, used, stored, transmitted, corrupted, lost and destroyed. The formal definition of cyber security relies on two sets of parameters:

— Threats, Vulnerability, Assets and Residual risk

— Availability, Integrity and Confidentiality

Cyber security has many technical components, it depends on human behaviour and it is influenced by the presence of many players: management, staff, internal and external auditors, legal counsel, external interested parties and stakeholders. There are also those motivated to breach an organization's defences to access data and information.

Asset

An asset is anything to which an individual or an organization assigns value. Of specific relevance to cyber security, all of the following fall into the category of "asset": documents, data, databases, software, physical information technology assets (computers, networks, etc), proprietary processes, industry specific exclusive knowledge, reputation and image. The valuation of such assets constitutes an essential part of any approach to cyber security.

Residual Risk

For a given set of assets, vulnerabilities and threats, it is possible to assess the risk that these assets will be damaged or compromised. This is not unique to information: it is possible to design a building so that it can withstand an earthquake. The cost of doing so increases rapidly with the severity of the earthquake it should be able to survive.

The compromise between cost and survivability implies the acceptance of a residual risk.

Organizations operating critical infrastructures, as well as military, policy and emergency services would normally accept the lowest level of residual risk. Banks, airlines and major outsourcing service providers may be able to accept a slightly higher level or residual risk. Low-tech manufacturing would be expected to have a greater tolerance to risk than any of the above organizations.

Availability

This is defined as the property of a system (or of a specific system resource) to be accessible and usable whenever required by an authorised entity and according to performance specifications appropriate to the system. Availability is usually expressed as a percentage, interpreted as follows:

— 99.9% implies that a system will operate as expected other than for a total of approximately 8 hours in a year. The non-operational time excludes planned outages.

— 99.99% implies that the cumulative non-operational time does not exceed 50 minutes in a year

— 99.999% implies that the cumulative non-operational time does not exceed 5 minutes in a year Systems and facilities operating seven days a week, 24 hours a day, can achieve such availability targets – at a cost. Cost increases at a faster rate than availability gains, and so do the resources needed to manage it and the complexity of the facilities.

Integrity

This is defined as the property that data has not been changed, destroyed or lost in an unauthorised or accidental manner. In practice, there are additional aspects to integrity, dealing with the confidence in data values and the information these values represent (correctness integrity) and with the trustworthiness of the source of the values (source integrity). Attacks on the integrity of information can have as an objective fraud (e.g. falsifying the records in a payroll system) or a political motive (e.g. modifying the contents of a website).

Confidentiality

This is defined as the property that information (or data) is not made available or disclosed to unauthorised individuals, entities or processes. Techniques, such as encryption, are used to obscure the contents of information and data from parties who do not have access to decryption facilities.

Principles of Cyber Security

The three principles of cyber security are given below:

Principle 1: 100% security is unachievable

For every security system and device there is at least one way to bypass it. The knowledge of how this is done used to be restricted to very few people and not disclosed. In cyberspace this is no longer the case. In the context of Cyber security, it is accepted throughout the industry that:

— Whilst software is designed to perform specific functions, experts – and these include hackers and crackers – can make it do other things

— Perfect software does not exist – all software contains bugs—coding errors in computer programs.

Moreover, a substantial amount of software includes features that were not part of the design specification and in practice software is only tested to confirm that it performs the functions specified. It is rarely tested to identify if it performs other – unwanted –functions. Such functions may include back doors, logic bombs and unauthorised special access rights to specific individuals. In addition, in recent years, desktop software often includes hidden programs, which range from games to the list of the names of the software designers.

The same is true for the management of cyber security –however good the procedures and practices applied, these may contain gaps, may be the subject of human error or the target of malicious intent. In practice all of the following four statements are true:

— New software means new bugs

— Old bugs are not always fixed

— Fixes are not always installed

— Fixes may contain new bugs

The result is that you only find out how effective your cyber security is when a security incident occurs, and then only if it is detected! Organizations that handle cyber security proactively will often engage security auditors to carry out unannounced tests to determine if they can breach the defenses in place. Otherwise, the security incident will be caused by someone who has different motives. Once a security incident has taken place, it may be possible to identify weaknesses in the arrangements, investigate and repair them.

The biggest challenge of cyber security is that of overcoming an organization's "comfort zone": the belief that their arrangements are adequate because a security incident has not occurred in the past or has not been detected. Statements such as "we have a firewall ", "we use a 128 bit encryption key", etc. are, by themselves, no substitute for a set of robust security policies, tools, measures, controls and a determined approach to compliance.

Principle 2: Risk and expenditure need to be balanced

We all take measures to protect our property and ourselves. The degree to which we implement such measures is influenced by our assessment of potential risks and our willingness to accept the restrictions and the constraints that such measures will impose on our daily life and their cost. We need to recognise however that in real life:

— Whatever protective measures we take, there is no guarantee that they will be totally effective all the time

— The risks against which we seek to protect ourselves will change in time and the assessment process and protective measures taken need to change accordingly to be effective

— Security measures involve investments and recurrent expenditures. Both of these could be significant A fundamental component of the practice of cyber security is the assessment of the value of the assets to be protected, the threats and vulnerabilities to which they may be subject and the impact that a security breach could have. Finally, as in the case of household insurance, it is necessary to define the level of residual risk that can be accepted.

Principle 3: Security and inconvenience need to be balanced

In the world of security nothing is perfect. This is true for information as well as for the protection of our property and person. Every security measure added implies an additional process or activity to end-users. As these measures add up, they become obstacles to be overcome by each end user, regardless of whether they are multiple locks and burglar alarms or the need to remember several passwords. The workload of the Systems Administrator also increases as a result. Human nature is such that people will look for shortcuts to complex processes. It is not unusual for multiple or complex passwords to be written down. Worse still, these can be found on a Post-It™ note affixed in a visible place. This weakens, if not altogether invalidates, the whole security process.

Managing Cyber Security

Managing cyber security is more than a discipline: it is a way of life. Its purpose is to achieve and maintain a state of equilibrium between four factors:

What are the threats to protect against and how likely are these? These threats include all of the "bad guys" described above. Having identified them, it is necessary to understand what interest or grudges they may have in an organisation. This requires the assessment of the financial, social and operational impact of such a threat.

What are the vulnerabilities of the information infrastructure and operations of a particular organisation? These vulnerabilities include technologies, software and operational practices, all of which are vulnerable to attack by an expert. Just as important is the degree to which best practices are applied, for example in configuration management and change control. A less than robust response to an attack should also be considered vulnerability.

What is the value of the information assets to be protected? This is a hard question to answer, as there are no agreed metrics for the value of information, information systems and, often, intellectual property. The methods to determine this value invariably include the cost of employee time when unable to perform their function. In the U.S.A., the figure of 1 dollar a minute is widely used.

How much should be spent on providing information security? There is no right answer to this question. One of the many problems facing professionals is that budgets containing new expenditures to improve security are challenged by requesting a calculation of Return on Investment.

Executives should not only assign overall responsibility to a single manager, typically the Chief Information Officer, although in a growing number of organizations, information security is managed separately from the ICT function with an overall Chief Security Officer. In both cases, the person responsible for information security should be required to create and maintain a catalog of all known information systems and network vulnerabilities and certify in writing the security status of all the organization's systems. This is no different from requiring the Chief Information Officer to formally certify the organization's accounts. Questions that executives should consider reviewing in their own organizations include:

— Who is responsible for the organization's overall information security at how is this responsibility dealt with at the organization's various locations?

— Who does the person responsible for the overall information security report to?

— Who reviews this person's performance and monitors her/his effectiveness?

— How is security managed with contractors, temporary personnel and outsource service providers?

— Who is responsible for dealing with a security incident?

— Who is responsible for conducting information security tests and audits?

— What is the organization's policy with regards to compliance with security policies and practices? When there are unambiguous answers to all these questions, the executive would have acted with due diligence and established an organizational framework that will support the practice of information security throughout the organization.

Information Security management can be grouped into three main activities:

— Risk assessment, policy definition, planning and implementation

— Operation, audit, testing and certification

— Responding to an event, post-mortem and digital forensics The reader is referred to ISO 17799, an international standard on the Management of Information Security as a comprehensive guide to implementation. The next section presents an outline of what the standard contains and what it means in practice. In addition there are several technical standards such as X.509, defining digital certificates, and the X.800 series of recommendations of the ITU, the International Telecommunications Union, as well as a number of vendor developed proposed and de-facto standards, such as the proposed standard WS-Security jointly developed by IBM and Microsoft, recently joined by Verisign.

While standards and legislation are both important components and a strong base on which to build, these are not enough by themselves to provide security. An outline of the main activities in the management of information security is given in the sections that follow.

ISO Code Practice

The Geneva based International Standards Organization (ISO) published this document in 1999. Its precursor was the British Standard BS 7799 (Part I), the British Standards Institute Code of Practice for Information Security Management, first issued in 1995 subsequently adopted in slightly modified form by a number of other countries. ISO 17799 identifies and describes ten guiding principles as the basis of a system for the management of Information Security. Although described as a standard, ISO 17799 is not prescriptive, for example:

— It does not state "you must have a firewall", instead it says "precautions are required to prevent and detect the introduction of malicious software"

— It does not say that "your system must be the same as my system", instead it says that "It is essential that an organization identifies its security requirements"

Guiding Principle 1. Security policy

Purpose: To provide management direction and support for information security

The standard recommends the following framework:

— Establishment of a top-level management security forum

— Provision of individual security awareness training

— Risk management as a management approach

— Compliance with the appropriate legislation (e.g. Data Protection Act)

A policy document would normally contain sections on:

— The need for an organization to have a contingency plan

— The need for effective data back-up

— The avoidance of malicious software

— Procedures for controlling access to systems and data

— Procedures for the reporting of security incidents

— Procedures for non-compliance with the policy, malicious activity, inappropriate use, etc.

Guiding Principle 2. Security organization

Purpose: To manage information security within the organization with particular emphasis on:

1. maintaining the security of organizational information processing facilities and of assets accessed by third parties
2. maintaining the security of information when the responsibility for information processing and service delivery has been outsourced to another organization. Such a security organization needs to make provision for, at a very minimum:
   — Establishment of an internal forum for information security
   — Arrangements for the coordination of information security
   — Allocation of information security responsibilities to nominated functions/ individuals
   — Identification of the risks associated with third party access to data and information
   — Ensuring that security requirements are specified in contracts with third parties
   — Security requirements in outsourcing contracts

Guiding Principle 3. Asset classification and control

Purpose: To identify the scope of information security management and ensure that information assets are given an appropriate level of protection.

An organization implementing ISO 17799 must determine which of its information assets may materially impact the operation and delivery of the organization's activities or business if they were to be unavailable or degraded. This in turn, requires an analysis of the probability that a given threat will exploit a specific weakness to cause loss or damage to an asset or group of assets. Risk is defined by the combination of value, vulnerability and threat. All assets relevant to the scope of the Information Security Management System must be identified and have a nominated "owner" or custodian.

Guiding Principle4. Personnel security

Purpose: To reduce the risks of human error, theft, fraud or misuse of facilities, in particular,

1. by ensuring that all end-users are aware of information security threats and concerns and that they can support the organization's security policies in the course of their normal work

2. by working to minimise the damage caused by security incidents and malfunctions as well as to learn from such incidents Typically, the tasks to be undertaken to meet this requirement are:

    — The inclusion of security considerations and responsibilities in job descriptions and staff contracts

    — End-user training

    — Response methodologies and practices in the event of malfunctions and security incidents.

Guiding Principle 5. Physical and environmental security

Purpose: to prevent unauthorised access, damage and interference to business premises and information and, as a result:

1. prevent loss, damage or compromise of assets and/or an interruption to business activities
2. prevent the theft of information and/or information processing facilities Normal practices in the implementation of environmental security include:
   - Definition and implementation of a security perimeter
   - Physical access controls (e.g. smart cards, keypad and secret codes and their associated monitoring)
   - Definition of secure working areas and associated practices
   - Ensuring the continuity and security of power supplies
   - Practices for the disposal of equipment (which may contain licensed software and data falling under the scope of the security policy)

Guiding Principle 6. Communications and operations management

Purpose: To ensure the correct and secure operation of information processing facilities to:

1. Minimise the risk of systems failures
2. Protect the integrity of software and information
3. Maintain the integrity and availability of information processing and communications facilities
4. Ensure the safeguarding of information in networks
5. Ensure the protection of the supporting infrastructure
6. Prevent damage to assets and interruptions to business activities

7. Present the loss, modification or misuse of information exchanges between organizations The minimum components of such practices are:
   - Fully documented operational procedures (typically including Availability and Performance Management, Incident and Problem Management, Change Control and Configuration Management among others)
   - Clear assignments of responsibilities to individuals
   - Protection against malicious software
   - Housekeeping (for example, registering and maintaining the records of users, inventories, resource usage)
   - Network management
   - Media handling and its security
   - Exchanges of information and software with other parties Best practices in the above are extensively documented.

Guiding Principle 7. Access control

Purpose: To control access to information to:

1. Prevent unauthorised access to information systems
2. Prevent unauthorised computer access
3. Ensure the protection of networked services
4. Detect unauthorised activities
5. Ensure information security when using mobile computing and teleworking facilities

Even though individual users may have legitimate access to an organization's systems, data and information, their rights may not include universal access to all information assets. Therefore, an organization needs to define who has the rights to access what and when.

The usual activities associated with access control include:

— Definition of the access control requirements (focus on confidentiality)

— Managing the access rights of individual users

— Defining the responsibilities of individual users

— Defining the appropriate mechanisms for access to a) the network, b) applications, c) operating systems

— Policies and practices for monitoring system access and use

— Policies and practices for granting remote access from teleworking staff, from mobile devices, etc These issues require particular attention when these activities are outsourced and it is strongly recommended that the right to audit the outsourcer should be part of all such contracts.

Guiding Principle 8. Systems development and maintenance

Purpose: To ensure that security is built into information systems to:

1. Prevent loss, modification or misuse of user data in applications systems
2. Protect the confidentiality and integrity of information

3. Ensure information systems and support activities are conducted in a secure manner
4. Maintain the security of application system software and data throughout the lifecycle of such systems This would normally require:
   - Definition of the security requirements of systems and computer applications
   - Definition of the role of cryptographic controls
   - Ensuring the security of system files
   - Ensuring the security of development and support processes

As in the case of 7 above, applications development is an activity which is increasingly being outsourced, and the same recommendation applies: that the right to audit the outsourcer should be part of all such contracts.

Guiding Principle 9. Business Continuity Management

Purpose: To counteract interruptions of business activities and protect critical business processes from the effects of major failures or disasters. It is important to distinguish three distinct activities relating to this:

- *Disaster Recovery*: this is the responsibility of the parties providing communications and operations management, i.e. an essentially technical process that relies on the use of other, often distant, facilities with an adequate replica of the infrastructure.
- *Business Continuity*: the next level up from Disaster Recovery, where clearly defined and essential activities can continue to be carried out from another location. This is the responsibility of senior

management and involves a number of staff who must be contactable and ready to assume these responsibilities as and when required.

— *Crisis Management:* another senior management responsibility, which involves communicating with all stakeholders and other interested parties once a disaster has been invoked and the business continuity arrangements put in place.

Guiding Principle 10. Compliance

Purpose: To avoid breaches of any civil or criminal law or of statutory, regulatory or contractual obligations, and to comply with organizational security policies and maximise the effectiveness of system audit processes. This requires a thorough knowledge of the legislative framework in which the organization operates, as well as the review of the security policy from this perspective. System audit becomes an essential part of the compliance process.

Cyber Security in Cooperate Environment

The implementation, operation and management of information security is more than a discipline. It is a way of life and relies on four components, all of which equally important and indispensable. Processes are fundamentally important to all systematic and/or continuous operations. Standards such as those set by ISO are of great value. Processes must be systematically applied and reviewed in the light of experience to remove as many systematic errors and flaws as possible.

People (staff, contractors, consultants) are vital to all operations and services. They need to be present in adequate numbers and with appropriate skills, experience and motivation. Technology is readily available. However, products are not perfect, and also have relatively short life cycles. The market is very competitive and a high percentage of vendors come and go – they are either absorbed by a bigger company or simply go out of business. All of this makes Technology Assessment more important than ever before.

Culture defines the work environment and in order to succeed, it must be shared across the organization. Executives have a major role to play in establishing and maintaining an appropriate culture. Examples of cultures that have traditionally been successful in managing information security can be found in two main areas of activity:

— Intelligence, Defense and Police

— Banking, Foreign Exchange, Stock Markets and Insurance The cultural aspects considered to be critical for the successful management of information security include:

— Full support and commitment to security from the very top management

— Strong organizational discipline

— Clearly documented and communicated policies

— Clearly documented processes supported by audits

— Systematic compliance monitoring

— Consistent actions to deal with non-compliance

— Regular tests, audits and reviews

Organizations that have implemented ISO standards are well placed to expand the culture this standard entails.

Physical Security

Like the basic security measures taken in the home, physical security is a prerequisite. It serves to create an environment and visible culture of controlled access and preparedness for disruption and damage to equipment.

Best practices require the definition of, among others:

- Those individuals who may enter a computer room or data centre, and whether they can do so alone or accompanied at all times
- Those individuals who may physically access specific pieces of equipment, and under what circumstances
- The conditions under which other parties such as contractors, consultants, temporary staff, cleaners, etc may enter the facilities
- The conditions and practices for the disposal of equipment no longer required
- The conditions for transporting and storing physical media such as magnetic tapes containing data as well as the necessary provision of:
  - suitably selected, implemented, managed and monitored access control devices
  - access control and/or identity cards or devices
  - secure doors and other access points (e.g. for deliveries and removals)
  - flooding, fire and smoke detectors, lighting and closed circuit television
  - secured power supplies and appropriate backup (batteries and generators)

— suitable locked cabinets, cable trays and other similar engineering practices

These matters take on particular significance whenever the provision of computer room or data center services has been outsourced, in which case the right to audit the service provider becomes an important consideration.

Logical Security

Information security does not require the attacker to have physical contact with the victim. Logical security is achieved when several complementary mechanisms are used together in an effective manner.

Logical security complements physical arrangements by providing procedures, tools and software to:

— structure how data and information are accessed and by whom

— create secure copies of all software and data to support disaster recovery create appropriate audit logs

— implement appropriate encryption mechanisms

— detect attempts to breach security or actual events

— detect malicious software within the systems, in electronic mail and in media

The major components of logical security are:

— authentication

— administration

— authorization

— audit

Authentication is the first component: In order to prove to a computer system who you are, there are three possible approaches:

1. *Tell the system something you know:* a name and a password. Passwords are simple to implement but they have shortcomings:

   They can be disclosed to a third party, for example by a disgruntled or ex-employee. They can be subject to complex rules: minimum number of characters, not easy to guess terms or dates, mix of letters and numbers, changed every month, etc. In these cases there is a strong temptation to write passwords down, which defeats the object if someone else finds them

2. *Provide the system something you have:* an identity card or a token. Security can be increased by requiring, in addition to the password, some kind of physical device such as an electronic identity card or token.

3. *Give the system something you are*: Personal features such as a retinal scan or voice pattern, called "biometrics," can be used in truly high security environments. The technologies are complex and expensive. Despite this, their use is increasing.

Once the system knows who the user actually is, the natural next question is "what is this person allowed to do": the *Authorisation* process regulates access to resources, for example what transactions can be performed and what data can be seen, modified and created by the user. Such access privileges are based on a user's role and responsibilities in the organization. In the case of service providers such as libraries, e-commerce companies, etc. such privileges are determined by criteria such as contracts, subscriptions, credit worthiness, credit history, etc.

Administration is the process of maintaining users' profiles as well as managing the security definitions of a particular resource. This includes such activities as removing the access privileges of an employee who is leaving the company, changing the profiles and the list of systems a specific user is allowed to access following a promotion or transfer, etc. Particular care has to be taken to plan the strategy to be followed in the case of a replacement of the Administrator himself.

Audit is the confirmation that these security measures are reasonable and in working order. There is no way to know if a user is exceeding authorization without such audits. There is also no way to show where security measures should be strengthened without first knowing where they are weak. Audit is a vital complement to all security measures.

None of the measures above will be effective without a number of people-oriented features:

— Executive support for information security policies, measures and processes must be fully committed before a security incident takes place.

— Staff needs to be aware of the threats related to information security and their importance of information security to their organization

— Staff needs to be organised, skilled and trained for dealing with information security incidents

— All such training on information security must be consistent with the needs of the organization

— Due consideration must also be given to other people with access to the organization's information assets such as maintenance personnel, consultants, contractors, temporary staff, cleaners, and others.

The delicate issues of pre-recruitment security clearances, the right to privacy in the workplace, the conduct of investigations, etc., are major topics in their own right. The list below highlights those activities, which the executive must control in order to ensure the success of information security management.

Understanding Information Systems

Such an understanding should not be from a technical perspective or what kind of equipment staff have on their desk.

What is meant here includes a good knowledge of:

— what would be the impact of a major security incident on the image and reputation of the organization, on its financial and operational performance, etc?

— how critical to the organization and the constituencies it supports are the use of computer systems and facilities such as the World Wide Web, Internet mail, multimedia facilities, etc?

— how well does the organization comply with appropriate legislation (for example data protection)?

— what are the organization's legal liabilities associated with such matters?

The following are the prerequisites for the development of effective information security policies:

— *Conducting a risk assessment, in particular looking for vulnerabilities* : This is a process that should be carried out on a regular basis to look for glaring problems such as poor password practices, missing updates and patches in infrastructure facilities, unauthorised dial-up modems and other "back doors" to the corporate network

— *Developing and implementing proper policies:* This action is the first requirement of ISO 17799. Documented policies are essential if information security is to be successful. It is the only effective way to deal with the excuse, "I did not know". Such policies must be based on business needs and relate to business risk and must be understood and supported by the executive, whose commitment to security is essential. This will only occur when the executive recognises that information security is not just a "technical matter" that is fixed by installing a firewall.

It is usual practice that staff and other parties should sign an acknowledgement of receipt of such policies and a commitment to comply with them, including the acceptance of the measures the organization may take in the event of non-compliance. Like any other process oriented documentation there is a risk that the creation, maintenance and dissemination of such policies may create its own bureaucracy. Good judgment is necessary to keep things in proportion. The effort required to create and maintain workable policies should not be underestimated. Many templates for such policies are available and can be useful to establish such policies. However, the value of the policies will be determined by how successfully they are communicated and applied.

A document based on a template and kept in a bookshelf ("Shelfware") may satisfy an inexperienced auditor that one has a security policy, but it has no business value. The publication of a security policy must be supported by a security awareness campaign and the briefing of all staff and other interested parties. This is a particularly important step in the recruitment of new staff.

Define accountability for managing information security: The story of the job that needed to be done and the four people who were there at the time: Messrs. Anybody, Somebody, Everybody and Nobody is worth repeating:

Everybody thought that Somebody would do the job.

In fact, Anybody could have done it.

In the end Nobody did it.

It would be disastrous if information security were to be managed in this way and avoidance of such a situation requires recognition that information security is not just an "IT problem" and that executives do not abdicate their responsibilities in this area. Executives must define the business need and the value of the assets to be protected, make resources available to deploy the necessary security, test it and manage it, and remain its main client.

The CIO or other senior IT professional must play the roles of (a) champion of the information security measures and (b) chief coordinator for the organization.The CIO must be accountable for the way in which all technical aspects are implemented and operated including technical choices, how and where security is sourced, what resources are assigned to it and how well it performs.Other responsibilities of the CIO are arranging for network and other tests to identify security weaknesses and vulnerabilities, develop processes to improve the detection of malicious code and work to minimise false alarms.It is also essential that the security organization should implement measures to make sure that the information resources of the organization have not been the subject of external or internal attacks.

Implementing appropriate security tools and procedures: The technical implementation of security will require the selection and procurement of a variety of products. These must have a demonstrable track record of effectiveness. However, these products in and of themselves have limited value if they are not properly installed and configured. It is common practice for vendors to deliver these products in a standard configuration referred to as "Out of the Box" or "Shrink-wrapped", which include, amongst other features, an initial User ID and password for the security administrator, which is well known, particularly to hackers. These default values MUST be changed to approved criteria before these products are put into service. Similarly, the CIO will be responsible for the development, introduction and management of processes to support the administration and monitoring of compliance with the security policy. These processes would normally include the critical task of monitoring incidents, events and trends, as well as following industry's alerts and notifications.

Best practices for such processes are based on using a central administration and distribution facility to ensure that all endusers have the latest updates of virus protection software and that they are immediately notified of infections.

Allowing vendors and maintenance organizations on-line access to support 24/7: High availability operations rely strongly on the technical support of vendors. To maintain these high levels of availability the former practice of a four-hour guaranteed response time will simply not do. Vendors now rely on diagnostic features built into their equipment and software to provide real time information to their technical support organization, which typically operates from multiple locations, 24 hours a day 7 days a week, by direct online communications. This implies an exchange of data between your facility and that of the technical support organization of the vendor. This is a back door into your organization and the security aspects of such access must be clearly specified in the contracts with the vendor and subject to audit by your chosen auditors.

Guidelines for Safe Computing

Privacy Issues

Life on the Internet is a different experience. There are many parties who are interested in who you are and what you do on the Web, all with different intentions. It is because of this that initiatives such as the Electronic Privacy Information Center (EPIC) and the World Wide Web Consortium (W3C) Platform for Privacy Preferences (P3P) were launched.Among the many examples of potential intrusions on your personal privacy include: Details of your hardware and software configuration, the browser you use, your assigned IP (Internet Protocol) address are readily available to the websites you visit. The IP address is usually sufficient to give an indication of your physical location. Your IP address – which is included in every e-mail you send, can be used to reveal at least some information about your geographical location, and this may be useful when trying to trace a suspect message received.

The owner of a Website will want to know, for example, when you access the Website, what pages and documents you look at, whether you download items or not, whether you look at advertisements, etc. To do this, they place cookies on your computer, and employ spy-ware and other devices to track such use.

The owner of a website who specialises in advertising, wants to know your e-mail address and so does a spammer. Many websites require individuals to register in order to provide access, usually free of charge to their site's content. Such registration requires details of name, address, and sometimes other personal information such as age and marital status and e-mail address. The issue of potential invasion of privacy is raised when such information willingly provided by the visitor to the Website is subsequently matched against other commercially available sources of information. The owner of a website dealing with electronic commerce needs to know your name, address, e-mail address, credit card number and period of validity and other related information.

There are other people whose interest may be somewhat less benign. Generally known under the name of "Pretexters" they may pose as representatives of survey firms, banks, Internet service providers and even government agencies to get you to reveal your Social Security number or equivalent, mother's maiden name, financial account numbers and other identifying information. Legitimate organizations with which you do business have the information they need and will not ask you for it. It is interesting to note that hardly any websites provide their visitors with the ability to validate what personal information is held in the databases. In Europe this is in fact against the relevant Data Protection legislation, which allows for (at least limited) access to such information.

E-Mail related privacy issues

Who is reading your e-Mail? Tools whcih are used to monitor the contents of e-mail messages (such as Carnivore and Echelon) may also used by an employer to monitor the content of messages for abusive or improper language, personal rather than business use, etc. Not all employers have clearly articulated policies about their rights and yours, and without such policies, many problems can arise, largely influenced by the national legislation concerning the rights of individuals. Such matters can become quite complex when, in the case of a telecommuter, the employer's e-mail system is used by a family member for personal matters.

Is someone forwarding your e-mails without your knowledge? This is perhaps the most common source of trouble – and there have been many articles in the press – when an e-mail between two parties, intended to be a private exchange and essentially a confidential matter, is subsequently distributed by the recipient to third parties without the knowledge or consent of the sender.

Is someone sending e-mail on your behalf ? The first indication you may have that someone is spoofing your mail or has stolen your account may be when you get into very serious trouble. If innocent, your only recourse is to ask for a full investigation, which may or may not be conclusive.

Are you receiving fake e-mail? As above, you may not know unless there is something suspicious about the content or it turns out to contain malicious software.

Again, should this happen, it is advisable to arrange for an investigation.

Measures to Protect the Systems

However good they are, it is imperative that the tools and technologies used to protect systems should be:

— installed correctly

— regularly maintained

— configured to operate at their maximum performance.

Protection from malicious code

The best form of protection against malicious code is the use of trusted quality Anti-Virus software. Such software is available commercially from a number of vendors as well as in the form of Freeware or Shareware. In general terms, even the most expensive commercial anti-virus software represents a fraction of the value of your computer, all of its software and, in particular, your data.

The practice of implementing a personal Firewall is also spreading and it is worth considering if you access the Internet through a dial-up connection. For any form of permanent connection, the use of a personal firewall is strongly recommended. A personal firewall consists of software that protects a single Internet-connected computer from intruders. This protection is especially useful for individuals with "always-on" connections such as DSL or cable modem.

As in the case of anti-virus software, personal firewalls are available from several vendors and some of them can be downloaded from the Internet free-of-charge.

Software is not static, and both anti-virus products and personal firewalls are frequently revised and improved by their vendors.

These improvements come in three distinct shapes:

— *Patch (sometimes called a "fix"):* A quick-repair job for a piece of programming. Problems (bugs) are invariably found. A patch is the immediate solution that is provided to users; it can be usually downloaded from the software maker's website. The patch is not necessarily the best solution for the problem and the product developers often find a better solution later

— *New Release:* A full edition of a software package that incorporates all patches and repairs, to a higher standard of resolution and, sometimes includes additional functionality.

— *Upgrade:* A full edition of a software package that brings substantial new features to previous releases.

Whilst patches are usually free of charge to licensed users, new releases and upgrades must be purchased. Owners of previous versions of the software usually, but not always, can upgrade at a reduced cost. The use of original, fully licensed software is essential in order to obtain such updates as well as technical support from their suppliers.

Privacy Protection

Configure your personal computer features to avoid disclosure You must configure your web browser to ensure that information you do not wish to share is not inadvertently made public: In your browser's configuration tool (which may be referred to as Options, Setup or

Preferences, depending on which browser you use, you have the choice of using a pseudonym instead of your real name and of not entering an e-mail address or other personally identifiable information.

It is also a good practice to look at other "Internet-defaults" in your computer for example in Windows the "Internet Control Panel" and with an Apple "Configuration Manager" and "Internet Config". These can be made equally anonymous if they contain any fields for personal information. In a domestic environment where a computer is shared by several people, it is important to set out clear rules so that everyone knows NOT to reveal personal information other than on an approved, website-by-website basis.

Policies for staff monitoring

What you do in your home, through your personal access to the Internet and the Internet Service Provider of your choice, is usually your own business, unless your employer has advised you otherwise. Using your employer's corporate network from your home, or surfing the Web, downloading software and doing your personal e-mail, may be in conflict with the employer's security policies and practices. These policies should normally be clearly disclosed to all staff.

Privacy at work is a major topic in its own right, for which there are no fixed rules. Legislation on this matter is either incomplete or ambiguous with the exception of criminal or civil investigations when there is "sufficient cause". Otherwise, it is a matter for very clear communications between management and employees. It's wise to assume that there is NO privacy at work, and that this applies no only to computer systems, e-mail, etc., but also to the use of telephones and fax machines.

Cookie manager

Whilst cookies are well-defined standard features of the Internet, and when legitimately used, quite convenient. They can be abused. An example is the disclosure of information about your browsing habits to other interested parties, such as advertisers. Moreover, cookie files in your computer constitute a record of your usage of the Internet that you may wish to, at the very least, have some control over. The mechanism to do this is cookie management software.

The latest versions of browsers include a cookie manager, which allows you to decide which cookies you wish to accept, view the cookies on your hard disk and to delete those you wish to remove. There are many other cookie managers that can be downloaded from the Internet, either free or requiring a modest registration fee.

User IDs/Passwords or physical devices

It is always a good idea to protect your computer, particularly notebooks and other small devices to prevent access by others. Such protection can take many forms ranging from a well designed User ID and password to the use of physical devices such as Smart Cards or small pieces of hardware (commonly referred to as "dongles") that need to be physically plugged in, usually in a parallel port.

A good password needs to meet two requirements: it should not require you to write it down and it should not be easily guessed (first name, date or birth, name of a child) or broken (such as with a dictionary attack tool).

Generally accepted criteria are that a password should be at least six characters long and contain both characters and numbers. Some systems are case sensitive and will also differentiate between upper-case and lower-case letters. Regrettably, these criteria can be incompatible with the human memory and our need to write such passwords down to be able to remember them when needed. Memorising multiple passwords becomes an even bigger headache unless you create a personal mnemonic system as an aid. It is also good practice to password protect specific documents that you do not wish others to share.

Encryption and other privacy tools

Hiding your text or files with a password is a good practice but not necessarily a highly secure one. There are two important kinds of encryption:

1. Digital Signatures
2. Cryptography

Digital Signatures, allow you to verify that a message was written by the person it claims to be from and that it has not been modified during transmission.

Digital signatures use a pair of keys, a public one which you provide to everyone (for example by posting it on your personal web page) and a private or secret key, known only to one individual and kept in this person's personal computer in encrypted form requiring a "pass-phrase" to activate it. Anyone can send a private message encrypted with the public key. Only the genuine recipient of this message can read it with the private key. To send a personal digital signature to someone else, one must use the private key. The recipient can confirm that it came from this individual by testing it with the public key. It is essential that whatever software is used to create digital signatures be trusted to use secure techniques and be a robust well-supported and studied design. A product such as Pretty Good Privacy (PGP) is widely acknowledged to meet these requirements and is available free of charge for non-commercial use. Tools are available to create a secure space on a hard disk to store sensitive information, often requiring a private key to provide access to it.

A Digital Certificate is an electronic file that uniquely links a person to a public key and is a device extensively used in electronic commerce. The subject of Public Key Infrastructure (PKI), its operation and trustworthiness is beyond the scope of this publication.

Cryptography, is the second mechanism for ensuring privacy since the invention of writing and has been in used in many different forms. Cryptography is usually reserved for the most highly confidential messages and has a counterpart in Cryptanalysis, the process of braking ciphers – something that is not always possible (at present).

Sophisticated encryption devices and software are currently classified as weapons by several countries and require an export license, which, in the U.S.A. is issued by the State Department –an authorization that appears difficult to obtain. In reality, exporting software either on a floppy disk or by a file transfer is not difficult and is used to circumvent the authorization process. Encryption is used to protect information about credit card details in transmission to the website. However it does not ensure that the website stores the information securely. Many ecommerce and other websites have been broken into by crackers, and as a result thousands of credit card details have been stolen, as was the case at the 2001 meeting of the World Economic Forum at Davos, Switzerland.

Credit card number details should never be disclosed without making sure first that the connection is in fact encrypted – this is usually indicated by an icon such as a closed lock or padlock or an unbroken key as well as by a web address (URL which begins with https//:) — if the web address does not have this "s" at the end of the "http" is not a secure site.

Protecting your use of e-mail

E-mail messages to unknown parties such as newsgroups, chat rooms and other public spaces need not be in your real name. For these situations, it is convenient to have one or more alternate accounts, often, but not necessarily, using a pseudonym. Addresses that are widely posted become targets for on-line junk mailers, known as spammers. If you become their target, simply ditch the account and open a new one from one of the many free offerings available.

Understanding headers e-Mail headers can tell you many things: the route a message took to get to your e-mail account, where the message originated, what e-mail program was used to send it, and more. But how do you know what the header contains? Most e-mail programs give you an option to "Show all headers", and in Microsoft's Outlook Express it's just a matter of pressing Ctrl+F3 while selecting a message. This will open a separate window, where you can view all the header information. In Netscape Messenger, you can select the

View > Headers, and make a selection from Brief, Normal or All. There are a wide variety of e-mail headers and some programs use/display different headers than others. The principles are the same.

Safe Computing Practices

Ensure that you have all the material necessary to rebuild your software and:

— Consider not being "permanently connected" as you are with DSL and cable modems. Such connections use a static IP address that makes them especially vulnerable to potential hackers.

— Ensure your Internet browser is sufficiently recent to incorporate security features and make certain these are correctly configured in your computer.

— Keep copies of all original and licensed software, together with appropriate ID codes and documentation needed to obtain updates and technical support.

— Ensure that your freeware is from a reputable and recommended source and that your shareware meets the same criteria as freeware AND is registered with the provider.

— Look for and install updates to virus definitions, personal firewalls, browsers and other software on which the security of your computer depends.

— Monitor alerts and developments in malicious software from the Press or appropriate websites. Take appropriate action immediately if a patch is required for your computer.

— Consider upgrading your software to a newer version or major new release if it contains features that will enhance your confidence in the security of your arrangements

— Enable anti-virus software and personal firewalls to operate in the background all the time. Moreover, test for the presence of viruses, Trojan horse and other malicious software on a regular basis: this vigilance should reflect the value of the software and data in your computer to your personal life.

— Remove all malicious software found – do not share it with anyone else

— Back up data. This requires very systematic and comprehensive back-ups. There is a wide variety of commercial software available to facilitate this process. Should the worst happen you would have access to your back-up files.

There are of course other risks to consider, such as those of an electric power surge, hardware failure (loss of the hard disk), or worse, the loss or theft of your computer. Power supply protection devices come in a wide price range, from a simple surge arrestor to an uninterruptible power supply (UPS) containing batteries that takes over should the mains electricity be turned off. Here, expenditure should match the need and the likelihood of such an event. Should your hard disk fail without a complete backup, there are companies specializing in data recovery. Their services also cover situations where the damage was caused by fire or water. Losing a notebook computer containing unprotected, unencrypted data is, regrettably a common occurrence. There is little that can be done to recover the computer and prevention is definitely better than cure.

Personal matters

Security is based on two very simple rules:

1. Trust No One
2. No Disclosure

The protection of personal information and privacy rely strongly on a little knowledge and a lot of common sense. The following are all simple to implement and quite effective:

— Beware of downloading and running programs (games, screen savers, etc) from sources that cannot be vouched for.

— Don't give your credit card number unless the website URL is https AND the padlock is showing in the browser screen, AND the web-site is trusted

— Beware of offers that appear too good to be true – they usually are, e.g. rewards or prizes in exchange for your contact or other information.

— Never reply to spammers: this confirms that your address is active and read – the result is that this will become known to more spammers. Clever spammers rely on e-mail software to tell them you have read the message. You should disable your e-mail package's automatic return receipt requests.

— If the problem becomes serious, contact your ISP with copies of the spam-mail so that they can forward your complaint to the spammer's ISP.

— Use and maintain well designed User IDs and passwords –cycling criteria

— Keep copies of your user ID and password in a secure and confidential place

— Attachments are files sent together with an e-mail message. Such files can consist of text document, digital photographs or other images, computer programs and many other useful items. They can also contain malicious code. Care should be exercised at all times when dealing with attachments, even if these appear to come from a trusted source.

— If there is the slightest doubt about the legitimacy of an attachment, don't open it until you can validate with the sender that it is OK to do so.

Responding to a Security Incident

You discovered that your organization's information resources have been compromised.

Scenario 1: An obvious problem, the result of a logical bomb being activated, a virus, worm or Denial of Service Attack, etc. The systems in your organization no longer work, data has been lost or corrupted and the staff is unable to work productively. In the first instance, someone, usually on behalf of the Chief Information Officer or IT Manager will have to act quickly and effectively to contain the damage and restore operations. In situations where information systems and facilities are critical to an organization, the only viable answer is that of having in place an Emergency Response Team of empowered and trained staff – capable of being mobilised in a very short time regardless of day of the week and time of day.

Dealing with a difficult situation is not a good time to improvise. An effective response to an incident will include six specific groups of tasks, namely, preparation, identification, containment, eradication, recovery and follow-up In addition, it is very useful to have an emergency plan based on common sense to handle the situation in the event of an unpleasant situation. A typical emergency plan would contain steps such as:

— *Don't panic.* Any incident raises stress levels all round. Communication and coordination become difficult and calm, particularly from senior management can help others to avoid making critical errors.

— *Take notes.* The managers responsible for security should create a set of record-keeping forms to be used in the event that the security incident becomes a matter for a court of law. These notes may become legal evidence. Good records should focus on Who, What, When and Where. Whenever possible, How and Why should also be part of the record.

— *Get help.* The first person to notify is your security coordinator. The telephone directory of the organization is a vital tool and, to complement the notes mentioned above, keep notes about each person contacted and what was said.

— *Apply a "need to know" policy.* Disclose, if you must, the details of the incident to the minimum number of people possible. Remind them that they are trusted individuals and that discretion is essential. Do not speculate.

— *Use trusted communications.* If the computers may have been compromised, avoid using them for incident-handling discussions. Use telephones and faxes instead. Do not send information about the incident by electronic mail, talk, chat, or news; the information may be intercepted by the attacker and used to worsen the situation. When computers are being used, encrypt all incident handling e-mail. Contain the problem. Take all possible steps to prevent the problem from getting worse. Generally that means removing the system from the network, though keeping connections open may help to catch an intruder.

— *Make a backup of the affected system(s) as soon as possible.* Use new, unused media. If possible make a binary, or bit-by-bit backup.

— *Fix the problem.* Identify what went wrong if you can. Take steps to correct the deficiencies that allowed the problem to occur. Restore normal service. After checking your backups to ensure they are not compromised, restore your system from backups and monitor the system closely to determine whether it can resume its tasks.

— *Learn from the experience.* You don't want to get caught unprepared the next time.

Scenario 2: Your organization does not know that it has been attacked. This could take the form of stolen data, a defaced website, the rerouting of external traffic, unknown software such as a Trojan Horse or a back door or the defrauding of the organization. In this scenario, the time of improper action may have preceded discovery by a substantial period of time, and many such events are discovered by chance rather than by design or audits. Upon discovery, the CIO will have to take measures in line with a corporate policy for such matters, as it will be necessary to obtain evidence and comply with the legal requirements of digital forensics. In addition, the offending attack needs to be dealt with. To investigate or not to investigate? That is the question. There are no fixed and immutable rules to help decide whether or not an attack regardless of the scenario should be followed by a detailed analysis of the attack, its causes, how security was breached and subsequent reporting.

In the case of Scenario 2, it is always best that an investigation should be conducted and that the CIO should in fact take the initiative before the chief executive asks the internal or external auditors to do so. Such an investigation should also determine if the security measures taken are consistent with the minimum requirements of the organization. For the IT manager concerned, the best outcome of such an investigation is one that confirms reasonable measures had been taken and that the security breach could have been prevented only by measures that would have been inconsistent with the organization's assessment of threats, vulnerabilities and residual risks.

Even under the most benevolent management regime, this outcome should occur no more than twice; the first time was bad luck, and the second time a coincidence. In many organizations, a second security breach would not be considered acceptable. The investigation may well show that the measures taken were inadequate and that the CIO or IT manager was negligent in the execution of his duties. This generally turns out to be career limiting. If the findings reveal that the CIO or IT manager was grossly or willfully negligent this opens the possibility of legal action leading to punitive damages.

Conduct intrusion detection tests

Some 15 years ago, a leading IT journal, Datamation, carried on its cover the following text: "How good is your I.T. shop? Find out before your boss does." This message remains valid today, and in the particular case of information security, it is strongly recommended that regular and serious tests be carried out to validate security arrangements before someone else exploits any weaknesses. Such tests may include one or all of the following:

— Pre-announced tests carried out by staff

— Pre-announced tests carried out by a trusted third party

— Unannounced tests by staff and/or a trusted third party

— Intrusions detected by an unknown and thus untrusted third party (hacker)

— Security tests performed during a test of the Disaster Recovery Plan

It needs to be recognised that successful tests do not constitute a guarantee. They simply mean "so far so good". At the end of such tests, any successful security breach regardless of its nature virus attack, Denial of Service attack, intrusion leading to access to data, or other, should be the subject of a detailed review of the technical and procedural weaknesses in the arrangements.

Have independent security audits carried out

It is a fact of life that many organizations do not conduct Information Systems and Technology audits with a frequency and scope that reflects the critical dependence they have on these technical means. Because of such dependence, the nature of IT audits has changed dramatically in the last few years and the IT Governance

Institute in the United States of America has issued what has effectively become the Open Standard for the Audit of IT, including all appropriate controls and security. These are referred to as COBIT (Control Objectives for Information Technology) and have been widely adopted in many countries. Similarly, ISO 17799 lends itself to form the framework for security-focused audits of Information Technology.

An organization has several choices. It can arrange for:

— Audits to be carried out by the organization's internal auditors – whenever these have adequate resources to conduct IT and, in particular, security audits

— Audits to be carried out by the organization's external auditors

— Specialised security audits to be carried out by a trusted third party

— Security audits and reviews as required for certification to ISO 17799

In the latter two cases, trust is a vital component of the audit arrangements as the auditors will, in the course of their work, have access to every detail of the security arrangements, their vulnerabilities and weaknesses. The contracts relating to such audits must include appropriate non-disclosure clauses and conditions.

Restore systems and facilities

This action is needed to restore a compromised system to normal operation and allow staff to have access to that system again, possibly even before a full analysis is completed and all corrections are made. In this case, the risk of doing so needs to be managed and monitored, in particular focusing on continued analysis of the incident, elimination of any intruders' access, and acknowledge the vulnerability to similar types of intrusion.

One of the purposes of a response process is to eliminate vulnerabilities that allow a security incident to occur and to return affected systems to full operational status. The first step towards restoring a system is the determination of the requirements and timeframe for returning the system to normal operations. This cannot be achieved without the involvement of senior management. If the system affected is mission-critical to the organization, analysis will have to continue in parallel and the system must be upgraded as soon as possible, accepting that until then the system is vulnerable to another incident of the same type. Increasing the level of system monitoring would help identify the emergence of another incident.

Any such restoration must use the latest trusted backup of user data from backup media known to be secure, as the incident may have altered user data and application program areas. Examples where this may occur include:

— The installation by an intruder of back doors to provide future access. For example, an intruder might install a program in a local user directory that is called each time the user logs in, providing an unprotected login shell that can be accessed by anyone via the Internet.

— The modification of user data to sabotage the user's work. For example, an intruder makes small unnoticed changes to spreadsheets. Depending on how the spreadsheets are used, this can cause minor to major damage. Users must be asked to check for unexpected changes to their files or data and be warned about the risk of compromise. All executable and binary files residing in user areas should be handled in the same way as system executables and binary files. If no authenticated validation is available, they must be reinstalled from the original distribution media. As the process continues, only those services required by the users of the system should be restored, i.e. not all available services.

The restored system should now be validated through tests such that the results can be compared with the results of prior tests. Once a system has been compromised, particularly by an intruder, this becomes well known in the hacker community, and as a result, the system may become a target for future attacks. Improved monitoring may reveal new attacks more easily and provide the opportunity to defeat the attacker.

Have robust and tested disaster recovery

If systems cannot be restored quickly enough to meet operational requirements, it may be necessary to invoke contingency plans and disaster recovery arrangements. The traditional practice of Disaster Recovery originated with the centralised data center and makes provision for similar facilities to be available at a separate location in the event that a data center becomes unusable as a result of fire, flooding, hurricane, etc.Depending on the criticality of the services provided by the data center, the time to recover information systems and facilities would normally range between several days (cold site recovery) and minutes (hot site recovery). There is a substantial difference in the cost of such arrangements.

As the number of technologies in a data center and in an organization's building increases, so does the complexity of disaster recovery. The logistics of moving people, data and software to another location, communicating the situation to managers, end users and other interested parties, and getting things back to work are challenging. Detailed documentation must communicated to all parties likely to be involved and, most important of all, regularly tested. Failure to test Disaster Recovery plans invariably results in having to resolve serious problems while already in crisis mode.

Global connectivity and the growing criticality of information systems and technology are gradually forcing organizations to plan for shorter and shorter recovery times, which result in greater complexity and higher cost.In addition, it is now not enough to simply recover information systems, it is also essential to guarantee some level of business continuity – the availability of facilities for employees and managers to continue to perform essential tasks in a place other than their offices, which may not be accessible or available.

Outsourcing of Information Systems

Outsourcing, the contractual transfer of responsibility for the performance of some tasks or services has been a major trend in Information Technology over the course of the last decade. Given that IT requires a growing number of staff with specialised skills and experience, many organizations choose to rely on others, whose core expertise is in the area of IT service delivery, even if this appears more expensive than an in-house arrangements. Outsourcing contracts need to be very specific as to the responsibilities of both parties, in particular with regard to cyber security and the actions to be taken in the case of a security incident.

Outsourcing does not absolve the organization from its responsibilities concerning cyber security, in particular, defining the value of the assets to be protected, creating an awareness of cyber security issues with their employees, contractors, etc. It is recommended that the contract with an outsourcing company should make provision for the ability to audit the outsourcer by the client's chosen auditors. Whilst responsibility for implementing a disaster recovery plan rests with the outsourcing vendor, arrangements for business continuity remain firmly with the organization.

5

Global Efforts to Combating Cyber Crime

The important role of information and communications technologies in today's society is no longer underestimated. These systems play critical roles in financial transactions – SWIFT (Society for worldwide inter-bank fund transfers) moves trillions of US dollars per day in electronic form; critical infrastructures are highly computerized and the amount of confidential personal information held in electronic form is just prodigious.

The lack of awareness about the scope and impact of information insecurity, and the absence of an effective ICT security strategy in many organizations, pales into insignificance in the face of the unconscionable gaps in the legislation on this issue. The gaps in legislation are easily exploited by the cyber-criminal in the full knowledge that punishment, if ever caught, would only be minor. Proper legislation would have to lie in two distinct areas –national legislation to cover issues of internal responsibility and liability, and international legislation relating to the inter-state aspects of jurisdiction, ownership, responsibility, and liability.

Since the 1970s, there has been a growing consensus that existing criminal laws covering the variety of crimes that can be committed with a computer either do not cover some computer abuses or are not strong and clear enough to discourage computer crimes and allow expeditious prosecution.

National Efforts

The history of computer-related crime begins with the history of computers. The first published accounts of computer manipulation, sabotage, espionage, and the illegal use of computer systems date back to the published press and scientific literature of the 1960s. These early computer crimes differed in type and scale from cybercrimes:

> Early computers were dedicated mainframes—and users were generally directly wired into the computers. Thus, early computer crime cases were characterized by authorized users manipulating computer programs to, for example, steal money from a bank or other employer. Other typical early computer crimes included attacks on telephone systems and networks . . . or diversion of money through electronic funds transfers. Because early users of computers were highly centralized and not very interconnected, the opportunity for computer crime tended to be limited to misuse of systems by authorized users. The nature of early computer offenses likewise was limited by the talents of the users and the nature of the non-distributed computer systems. . . . [P]rosecutors and judges were forced to deal with computer miscreants by resorting to ordinary criminal law concepts of theft, destruction of property, trespass and criminal mischief. At that time, computers tended to be large, dedicated stand-alone machines, and access . . . was generally

> restricted by limiting access to the physical terminals which were connected to the mainframe computer. As a result, virtually all computer crimes were committed by insiders or quasi-insiders. Legitimate computer users with authorized access to the computers, software developers, vendors and other authorized users were the primary perpetrators of these computer crimes. . . . .

The first empirical computer crime studies to apply criminological research methods were conducted in the 1970s. These studies verified a limited number of cases, suggesting that many more have gone undetected or unreported.

In the United States, the Senate Governmental Affairs Committee held hearings on the need for computer crime legislation in 1976, which prompted Senator Abraham Ribicoff in 1977 to introduce the Federal Computer Systems Protection Act as the first proposal for federal computer crime legislation. The bill, revised and reintroduced in 1979, declared any "knowing, willful manipulation or attempted manipulation: of "any computer owned or operated by the United States, certain financial institutions, and entities affecting interstate commerce, for the purpose of `devising or executing any scheme or artifice to defraud,' or of `obtaining money, property, or services...by means of false or fraudulent pretenses, representations, or promises'" to be "a crime and could have a jail sentence of up to 15 years." The 1979 bill died in committee, but it was influential in promoting the subsequent enactment of federal computer crime legislation and in encouraging the adoption of such legislation in two states, Arizona and Florida.

The 1980s witnessed cases of hacking, viruses, and worms, as well as program piracy, cash dispenser manipulation and telecommunication abuses. Vulnerabilities of an information-based society and limitations of existing computer security approaches, as well as the limitations of law and enforcement efforts were widely publicized in the 1990s. Computer crime has expanded in scope far beyond mere economic crime, and can be expected to include attacks against national infrastructure, security and social well being.

Computer-related criminal law has undergone similar changes, in response to the criminal evolution enabled and enhanced by information technology. Legal reforms have taken place in many countries (mostly European) since the 1970s, reflecting not only changes in technology, but also a change in legal paradigms. Prior to the mid-twentieth century, all countries' criminal codes focused principally on the protection of tangible objects. However, the emergence of an information-based society placing great value and dependence on incorporeal values and information has predicated the development of new laws to protect incorporeal values.

The first wave of law reform in most western legal systems addressed the protection of privacy, in response to emerging vast capabilities for collecting, storing and transmitting data by computer equipment. Administrative, penal and civil legislation was enacted to protect data and associated citizens' rights to privacy the following countries: Sweden, USA, Germany, Austria, Denmark, France, Norway, Luxembourg, Iceland, Israel, Australia, Canada, the United Kingdom, Finland, Ireland, Japan, Netherlands, Portugal, Belgium, Spain, Switzerland, Spain, Italy and Greece. This concern with privacy prompted constitutional amendments in Brazil, the Netherlands, Portugal and Spain.

The second wave of computer-related law reform originated in the 1980s and encompassed economic crimes. This wave was precipitated by the inadequacy of the existing traditional criminal provisions, which protect exclusively physical, tangible and visible objects against traditional crimes, in the advent of cybercrime. The new laws addressed the new capabilities of computer related crimes to violate traditional objects through new media (such as stealing money by manipulating bank accounts), to involve intangible objects (such as computer programs), and to employ new methods of committing crimes made possible by increasing use and reliance on computer systems and networks.

The following countries enacted new laws against computer-related economic crimes (including provisions against illegal access to computer systems) to deal with the new criminal realities: Italy, Australia, UK, USA, Canada, Denmark, Germany, Sweden, Austria, Japan, Norway, France, Greece, Finland, Netherlands, Luxembourg, Switzerland, Spain and Malaysia.

A third wave of amendments and additions to national laws also took place in the 1980s. This effort was directed toward providing better protection of intellectual property in the realm of computer technology. These laws include copyright protection for computer programs, including criminal copyright law and legal protection of topographies.

National legislation concerning illegal and harmful content emerged as a fourth wave in the 1980s. This type of legislation began to expand significantly with the ubiquity of the Internet, beginning in the mid-1990s. Content-related legislation has covered such topics as dissemination of pornography and pedophilia, hate speech and defamation, and the responsibility of service and access providers. The nature of content deemed illegal as well as methods for enforcement vary significantly according to national attitudes and legal systems.

International Efforts

Various international and supranational organizations have recognized the inherently transborder nature of cybercrime, the ensuing limitations of unilateral approaches, and the need for international harmonization of legal, technical, and other solutions. In particular, the Organisation for Economic Cooperation and Development (OECD), the Council of Europe, the European Union, the United Nations, and Interpol have played leading and important roles in building international awareness and cooperation in this regard.

The first comprehensive inquiry into the criminal law problems of computer crime on the international scale was initiated by the (OECD). In 1983, a group of experts met and recommended that the OECD take the initiative in trying to achieve the harmonization of European computer crime legislation. From 1983 to 1985, the OECD carried out a study of the possibility of an international application and harmonization of criminal laws to address cybercrime and abuse. The study resulted in the 1986 report *Computer-related Crime: Analysis of Legal Policy*, which surveyed existing laws and proposals for reform and recommended a minimum list of abuses that countries should consider criminalizing. This list was compiled as a result of a comparative analysis of substantive law around the world and outlined commonly recognized acts, which could constitute a shared basis for the different approaches taken by member states:

(1) the input, alteration, erasure and/or suppression of computer data and/or computer programs made wilfully with the intent to commit an illegal transfer of funds or of another thing of value;

(2) the input, alteration, erasure and/or suppression of computer data and/or computer programs made wilfully with the intent to commit a forgery;

(3) the input, alteration, erasure and/or suppression of computer data and/or computer programs, or other interference with computer systems, made wilfully with the intent to hinder the functioning of a computer and/or of a telecommunication system;

(4) the infringement of the exclusive right of the owner of a protected computer program with the intent to exploit commercially the program and put it on the market;

(5) the access to or the interception of a computer and/or telecommunication system made knowingly and without the authorization of the person responsible for the system, either by infringement of security measures or for other dishonest or harmful intentions.

From 1985 to 1989, the Select Committee of Experts on Computer-Related Crime of the Council of Europe discussed the issues raised by cybercrime and drafted Recommendation 89(9), adopted September 13, 1989. Recommendation 89(9) emphasized the importance of an adequate and quick response to cybercrime, the transborder nature of which requires harmonization of law and practice and improved international legal cooperation. It further emphasized the need for international consensus in criminalizing and addressing certain computer-related offenses. The Recommendation featured a "minimum list" of crimes to be prohibited and prosecuted by international consensus, as well as an "optional list" that describes prominent offenses on which international consensus would be difficult to reach. The "minimum list" includes:

— *"Computer Fraud"*: The input, alteration, erasure or suppression of computer data or computer programs, or other interference with the course of data processing, that influences the result of data processing thereby causing economic or possessory loss of property of another person with the intent of procuring an unlawful economic gain for himself or for another person;

— *"Computer Forgery"*: The input, alteration, erasure or suppression of computer data or computer programs, or other interference with the course of data processing, in a manner or under such conditions, as prescribed by national law, that it would constitute the offense of forgery if it had been committed with respect to a traditional object of such an offense;

— *"Damage to Computer Data or Computer Programs"*: The erasure, damaging, deterioration or suppression of computer data or computer programs without right;

— *"Computer Sabotage"*: The input, alteration, erasure or suppression of computer data or computer programs, or other interference with computer systems, with the intent to hinder the functioning of a computer or a telecommunication system;

— *"Unauthorised Access"*: The access without right to a computer system or network by infringing security measures;

— *"Unauthorised Interception"*: The interception, made without right and by technical means, of communications to, from and within a computer system or network;

— *"Unauthorised Reproduction of a Protected Computer Program"*: The reproduction, distribution or communication to the public without right of a computer program which is protected by law;

— *"Unauthorized Reproduction of a Topography"*: The reproduction without right of a topography protected by law, of a semi-conductor product, or the commercial exploitation or the importation for that purpose, done without right, of a topography or of a semi-conductor product manufactured by using the topography.

The optional list involves:

— *"Alteration of Computer Data or Computer Programs"*: The alteration of computer data or computer programs without right;

— *"Computer Espionage"*: The acquisition by improper means or the disclosure, transfer or use of a trade or commercial secret without right or any other legal justification, with intent either to cause economic loss to the person entitled to the secret or to obtain an unlawful economic advantage for oneself or a third person;

— *"Unauthorised Use of a Computer"*: The use of a computer system or network without right, that either: (a) is made with the acceptance of a significant risk of loss being caused to the person entitled to use the system or harm to the system or its functioning, or (b) is made with the intent to cause loss to the person entitled to use the system or harm to the system or its functioning, or (c) causes loss to the person entitled to use the system or harm to the system or its functioning;

— *"Unauthorised Use of a Protected Computer Program"*: The use without right of a computer program which is protected by law and which has been reproduced without right, with the intent, either to procure an unlawful economic gain for himself or for another person or to cause harm to the holder of the right."

In 1990, the Eighth United Nations Congress on the Prevention of Crime and the Treatment of Offenders addressed the legal problems posed by cybercrime. The Congress produced a resolution calling for Member States to intensify their efforts to combat computer crime by modernizing their national criminal laws and procedures, improving computer security and prevention measures, and promoting the development of a comprehensive international framework of guidelines and standards for preventing, prosecuting, and punishing computer-related crime in the future. Most notably, the resolution called for Member States to intensify their efforts toward the modernisation of national criminal laws and procedures, including measures to:

(a) Ensure that existing offences and laws concerning investigative powers and admissibility of evidence in judicial proceedings adequately apply and, if necessary, make appropriate changes;

(b) In the absence of laws that adequately apply, create offences and investigative and evidentiary procedures, where necessary, to deal with this novel and sophisticated form of criminal activity;

(c) Provide for the forfeiture or restitution of illegally acquired assets resulting from the commission of computer-related crimes.

In 1990, the Third Committee of the United Nations General Assembly drafted a resolution inviting governments to be guided by the resolutions adopted at the Eighth United Nations Congress in "the formulation of appropriate legislation and policy directives." The General Assembly adopted this resolution on December 14, 1990.

In 1992, the Council of the OECD and 24 of its Member countries adopted the Recommendation of the Council Concerning Guidelines for the Security of Information Systems, intended to provide a foundational information security framework for the public and private sectors. The *Guidelines for the Security of Information Systems* were annexed to the Recommendation. This framework includes laws, codes of conduct, technical measures, management and user practices, and public education provisions.

The *Guidelines* focus on the implementation of minimum standards for the security of information systems. In parallel, however, the *Guidelines* request that Member States establish adequate penal, administrative or other sanctions for misuse of information systems, and develop means for mutual assistance, extradition and other international cooperation in matters of security of information systems.

In 1995 the United Nations Manual on the Prevention and Control of Computer-Related Crime was published. The *Manual* examines the phenomenon of computer crime, substantive criminal law protecting the holder of data and information, substantive criminal law protecting privacy, procedural law, crime prevention in the computer environment, and the need for and avenues to international cooperation.

In 1995, Interpol held its first international conference on computer crime. The conference confirmed a high level of concern in the law enforcement community over the propagation of computer crime; Conference participants were especially troubled by the lack of a worldwide mechanism to address such crime effectively and efficiently. Interpol held subsequent conferences on computer crime in 1995, 1996, 1998 and 2000. Interpol's approach to cybercrime has been to harness the expertise of its members in the field of Information Technology Crime (ITC) through the vehicle of a 'working party' or a group of experts. In this instance, the working party consists of the Heads or experienced members of national computer crime units. These working parties have been designed to reflect regional expertise and exist in Europe, Asia, the Americas and in Africa. All working parties are in different stages of development.

The first Interpol working party, the European Working Party on Information Technology Crime, was established in 1990; the other three working parties were established later. Interpol has also established a Steering Committee for Information Technology Crime, which coordinates and harmonizes the initiatives of the various working parties.

In 1995, the Council of Europe adopted Recommendation No. R (95)13 of the Committee of Ministers to Member states, spelling out the principles that should guide states and their investigating authorities in the field of information technology. The principles cover search and seizure, technical surveillance, obligations to co-operate with the investigating authorities, electronic evidence, use of encryption, research, statistics and training, and international cooperation.

In 1996 and 1997, the European Commission issued several documents dealing with harmful and illegal content online and with the safe use of the Internet. On April 24, 1997, the European Parliament adopted a resolution on the European Commission's "communication on illegal and harmful content on the Internet, supporting the initiatives undertaken by the Commission and stressing the need for international co-operation in various areas, to be initiated by the Commission." And in April of 1998 the European Commission presented the European Council with a report on computer-related crime for which it had contracted.

In 1997, the Justice and Interior Ministers of the Group of Eight (G8) met in Washington and adopted ten Principles to Combat High-Tech Crime:

I. There must be no safe havens for those who abuse information technologies.

II. Investigation and prosecution of international high-tech crimes must be coordinated among all concerned States, regardless of where harm has occurred.

III. Law enforcement personnel must be trained and equipped to address high-tech crimes.

IV. Legal systems must protect the confidentiality, integrity, and availability of data and systems from unauthorized impairment and ensure that serious abuse is penalized.

V. Legal systems should permit the preservation of and quick access to electronic data, which are often critical to the successful investigation of crime.

VI. Mutual assistance regimes must ensure the timely gathering and exchange of evidence in cases involving international high-tech crime.

VII. Transborder electronic access by law enforcement to publicly available (open source) information does not require authorization from the State where the data resides.

VIII. Forensic standards for retrieving and authenticating electronic data for use in criminal investigations and prosecutions must be developed and employed.

IX. To the extent practicable, information and telecommunications systems should be designed to help prevent and detect network abuse, and should also facilitate the tracing of criminals and the collection of evidence.

X. Work in this area should be coordinated with the work of other relevant international fora to ensure against duplication of efforts.200 The Ministers also adopted the Action Plan to Combat High-Tech Crime in which, among other things, they pledged to "[r]eview our legal systems to ensure that they appropriately criminalize abuses of telecommunications and computer systems and to promote the investigation of hightech crimes."

In 1997, the OECD Directorate for Science, Technology and Industry directed a five-year review of the progress that had been made toward implementing the 1992 *Guidelines for the Security of Information Systems*, discussed above. The review was conducted by means of a questionnaire issued to OECD Member countries. The review disclosed, among other things, that the responding countries had experienced difficulties in developing laws and procedures relating to information security because of "differences in the various legal systems and how they deal with security matters . . . such as . . . computer crimes." The general consensus was that the *Guidelines* were still adequate and did not need to be revised.

In 1997, the Council of Europe's European Committee on Crime Problems (CDPC) created a new Committee of Experts on Crime in CyberSpace (PC-CY). The Committee of Experts on Crime in Cyberspace was assigned to examine—"in light of Recommendations No R (89) 9 . . . and No R (95) 13"—the problems "of criminal procedural law connected with information technology" including, *inter alia*, "cyberspace offences" and "other substantive criminal law issues where a common approach may be necessary for the purposes of international co-operation". The new Committee was also given the task of drafting "a binding legal instrument" dealing with these issues.

The Council of Europe's Committee of Experts on Crime in Cyber-Space took this assignment to heart, preparing a Convention on Cyber-Crime. The preparation of the Convention was a long process, taking four years and twenty-seven drafts before the final version, dated May 25, 2001, was submitted to the European Committee on Crime Problems at its 50th Plenary Session, June 18-22, 2001.

The Chapter II of the Draft Convention on Cyber-Crime "measures to be taken at the national level," is divided into Section one, "substantive criminal law" and Section two, "procedural law." The Explanatory Memorandum accompanying the Draft Convention indicates that Section 1 seeks to: improve the means to prevent and suppress computer- or computer – related crime by establishing a common minimum standard of relevant offences. This kind of harmonisation alleviates the fight against such crimes on the national and on the international level as well. Correspondence in domestic law may prevent abuses from being shifted to a Party with a previous lower standard. As a consequence, the exchange of useful common experiences in the practical handling of cases may be enhanced, too. International cooperation is facilitated e.g. regarding requirements of double criminality.

Parties to the Convention would agree to adopt legislation and other measures necessary to establish certain activities as cybercrimes under domestic law. The activities are set out in five titles to Chapter II:

(1) illegal interception of and/or interference with computer data, illegal access to and/or interference with computer systems, and the misuse of devices to commit any of these offenses;

(2) computerrelated forgery and fraud;

(3) child pornography;

(4) the infringement of copyright and related rights; and

(5) provisions governing the imposition of aiding and abetting and corporate liability.

Parties also agree to establish "effective, proportionate and dissuasive criminal . . . sanctions" for the commission of any of the specified offenses. The Parliamentary Assembly of the Council of Europe approved the Draft Convention on Cyber Crime at its April, 2001 session, and it was opened for signature by the member states on November 23, 2001.

In May of 2000, the G8 held a cybercrime conference to discuss "how to jointly crack down on Internet crime."

The conference, which brought together "about 300 judges, police, diplomats and business leaders from the G8 states—the United States, Japan, Germany, Britain, France, Italy, Canada and Russia, drafted an agenda for a follow-up summit to be held in July. At the July, 2000 summit, the G8 issued a communiqué which declared, in pertinent part, that it would "take a concerted approach to high-tech crime, such as cyber-crime, which could seriously threaten security and confidence in the global information society." The communiqué noted that the G8's approach to these matters was set out in paragraph eight of the Okinawa Charter on Global Information Society:

> "International efforts to develop a global information society must be accompanied by co-ordinated action to foster a crime-free and secure cyberspace. We must ensure that effective measures, as set out in the OECD Guidelines for Security of Information Systems, are put in place to fight cybercrime. G8 co-operation within the framework of the Lyon Group on Transnational Organised Crime will be enhanced. We will further promote dialogue with industry. . . . Urgent security issues such as hacking and viruses also require effective policy responses. We will continue to engage industry and other stakeholders to protect critical information infrastructures. The G8 also pledged to establish a "Digital Opportunity Taskforce" which would explore how to integrate the efforts of the G8 members into "a broader international approach." The Taskforce held meetings during the late 2000 and early 2001 and submitted a report containing their Proposed Plan of Action to the personal representatives of the G8 leaders in May, 2001. The report did not address cybercrime, but focused instead on the need to overcome the "digital divide." In June of 2000, an Action Plan prepared by the European Commission and the European Council was adopted by the Feira Summit of the European

> Council. Among other things, the Action Plan called for the "establishment of a co-ordinated and coherent approach to cybercrime by the end of 2002."

A Commission report issued subsequently explained that, "an EU legislative instrument approximating substantive criminal law in the field of computer-related crime has been on the EU agenda" since October, 1999. The report noted that the "Commission has followed the work of the Council of Europe on" the Draft Convention on Cyber-Crime discussed above. It also explained that the European Union's planned approximation on substantive cybercrime law "could go further than the C.o.E Convention, which will represent a minimum of international cooperation", could "be operational within a shorter period of time" and "would bring computer crime within the realms of EU law and introduce EU law enforcement mechanisms." This portion of the report then goes on to announce four measures the European Commission plans to take:

1) introduce a proposal for a Council Framework Decision that will include provisions for the approximation of laws on child pornography on the Internet, laws that go further than the measures contemplated by the Council of Europe's Draft Convention on Cybercrime;

2) bring forward a proposal to approximate high tech offenses, notably "hacking and denial of service attacks", which will include standard definitions and "go further than the draft Council of Europe Convention by ensuring that serious cases of hacking and denial of service attacks are punishable by a minimum penalty in all Member States";

3) "examine the scope for action against racism and xenophobia on the Internet with a view to bringing

forward a proposal for a Council Framework Decision . . . covering both offline and on-line racist and xenophobic activity";

4) consider "how to improve the effectiveness of efforts against the illicit drugs trade on the Internet."

Cumulatively, national efforts and those of international organizations have reinforced each other, achieving nearly global attention to the problems of cybercrime and terrorism, and promoting international harmonization of legal approaches. National efforts at combating cybercrime encompass different levels of sophistication and priority, but are present in at least 40 major countries. These countries represent all parts of the world and run the gamut of advanced, industrialized and developing nations. Many countries are developing specialized police capabilities through equipment, training and laws.

International and supranational organizations have significantly contributed to the harmonization of criminal law as well as of underlying civil and administrative law in all of the areas of computerrelated criminal law reform. Ulrich Sieber, author of the cybercrime study commissioned by the European Commission, found a close interrelationship between law reform at the national level and activities on the international and supranational level. As Sieber explained, "the preparation of the respective initiatives had a considerable impact on national laws by bringing the major national players together."

The European Community's power to adopt binding directives opened a new age of legal harmony in Europe, and the process continues. Similar efforts are taking place in other parts of the world. But even as these efforts progress, global cybercrime law continues to be a patchwork of new laws, old laws and no laws. Experts emphasize the persistent need for the development of comprehensive, consistent national legal frameworks that can be integrated into a global cybercrime strategy; the existence of such laws is a fundamental prerequisite for investigation, as well as for prosecution.

Consensus Crimes

The notion of consensus crimes is oxymoronic insofar as it implies there are fundamental differences in the way nations go about defining the conduct that will result in the imposition of a society's harshest sanctions. In fact, there is a great deal of consistency, across geography and across time, in how countries delineate outlawed behaviors. This consistency derives from the function of criminal law: to maintain social order within a society. To do that, countries must establish prohibitions that are designed to maintain the integrity of certain vital interests: the safety of persons; the security of property; the stability of the government; and the sanctity of particular moral principles.

No society can survive if its constituents are free to harm each other at will, to appropriate each other's property, to undermine the political order and/or to flout the moral principles the citizenry hold dear. Every society will therefore formulate penal prohibitions defining :

(i) crimes against persons (e.g., murder, assault, rape);

(ii) crimes against property (e.g., theft, arson, fraud);

(iii) crimes against the state (e.g., treason, rioting, obstruction of justice); and

(iv) crimes against morality (e.g., obscene materials, defiling a place of worship).

The greatest degree of consistency will be found in the first two categories which represent the *malum in se* crimes, the absolute prohibitions a society must establish if it is to maintain a modicum of social order because they involve the direct infliction of harm by one person upon another or others.

There will be consistency as to a core of offenses in the third category, e.g., treason, riot, and obstructing justice, because every society must also ensure the stability of its political order. But there will be more overall deviation in this category because nations vary in terms of the extent to which they feel it necessary to discourage political dissidence. Finally, there will be a great deal of inconsistency as to offenses in the fourth category because they are the product of a society's values and religious principles and, as such, tend to be much more idiosyncratic in nature.

Any effort to devise consensus crimes as an instrument for harmonizing national cybercrime laws needs to take account of, and build upon, consistencies that exist in the articulation of terrestrial crimes. The more these consensus crimes mirror the definitions of traditional crimes, the more likely it is that countries will be willing to incorporate them into their penal codes. It will, for example, be easier to devise consensus crimes that deal with *malum in se* offenses such as burglary, larceny and property damage than with crimes such as pornography or gambling because the definitions of the former will be far more consistent across national boundaries than the latter.

All countries will outlaw acts falling into the first category, and will do so in relatively standard terms because the prohibitions are directed at a finite range of conduct. As to pornography and gambling, countries will vary widely in their prohibitions of the former, and some will, and some will not, prohibit the latter. Building upon previously existing legal concepts also makes the process more efficient and more effective; trying to create new law from scratch is a very timeconsuming process, and the technology and the threat is constantly marching on. For another, identifying fundamental consistencies in the structure of penal codes can help to identify those areas where consensus crimes are most likely to be needed.

Unlike civil statutes, which tend to prescribe standards and behaviors, criminal statutes are prohibitionary, i.e., they prohibit the behaviors used to achieve specified results. A criminal statute is designed to prevent a forbidden result, or "harm," by outlawing it and imposing a more or less heinous penalty upon those who achieve (and who endeavor to achieve) that result. The focus of such a statute is therefore on the prohibited result, and its ability to encompass the use of computer technology in achieving that result will depend on the extent to which the statute is phrased in terms that transcend the differences between physical reality and virtual reality.

Crime agianst Persons

The purpose of developing consensus crimes is to provide a means of filling the gaps in a country's existing penal law that do not allow the prosecution of cybercrimes. Gaps exist either (a) because a country has not yet outlawed entirely "new" types of criminal activity (such as cyberstalking) or (b) because the language a country has employed to define traditional crimes is so based in physical reality it cannot encompass the use of computer technology to commit those crimes.

Since both homicide and rape, perhaps the oldest forms of criminal activity, are crimes that are firmly grounded in physical reality, neither falls into the first category; every country will have long ago outlawed the acts of taking another person's life and of forcibly having sexual intercourse.

Homicide does not fall into the second category because homicide crimes are defined in terms of a prohibited result—the death of another person or persons—that transcends the differences between physical and virtual reality. The focus is on the result—the method is for the most part irrelevant. Penal codes do not, for instance, parse the result into "homicide by gun," "homicide by strangulation," "homicide by poison" and so on; they simply prohibit causing the death of another human being. Existing homicides statutes should therefore encompass the use of computer technology to cause the death of another person or persons.

Rape will not fall into the second category as long as it continues to prohibit coerced physical sexual intercourse between two or more people because such an act cannot be consummated in cyberspace or via the medium of computer technology; existing rape statutes should therefore apply even if computer technology were somehow to be used as the means of perpetrating rape (to identify a victim, say).

As to other physical crimes against persons, assault-type statutes and kidnapping statutes should be able to encompass whatever role computer technology comes to play in the commission of these crimes; as should child abuse and suicide statutes. The same should generally be true for statutes defining non-physical crimes against persons, such as invasions of privacy and defamation. So far, the truly problematic crimes in this category are those targeting harassment or intimidation: The prohibited result is usually a direct threat to cause physical harm to the victim or the victim's family; statutes that prohibit the generic communication of such a threat should reach the use of computer technology to that end.

Unfortunately, the Internet and its facilitation of anonymous communication have generated varieties of harassment that do not involve the transmission of a direct threat to cause physical injury and so cannot be prosecuted under existing law; to reach this type of conduct, nations will have to enact statutes that broaden the prohibited result.

Crimes against Property

The prohibited results are wrongfully taking another's property (embezzlement, theft, robbery, fraud, forgery); wrongfully damaging or destroying another's property (vandalism, arson); and wrongfully intruding upon another's property (trespass, burglary). Since crimes against property are also among the oldest types of criminal activity, prohibitions directed at these results are standard features of every penal code.

Computer technology makes the application of these prohibitions problematic in certain respects. Unlike the harassment statutes discussed in the preceding paragraph, the problem here lies not with the characterization of the prohibited results but with the conceptualization of "property." The formulations of offenses falling into this category have always been predicated upon the notion that "property" is a real-world, physical construct, i.e., a tangible item.

Conceptualizing property in this way imposes significant limitations upon the application of theft, damage and intrusion statutes to conduct occurring in and via cyberspace because in cyberspace property becomes an intangible item. Cyberspace property can consist, for instance, of electronic data which has value because it represents funds one can expend in the "real world"; cyberspace property also consists of software, of domain names and of "pure" information, all of which are valuable in and of themselves.

Some transgressions against intangible property can be prosecuted using traditional crimes against property statutes, but some cannot. If a hacker breaks into a bank's computer system and electronically transfers $1 million from Bill Gates' account into an account she controls, this is theft, even under traditional theft statutes; the possession and use of the funds has been completely transferred from Gates to the hacker even though at no time did the hacker have physical possession of real currency.

But if a hacker breaks into the computer system of a biotech research corporation, copies secret information about the company's research and takes the copies, this is not theft in the traditional sense because the company has not been totally deprived of the information; it still has its property, though the value of that property has no doubt been diluted by the thief's actions.

The same tends to be true of property damage or destruction statutes, which were drafted to prohibit the acts of damaging or destroying tangible property; it may, for example, be impossible to use a vandalism statute to prosecute a hacker who defaces a web site. Property intrusion statutes also suffer from the same defect in characterization, though it plays a somewhat different role in this context.

Criminal trespass and burglary statutes were developed to deal with persons who physically entered a material space—real world property—without being authorized to do so. Since these statutes require an actual physical intrusion into a tangible physical area, they cannot be used to prosecute a hacker who metaphorically "breaks into" a computer system; while the computer system is itself a form of real world property, and while the hacker does in a sense "enter into" that system, the concepts traditionally used to operationalize the trespass crimes simply do not apply to the hacker's conduct. Consensus crimes are, therefore, needed to update the traditional categories of crimes against property.

Computer technology has also produced an activity which has all the hallmarks of a crime against property but which does not fit into any of the existing offense categories. When a commercial web site is attacked, the site becomes inaccessible to visitors and the operator of the site loses some volume of business. The victim has clearly been deprived of "property," in the form of the lost revenues, but this is not theft because the attacker has not been enriched; the attacker has not appropriated any property from the victim. It is not vandalism because the web site has not been physically damaged or destroyed; and it is not trespass because the attacker never penetrates the victim's web site—the attack is mounted from the outside. It is, however, a crime against property; just as in traditional crimes against property, the victim sustains a loss as the result of the criminal's acts. This, then, is an area in which a consensus crime must be devised to deal with a "new" type of cybercrime.

Crime against State

Crimes against the state consists of a set of core offenses every country will outlaw plus another set of distinctive offenses found in one or more nations. The core offenses include the crimes of treason, counterfeiting, rioting, and obstructing justice.

Treason, the act of levying war against one's country or supporting its enemies, is a crime the prohibitions of which, like those directed at homicide, are very much focused on a specific result; traditional treason statutes should therefore encompass the use of computer technology to achieve this result, so that neither new, cyber-treason statutes nor modifications in existing statues will be required.

Traditional rioting statutes may not encompass the use of computer technology to instigate rioting or other forms of public disorder, so this is an area where new legislation can be needed. Computer technology should not affect the application of traditional counterfeiting statues since, as one author noted, "[u]sing a computer, a scanner, graphics software, and a high-quality color laser printer for forgery or counterfeiting is the same crime as using an old-fashioned printing press with ink".

Obstructing justice is an area where existing laws may need to be modified: Statutes in this area prohibit, among other things, creating, modifying or destroying evidence; to the extent that such statutes conceptualize evidence solely as a tangible commodity, they will need to be modified to include acts directed at electronic evidence. Also, existing obstruction of justice statutes may not address acts such as, for example, hacking into a court system's computers and altering or deleting charges against a perpetrator or warrants issued for his arrest.

While it might seem that these issues are a matter of local concern, and therefore not the likely focus of consensus crime categories, that is in fact not the case; the transnational character of cybercrime means that countries depend upon each other, in large part, to gather and preserve evidence and, to a lesser extent, to facilitate the identification and apprehension of known offenders. If a cybercriminal can exploit loopholes in one country's obstruction of justice laws, this can have a negative impact on other countries, the citizens of which have been victimized by that cybercriminal's activities.

Crimes agianst Morality

Crimes against morality is the one in which there will be the least consistency in the creation and definition of offenses. This lack of consistency has two implications for the articulation of consensus crimes: the lack of consistency means that what is a crime in some countries (gambling, say) is not a crime elsewhere, so this category is *generally* not likely to be a source of consensus crimes; the lack of consistency also means that it would *generally* be difficult to gain acceptance for consensus crimes developed for this category.

The qualifications are necessary because it is sometimes difficult to decide whether an activity—such as child pornography—is a "crime against persons" or a "crime against morality." Child pornography, at least non-virtual child pornography, clearly falls into both categories: a crime against persons is committed when real children are used to produce child pornography; and the creation, distribution and possession of child pornography is considered a crime against morality in many nations, just as the dissemination of adult pornography is often considered to be a crime against morality.

Child pornography in some guise is therefore an area that will almost certainly be the focus of one or more consensus crimes. Victimless crimes like the use of drugs and alcohol, gambling and prostitution fall into the category of crimes against morality, but this type of prohibition tends to be so tied into parochial standards of morality it is unlikely to yield consensus crimes. The same is true of offenses that prohibit acts directed at religious observances or symbols. There are other activities that, like child pornography, do not fit neatly into any one category.

Terrorism is one: it can be considered a crime against persons because terrorist acts inflict injury and death, a crime against property because property is often damaged by terrorist acts, and/or a crime against the state because the terrorist's goal is to undermine the stability of that state by generating chaos and destruction.

The characterization of terrorism is further complicated by the fact that nations disagree as to what is, and is not, a terrorist act; the British described the American revolutionaries as terrorists but to modern Americans they were heroic freedom fighters. For that reason, perhaps, countries tend to prosecute terrorist acts as crimes against persons and crimes against property, reducing the acts to their constituent results instead of treating them as a distinct category of criminal activity. This suggests terrorism is not a likely candidate for a consensus crime.

Analyzing consistencies in the articulation of traditional crimes suggests that consensus crimes are needed and are likely to be accepted in these areas:

defining "new" crimes against persons, for example, online stalking and harassment; revising extant crimes against property so they encompass acts directed at intangible property; defining "new" crimes against property that encompass denial of service attacks and other emerging types of property damage; revising obstruction of justice crimes so they encompass, *inter alia,* the creation, alteration, admissibility and destruction of electronic evidence; defining "new" crimes directed at obstructing justice, such as tampering with court records; and revising some crimes against morality, notably child pornography, to encompass the use of computer technology.

Since the property crimes are the most consistently problematic, and since the business community and global financial markets have an enormous stake in ensuring the safety of property, this area will no doubt be among the first of these to be addressed. The analysis of consistencies in the articulation of traditional crimes also suggests that consensus crimes are otherwise not likely to be developed (a) because cybercrime can be prosecuted under existing offense-definitions or (b) because there is a lack of agreement between nations as to what should and should not be criminalized. And while it may seem as if consensus might be an impossible goal to reach, evidence would suggest that more and more nations around the world are moving towards consensus in their approaches to crime in cyberspace.

Efforts to Build Consensus

Though some might look at the recently adopted Council of Europe Treaty on Cybercrime and suggest that the notion of building consensus on crime in cyberspace is a relatively new phenomenon, a review of history clearly shows consensus has been building over the last two decades. Indeed, the need for building consensus is apparent to those involved in combating cybercrime. Thus, there have been a series of efforts undertaken to build consensus around a set of core crimes.

In 1986, the Organization for Economic Cooperation and Development issued a report that contained a list of acts countries should criminalize; aside from software piracy, the acts involved attacks on computers, computer systems or computer data. In 1989, the Council of Europe's Select Committee of Experts on Computer-Related Crime issued a similar list, which became the foundation of the Convention on Cyber Crime.

In 1990, the Eighth United Nations Congress on the Prevention of Crime and the Treatment of Offenders produced a resolution that called for Member States to modernize their laws by, among other things, creating offenses, where necessary, to "deal with this novel and sophisticated form of criminal activity". While the United Nations' work in 1990 produced a number of resolutions related to cybercrime, information security, and the protection of privacy, it wasn't until 1994 that the UN published its Manual on the Prevention and Control of Computer-related Crime, wherein specific computer related crimes were introduced and explained to member nations. The UN *Computer Crime Manual* was not put forth as a treaty remedy per se, rather it was educational in nature. The manual however did recognize the need for consensus vis-à-vis cybercrime:

Given the international scope of telecommunications and computer communications, the transborder nature of many computer crimes and the acknowledged barriers within current forms of international cooperation, a concerted international effort is required to address the problem effectively. Attempts to define computer crime, or at least achieve common conceptions of what is comprises, and to harmonize the procedural processes for sanctioning it have a number of benefits.

The benefits of building consensus around offenses to be prohibited in cyberspace has been building for sometime. As time passed, the call for consensus became not only louder and more clear, but also more specific and well honed. That is to say, supra national cooperative bodies continued to present with greater and greater detail not only substantive criminal laws to be adopted to combat cybercrime, but a number of procedural legal changes as well.

In 1997, Ministers of the Group of Eight adopted an Action Plan to Combat High-Tech Crime in which the Member States each pledged to review their legal systems to ensure that they "appropriately criminalize abuses of telecommunications and computer systems". Work of the G8 is ongoing and a number of subsequent conferences, meetings, and sub-group get-togethers have taken place.

In 2000, the European Commission issued a report announcing anti-cybercrime measures the Commission planned to take; these measures focused on the adoption of penal law outlawing various activities, which not only included attacks on computer systems but also addressed the use of the Internet to disseminate child pornography and hate speech and its role in promoting the trafficking of illegal drugs.

There have been a number of attempts seeking to promote the definition of consensus crimes; for the purposes of this discussion it is sufficient to analyze two such efforts, because they illustrate the types of activities these attempt focus on. They are (a) Council of Europe Convention and (b) The CISAC Convention.

Council of Europe Convention: The consensus crime provisions of the Council of Europe's Convention on Cyber Crime conform to the propositions set out above. The Convention does not itself define the crimes as to which it seeks consensus; instead, the Convention lists nine offense categories, and parties to the Convention agree to "adopt such legislative and other measures" as are necessary to define the activity encompassed by each category "as criminal offences under [their] domestic law."

The nine categories represent eight property crimes and one non-property crime: illegal access; illegal interception; data interference; system interference; misuse of devices; forgery; fraud; child pornography; and copyright infringement and related offenses.

The first five offense categories are all concerned with outlawing "new" crimes against property; they do this, for the most part, by requiring signatory nations to adopt legislation creating electronic versions of existing property crimes. The illegal access provision requires them to make electronic trespass, or hacking, illegal. The illegal interception provision requires the creation of an electronic invasion of privacy/burglary offense that prohibits unauthorized intrusions resulting in the appropriation of "property" in the form of data.

The data interference provision requires the creation of a property damage offense, the "property" again being data. The system interference provision deals with conduct which has no analogue in terrestrial crime, so it requires signatory nations to create a entirely new offense (or offenses) that criminalize denial of service attacks and the dissemination of viruses and other malicious codes.

Finally, the misuse of devices provision requires signatory nations to outlaw electronic burglary tools, that is, to make it a crime to produce, sell, procure, import and/or distribute tools to be used in committing any of these four property crimes. This is, first of all, an inchoate offense that targets preparatory steps taken toward committing the target crimes; it also imposes aiding and abetting liability upon those who provide tools that are actually used to commit one of these crimes; and it imposes an inchoate, attempt-to-aid-and-abet liability upon those who produce and distribute such tools regardless of whether they are actually used to commit one of those crimes.

Three of the next four offense categories also deal with property crimes, but they are not concerned with defining "new" crimes: One requires signatory nations to outlaw computer-related fraud, another does the same for computer-related forgery, and the third requires nations to criminalize computer-related infringements of copyrights and related rights. All three deal with updating traditional property crimes to incorporate the use of computer technology as a tool for committing the crime; infringement of copyright and related rights is, after all, simply a form of theft, i.e., the misappropriation of intangible property.

The non-property crime is child pornography: The Convention requires signatory nations to "modernize" their law so it "more effectively circumscribe[s] the use of computer systems" to produce, distribute and/or possess child pornography. The architects of the Convention recognized that most countries already criminalize these activities, but thought it advisable to emphasize that laws need to be modernized to address "the ever-increasing use of the Internet as the primary instrument for trading such material."

The CISAC Convention: The CISAC Convention is unofficial, the product of a conference held at Stanford University in 1999, but its rather different approach to the development of consensus crimes is still instructive. The provisions of the Convention are to some extent consistent with the propositions set out above, but there are some notable departures.

Like the Council of Europe Convention, the CISAC Convention does not define the crimes as to which it seeks to establish consensus; instead, parties to the Convention agree to "adopt such measures as may be necessary" to criminalize conduct falling into seven offense categories. Specifically, they would agree to criminalize the following: illegal entry into a computer system; manipulating data to disrupt the functioning of a computer system; manipulating data to cause "substantial damage" to persons or property; interfering with computer security measures; manufacturing or distributing a device used to commit an offense defined under the Convention; using computer technology to engage in activity outlawed by a list of treaties; and committing any of the above offenses "with the purpose of targeting the critical infrastructure" of any nation that is a party to the Convention.

The drafters of the CISAC Convention did not include provisions directed at computer-related forgery, fraud, theft or conversion because "they are in general already encompassed in extradition treaties". The first four offense categories are concerned with "new" types of crimes against property: the illegal entry provision requires parties to make computer trespass a crime; the manipulating data provisions require them to make computer-related property damage (damaging a computer system or using a computer system to damage property) a crime; and the evading computer security provision requires parties to criminalize one step in the commission of a computer-trespass/burglary offense.

The "computer damage" projected that consensus crimes would concentrate on crimes against property and would not focus on crimes involving physical injury to persons. This provision, however, requires parties to define a crime against persons along with a crime against property.

The fifth offense category is analogous to the "electronic burglary tools" provision included in the Council of Europe's Convention, but the CISAC version sweeps more broadly in that it requires parties to criminalize the manufacture or distribution of devices that can be used to commit *any* crime defined pursuant to the Convention. Like the Council of Europe provision, this offense category is directed at conduct that can facilitate (i.e., aid and abet) the commission of such a crime. But since this provision, like the Council of Europe's version, does not require that the device have been used to commit a crime, it actually imposes both aiding and abetting liability and inchoate liability for attempting-to-aid-and-abet the commission of such a crime.

Unlike the Council of Europe's version, this offense category does not impose inchoate liability for the act of acquiring a device as a preparatory step toward committing such a substantive crime. The CISAC provision does require parties to criminalize using such a device to commit a crime defined pursuant to the Convention, which is analogous to making it a crime to use a firearm in the course of committing a felony.

The last two offense categories are unlike anything in the Council of Europe's Convention. The first requires parties to make it a crime to use a computer "as a material factor in committing an act" outlawed by any of several treaties. The treaties impose criminal liability for engaging in specified acts of terrorism, drug trafficking, hostage-taking, aircraft high-jacking and sabotage. Since the treaties already criminalize these acts, this offense category is, like the provision noted in the previous paragraph, analogous to statutes that make it an offense to use a firearm to commit a felony.

The final offense category requires parties to make it a crime to commit any of the above offenses "with a purpose of targeting the critical infrastructure of any State Party" to the CISAC Convention. To comply, parties would have to create the separate crime of "using a computer or computer system to commit [one of the specified offenses] for the purpose of attacking the critical infrastructure" of specified nations. This would mean, for example, that someone who uses a device outlawed under the fifth offense category to by-pass computer security measures and illegally gain entry into a computer system to attack the critical infrastructure of a qualifying nation has already committed four crimes under the CISAC Convention. If the offender were to go further and use the computer system to cause "substantial damage" to property, he or she would have committed five crimes under the Convention, and if the damage to property were of a type outlawed by one of the incorporated treaties, the perpetrator would have committed at least six.

This type of layering, or compounding, of liability for a single course of conduct is unusual, found in statutes that attack complex, larger-scale criminal activity. Traditional criminal statutes are based on the premise that it is sufficient to articulate one offense that encompasses a single, sequential course of conduct; complex criminal statutes parse conduct into segments and allow the imposition of liability for each segment.

The CISAC Convention is only incidentally concerned with crimes against property or persons, as such; its primary focus is on outlawing the use of computer technology to commit terrorist and terrorist-style acts. The Convention eschews traditional (fraud, forgery, theft, burglary) and non-traditional (copyright infringement) crimes against property, as well as child pornography. The *Commentary* for the Convention explains that the drafters did not address copyright infringement or child pornography because "their inclusion [might] prove controversial." It goes on to note, though, that "a sufficient consensus for including some of these offenses—especially the use of computers for sexual exploitation of minors—may exist", and that offense categories directed at these crimes could be added to the Convention.

The CISAC Convention's focus on terrorism also runs counter to the prediction that terrorism would not be a good candidate for a consensus crime because countries disagree on what "terrorism" is. The drafters of the Convention dealt with this issue in two ways: They built upon a level of existing consensus by incorporating the provisions of treaties that have already defined a variety of terrorist acts. They also expanded upon those definitions by adding computer-related acts directed at "the critical infrastructure" of a signatory party, assuming, perhaps, that nations would find this expansion acceptable because it reaches conduct designed to undermine national integrity.

Limits of Penal Law Constistency

Penal law has evolved to maintain order *within* a society. Each nation-state is concerned with fulfilling its obligations to its citizens (protecting their lives, property and morality) and with ensuring its own survival. As noted earlier, prohibitions barring crimes against persons and property arose because no nation can survive if its citizens are free to prey upon each other. But what if they prey upon citizens of *another* society? What if the citizens of Nation A use cyberspace to prey upon the citizens of Nations B and C? Is this a matter that is likely to be of great concern to Nation A? There are no ready answers to these questions, but there are historical precedents for this type of behavior that may shed some light on what will ensue in cyberspace. The most analogous of these involve high-seas piracy and intellectual piracy.

High-seas piracy has been around for centuries; indeed, until the seventeenth century it was "widely sanctioned" in most countries, a "national industry." Early in the seventeenth century, the nations of Europe banded together to battle the "infidel" Turkish pirates who had expanded from the Mediterranean into the North Atlantic; by the end of the century, increased trade was transforming attitudes toward piracy. "The advantage to be derived from stealing from one another was giving way to the greater advantage of stable commercial relations."

In the eighteenth century, European countries began a war on piracy that included warning other nations "to cease sponsoring pirate expeditions and to crack down on . . . pirates operating . . . from their territories." These efforts were not immediately successful, in part because many non-European nations and even some European colonies resisted, regarding them as unwelcome infringements. This was certainly true in the American colonies, where "business executives and public officials alike continued to provide havens . . . for pirate ships for decades after London ordered a halt to such activities".

Piracy therefore persisted well into the nineteenth century; it was not until 1849, for instance, that British forces finally eliminated pirate bases in Crete and Borneo after local rulers refused to act, and pirate havens in the West Indies survived until the 1820s. But by the end of the nineteenth century, piracy had been pretty much eliminated around the world: "As . . . the high seas ceased to be perceived as a no-man's-land, larceny at sea became less justifiable." The prohibition against piracy has been described as the first consensus crime. High-seas pirates looted tangible property—gold, silver, jewels and other objects.

For intangible, intellectual piracy to develop there had to be a means by which intellectual property could be widely produced, marketed and controlled. That process began with the printing press, brought to England in 1476; by 1534, a Crown decree forbade anyone from publishing without a license and approval from royal censors. This measure was meant to promote censorship, not protect property; but by the sixteen century, Britain had begun to protect intellectual property, a process that culminated in the adoption of the first copyright law, the Statute of Anne, in 1709. The statute barred the reproduction of a published work without the copyright owner's consent and shifted ownership of copyrights from publishers to authors.

The Statute of Anne is generally considered to have provided the model for modern copyright law "in the Western World"; it was widely copied by other countries, including the United States. Its initial effort—the Copyright

Act of 1790—gave "citizens" and "residents" the "sole right" to publish their work but did not prohibit importing, selling or publishing works "written . . . or published by any person not a citizen of the United States, in foreign parts". When the Act was adopted, there were no American authors who needed international copyright protection, and this approach - meant to foster the growth of an American publishing industry—let publishers infringe British copyrights "without paying royalties to authors from a country against which the United States had just revolted." For a century, American publishers pirated the works of foreign authors, which eventually had an unforeseen result: Pirated works could be sold so cheaply they created a market "that provided high quality foreign books at a price lower than an American author could match." In 1891, the complaints of American authors finally led to the adoption of the Chace Act, which gave non-resident foreign authors copyright protection under American law.

Both episodes involved instances in which societies were willing to allow their citizens to steal from citizens of other societies. In both, the focus was on crimes against property, not against persons; the motivation was purely economic. In both the conduct took place at the "margins" of the law: high-seas piracy occurred outside the territorial boundaries of any nation and therefore outside the scope of any laws; eighteenth-century American intellectual property piracy occurred at a time when the legal status of intellectual property as "property" was still evolving. Both types of conduct were outlawed when they became economically disadvantageous for the host countries; high-seas piracy was criminalized when it became a threat to the economic advantages derivable from legitimate commerce; and America prohibited intellectual piracy of foreign works when it began to undermine the economic prospects of native authors and the value of domestic intellectual property.

One can, therefore, hypothesize that countries may be inclined to tolerate their citizens' victimizing citizens of other nations if (a) the conduct takes place at the "margins" of the law, that is, involves activity that is not definitely proscribed by an applicable set of legal standards and (b) results in a benefit to the victimizing nation. The former gives the victimizing nation at least plausible deniability when confronted with its tolerance of illegal activity; the latter is an obvious motive for tolerating the activity at issue, and may even reinforce the rationale given for tolerating that activity. That is, as to the latter proposition, the victimizing nation may assert, and may believe, that the activity in question is simply a reallocation of scarce resources from a wealthy nation to a poorer nation.

Curent Consensus on Core Crimes

To meet the challenge posed by cybercrime, many countries have reviewed their domestic criminal laws to determine if it is adequate to combat this new phenomenon. Consequently, a number of countries have already amended their criminal laws, including the United States, Austria, Denmark, France, Germany, Greece, Finland, Italy, Turkey, Sweden, Switzerland, Australia, Canada and Japan. And other countries, including Spain, Portugal, the United Kingdom, Malaysia and Singapore have enacted new legislation to prevent computer-related crimes.

The United Nations Asia and Far East Institute for the Prevention of Crime and the Treatment of Offenders (UNAFEI) recently surveyed 185 United Nations members as to whether they have "amended their substantive criminal law in order to make it apply to all kind of noxious or otherwise illicit behavior that can be committed by means of, through or against computer systems and networks".

The questionnaire used in the survey sought information on three categories of cybercrime: (a) the "confidentiality, integrity and availability" crimes, e.g., crimes in which a computer system or data contained within the system is the target of the criminal activity; (b) computer-related fraud and forgery; and (c) pornography and child pornography. Thirty-seven nations replied to the survey.

With regard to the first category of offenses, over 60% of the responding nations indicated that their laws criminalize the unauthorized destruction of computer data, the unauthorized alteration of computer data and unauthorized acts rendering computer data inaccessible to its rightful owners. The criminal law of 51% of the responding countries penalized the unauthorized acquisition of data from a computer system, but in 32% of the responding countries unauthorized acquisition is criminalized only if it is preceded by an act of gaining unauthorized access to a computer system. In 29% of the responding countries, the law draws distinctions between the type of data that is obtained without authorization. France and China, for example, emphasize the protection of data that pertains to national security, state affairs and science and technology, while Spain makes "special reference" to the protection of personal data.

As to computer facilitated fraud and forgery, 62% of the responding countries indicated that their penal laws encompass computer-related fraud. And 43% of the respondents reported that their laws criminalized computer-related forgery. Finally, 67% of the responding countries indicated that their laws criminalize the use of computer technology to possess and/or distribute pornography, while 70% reported that their laws criminalize the use of such technology to possess or distribute child pornography.

The survey found, however, that "in most countries pornographic or pornographic material is not very precisely defined in criminal law." It also found that countries varied in the way their criminal law defined a "child:" for example, in Germany a child is a person "under the age of fourteen years", in Norway a child is anyone under the age of 16 and in Sri Lanka a child is anyone under the age of 18. A number of the countries responding to the survey—including Finland, France and Iceland—have not identified a specific age that defines the outer limits of childhood for the purposes of applying laws criminalizing child pornography.

Countries are moving to adopt consensus crimes in certain areas. Consensus cybercrimes were the most likely to be adopted with regard to acts targeting property and but were also likely to be adopted to address "new" crimes against persons, online child pornography and new acts intended to obstruct justice. Significant progress has been made toward achieving consensus with regard to outlawing cybercrime against property, and there is also a solid, and growing, consensus on outlawing the use of computers and the Internet to produce and disseminate child pornography.

There are areas in which consensus will not be achieved. Crimes against morality are the most systemically idiosyncratic types of crime because they are intrinsically bound up with a nation's religious and moral principles. It is true that the essentially-irresistible proliferation of the Internet will lead to some eroding of national moral proscriptions, some leveling in the definitions of crimes against morality, because it is more difficult for nations to maintain stringent standards of moral interdiction when their citizens are exposed to the permissive standards in force elsewhere.

Countries have tried to avoid this outcome by restricting or eliminating access to the Internet, but that is likely to prove futile. The effects of this are apparent with regard to gambling, which already enjoys vastly increased legal and social acceptance as a result of online gambling. This does not, of course, mean that a "reverse consensus" will develop which calls for the elimination of crimes against morality; indeed, the opposite will continue to be the case as, for example, online sales of alcohol and/or tobacco find acceptance in some countries but are outlawed in others.

Past efforts to develop consensus crimes have been notably unsuccessful with regard to the articulation of offenses directed at gambling and other crimes against morality. The same is true of a related area that involves the limitations which are placed on what can be disseminated online.

Consensus generally exists as to the imposition of one such limitation, namely, prohibitions on creating, posting and disseminating child pornography, but child pornography seems destined to be a special case. Many countries do, of course, censor what can be posted on the

Internet; some make it a crime to post prohibited material. The forms this censorship assumes range from sweeping prohibitions designed to block the dissemination of political statements to narrowly-crafted statutes criminalizing the publication of particular types of material - such as racist/hate speech—on the Internet. Relatively few countries fall into the first category but many outlaw the dissemination of racist/hate speech, which might lead one to assume that consensus could be achieved in this area. Indeed, a provision to this effect was proposed for inclusion in the Council of Europe's Convention on Cyber Crime.

Consensus will almost certainly not be achieved with regard to content-based restrictions other than those targeting child pornography; and prohibitions on child pornography can be distinguished, to some extent at least, from other content-based prohibitions because the primary impetus behind laws against child pornography has traditionally been to address a crime against persons, i.e., the use of children in the production of pornography. Nor will it be achieved with regard to prohibitions targeting online terrorism. The obstacle here is the divergent views countries take as to what is and is not a terrorist act. But while the failure to establish consensus crime categories encompassing terrorism *qua* terrorism may let the perpetrators of some terrorist acts avoid prosecution, nations can still pursue and prosecute them for the underlying crimes against persons and crimes against property they commit as part of terrorist agendas.

Action Plan for Deterrence of Cyber Crime

Cyberspace in the early 21st Century can be looked upon as a Frontierland. In human history there have been many such Frontierlands as a result of exploration and/or innovation. The characteristics that define a Frontierland include:

— *Uncharted territory* – there are no detailed maps showing boundaries or landmarks – those venturing into Frontierland need to think and behave as explorers.

— *Unclear or undefined ownership* – many Frontierlands have been claimed in the name of a ruler, whose explorers first stumbled by design or by luck upon such lands. Others are fought for until ownership, or at least control, is achieved by a dominance established by the most powerful contender

— *Lack of legislation* – an orderly and fair society does not emerge until the Frontierland has been explored, settled and disputed for some time. Disputes and other matters dealt with through a legal code elsewhere are handled more pragmatically in Frontierland. It may be rough justice but that's all there is.

— *Adventurers* – The above three characteristics can be seen as a problem by those whose reference framework is one of an orderly society and the rule of law. They are also seen as opportunities by those willing to take risks. Indeed, many adventurers in past Frontierlands became highly successful, and are often remembered with reverence. Those who failed, however, have been forgotten long ago.

Some Frontierlands are readily recognized as such and quite well known through literature and cinema, such as the North American "Wild West" of the mid-19th century. However, if the above characteristics are accepted as valid, humanity is still grappling with other Frontierlands, such as those of Nuclear, Biological and Chemical material, and is beginning to be concerned with emerging Frontierlands including Genetics, Nanoengineering, and Robotics.

Like all technologies, these can be used to benefit humanity and make a better world, and yet also have the potential to be used as weapons. Chemical weapons were used in World War I and nuclear bombs were first used in World War II. Work towards treaties on the use of such weapons, remains in progress and not every country is ready to ratify the treaties that emerge. Information Security also falls in this category, although as an emerging issue as the technologies of chemical, bacteriological and nuclear weapons have been in existence many years before cyberspace and their potential as weapons of mass destruction much easier to understand than the potential of information to disrupt society. New Frontierlands of this kind will continue to emerge and, given the worldwide acceleration of technical and scientific innovation, they will do so at shorter intervals than hitherto.

As our knowledge and understanding of Frontierland increase, they make available better charts of the territory. Each Frontierland will have its distinctive charts and what works for one Frontierland will, in all likelihood, be unsuitable for a new Frontierland. Frontierland becomes fit for civil society in a number of steps. For security in cyber-space these steps are three: Best Practices, Standards and Legislation.

Best practices

For managing Information Security, these first charts consist of widely accepted best practices. These often start as extensions to previous tried and tested practices. In many areas these remain as "best practices" and are never standardized. One specific cyber-space example can be found in the practices of "disaster recovery" and "business continuity":

As information and communications technology play a more critical role in the day-to-day activities of an organization, it becomes necessary to make arrangements for the event that these technologies become inoperational for a period of time greater than the organization can accept without major disruption to its activities.

Financial institutions, banks, airlines, critical infrastructures (electricity, water) have plans that allow them to resume operations in the case of a major ICT problem within, at most, a few hours. The original plans were designed to cope with catastrophic events in a computer room or data center (flooding, hurricanes, fire, major hardware failures). The emergence of cyberspace and the possibility of remote sabotage, denial of service attacks or similar events, have required that disaster recovery plans be updated and extended to deal with a new collection of disruptive events. There are many sources of best practices, some free of charge and others at low cost, developed by practitioners and professional associations. A list of such sources is included in the references.

Nevertheless, the following deserve specific mention here:

— *ITIL Security World:* The Information Technology Infrastructure Library, originally produced by the U.K. Central Computing and Telecommunications Agency's, now an automous agency, in extensive use around the world;

— *COBIT:* The Control Objectives for Information Technology guidelines published by the Information Systems Audit and Control Association (ISACA) are very highly regarded.

— *SANS:* the Systems And Network Security Institute professional training association has several books on offer (priced at around 30 US dollars each) on many technical aspects of information security and run frequent training courses in the US and elsewhere;

— *CASPR:* the Commonly Accepted Security Practices and Recommendations. The owners of this website intended to provide comprehensive best practices on information security in the year 2002.

The international community has a great opportunity to launch a project to seek the agreement of the above, and similar, organizations to select, translate and disseminate these best practices in languages other than English. Having access to best practices and applying them systematically are fundamentally different things. There are two complementary approaches to validating how well these are applied: Tests and Audits. For activities such as disaster recovery and the robustness of defences against penetration, tests are the only effective method to determine whether things will work when called upon. Although such tests are complex and usually disruptive, there really is no alternative.

Standards for information security

When the charts become sufficiently detailed and incorporate the experience of many parties, they can be formalized into "official" charts referred to as standards. Standards play an important role in the transformation of a Frontierland into an orderly society, where the rules of interaction are defined and widely applied. For example the technical and operating standards defined by the Internet Engineering Task Force enabled the Internet to become a global network in a relatively short time. Access to an Internet Café or a contract with an Internet Service Provider, then become the "passport" that grants an individual access to this portion of Cyber-space.

There are four sources of standards and recommendations:

1. The International Standards Organization (ISO), often in collaboration with International Organizations such as the International Telecommunications Union (ITU) or with national standards organizations such as the British Standards Institute.

2. Other national and regional organizations:

   — NATO Orange and Red books for trusted computer systems first produced in the late 1980s.

   — Other bodies working on standardization include ETSI (European Telecommunications Standardization Institute), under the auspices of the Council of Europe.

   — An appropriate example of a national standards body is the National Institute of Standards and Technology of the U.S. Government and its Computer Security Resource Centre

3. Professional associations, such as the Institution of Electrical and Electronic Engineers (IEEE), based in the United States but with a worldwide membership and the Internet Engineering Task Force (IETF), also with a worldwide membership.

4. Vendor associations such as ECMA, the European Computer Manufacturers Association or vendors whose products in such ubiquitous use that their architecture and software become the dominant technology and as such, de-facto standards.

National and Regional Legislation

The protection of society against breaches of information security can no longer be a simple matter of trust: it has become a legal issue. However, technology advances faster than legislators' ability to formulate, validate and put in place adequate laws and regulations. This implies that we shall continue to live in Frontierland for a considerable time.

Private Sector Initiatives

A number of non-governmental organizations have taken great interest in the matter, despite the clear fact that legislation falls within the purview of legislators and governments alone. Among the more prominent of these private sector organizations are:

— The International Chamber of Commerce (ICC).

— The Global Business Dialogue on Electronic Commerce (GBDE).

— The Information Technology Association of America (ITAA).

— The World Information Technology and Services Alliance (WITSA).

— The Global Internet Project (GIP).

— The Global Information Infrastructure Commission (GIIC).

Some of these organizations have established working groups and task forces to work in a focused fashion on the question of the gaps in legislation. As this whole subject of legislation moves forward, these and other parts of the private sector and civil society will have to be brought into the negotiating loop in the interest of durable laws.

National legislation

Many countries have been introducing national legislation on all or at least some of the aspects concerning either cyber-crime or cyber- security. Almost all of these are developed countries. Developing countries are noticeably absent. There is relatively little legislation on issues relating to fraud, money-laundering, identity theft, etc., though the United States does have laws that address parts of the problem.

Multi-national and regional legislation

There are three major initiatives that need to be studied carefully:

— The Council of Europe Convention on Cyber-crime of 2001

— The G-8 Lyon Group recommendations of 1999 to combat trans-national organized crime

— The OAS Final Report of 2000 on the two meetings of their Attorneys General and Ministers of Justice and Interior.

The Council of Europe Convention on Cyber-crime

The major event of 2001 was the emergence of the Council of Europe Convention on Cyber-Crime. This convention addresses unauthorised access, system interference and sabotage, data interception and data modification, data theft and misuse and aiding and abetting cyber criminals. Its three primary groups of provisions are designed to enable signatory nations to implement computer-related criminal law standards. These three groups of provisions cover:

— The outlawing of unauthorised computer intrusion, the release of malicious code, the use of computers to commit acts which are already crimes (e.g. fraud),

— The development of procedures to capture and retrieve online and other information by issuing "retention orders"

— The cooperation between national governments to share electronic evidence

Reaction 1: Signature and ratification of the Convention : By mid 2002, 33 States had signed, but not ratified, the Council of Europe Convention on Cyber-crime: These included 29 of the 44 members of the Council and four non-members who participated in the negotiations.

The 29 Council Members that have signed the convention are: Albania, Armenia, Austria, Belgium, Bulgaria, Croatia, Cyprus, Estonia, Finland, France, Germany, Greece, Hungary, Iceland, Ireland, Italy, Macedonia, Malta, Moldova, the Netherlands, Norway, Poland, Portugal, Romania, Spain, Sweden, Switzerland, Ukraine and the United Kingdom.The convention will enter into force when it has been ratified by five states, of which at least three must be members of the Council. The EU hopes to complete the ratification process by the middle of 2003.

Reaction 2: Misgivings: There have been many concerns expressed about the Council of Europe's Convention on Cyber-crime. Among them:

The Council is understood to be drafting an additional protocol for the convention that would treat xenophobic or racist acts committed in cyberspace as criminal offences. However, the United States indicated that such a protocol would be in contravention with its legislation on the freedom of speech. A pending area is a proposed extension to the convention to permit the interception and decoding of electronic messages between individuals suspected of terrorist activity. Another area of criticism of the convention is that more countries would have to sign and ratify the convention and abide by its mandates in order for it to be an effective deterrent. Critics note that none of the countries that have signed the convention so far are "problem countries" in which cyber-criminals can act with impunity. It is known that hackers and other attackers route their traffic through portals and facilities in countries that have not signed the convention.

Civil liberties groups have also expressed concern that the convention undermines individual rights to privacy and extends the surveillance powers of the signatory governments. Critics in the United States indicate that the provisions of the convention are incompatible with current U.S. law. Critics in Europe are concerned that the provisions of the convention allow the transfer of personal data to countries outside Europe, notably the United States and express the belief that the U.S. has less protective legislation regarding the use of such information and that it also may enable "foreign" countries to issue warrants seeking evidence and extradite and prosecute foreign nationals for cyber-crimes. In addition, lobbyists acting on behalf of business and consumer groups are concerned that the provisions of the CoE Convention could increase the cost of e-business, delay or impede the development of security technologies, limit the export of encryption products, and reduce consumer confidence in ecommerce.

G-8 initiatives

The Lyon Group established by the G-8 in 1995 has worked on 40 recommendations to combat trans-national organized crime. One of these recommendations calls on members to "review their laws to ensure that abuses of modern technology are criminalized". In 2002 the G-8 considered (but did not adopt) nine non-binding principles for information security:

— The creation of emergency watch and warning networks.

— The sharing of critical infrastructure information between the public and private sectors.

— Legal systems to ensure that such sharing of information is actually possible.

— Legal systems to enable the sharing of such information with third countries.

— The creation of secure and stable governmental communications for situations of emergencies.

— The mapping of critical infrastructures, and their interdependence.

— Legal systems to ensure against data destruction.

— The coordination of work among all stakeholders.

— Training exercises to enhance response capabilities.

Global International Legalisation

Global international legislation is needed because cyberspace does not have the same geopolitical borders as nation states and cybercrime does not require a physical presence at the scene of crime. There must be no non-signatories, as any loophole will be immediately exploited by the cyber-criminal and cyber-terrorist. There are two interesting older initiatives to address this issue, and much can be learnt from both.

The first can be seen in a document entitled, "International review of criminal policy. United Nations Manual on the prevention and control of computer-related crime" is. The original is a document of the UN Office in Vienna, Center for Social Development and Humanitarian Affairs, under the title "International Review of Criminal Policy - Nos. 43 and 44" of 1994. This manual is widely quoted in websites dealing with cyber-law. It calls for further international work and presents a good statement of the problem. Its two final paragraphs are quoted below in italics, as they remain relevant and as actionable as they were when first written. They state:

"At the international level, further activities could be undertaken, including the following:

1. Within regional groups or associations, conducting comparative analyses of substantive and procedural law relating to computer crime;

2. Attempting to harmonize substantive and procedural law among the States of a region by developing guidelines, model law or agreements;
3. When negotiating or reviewing treaties on extradition, mutual assistance or transfer of proceedings, whether bilateral or multilateral, addressing the following issues, taking into account human rights, including privacy rights, and the sovereignty of States:
4. Ensuring a jurisdictional base for the prosecution of trans-border, computer-related crime and enacting mechanisms for resolving jurisdictional conflicts;
5. Imposing obligations to extradite or prosecute offenders;
6. Facilitating mutual assistance, particularly regarding synchronized law enforcement, transborder search and seizure and the interception of communications.

"To ensure that human rights principles, privacy rights and international legal principles are effectively balanced, model treaties on criminal matters, such as those developed by the United Nations, can provide valuable guidelines. The implementation of security and crime prevention measures should be concomitant with technological development. The time to act is now."

The second initiative to create a formal framework for cyber-space was put forward in 1994 by the Progress Freedom Foundation. This is a document entitled "Cyber-space and the American Dream. A Magna Carta for the Knowledge Age" authored by Esther Dyson, George Gilder, George Keyworth and Alvin Toffler.

Some work has been done by different elements of the United Nations System, like the United Nations

Conference on Trade and Development (UNCTAD), the World Intellectual Property Organization (WIPO), the World Trade Organization (WTO), etc, but no truly coordinated global work exists at present. The United Nations General Assembly has several resolutions dealing with its desire to see progress on this issue. Among these are:

— Resolutions 55/63 and 56/121 on Combatting the Criminal Misuse of Information Technology, which noted the value of the G-8 principles, and urged states to take these principles into account.

— Resolutions 53/70, 54/79, 55/28, and 56/19, all of which call on Member States of the United Nations to promote the multi-lateral "consideration of existing and potential threats in the field of information security, as well as possible measures to limit the threats emerging in this field".

The Law of Cyber-Space

The current national and international legislation is completely insufficient to address the scope and complexity of the subject of cyber-threats and cyber-attack. So that a determined effort has consequently to be made to identify the shortcomings in existing legislation, and to draft and adopt a comprehensive Law of Cyber-Space. Such a Law of Cyber-Space would have to address the following issues, among others:

— Definition of cyber-space

— Sovereignty and jurisdiction

— Right to access

— Cyber-hooliganism

— Cyber-crime
— Cyber-terrorism
— Cyber-war
— National security
— Standards of evidence
— Intellectual property
— Software, including encryption
— Data protection
— Malicious code
— Electronic commerce
— Telecommunications regulation
— Obscene publications and related matters
— Civil liberties and right to privacy
— Anonymity
— Regulatory and investigative powers
— International cooperation mechanisms
— Trans-national extradition
— Treaty secretariat

Obviously all this cannot be done within the framework of national legislation alone. Different countries have different legal systems, standards and rules, and therefore harmonization would be almost impossible. Some countries might opt to stay out of the system, and would then become "offshore" havens for cybercrime and cyber-terrorism. It cannot be done in regional forums either, as the problem has global dimensions that cannot be defined in regional terms. The manner in which cyber-space envelops the globe, and manages to freely cross borders without let or hindrance, makes it absolutely essential that the parameters of the future Law of Cyber-Space will have to be developed and negotiated in a global forum for a global consensus on a global problem. As the only truly universal international organisation that we have today, the United Nations can provide the broadest and most neutral and legitimate platform for bringing together governments and other key stakeholders to undertake this effort. Only this institution can provide the forum for discussion and debate on the complexities of the subject, and coalesce the expertise that exists around the world for a proper drafting of relevant legislation that can fill the existing and growing void in cyber-law. It has done it before, in the nearest equivalent to cyber-space, when the United Nations negotiated and agreed on a Law of the Seas. That took almost a decade of negotiations, but the endresult was worthy of the time spent, and the consensus has withstood the passage of time.

A complication arises from the fact that both the Private Sector and Civil Society have major stakes in these negotiations. Since the United Nations is essentially an inter-governmental organisation, the question is how its Member States will adequately incorporate the interests of the Private Sector and Civil Society in the processes for the development and negotiation of a Law of Cyber-Space.

As the United Nations gains experience in building relationships with the Private Sector and Civil Society, innovative ways and means can be devised to ensure the full engagement of all key stakeholders in cyber-space, in a process whose outcome would be mutually beneficial, and which would create a solid foundation and a conducive environment for the positive use of cyber-space for the economic and social development of all countries.

6

Cyber Crime Laws Around the World

This chapter surveys the extent to which countries have adopted legislation that specifically targets the commission of computer-related crime. It does not attempt to analyze the extent to which a country's traditional penal legislation can be applied to prosecute those who use computer technology to commit such traditional offenses as theft, fraud and forgery.

Western Europe

Austria

Austria's Privacy Act 2000, which into effect on January 1, 2000, establishes penalties for unlawful acts directed at data. Specifically, it provides that a fine shall be assessed for doing any of the following:

(1) willfully obtaining or maintaining unlawful access to a data application;

(2) intentionally transmitting data in violation of the Data Secrecy Clause, especially if he or she was given access to it for other purposes;

(3) using data contrary to a legal judgment or decision, failing to correct false data or failing to delete data; and

(4) intentionally deleting data.

Belgium

In November, 200, the Belgian Parliament adopted new legislation which would insert a series of new articles, which deal with computer crime, into the Belgian Criminal Code. The articles make "computer forgery, computer fraud, hacking and sabotage . . . criminal offences in their own right". Belgium's approach to computer forgery—defined by new Article 210(b) of the Criminal Code—differs from that taken elsewhere: "Instead of conferring the quality of `a written document' upon data stored in a computer system," the new article creates the distinct crime of computer forgery, which consists of "the falsification of computerised information." The new offense does not "require the particular intention of pecuniary gain or intention to cause harm" because these acts are covered by the new articles on fraud and sabotage. It encompasses the completed act or the attempt to "`intentionally hide the truth by means of computerised manipulations of legally pertinent data, or the use of such data'". The forgery or attempted forgery must cause "the modification of the legal effect of such data."

Unlike the forgery offense, the new computer fraud offense—codified in Article 504(4)—requires that the "computerised manipulations have procured . . . a fraudulent pecuniary advantage" for the perpetrator or someone else. The computer sabotage offense—codified as Article 550(3)—requires that the perpetrator act with the intent to cause harm. It fills what had been a gap in Belgian criminal law:

In the past, the notion of sabotage required the destruction or damage of physical objects. The destruction or damage of computerised data is not covered by the existing Criminal Code. The new article therefore criminalises any manipulation of data with the intent to cause harm.

If the data manipulation causes damage to the computer system or affects its functioning, the behavior is punished more severely than simply causing damage to data. "Impeding the correct functioning of a computer system is now . . . considered as causing damage." The new offense can also be used to prosecute "those who create or spread viruses, or who create programmes which create viruses." Finally, the new hacking provision penalizes "both internal and external hacking", e.g., both the acts of breaking into a computer system from outside and that of exceeding one's lawful access to a computer system. "No particular intention is required of an external hacker . . . (although the intention to defraud is an aggravating circumstance), whereas the activities of the internal hacker must be motivated by a fraudulent intention or an intention to cause harm in order to be sanctioned." The article also makes it a crime to attempt to break into a computer system.

Denmark

Section 263(2) of the Danish Criminal Code makes it an offense to, "in an unlawful manner," obtain "access to another person's information or programs which are meant to be used in a data processing system". The basic sanction is imprisonment "for a term not exceeding 6 months", but if the offense is committed with the intent to "procure or make oneself acquainted with information concerning trade secrets of a company or under other extraordinary aggravating circumstances," the penalty is increased to "imprisonment for a term not exceeding 2 years." Section 279 of the Danish Penal Code outlaws using a computer to commit fraud. Specifically, it declares that anyone who, "for the purpose of obtaining for himself or for others an unlawful gain" unlawfully alters, adds or erases "information or programs for the use of electronic data processing, or who in any other manner attempts to affect the results of such data processing" is guilty of computer fraud.

The basic sanction is imprisonment for up to "one year and six months", but the penalty can be increased—to as much as eight years imprisonment—when the crime was of "a particularly aggravated nature" or where the perpetrator committed "a large number of such offences". Two provisions of the Danish Criminal Code can be used to prosecute someone who uses a computer to cause damage. Section 193(1) is essentially an anti-terrorism provision, making it a crime unlawfully to cause "major disturbances in the operation of public means of communication, of the public mail service, of publicly used telegraph or telephone services, of radio and television installations, of data processing systems or of installations for the public supply of water, gas, electricity or heating".

The offense is punishable with imprisonment for up to four years; if mitigating circumstances are shown or if the offense was committed through negligence, the penalty is reduced to a fine or "simple detention". Section 291(1) makes it a crime to destroy, damage or remove "objects belonging to others". The basic penalty is a fine or imprisonment for up to one year, but if the damage is "very serious" and the perpetrator has previous convictions for similar acts, the sanction can be increased to imprisonment for up to four years.

Finland

Finland outlaws the creation and dissemination of computer viruses under the aegis of an offense called "criminal computer mischief." It has also criminalized computer fraud and damage to computer data. It also enacted an omnibus provision entitled "data and communications offenses" which outlaws hacking and the interception of electronic communications, among other activities.

France

France has outlawed hacking and cracking since 1993.

Germany

Germany has criminalized computer sabotage and computer fraud, along with data theft and data alteration or destruction.

Greece

The Greek Penal Code "protects 'secrecy' and punishes everyone, who unlawfully copies, prints, uses, discloses to a third party, or by any means violates secret data or computer programs." It also criminalizes unauthorized access to computer systems and computer programs, as well as and computer fraud.

Iceland

Iceland has criminalized unlawfully obtaining access to data or to programs stored as data.

Ireland

Section 2(1) of the Criminal Damage Act makes it an offence for anyone to damage property belonging to another or to be reckless as to whether such property would be damaged. Section 5 of the Act makes it a crime for someone to operate a computer "without lawful excuse" (a) "within the State with intent to access any data kept either within or outside the State" or (b) "outside the State with intent to access any data kept within the State". Such a person commits the offense regardless of "whether or not he accesses any data". This provision also encompasses the dissemination of viruses. Curiously, the Act nowhere defines "computer", though it does define "data" as "`information in a form in which it can be accessed by means of a computer and includes a program'".

Italy

Article 615.5 of the Italian Penal Code makes it a crime to disseminate programs aimed at damaging or interrupting the operations of a computer system. Article 615 also criminalizes hacking and the unlawful possession and distribution of computer access codes.

Luxembourg

Luxembourg makes it an offense either to fraudulently gain access to a computer system or to alter, suppress or modify data contained in such a system.

Malta

On January 8, 2001, the Parliament enacted the Electronic Commerce Act, which adds a new section, entitled "Computer Misuse", to the Maltese Criminal Code. Aside from definitional and procedural provisions, the new Computer Misuse section of the Criminal Code creates offenses falling into two categories, unlawful access to information and misuse of hardware.

The Netherlands

The Netherlands has outlawed hacking.

Norway

Norway has outlawed hacking and a form of cyberterrorism.

Portugal

Portugal has outlawed hacking, which becomes an aggravated offense if the perpetrator obtains information by violating security measures or obtains access to trade secrets or other information protected by law.

Spain

Spain has criminalized the interception of e-mail or "any other communications signal" and the copying, use or modificaton of "private personal or family data of another individual". Spain has also outlawed computer fraud and the unauthorized use of telecommunications terminal equipment.

Sweden

Sweden has made "data trespass" a crime.

Switzerland

Article 143(a) of the Swiss Penal Code makes hacking a crime.

United Kingdom

The centerpiece of the United Kingdom's approach to cybercrime is the Computer Misuse Act of 1990. The Act creates three distinct offenses: unauthorized access to computer material; unauthorized access with intent to commit or facilitate commission of further offenses; and unauthorized modification of computer material. Like Ireland's Criminal Damage Act, described above, the Computer Misuse Act makes no effort to define "computer", though it does define "access." One criticism leveled at the Computer Misuse Act is that it needs to be revised, since it "takes not account of the Internet, and has not yet been updated to cover offences such as denial of service (DOS) attacks."

Russia and Esatern Europe

Countries of Central and Eastern Europe have generally made less progress in reforming their legal systems to incorporate cybercrime, though Russia stands as an exception. Russia has developed an extensive legal framework to detect, punish, and prevent computer crime, but implementation remains problematic. Other countries of Central and Eastern Europe have also started addressing cybercrime as part of the larger on-going legal reforms in the region. Romania and Poland have draft laws underway that include computer-related provisions.

Albania

A study published in December of 2000 found that Albania had no cybercrime specific laws in place. It noted, however, that the Albanian Authority for the Regulation of Telecommunications had begun discussions "on the topic of cyber laws, with the goal of preparing protocols of collaboration and exchanging information."

Bosnia

The Federation of Bosnia and Herzegovina has implemented an article in their criminal code to criminalize computer data theft. Article 193(2) of the Criminal Code, which went into effect on November 20, 1998, makes it illegal to break into a computer database containing personal data, use such data, or make such information available to another person.

Bulgaria

The Bulgarian criminal code has established crimes involving computers in two separate categories; crimes against intellectual property and general economic crimes. Article 172a, which covers crimes against intellectual property, criminalizes reproducing or distributing another's property without the copyright holders consent. The punishment for this type of crime is imprisonment of up to three years and a fine from 1000,00-3000,00 levas, however, if the crime is a second offense or causes substantial harm, the punishment is up to five years imprisonment and a fine of 3000,00-5000,00 levas. Under general economic crimes in the criminal code, Article 227 forbids using a mark, industrial design, or topology of integrated circuits in commercial activities. The punishment for this crime is imprisonment of up to three years and a fine of up to 5000,00 levas.

Czech Republic

In 1999, the Ministry of the Interior of the Czech Republic issued a report that surveyed cybercrime analyzed the adequacy of the legislation available to combat it. In the paragraph below, the report discusses "crime in information technology" and notes the extent to which is can be pursued using existing law:

> *Hacking in IT and programmes*
>
> § 152 of the Criminal Code - Infringement of copyright
>
> § 182 of the Criminal Code - Impairing and endangering the operation of public utility facilities

§ 249 of the Criminal Code - Unauthorised use of other people's articles

§ 257a of the Criminal Code - Damaging and misusing records in information stores

Unlawful conduct in the electronics trade

§ 121 of the Criminal Code - Harming the consumer

§ 127 of the Criminal Code - Breaching the binding regulations of economic relations § 128 of the Criminal Code - Misuse of information in business relations § 250 of the Criminal Code – Fraud The report emphasizes that cybercrime can also "involve e.g. vice crimes, certain crimes against the Republic and the security of the Republic, and other crimes, especially economic ones." And it explains that various entities are working to develop legislation which will target other areas of cybercrime.

Estonia

Estonia recently adopted legislation outlawing computer fraud, sabotage and related offenses. The computer fraud provision makes it a crime to receive "proprietary benefits through entry, replacement, deletion or blocking of computer programs or data" which "influences the result of the data processing operation. The computer sabotage provision makes the "[u]nlawful replacement, deletion, damaging or blocking of data or programs in a computer" and/or the "unlawful entry of data or programs in a computer" a crime if "significant damage is thereby caused". Another provision makes it illegal to disseminate computer viruses; the basic punishment is a fine or up to one year's imprisonment, but if the offense is repeated or is committed "in a manner which causes significant damage" the allowable period of imprisonment rises to three years. Another provision makes it ulawful to damage or block computer network connections. It is also illegal to distribute "the protection codes of a computer, computer system or computer network, if committed for the purpose of personal gain and in a manner which causes significant damage or results in other serious consequences."

Hungary

So far, Hungary's only cybercrime-specific penal legislation is a provision criminalizing computer fraud.

Latvia

Latvia has outlawed the following: "arbitrarily accessing computer systems;" the unauthorized acquisition of computer software; damaging computer software; disseminating a computer virus; and violating "safety provisions regarding information systems."

Poland

The Polish Penal Code criminalizes the following: unauthorized access to information; damaging, destroying or deleting information; and destroying, deleting or altering information "having a particular significance for national defense, transport safety, [or] operation of the government". Other provisions make it a crime to connect to a computer network to gather information for the benefit of a foreign intelligence service and to interfere with the automatic processing, gathering or transfer of information. Finally, Poland also criminalizes improper access to and/or use of personal information, as well as the act of failing to protect such data when one is under an obligation to do so.

Romania

The Romanian Criminal Code contains no special legislation on computer crimes. Several years ago, the government drafted "The Code for Information Technologies Development and Use." The draft Code stipulated that "IT offenses" would be punishable by imprisonment for terms ranging from two to ten years, depending on the offense and its severity. The offenses include: unauthorized access to an information system for the capture, storage, processing and distribution of data and/or programs or for altering, damaging and destroying hardware, data and/or software; data embezzlement, program disturbance, alteration and erroneous data transmission resulting in data flow disturbance; and computer fraud. An accidental entry into data flows that caused any of the above-mentioned types of damage would be criminalized if the perpetrator did not immediately acknowledge the act to the Romanian Authority for Informatics. Infringements, such as disobeying the recommendations or authorizations of Romanian Authority for Informatics, would be punished by fines. The Code for Information Technologies Development and Use was submitted to the European Commission, with comments received in March of 1998. The second revised Code was approved by the Government and forwarded to the Romanian Parliament in 1999, but Parliament has so far not acted upon it.

Russia

Prior to 1997, the Criminal Code of the Russian Federation included no specific provisions regarding computer crimes. The new Penal Code of the Russian Federation, which entered into force in 1997, directly addresses computer crimes. Chapter 28 of this Code is entitled "Crimes in the Domain of Computerized Information" and includes articles on unauthorized access to computerized information; the creation, use, and promulgation of harmful computer software; and breach of operating rules for computers, computer systems and networks.

Slovenia

There is no special legislation dealing with computer crime in force in Slovenia. Slovenia expects to ratify the Convention on Cybercrime soon, which would obligate it to prosecute the offenses specified by the Convention. The Slovene Penal Code generally enables the prosecution of all the offenses listed in the Convention, though small amendments may be necessary to ensure full compliance with the Convention. Greater amendments will likely to bring the Slovene Criminal Procedure Code into compliance with the Convention.

Yugoslavia

Yugoslavia has enacted several laws attempting to address cyber crimes. These include laws on the information system of the government agencies and organization of FRY ("Official Gazette of FRY" No.59/98) and laws on the protection of personal data ("Official Gazette of FRY", No. 24/98).

North America

Canada

Canada criminalizes a number of computer-related offenses, including computer mischief; data theft; invasion of privacy; computer fraud; and hacking/cracking and virus dissemination.

United States of America

Cybercrime legislation has been adopted at both the state and federal levels. The survey below concentrates on federal legislation, both because of its more general applicability and because the idiosyncrasies of the legislation adopted by the fifty states is quite outside the ambitions of this endeavor.

Federal legislation:

Computer intrusions and other computer-related crimes: Section 1030 of Title 18 of the U.S. Code defines a number of computer-related offenses, e.g., hacking, cracking, virus dissemination, fraud, password trafficking, extortion and fraud. The statute reaches conduct targeting a federal or "protected computer." A "protected computer" is (a) a computer that is used exclusively by a financial institution or the federal government or that is used, albeit nonexclusively, by a financial institution or the federal government and the conduct constituting the offense affects that use; or (b) a computer that is used in interstate or foreign commerce or communication. The statute reaches conduct that inflicts damage to individuals or to artificial entities.

As to substantive offenses, § 1030(a) makes it a federal crime to do any of the following:

a. To (i) knowingly access a computer without authorization or by exceeding authorized access and thereby obtain information that is protected against disclosure which the perpetrator has reason to believe could be used to the disadvantage of the U.S. or to the advantage of any foreign nation and (ii) willfully either deliver that information to a person not entitled to receive it or retain the information and refuse to deliver it to the federal agent entitled to receive it;

b. To intentionally access a computer without authorization or by exceeding authorized access and thereby obtain (i) information contained in a financial record of a financial institution, or of a card issuer or contained in a file of a consumer reporting agency on a consumer, (ii) information from any federal department or agency, or (iii) information from any protected computer if the conduct involved an interstate or foreign communication;

c. To intentionally and without authorization access (i) a computer used exclusively by a federal department or agency or (ii) a computer not used exclusively by a federal department or agency when the conduct affects the computer's use by or for the federal government;

d. To knowingly and with the intent to defraud access a protected computer without authorization or by exceeding authorized access and thereby further the intended fraud and obtain anything of value unless the object of the fraud and the thing obtained consist only of the use of the computer and the value of that use does not exceed $5,000 in any one-year period;

e. To (i) knowingly cause the transmission or a program, information, code or command and thereby intentionally cause damage to a protected computer; (ii) intentionally access a protected computer without authorization and thereby recklessly cause damage; or (iii) intentionally access a protected computer without authorization and thereby cause damage;

f. To knowingly and with intent to defraud traffic in any password or other information used to access a computer if (i) the trafficking affects interstate or foreign commerce or (ii) the computer to which access can be gained is by or for the federal government;

g. To transmit in interstate or foreign commerce any threat to cause damage to a protected computer with the intent to extort money or any thing of value from any person, firm, association, educational institution, financial institution, government or other legal entity.

Unauthorized access to stored electronic communications: Section 2701(a) of Title 18 of the U.S. Code makes it an offense either (a) to intentionally access without authorization a facility through which an electronic communication is provided or (b) to intentionally exceed an authorization to access such a facility and thereby obtain, alter or prevent authorized access to a wire or electronic communication while it is in electronic storage. The basic punishment is a fine, imprisonment for not more than six months, but the penalties increase if the offense was committed for purposes of commercial advantage, malicious destruction or damage or private commercial gain. If the offense is committed for the purpose of commercial advantage, malicious destruction or damage or private commercial gain, the allowable period of imprisonment rises to not more than one year for a first offense and to not more than two years for a subsequent offense.

Sending obscene/offensive material to minors or sending harassing messages: Section 223(a) of Title 47 of the U.S. Code makes it an offense to use a telecommunications device in interstate or foreign communications to:

(1) make, create solicit and initiate the transmission of "any comment, request, suggestion, proposal, image, or other communication which is obscene, lewd, lascivious, filthy, or indecent, with intent to annoy, abuse, threaten, or harass another person";

(2) make, create solicit and initiate the transmission of "any comment, request, suggestion, proposal, image, or other communication which is obscene or indecent, knowing that the recipient of the communication is under 18 years of age, regardless of whether the maker of such communication placed the call or initiated the communication";

(3) make a telephone call or "utilize a telecommunications device, whether or not conversation or communication ensues, without disclosing his identity and with intent to annoy, abuse, threaten, or harass any person at the called number or who receives the communications";

(4) make or cause "the telephone of another repeatedly or continuously to ring, with intent to harass any person at the called number";

(5) make repeated telephone calls or repeatedly initiate communication "with a telecommunications device, during which conversation or communication ensues, solely to harass any person at the called number or who receives the communication"; or

(6) knowingly permit any telecommunications facility under his or her control to be used to commit any of the previously-listed activities. The penalties for these offenses include fines, imprisonment for up to two years, or both.

Section 223(b) of Title 47 of the U.S. Code makes it an offense: (a) for any person knowingly to use a telephone to make an obscene or indecent communication for commercial purposes or to allow a telephone facility under his or her control to be used for this purpose, or (b) for any person knowingly to use a telephone to make an indecent communication for commercial purposes which is available to anyone under the age or eighteen or to allow a telephone facility under his or her control to be used for this purpose.

The Supreme Court invalidated portions of this statute relating to "indecent" communication by means of a telecommunication device and "patently offensive" communications through use of interactive computer service to persons under the age of 18 on First Amendment grounds in *Reno v. ACLU,* 521 U.S. 844 (1997).

Child Online Protection Act (COPA): Section 231(a)(1) of Title 47 of the U.S. Code makes it an offense to "knowingly and with knowledge of the character of the material, in interstate or foreign commerce by means of the World Wide Web, make any communication for commercial purposes that is available to any minor and that includes any material that is harmful to minors." It is an affirmative defense that the defendant in good faith restricted minors' access to material that is harmful to them by requiring the use of a credit card or other method of indicating age or by employing "any other reasonable measures that are feasible under available technology." In

ACLU v. Reno, 217 F.3d 162 (3d Cir. 2000), the Third Circuit upheld the issuance of an injunction barring enforcement of the statute; the Supreme Court has granted certiorari to review the decision.

Transmitting information about a minor: Section 2425 of Title 18 of the U.S. Code makes it an offense knowingly to initiate "the transmission of the name, address, telephone number, social security number, or electronic mail address of another individual," knowing that person has not attained the age of sixteen, "with the intent to entice, encourage, offer, or solicit any person to engage in sexual activity for which any person can be charged with a criminal offense". The statute also makes it a crime to attempt to violate its provisions.

Fraud in connection with access devices: Section 1029 of Title 18 of the U.S. Code makes it an offense to engage in certain activities involving "access devices," which it defines as "any card, plate, code, account number, electronic serial number, mobile identification number, personal identification number, or other telecommunications service, equipment, or instrument identifier, or other means of account access that can be used . . . to obtain money, goods, services, or any other thing of value". The statute also prohibits activities involving counterfeit access devices, which it defines as "any access device that is counterfeit, fictitious, altered, or forged, or an identifiable component of an access device or a counterfeit access device."

Section 1029 makes it an offense to do any of the following: (a) knowingly and with the intent to defraud produce, use or traffic in a counterfeit access device; (b) knowingly and with the intent to defraud traffic in or use one or more access devices during any one-year period and thereby obtain anything of a value aggregating $1,000 or more; (c) knowingly and with the intent to defraud possess fifteen or more devices which are counterfeit or unauthorized access devices; (d) knowingly and with the intent to defraud produce, traffic in, have custody or control of or possess access device-making equipment; (e) knowingly and with the intent to defraud effect transactions with one or more access devices issued to another person or other persons to receive anything of value during any one-year period of a value aggregating $1,000 or more; (f) without the authorization of the issuer of an access device, knowingly and with the intent to defraud solicit someone for the purpose, either, of offering an access device selling information regarding or an application to obtain an access device; (g) knowingly and with the intent to defraud use, produce, traffic in, have custody or control of or possess hardware or software knowing it has been configured to insert or modify telecommunications identifying information associated with or contained in a telecommunications instrument so that the instrument can be used to obtain telecommunications service without authorization; or (h) without the authorization of a credit card owner or its agent, knowingly and with the intent to defraud cause or arrange for another person to present one or more records of transactions made by an access device to the owner or its agent for payment.

State legislation

Hacking/cracking: Most states make it a crime to purposely access a computer, computer system or network without authorization. Most make it a more serious crime to purposely access a computer without authorization and alter, damage or disrupt the operation of the computer and/or the data it contains. Some states have a "misuse of computer information" statute which prohibits copying, receiving or using information that was obtained by violating a hacking or cracking statute. New York has what is in effect a cyber-burglary statute that makes it a crime to break into a computer or computer system "with an intent to commit or attempt to commit or further the commission of any felony".

Viruses and other harmful programs: A few states outlaw the creation and transmission of virii and other harmful programs, and bills to this effect have been introduced elsewhere. Miscellaneous computer offenses: A few states make it a crime to introduce false information into a computer system for the purpose of "damaging or enhancing" someone's credit rating. A surprising number have an "offense against computer equipment or supplies," which consists of modifying or destroying "equipment or supplies that are used or intended to be used in a computer, computer system, or computer network". Even more make it a crime to deny, disrupt, degrade, interrupt or cause the denial, disruption, degradation or interruption of computer services or of access to a computer. A few make it a crime to destroy computer equipment. Several states outlaw "computer invasion of privacy," which consists of using a "computer or computer network with the intention of examining any employment, medical, salary, credit, or any other financial or personal data relating to any other person with knowledge that such examination is without authority". Others make it a crime to disclose someone else's computer password.

Offenses targeting children: A number of states make it a crime to use a computer to solicit or lure a minor to engage in an "unlawful sex act." Several states make it a crime to use a computer to compile information about a child "for the purpose of facilitating, encouraging, offering or soliciting a prohibited sexual act" from that child. These statutes are part of an effort to outlaw child pornography. Many states prohibit using a computer to create, store and/or distribute child pornography, and many also prohibit using a computer to send obscene material to a child. Pennsylvania makes it an offense to use a computer to communicate with a child for the purpose of engaging in prostitution.

Stalking and harassment: Only about sixteen states outlaw online stalking or harassment, and several of them require that an offender transmit a "credible threat" to injure the victim, the victim's family or "any other person." Other statutes are broader, making it a crime to use a computer to "engage in a course of conduct" that would cause a "reasonable person" to "suffer intimidation or serious inconvenience, annoyance or alarm," as well as fearing death or injury to themselves or to members of their family. Some states have expanded their "obscene phone call" statutes so they encompass using the telephone or an "electronic communication device" to contact someone and threaten to injure that person or his/her family, to use obscene language or to make repeated contacts in an effort to annoy the person. A New York court has held that a similar provision encompasses harassing or threatening messages sent via the Internet. Bills have been introduced to make online stalking and/or harassment an offense in states where it is not currently outlawed.

Fraud and theft crimes: A substantial number of states outlaw using computers to commit fraud, i.e., using a "computer, computer system, computer network, or any part thereof for the purpose of devising or executing any scheme or artifice to defraud" or for "obtaining money, property, or services by means of false or fraudulent pretenses, representations, or promises". States tend to incorporate embezzlement crimes into their computer fraud statutes, rather than creating separate "computer embezzlement" provisions. A substantial number of states also outlaw "computer theft," which can encompass any of several discrete offenses: information theft; software theft; computer hardware theft; and theft of computer services. It can also encompass using a computer to commit a theft in a more traditional sense, e.g., to steal property other than data or computer hardware or software. A few states prohibit the unlawful possession of computer data and/or computer software. Some have "identity theft" statutes, which make it a crime to "knowingly and with intent to defraud for economic benefit" obtain, possess, transfer, use or attempt "to obtain, possess, transfer or use, one or more identification documents or personal identification number of another /person other than that issued lawfully for the use of the possessor."

A few states outlaw computer forgery, which is defined as follows: "Any person who creates, alters, or deletes any data contained in any computer or computer network, who, if such person had created, altered, or deleted a tangible document or instrument would have committed forgery . . . shall be guilty of the crime of computer forgery." At least one state makes it a crime to possess "forgery devices," which include computers, computer equipment and computer software "specifically designed or adapted to such use".

Crimes against government: Only a few states have make it a crime to use computers to obstruct law enforcement or the provision of government services. Illinois forbid using a computer to cause a "disruption of or interference with vital services or operations of State or local government or a public utility". Several states make it a crime to use a computer to interrupt or impair the delivery of essential services (e.g., services of a public or private utility, medical services, communication services or government services) or to otherwise endanger public safety. Some states make it a crime to use a computer to obtain information "with the state or any political subdivision which is by statute required to be kept confidential". West Virginia prohibits the unauthorized accessing of information stored in a computer owned by its state legislature. Rhode Island makes it a crime to use a computer to destroy evidence for the purpose of obstructing an official investigation.

Internet gambling: On June 4, 2001, Nevada legislators approved a bill that would make Nevada the first state to offer legalized Internet gambling. On June 14, 2001, Nevada's governor signed the bill, thereby setting up what may be an interesting legal challenge, since some contend that online gambling, even if legal under Nevada law, would violate federal law.

South and Central America and the Carribbean

Argentina

In responding to a 1999 survey administered by the Permanent Council of the Organization of American States' Government Experts on Cyber Crime, Argentina indicated that its law did not then penalize "the unauthorized destruction, modification, alteration, access, usage or other similar interference to or of a computer system or program". Asked if its law penalized the "unauthorized erasure, alteration, rendering inaccessible, acquisition, or other similar interference to or of information or data from a computer system or program", Argentina replied that it did to some extent, since "[I]n the area of criminal tax law, Criminal Tax Act No. 24,769, article 12, addresses the fraudulent alteration of records." The questionnaire also asked countries if their law criminalized the "unauthorized interception of the transmission in any manner or mode of computer data or information".

Argentina's response was that its law did not specifically outlaw this but that "Article 197 of the [Argentine] Penal Code punishes the interception of telephone communications. Therefore, if data is transmitted via telephone, unauthorized interception could be considered criminal." However, there appears to be a loophole in the Argentinean law, which allows the defacing of webpages because they are not considered material objects.

Barbados

Barbados has not enacted any specific cyber crime legislation.

Brazil

On July 14, 2000, amendments to Brazil's Penal Code were enacted, to go into effect ninety days after the date the amendments were published. The amendments created two new offenses: the "entry of false data" into an information system; and the unauthorized modification or alteration "of the information system or computer program by an employee". Brazil also has a number of cybercrime laws that predate these amendments. Its criminal law defines computer data as "information stored by means of electronic, video or voice equipment, whereas a data base is a collection of information stored by means of electronic, video or voice equipment, which permits the search of said data by manual or electronic procedures of any kind".

Brazilian law defines a computer program as an organized series of instructions in natural or codified language contained on a physical medium of any kind, which requires the use of electronic data processing machinery, devices, instruments or ancillary equipment, based on digital or analog technology, to operate it for certain purposes. The gaining of unauthorized access to a computer system or a violation of the secrecy of a computer system, belonging to either a financial institution or securities dealer is a crime under Article 18 of Law No. 7492, dated June 16, 1986, which defines crimes against the national financial system.

Computer trespass is covered by several Brazilian laws: The violation of data by means of clandestine or hidden access to a computer program or system is also a crime, punishable by imprisonment of six months to one year as is violation of the secrecy of data by gaining access to information contained in the system or physical medium of a third party. If such access results in undue economic benefit to the detriment of the principal of the system, such an act is penalized as stellionate, which is described in Art. 2 of that Law.

Obtaining undue access to a computer system or to an integrated computer network is a crime punishable by a prison term of three to six months, or a fine. If access is gained through wrongful use of the password or code or magnetic identificatino procedure of a third party, the crime is punishable by imprisonment from one to two years and a fine. If, in addition, it results in economic damages to the principal, it is punished with imprisonment of one to three years and a fine. If the purpose of the access is to cause damage to another or to obtain an undue advantage or benefit, the crime is punishable by imprisonment of two to four years and a fine. Further, if the integrated computer network or system belongs to a public corporate entity under Brazilian law, or to a decentralized agency, public enterprise, semi-public company, or foundation instituted or maintained by the national government, or independent social services, the punishment is enhanced by one-third.

Brazil has several laws prohibiting the interception of telephone, data, or telematic communications. These laws ensuring privacy and criminalizing data interception are outlined in both the Brazilian Federal Constitution as well as in public law.

On August 8, 2001, "Project de Lei da Camara n. 84/ 1999," a bill specifically targeted at cybercrimes, was submitted to the House of Representatives. If the House passes the bill it will be sent to the President for his approval.

Chile

Chile's Law on Automated Data Processing Crimes no. 19.223, published June 7, 1993 criminalizes espionage on automated systems.

Costa Rica

Costa Rican law does not currently have specific laws that prohibit computer trespass, tampering with a computer system, or computer related theft. These crimes, when possible, would be prosecuted other under general criminal statues such as theft.

The Costa Rican Penal Code however is currently undergoing substantial revision. The Costa Rican Attorney General has indicated that "it would be advisable to introduce categories that specifically protect legal interests related to computers, so that the special nature of the matter can be taken into account when the punishment is established." The proposed comprehensive Penal Code reform (Draft law No. 11,871) provides protection for a number of legal interests tied to "cybercrimes," but does not do so in a special way or cover the subject in a separate section. Instead, this is included in defined crimes against privacy (Title IV: Offenses Related to the Violation of Privacy) in Chapter I, the heading of which is "Tampering with Personal Data and Communications."

Cuba

A study published in December of 2000 found that while Cuba currently had no cybercrime specific laws in place, a working group from the Ministry of Justice was drafting cybercrime legislation. In looking at the need for new legislation addressing cybercrimes, the working group found that "a great number of them" are covered by Cuba's present Penal Code, but still developed some modifications that might improve the Penal Code's ability to address cybercrimes. One such modification would make the use of a computer to commit a crime an aggravating factor, just as the use of a firearm is an aggravating factor under the laws of many countries. The working group also drafted possible revisions of three existing offenses and sections defining new crimes.

Ecuador

There are no criminal laws in Ecuador which prohibit "computer crimes" such as computer trespass, vandalism, or interception of computer communications. Ecuador's penal code does not speak of cybercrime. Ecuador does however monitor and investigate computer piracy, defined as the use of computers to duplicate computer programs or phonographic works in violation of copyright law. Thus, Ecuadorian law punishes only the alteration or modification of electronic information as regards copyright provisions, under Articles 26 and 324 of the Intellectual Property Act. The Government of Ecuador could provide no specific data on any particular computer crimes which might have occurred in the country. Statistics on computer crime are not available, since these crimes are in a gray area and hard to trace.

Since there are no laws prohibiting most common forms of computer crime in Ecuador, the government has stated that it has no jurisdiction to investigate and prosecute these matters. The only exception once again is computer piracy, to which the procedure established under Decision 351 of the Andean Community of Nations and the Ecuadorian Intellectual Property Act is applied. Furthermore, in Ecuador, the seizure of intangible computer data is not permitted, because there is no law expressly permitting it.

El Salvador

There are no laws on the books in El Salvador which prohibit the alteration, interception, or destruction of computer information. Computer systems are not defined nor referenced within El Salvadorian criminal law. Despite the lack of substantive law relative to computer crime in El Salvador, training courses on the subject have been started and are in progress in the Office of the Attorney General of the Republic.

Mexico

Article 211(1) to 211(7) of the Mexican Federal Penal Code prohibits the copying, modification, destruction or damaging information, databases, or computers or information systems.

Nicaragua

A study published in December of 2000 found that Nicaragua had no cybercrime specific laws in place.

Panama

In the Republic of Panama there are no specifically defined and punishable crime relating to computer crime. There is, however, the concept of "damage," within the meaning of "crimes against property," in which computers are considered as the property of another. The Criminal Code of the Republic of Panama does penalize the destruction of a computer system, seen from the perspective that the computer system is another person's property. This is the sense of Article 200 of the Criminal Code, relating to "damage" under the heading "Crimes against property." It is unknown, however, whether any prosecutions have taken place under this theory in Panama to date. The Criminal Code of the Republic Panama does not specifically penalize the unauthorized destruction, modification, alteration, access, usage, or other similar interference to or of a computer system or program, from the perspective of "cybercrime."

Peru

In April of 2000, Peru added two computer crime provisions to its Penal Code. The provisions criminalize the unauthorized use of a computer system and damaging, altering or destroying data or computer programs.

Trinidad and Tobago

At this time, there is no specific computer crime legislation, but Trindad and Tobago are in the process of finalizing specific legislation – The Computer Misuse Bill, 1999. This bill provides the following offenses and penalties:

Clause 5 – Unauthorized modification of computer material;

Clause 3 – Unauthorized access to computer material

Clause 6 – Unauthorized use or interception of computer service

Clause 7 – Unauthorized obstruction of use of computer

Clause 8 – Unauthorized disclosure of access code

Clause 10 – Unauthorized receiving or giving access to data.

Venezuela

Venezuelan law does not criminalize the destruction, modification, alteration, or interference to or of a computer system or program. In the case of interference and other harmful activity that targets information and data of computer systems or programs, penalties exist in Venezuela that are applicable to the content of communications. These provisions are expressed in Articles 2 and 4 of the Law on the Protection of the Privacy of Communications, which states:

> *Article 2.* Anyone who arbitrarily, clandestinely, or fraudulently records or intercepts a communication between two persons, or interrupts it or blocks it, shall receive a prison sentence of three to five years.
>
> *Article 4.* Anyone who, in order to obtain some benefit for himself or others or in order to produce damage, forges or alters the content of a communication, shall receive a prison sentence of three to five years, provided that he used said content or allowed others to use it.

The same penalty shall be imposed on anyone who uses or exploits the content of a forged or altered communication, or even though that person did not participate in its falsification or received it from an anonymous source.

Venezuelan criminal law does penalize the unauthorized interception and transmission of computer data and information. Article 2 of the Law on the Protection of the Privacy of Communications published in Official Gazette No. 34,863 of December 16, 1991 states:

> *Article 2*
>
> Anyone who arbitrarily, clandestinely, or fraudulently records, or obtains information about a communication between two persons, or interrupts it or blocks it, shall receive a prison sentence of three to five years.

> Anyone who discloses, in whole or in part, using any means of communication, the content of the communications indicated in the first part of this article shall receive the same penalty, unless the act constitutes a more serious offense. In that regard, the Organic Draft Law on the General Telecommunications System also establishes administrative sanctions for cases of interference with telecommunications systems, as can be seen in the wording of this law:
>
> *Article 145*
>
> A fine of 100 to 1,000 taxation units shall be imposed on anyone who intentionally causes interference that is prejudicial to the operators or users of telecommunications services. If this interference results in the interruption of a legally installed telecommunications service, the fine shall be 500 to 2,000 taxation units.

Asia

Bangladesh

Bangladesh's responses to a United Nations survey on cybercrime law indicate that it has not adopted cybercrime-specific penal legislation.

Burma (Myanmar)

In September 1996, the country enacted the Computer Science Development Law. This legislation includes titles, definitions, and objectives for computer development within Burma (Myanmar). This act also contains a section on prior sanctions and licenses, as well as offences and penalties.

People's Republic of China

The bulk of China's cybercrime provisions are contained in its "Computer Information Network and Internet Security, Protection and Management Regulations", which were promulgated to "strengthen the security and the protection of computer information networks and of the Internet, and to preserve the social order and social stability." The prohibited activities are set forth in four Articles of the Regulations, to wit:

Article 4: No unit or individual may use the Internet to harm national security, disclose state secrets, harm the interests of the State, of society or of a group, the legal rights of citizens, or to take part in criminal activities.

Article 5: No unit or individual may use the Internet to create, replicate, retrieve, or transmit the following kinds of information:

(1) Inciting to resist or breaking the Constitution or laws or the implementation of administrative regulations;

(2) Inciting to overthrow the government or the socialist system;

(3) Inciting division of the country, harming national unification;

(4) Inciting hatred or discrimination among nationalities or harming the unity of the nationalities;

(5) Making falsehoods or distorting the truth, spreading rumors, destroying the order of society;

(6) Promoting feudal superstitions, sexually suggestive material, gambling, violence, murder,

(7) Terrorism or inciting others to criminal activity; openly insulting other people or distorting the truth to slander people;

(8) Injuring the reputation of state organs;

(9) Other activities against the Constitution, laws or administrative regulations.

Article 6: No unit or individual may engage in the following activities which harm the security of computer information networks:

(1) No one may use computer networks or network resources without getting proper prior approval

(2) No one may without prior permission may change network functions or to add or delete information

(3) No one may without prior permission add to, delete, or alter materials stored, processed or being transmitted through the network.

(4) No one may deliberately create or transmit viruses.

(5) Other activities, which harm the network, are also prohibited.

Article 7: The freedom and privacy of network users is protected by law. No unit or individual may, in violation of these regulations, use the Internet to violate the freedom and privacy of network users.

For violations of Articles 5 and 6, "the Public Security organization gives a warning and if there [is] income from illegal activities, confiscates the illegal earnings." Violations of Articles 4 and 7 are "punished according to the relevant laws and regulations."

Article 287 of the criminal code makes in an offense to "use a computer for financial fraud, theft, corruption, misappropriation of public funds, stealing state secrets or other crimes". In January of 2000, China implemented "State Secrecy Protection Regulations For Computer

Information Systems on the Internet". These Regulations are intended to "to strengthen the management of secrets for the computer systems on the Internet and to ensure the safety of state secrets." They establish a series of procedures which are designed to prevent the advertent or inadvertent disclosure of China's "state secrets," a term which is "used very loosely and can mean any information not officially approved for publication."

Hong Kong

Telecommunication Ordinance § 27A prohibits unauthorized access to a computer by telecommunication. Section 161 of the Crimes Ordinance covers obtaining access to a computer with criminal or dishonest intent. Section 60 of the Crimes Ordinance, which prohibits damaging or destroying property, encompasses the misuse of a computer, which is defined as follows:

'misuse of a computer' means:

(a) to cause a computer to function other than as it has been established to function by or on behalf of its owner, notwithstanding that the misuse may not impair the operation of the computer or a program held in the computer or the reliability of data held in the computer;

(b) to alter or erase any program or data held in a computer or in a computer storage medium;

(c) to add any program or data to the contents of a computer or of a computer storage medium, and any act which contributes towards causing the misuse of a kind referred to in paragraph (a), (b) or (c) shall be regarded as causing it.

Also, burglary, which is defined by § 11 of the Theft Ordinance, encompasses causing damage to a computer as part of its prohibition on entering a building with the intent to commit an offense consisting of theft, causing bodily harm or "doing unlawful damage to the building or anything therein."

India

India's cybercrime legislation is set out in "The Information Technology Act, 2000". The offenses are set out in Chapter XI of the Act. They include: tampering with computer source documents; unauthorized access; damaging or destroying computer data; publishing obscenity; disclosing confidential information without authorization; publishing a false digital signature certificate; and creating or publishing a digital signature certificate for fraudulent purposes.

Japan

Japan's cybercrime legislation is contained in two enactments, the "Unauthorized Computer Access Law," and the "Computer Crime Act." The Unauthorized Computer Access Law creates two offenses: unauthorized computer access and facilitating unauthorized computer access.

The Computer Crime Act creates five: computer forgery; disrupting the operations of a business computer; computer theft; computer fraud; and destroying computer records. In April of 2002, Japanese officials announced that they intended to put forward legislation which would criminalize the online transmission of child pornography;

while the sale and distribution of child pornography is already illegal in Japan, the law does not outlaw "show[ing] pornographic images of children on . . . websites."

Malaysia

Malaysia's cybercrime legislation is contained in the "Computer Crimes Act 1997." The Act creates four offenses: unauthorized access; unauthorized access with intent to commit or facilitate commission of further offense; unauthorized modification of the contents of a computer; and wrongful communication. It also criminalizes aiding and abetting and attempting to commit any of these offenses.

Mauritius

Mauritius' cybercrime legislation is the product of its "Information Technology Act 1998". Section 4 of the Act amended the Mauritius Criminal Code to add two new offenses: a data protection and security offense; and computer misuse.

Pakistan

Pakistan enacted the PAK Ordinance, which specifically addresses hacking, and virus related offenses. The PAK fails to address obscenity, cyber fraud, intellectual property rights, content filtering, censorship and Spamming. Instead, it leaves these offenses to be covered under existing common law. Section 32 of the Pak makes international offenders liable.

Philippines

Six weeks after the dissemination of the "Love Bug" virus, the Republic of the Philippines adopted the "Electronic Commerce Act" which, among other things, created several new cyberoffenses. The offenses are set out in § 33(a) of the Act, which states that the following "shall be penalized by fine and/or imprisonment":

> Hacking or cracking which refers to unauthorized access into or interference in a computer system/server or information and communication system; or any access in order to corrupt, alter, steal, or destroy using a computer or other similar information and communication devices, without the knowledge and consent of the owner of the computer or information and communications system, including the introduction of computer viruses and the like, resulting in the corruption, destruction, alteration, theft or loss of electronic data messages or electronic document shall be punished by a minimum fine of one hundred thousand pesos (P100,000.00) and a maximum commensurate to the damage incurred and a mandatory imprisonment of six (6) months to three (3) years.

Singapore

Singapore's cybercrime legislation appears in the Computer Misuse Act which was adopted in 1998. Part II of the Act created six new offenses: unauthorized access; access with intent to commit or facilitate commission of an offense; unauthorized modification of computer material; unauthorized use or interception of computer service; unauthorized obstruction of use of computer; and unauthorized disclosure of access code. The Computer Misuse Act also criminalizes aiding and abetting and attempting to commit any of these offenses.

South Korea

South Korea has two methods of implementing computer crime laws. They have established numerous articles within their criminal code, which went into effect on July 1, 1996, and they have implemented the Promotion of Utilization of Information and Communications Network Act, which went into effect on July 1, 1999.

Within the criminal code, Article 141-1 criminalizes the destruction of documents of public offices, including electromagnetic records. Article 227-2 makes it a crime to falsify or alter electromagnetic documents of a public official or a public office. Article 232-2 criminalizes falsification or alteration of private electromagnetic records. Article 314-2 makes it a criminal offense to interfere with business by damaging or destroying any data processors, including computers or electromagnetic records. Article 347-2 make it a crime to commit fraud by the use of a computer. Article 366 makes it a crime to damage, destroy, or conceal another person's property, including electromagnetic records.

Within the Promotion of Utilization of Information and Communications Network Act; Chapter V, Article 19 secures the safety of information, the truthfulness of the information, and protects users against unwanted advertising. Article 20 imposes obligations on providers of information and communications services, forbidding them from committing acts that are harmful to the security of the state, acts detrimental to public safety and moral, injurious to the economic order of the state, hurtful to the development of the economy, and criminal activities. Article 21 restricts the outflow of key information, enabling the Minister of Information to take any necessary measures to prevent information leaks to foreign countries. Article

22 makes it a criminal act to damage information of other's, infringe upon the information, steal, or leak the secrets of other persons. Chapter VII; Articles 28 and 29 of the Act provides for penal provisions for violators of the Act.

Taiwan

In 1997, Taiwan amended its Criminal Code to include prohibitions directed at several varieties of cybercrime. The revised Criminal Code does not make simple hacking an offense, but it does criminalize the following: disclosure of secrets; offenses against e-mail; causing damage or injury; disrupting the operation of a computer or computer system; computer fraud; computer forgery; and theft.

Vietnam

Vietnam has recently enacted new legislation to prosecute Internet related crimes. Included in the new legislation is Article 41 which addresses administrative breaches of regulations, Article 224 of the Penal Code which covers the creation, spread and scattering of electronic virus programs, Article 225 encompasses breaching regulations on operating, exploiting and using computer networks, and Article 226 on illegally using information in computer networks.

North Africa and the Middle East

Egypt

A study published in December of 2000 found that Egypt had no cybercrime specific laws in place.

Iran

A study published in December of 2000 found that Iran had no cybercrime specific laws in place. It noted that "for the past six years Iran has examined various aspects of cyber law," including "computer offenses", but so far no laws have been adopted. In June of 2001, the Iran Telecommunications Company issued regulations "to filter all materials presumed immoral or contrary to state security, including the Web sites of opposition groups," and to bar Internet access for those under eighteen.

Israel

Israel's cybercrime legislation appears in its Computers Law, 5755, which has been in effect since 1995. The Computers Law creates the following offenses: disrupting or interfering with the operation of a computer; disseminating "specious information" or "specious output"; unauthorized access; unauthorized access to commit another offense; and disseminating viruses or other harmful programs.

Jordan

A study published in December of 2000 found that Zimbabwe had no cybercrime specific laws in place. Subscribers to Internet services are explicitly required to abide by the laws applicable in Jordan, especially pertaining to publications, limitations on opinions expressed, and all the relevant Jordanian laws.

Kazakhstan

A study published in December of 2000 found that while Kazakhstan currently had no cybercrime specific laws in place, "state bodies" were "developing a law regarding cyber offenses."

Lebanon

Lebanon has yet to enact specific cyber crime legislation. However, through funds from the World Bank, Lebanon has drafted the National Information Technology Policy and Strategy document. The approach of this policy is for the government to take responsibility for key regulatory functions including privacy, intellectual property, security, and information content.

Morocco

A study published in December of 2000 found that Morocco currently had no cybercrime specific laws in place, but that an "inter-ministerial commission sponsored by the Prime Minister" was "working on security issues."

Oman

Rules and regulations of an ISP entitled GTO prohibit unauthorized or unlawful gaining or trying to gain access to any computer systems or networks through the use of the ISP services and any unlawful activities which are contrary to the social, cultural, political, religious or economical values of the Sultanate of Oman. Customers are also warned that any abuse and misuse of the Internet services through email or news or by any other means, including posting or soliciting obscene materials, hacking or trying to hack, shall result in criminal or civil lawsuits against the perpetrators. The ISPs also reserves the right to disconnect the service without notice.

Saudi Arabia

All communications are routed through a state proxy-server, which blocks access to sites deemed unacceptable for religious, moral, national security, or other reasons set out by the state.

Sudan

A study published in December of 2000 found that Sudan had no cybercrime specific laws in place. Sudan plans to "invite lawyers, legislators and computer professionals to a workshop" where the discussion will focus on the drafting of cybercrime legislation.

Syria

President Bashar al-Assad has pledged to take Syria into the computer age and Internet access is now available in the country.

Tunisia

Tunisia has not enacted any specific cyber crime legislation.

Turkey

Turkey's Criminal Code defines several types of cybercrime, to wit:

Article 525/a - (Annexed by Code 3756 Art. 21, 06.06.1991)

Whoever obtains programs or data or another component from an automatic data processing system illegally, shall be punished by imprisonment for one year to three years and a heavy fine of 1,000,000 to 15,000,000 liras.

Whoever uses, transfers or copies programs, data or another component in anautomatic data processing system, with the purpose of harming anybody, shall suffer the punishment in the above mentioned paragraph.

Article 525/b - (Annexed by Code 3756 Art. 22, 06.06.1991)

Whoever destroys or changes or deletes or prevents from operating or ensures incorrectly operating an automatic data processing system or data or another component, completely or partially, for the purpose of harming anyone or deriving a benefit for himself or anybody else, shall be punished by imprisonment for two years to six years and a heavy fine of 5,000,000 to 50,000,000 liras.

Whoever derives a legal benefit for himself or anybody else, using an automatic data processing system, shall be punished by imprisonment for one year to five years and a heavy fine of 2,000,000 to 20,000,000 liras.

Article 525/c - (Annexed by Code 3756 Art. 23, 06.06.1991

Whoever puts data or other components into an automatic data processing system or alters existing data or other components, in order to generate a counterfeit document for the purpose of using as evidence in jurisprudence, shall be punished by imprisonment for one year to three years. Whoever uses knowingly the abovementioned-altered one shall be punished by imprisonment for six months year to two years.

United Arab Emirates

There currently is no cybercrime legislation in the United Arab Emirates, though a draft cybercrime law is in process. Etisalat, the Emirates Telecommunications Corporation, has promulgated "terms and conditions" for the use of its services and an "acceptable use policy",; it reserves the right to initiate "such criminal or civil proceedings" as it deems necessary to secure the enforcement of these regulations.

Sub-Saharan Africa

Gambia

A study published in December of 2000 found that Gambia currently had no cybercrime specific laws in place. Gambia is "planning a national information technology initiative" which might produce such legislation," although the capacity for drawing up a legal framework is limited."

Kenya

Kenya has not enacted any specific cyber crime legislation.

Lesotho

A study published in December of 2000 found that Lesotho, too, currently had no cybercrime specific laws in place. It has established "special interest groups to look at the various aspects of information security relating to e-commerce.

Nigeria

A study published in December of 2000 found that Nigeria had no cybercrime specific laws in place.

South Africa

A study published in December of 2000 found that South Africa had no cybercrime specific laws in place.

Zambia

A study published in December of 2000 found that Zambia currently had no cybercrime specific laws in place. It also noted that Zambian officials had prepared a draft Telecommunications and Information Technology Council Act.

Zimbabwe

A study published in December of 2000 found that Zimbabwe had no cybercrime specific laws in place.

Australia, New Zealand and the Pacific Islands

Australia

Australia's Crimes Act 1914 establishes four cyber-offenses: unlawful access to data in Commonwealth and other computers; damaging data in Commonwealth and other computers; unlawful access to data in Commonwealth and other computers by means of Commonwealth facility; and damaging data in Commonwealth and other computers by means of Commonwealth facility.

Fiji Islands

The Fiji Islands have not enacted any specific cyber crime legislation.

New Zealand

A study published in December of 2000 found that New Zealand currently had no cybercrime specific laws in place. It noted that New Zealand was drafting a Crimes Amendment Bill (No. 6) which would address cybercrime.

7

Managing Cyber Crime: Recommendations of Information Security Permanent Monitoring Panel

The stability of modern society has been heightened by the ubiquitous nature of ICTs which pervades all aspects of human activity. Indeed the utilization of ICTs is a recognized prerequisite to improved corporate competitiveness, government efficiency, human development, and the development of knowledge societies and economies. The Internet and capabilities of broadband networks have integrated business, government, and defense interests and empowered small and medium-sized enterprises (SMEs), enabling them to compete on a global basis.

The benefits of ICTs, however, can be undercut by negative uses of these technologies in the form of cyber attacks, viruses and other malware, economic espionage, sabotage of data and systems, exploitation of networks, etc. Individuals and small groups can use ICTs against the interests of nation states. These cyber criminal acts can affect not only individual systems, but can also impact world peace and security and undermine development efforts. The resulting damage can ignite panic, cause a loss of confidence, create uncertainty, and destroy trust in modern society.

The challenges presented by cybercrime are directly proportional to the size of the problem. Since cybercrime was first identified and its dangerous potential recognized, the problem has shown rapid growth such that it challenges all ICT users—whether individuals, small businesses, multinational corporations, public sector entities, or nation states—and imposes responsibilities for cyber security upon them. The availability of tools to exploit ICT systems has markedly increased, thereby lowering the skill level needed to launch such attacks. Consequently, the number of incidents has risen dramatically.

The number of computer incidents reported to the Computer Emergency Response Team Coordinating Center (CERT/CC) of Carnegie Mellon Software Engineering Institute rose from six in 1988 when CERT/CC was formed to around 82,094 for 2002. Apart from the consequences for human development, there are three categories of harm flowing from cybercrime and attacks: economic consequences, disruption to critical infrastructures, and threats to national security and the capabilities of military and defense systems and first responders.

The economic damage and disruption associated with these incidents, compared to traditional crimes, is alarming. For example, the U. S. Association of Certified Fraud Examiners reported that in 2000, that the average sum of money taken in a bank holdup was US$14,000, but the average computer theft was US$2 million. According to the 2002 Computer Security Institute/Federal

Bureau of Investigation annual survey, the financial losses associated with U. S. computer crime rose from US$20,048,000 in 1997 to US$170,827,000 in 2002. Total losses incurred for the 1997-2001 time period was US$1,459,755,245.

Cyber attacks against critical infrastructures also pose a grave problem and threaten the global nature of cyberspace. Critical infrastructures are those systems that are vital to government operations, public safety, and national and economic security. The U. S. government considers the thirteen infrastructures as critical: agriculture, food, water, public health, emergency services, government, defense industrial base, information and telecommunications, energy, transportation, banking and finance, chemical industry, and postal and shipping. The potential for cyber attacks against these infrastructures by other nation states and terrorists has alarmed governments around the globe.

Because of the increasing dependency on ICTs, the vulnerability to cyber attacks against these infrastructures is steadily increasing. Since most of these infrastructures are owned and operated by the private sector, business's responsibility for cyber security with respect to these networks is heightened.

Combating cybercrime requires significant international cooperation and preventative measures, and this is especially important in deterring acts against critical infrastructure. Terrorists' use of ICTs to communicate and conspire and the feasibility of their launching attacks through information infrastructure is real.

In fall 2001, the Mountain View, California, police department requested FBI assistance in investigating suspicious surveillance of computer systems controlling utilities and government offices in the San Francisco Bay Area. The digital snooping was being done by Middle Eastern and South Asian browsers. The FBI found "multiple casings of sites" through telecommunications switches in Saudi Arabia, Indonesia, and Pakistan that focused on emergency telephone systems, electrical generation and transmission equipment, water storage and distribution systems, nuclear power plants, and gas facilities across the U. S. Some of the electronic surveillance focused on the remote control of fire dispatch services and pipeline equipment. Subsequently, information about those devices, including details on how to program them, was found on Al Qaeda computers seized this year.

The U. S. government has expressed concern that terrorists are targeting the junctures between physical and virtual infrastructures, such as electrical substations handling hundreds of thousands of volts of power or panels controlling dam floodgates. According to a recent Washington Post report, one Al Qaeda laptop found in Afghanistan had frequented a French website that contained a twovolume online "Sabotage Handbook" on tools of the trade, planning a hit, switch gear and instrumentation, anti-surveillance methods, and advanced attack techniques.

An Al Qaeda computer seized in January 2002 in Afghanistan contained models of a dam, complete with structural architecture and engineering software that enabled the simulation of a catastrophic failure of dam controls. Other computers linked to Al Qaeda visited Islamic chat rooms and had access to "cracking" tools to search networked computers and find and exploit security holes to gain entry or full command.

Additionally, evidence obtained from browser logs indicate Al Qaeda operatives spent time on sites that offer software and programming instructions for digital switches that run power, water, and transport and communications grids. Al Qaeda prisoners have reportedly admitted to planning to use such tools. These systems are especially vulnerable because many of the distributed control systems (DCS) and supervisory control and data acquisition (SCADA) systems that control critical infrastructure are connected to the Internet but lack even rudimentary security.

In addition, the technical details regarding how to penetrate these systems are widely discussed in technical fora, and experts consider the security flaws to be widely known. Since September 11, the U. S. Government has identified 192 groups, organizations, or individuals linked to terrorism. Also, it is well known that civilians often take political actions against websites or business systems.

In October 2000, the FBI issued an advisory warning that, due to high activity between Palestinian and Israeli sites, U. S. Government and private sector sites could become potential targets. Less than a month later, a group of hackers named Gforce Pakistan defaced more than 20 web sites and threatened to launch an Internet attack against AT&T. Other direct acts of cyberterrorism include attacks by pro-Israeli and pro-Palestinian hackers on their opposing side's web sites. Pro-Palestinian hackers attacked several Israeli government sites, including those of the Knesset (Parliament), Bank of Israel, the Prime Minister's Office, and the Israeli Army. The hackers also broke into several American-Israel Public Affairs Committee (AIPAC) databases, including one containing credit card numbers of members, then sent e-mails to 3,500 AIPAC members boasting of their intrusion.

ICTs in the wrong hands present a new threat to world peace and national security through the offensive use of these technologies in the form of cyber warfare and cyber attacks. Nation states have developed more sophisticated capabilities to launch attacks against critical infrastructures and impair the national security of another state and its ability to defend itself. In a recent classified report, the U. S. Central Intelligence Agency reportedly expressed concern that the Chinese military may be examining methods to attack defense and civilian computer systems in the U. S. and Taiwan. One way of conceptualizing the problem is by viewing these e-attacks as information warfare.

At present, there is neither an established classification of cyber weapons, nor clear definition of this term. The key concept for defining the subject area of information security is one of "informational weapons. "The U. S. Department of Defense (DoD) defines information warfare as, "Information operations conducted during the time of crisis or conflict to achieve or promote specific objectives over a specific adversary or adversaries" and defines information operations as "Actions taken to affect adversary information and information systems while defending one's own information and information systems. "

Cyberterrorism has been defined by a leading U. S. expert in testimony before the U. S. Senate to be: [T]he convergence of terrorism and cyberspace.... is generally understood to mean unlawful attacks against computers, networks, and the information stored therein when done to intimidate or coerce a government or its people in furtherance of political or social objectives. Further, to qualify as cyberterrorism, an attack should result in violence against persons or property, or at least cause enough harm to generate fear. Attacks that lead to death or bodily injury, explosions, plane crashes, water contamination, or severe economic loss would be examples.

Cyberwar is a very real technique of war, and likely to be used more and more as time passes. The U. S. , for example, has developed an "e-bomb" that utilizes high-velocity electromagnetic pulses that can permanently disable electrical and communication systems. The cyberwar and cybercrime problem will continue to pose a serious threat that will require a coordinated response from industry, intelligence, military and defense, national security officials, and law enforcement. Even more disconcerting is the fact that there is not only the potential – but the likelihood – of a combination of attacks that will impair economic interests, critical infrastructures, and military and defense capabilities.

According to a recently published UN report, "Cyber-crime and cyber-terrorism, and possibly cyber-war, will be an inevitable part of our future landscape. "Jurgen Storbeck, Director of Europol, has described the Internet as "a new sphere of life and a new scene of crime. "There is an age-old and perpetual race between attack and defense, and information infrastructure will provide no exception.

The legitimate interests of a state in countering cyber attacks and cybercrime, however, must be balanced against other international rights, such as those guaranteeing freedom of expression and human rights. Additionally, there is the concern that government regulation of and interference with Internet usage will impair the well-recognized ability of the Internet to foster democratization across the globe. The problems posed by cybercrime, cyber warfare, and cyberterrorism are of a universal and transnational character that touch upon all facets of the existence of states, society, business, and individuals. Information security underlies each of these challenges.

Recommendations of Information Security Permanent Monitoring Panel

In the framework of the seminars on Planetary Emergencies, the Information Security Permanent Monitoring Panel (PMP) was established in 2001, in order to examine the emerging threat to the functioning of information and communication technology (ICT) systems and to make appropriate recommendations. A set of thirteen Recommendations set out were adopted by the Panel in August 2002 and endorsed by the World Federation of Scientists. In September 2002, prior to the inauguration of the 57session of the UN General Assembly (UNGA), these Recommendations were submitted to the Secretary General of the UN, the President of the General Assembly, and the Presidents of the relevant Main Committees. In the opinion of the PMP, these Recommendations retain their validity, and the present Explanatory Comments are designed to provide them with new thrust and clarity.

Recommendations

Today, information security is an important priority for societies. Because of the global nature of cyberspace and the more active use of information and communication technologies (ICTs), this problem is of a universal and transnational character that touches upon all facets of the existence of states, society, and individuals. The vulnerability of global and national information infrastructures gives birth to new challenges to national and international security, business activity, and human rights. The problem of information security will not be resolved by the efforts of just one state or a group of states or on a regional basis. The solution of this problem demands a unified effort of the entire international community.

In light of the foregoing, the Panel accepted the following Recommendations:

1. Because of its universal character, the United Nations system should have the leading role in inter-governmental activities for the functioning and protection of cyberspace so that it is not abused or exploited by criminals, terrorists, and states for aggressive purposes. In particular it should: (a) respond to an essential and urgent need for a comprehensive consensus Law of Cyberspace; (b) advance the harmonization of national cybercrime laws through model prescription; and (c) establish procedures for international cooperation and mutual assistance.

2. Working to this end, the UN should give recognition to the work already accomplished by the negotiating parties to the Council of Europe Convention on Cybercrime (CoE Convention). The CoE Convention would draw greater strength if all parties who participated in its negotiation process were to sign the Convention if they have not already done so, and those who have were to accelerate the ratification and transformation processes. Immediately subsequent to

the entry into force of the Convention, signatories should take steps to nominate and notify their Authority for the handling of mutual assistance, to participate in the 24/7 network, and to take other steps to promote international cooperation in the defeat of cybercrime as the CoE Convention foresees.

3. Cybercrime, cyberterrorism, and cyber warfare activities that may constitute a breach of international peace and security should be dealt with by the competent organs of the UN system under international law. We recommend that the UN and the international scientific community examine scenarios and criteria and international legal sanctions that may apply.

4. Within the UN framework, we recommend that a special forum undertake the synthesizing of work on cyberspace undertaken within the UN system.

5. In this context, we recommend the UN and other international entities examine the feasibility of establishing an international Information Technology Agency with the indicative mandate to, inter alia:

   — Facilitate technology exchanges;

   — Review and endorse emerging protocols and codes of conduct;

   — Maintain standards and protocols for ultra-high bandwidth technologies;

   — Specify the conditions on which access to such ultra-high bandwidth technologies be granted;

   — Promote the establishment of effective inter-governmental structures and public-private interaction;

— Attempt to coordinate international standards setting bodies with the view of promoting interoperability of information security management processes and technologies;

— Facilitate the establishment and coordination of international computer emergency response facilities, including taking into account activities of existing organizations;

— Share cyber-tracking information derived from open sources and share technologies to enhance the security of databases and data sharing.

6. Nationally and transnationally, an educational framework for promoting the awareness of the risks looming in cyberspace should be developed for the public. Specifically, schools and educational institutions should incorporate codes of conduct for ICT activities into their curricula. Civil society, including the private sector, should be involved in this educational process.

7. Due diligence and accountability should be required of chief executive officers and public and private owners to institutionalize security management processes, assess their risks, and protect their information infrastructure assets, data, and personnel. The potential of market forces should be fully utilized to encourage private sector companies to protect their information networks, systems, and data. This process could include information security statements in filings for publicly traded companies, minimum insurance requirements for coverage of cyber incidents, and return on investment analyses.

8. In parallel, to the elaboration and harmonization of national criminal codes, there should also be an effort to work toward equivalent civil responsibility laws worldwide. Civil responsibility should also be established for neglect, violation of fiduciary duties, inadequate risk assessment, and harm caused by cyber criminal and cyber terrorist activities.

9. Among the specific and concrete actions that should be considered is the possibility that commercial off-the-shelf (COTS) hardware, firmware, and software should be open source or at least be certified.

10. Information security issues should also be addressed in forthcoming multilateral meetings. Regional organizations should also add to national and international efforts to combat attacks in cyberspace in their respective regional contexts.

11. International law enforcement organizations should assume a stronger role in the international promotion of cybercrime issues. The competences and functions of Interpol and, in the European context, Europol, should be substantially strengthened, including by examining their investigative options.

12. The international science community should more vigorously address the scientific and technological issues that intersect with the legal and policy aspects of information security, including the use of ICTs and their impact on privacy and individual rights.

13. The international scientific community, and in particular the World Federation of Scientists, should assist developing countries and donor organizations to understand better how ICTs can further development in an environment that promotes information security and bridges the Digital Divide.

Explanatory Comments to Recommendations

> **1. Because of its universal character, the United Nations system should have the leading role in inter-governmental activities for the functioning and protection of cyberspace so that it is not abused or exploited by criminals, terrorists, and states for aggressive purposes. In particular it should: (a) respond to an essential and urgent need for a comprehensive consensus Law of Cyberspace; (b) advance the harmonization of national cybercrime laws through model prescription; and (c) establish procedures for international cooperation and mutual assistance.**

A. Why Should the UN Have the Leading Role in Intergovernmental Activities on Cyberspace?

The interconnected global network of 600 million online usersserved by 15 million hostsconnecting nearly 200 countries presents increasingly daunting security challenges to governments, companies, and citizens. Although the Internet has brought enormous economic and social benefits, it has also ushered in a host of new problems. Negative repercussionsof the Internet boom – while not outweighing the benefits – include:

— Computer related fraud, forgery, and theft

— Violations of intellectual property rights

— Cyber-mediated physical attacks

— Sabotage of data

— Network attacks such as distributed denial of service attacks (DDoS)

— Malicious code (viruses, worms, and Trojan horses)

— Web defacements, including politically motivated hacking (hactivism)Unauthorized interceptions of communications, intrusion, and espionage

— Identity theft

— Spoofing of IP addresses, password cracking, and theft

— Online sexual exploitation of children and child pornography

— Computer harassment and cyber-stalking.

The motivation to commit cybercrime is also increasing exponentially. Ever increasing connectivity among Internet users around the globe compounds the risks because there will be more sophisticated communications infrastructure and an increased pool of bad actors and terrorists who can use technology to conspire and to commit widespread vandalism, fraud, economic espionage, and to launch attacks on networks and information systems.

The already pervasive and expanding nature of the Internet and ICTs requires a universal approach to the security of data, systems, and networks. According to a recent UN report on information security:

> The wide and pervasive integration of computers and embedded chips into modern society is what makes it vulnerable to cyber-attacks. Computers are now deeply integrated into the management and processing of our daily actions, and embedded chips are so omnipresent today that it is virtually impossible to determine even their actual numbers and locations. This became abundantly clear during the Y2K exercise, when businesses and governments spent billions to make sure computer systems would work when the year 2000 began.

The profound integration of computers and information technology is obviously the strength of modern life, but it is also its vulnerability. The greater the interconnectedness, reliability, and complexity, the greater the vulnerability and the ease for exploitation.

Information and communications systems are not only a potential target of criminals, terrorists, and military planners; they are also portals of physical vulnerability for the vast number of physical assets with controls linked to the Internet or managed by information technology systems. These direct and indirect vulnerabilities are amplified by the relatively small number of nodal exchange points (roughly 100 or so) on the Internet network, the existence and location of which is public knowledge.

Because the ubiquitous nature of the Internet and the built-in vulnerabilities of the global network require a global perspective, the UN is ideally suited to accept a role within its capabilities to lead inter-governmental activities regarding the security of cyberspace. Similarly, only a global consensus can address the updating of the laws of war to include the parameters of wars in cyberspace.

No multinational organization other than the UN has the membership and capability to address these issues in a meaningful way that will have global impact. Beyond security concerns, the utilization of ICTs in investigatory, tracking, and recording practices and control over communications and Internet usage poses a serious threat to international rights guaranteed under the international law of the UN, such as human rights, freedom of expression and other civil liberties. According to a senior UN official:

> As the only truly universal international organisation that we have today, the United Nations can provide the broadest and most neutral and legitimate platform for bringing together governments and other key stakeholders to undertake this effort. Only this institution can provide the forum for discussion and debate on the complexities of the subject, and coalesce the expertise that exists around the world for a proper drafting of relevant legislation that can fill the existing and growing void in cyber-law.

B. Why a Law of Cyberspace?

At the outset, one must acknowledge that the call for a body of law regulating cyberspace is not uniformly accepted in the legal community. The usual arguments are that

(1) there is no consensus concerning the many possible designs or architectures that may affect the functionality we now associate with cyberspace;

(2) very few bodies of law are defined by their characteristic technologies; and

(3) the best legal doctrine re-examines, expands, or applies existing doctrines to a new arena.

Whatever the validity of such comments concerning activities within single nation states, the capability of the Internet to cut across many national jurisdictions at lightning speed argues that we look anew. It recommends that nations seek a comprehensive re-examination of the many relevant, sometimes conflicting legal doctrines, practices, and procedures to produce a comprehensive, universal, and uniform legal framework for handling the issues colloquially called cyber law.

The Privacy & Computer Crime Committee, Section of Science & Technology Law of the American Bar Association, has recognized the need for international action to create a uniform body of law:

> A major component of information and infrastructure security is a nation's ability to deter, detect, investigate, and prosecute cyber criminal activities. Industrialized nations and multinational organizations have taken significant steps toward combating cybercrime. The glaring gaps in work to-date are: (1) inadequate international coordination and (2) woefully deficient legal frameworks and organizational capacity in developing countries necessary to combat cybercrime.

An initial framework that could serve as an excellent starting point for the development of a Model Law on Cybercrime has been developed in the Council of Europe. The CoE Convention on Cybercrime of 2001 (CoE Convention) has been signed by 36 countries. Although civil libertarians and privacy advocates continue to express concern that the CoE Convention undermines individual privacy and is inconsistent with provisions in U. S. law, it has been endorsed by the Group of Eight (G8) as a model to be followed by other countries. Other important work in this area has been done by the G8, the Organization for Economic Cooperation and Development (OECD), the Asia-Pacific Economic Cooperation (APEC), the European Union (EU), and the Organization of American States (OAS).

Furthermore, with the public revelation of President Bush's National Security Presidential Directive 16 ordering the U. S. government to develop cyber warfare guidelines and rules under which the U. S. could penetrate and/or disrupt foreign computer systems,cyber warfare has come out of the closet. As with other forms of warfare, there should be internationally accepted limitations on the form of conflict. Certainly, a meaningful codification of such activities should take place under the aegis of the international body with the widest membership, the United Nations.

The PMP concludes that, on a global basis, current national and international legal frameworks are insufficient and inconsistent across national jurisdictions to address the scope and complexity of the subject of cybercrime, cyberterrorism and cyber warfare. While efforts to combat cybercrime and cyberterrorism have been valiant and even successful in many areas, more is possible. We recommend a determined effort be made to draw upon the work performed to date in order to draft and adopt a comprehensive Model Law on Cybercrime and agreement on related procedural, administrative and cooperative considerations.

The UN has already performed excellent work in the development of model laws for electronic transactions and electronic signaturesand its institutional roots are based on established international rules for conflict. Such a Model Law would have to address numerous issues, ranging from technical and definitional (e. g. , what is cyberspace) to substantive (e. g. , legal provisions, jurisdictional issues, and standards of evidence) to procedural and administrative (e. g. , international cooperation mechanisms). It would also have to balance competing interests of sovereignty, national security, civil liberties, human rights, and freedom of expression. The UN should give separate consideration to determining the rules under which nation states may engage in cyber warfare and respond to cyberterrorism. The World Summit on the

Information Society may also be a forum for discussion on this subject.

C. How Comprehensive a Consensus is Needed?

Some argue that the CoE Convention on Cybercrime is adequate consensus for an international legal framework to be developed. A legitimate counterpoint, however, is that more countries would have to sign and ratify the Convention and abide by its terms in order for it to effectively deter cybercrime, significantly advance international cooperation on these issues, or lead to a harmonized global framework.

Out of about 200 countries, only 36 have signed the CoE Convention. Many of the countries who have not signed the CoE Convention either do not have any cybercrime laws, or have such inadequate ones, that criminals can essentially act with impunity. Since communications utilizing packet switched technologies often travel through many countries before reaching their destination (even on local-to-local communications), the CoE Convention does not provide a comprehensive enough consensus in this area.

However, despite some shortcomings, controversial points, and lacunae, the CoE Convention "no doubt constitutes a major drafting achievement by a representative cross section of the international community, and there is no private or public initiative in sight that could match it in legal status, completeness, quality and endorsement received. "This Convention deserves to be considered as a starting point for working toward a broader, universal agreement and Model Law.

D. *What are Some Areas of Conflict/Inconsistency?*

Multiple cases have arisen where Internet activities considered to be legitimate in one country violate the laws in another. Additionally, one country may not have the procedural laws to enable it to perform the requested assistance or law enforcement may not have the expertise to assist in the search and seizure of electronic evidence. Examples of areas of conflict include jurisdictional issues, extradition disputes, extra-territorial seizures, violations of content laws, and inconsistent hacking laws. These inconsistencies alone underscore the important role the UN could play in acting as coordinator on these issues.

Gelbstein and Kamal note that:

> Civil liberties groups have also expressed concern that the [CoE] convention undermines individual rights to privacy and extends the surveillance powers of the signatory governments. Critics in the United States indicate that the provisions of the convention are incompatible with current U. S. law. For example, by defining the sending of unsolicited e-mails as a criminal activity, the Convention is claimed "to criminalize behavior which until now has been seen as lawful civil disobedience. "E. How Might Harmonization of Cybercrime Laws Proceed Through Model Prescription?The UN Model Laws on Electronic Commerce and Electronic Signatures are considered to be the the global "standard" for legislation in these areas. They have been looked to and followed by industrialized and developing countries around the globe. UN action that would provide a global model law and an accompanying explanatory memoranda that nation states could use as a guide, along with an international agreement on procedural, administrative, and cooperative aspects, would make the global harmonization of cybercrime laws an achievable goal.

F. What are Examples of Procedures for International Cooperation and Mutual Assistance?

Certainly, one of the oldest and best known institutions for international cooperation and mutual assistance is Interpol. Founded in 1923, it has 178 member countries and maintains close working relationships with numerous intergovernmental bodies. The G8, Europol, OECD, UN, APEC, and OAS have all established mechanisms or launched initiatives to promote international cooperation and mutual assistance in the cyberspace arena. One of the best known practical examples of global-scale coordinated international cooperation and mutual assistance was seen in efforts to deal with the Y2K problem.

The Year 2000 (Y2K) experience gave rise to new ways in which governments and critical infrastructure sectors world-wide shared information to monitor incidents as they arose.... . The international governmental and industry organisations notable for establishing mechanisms for global monitoring of Y2K incidents affecting critical infrastructure sectors included the International Civil Aviation Organization (ICAO) and the International Air Transport Association (IATA), and the International Atomic Energy Agency (IAEA) and the World Association of Nuclear Operators (WANO). At the technical levels, there are numerous opportunities for information sharingboth in the public and private sectors.

Information sharing can be facilitated by public sector initiatives that:

(a) establish centers for sharing information on an anonymous basis or serve as an intermediary where the direct sharing of information among industry is difficult,

(b) create a central alert point for technical information and assistance regarding security risks and fixes, and

(c) organize a public/private group comprised of all stakeholders (industry, government, academia, NGOs) to begin a dialogue on ICT security risks and develop ways to work together.

In 1997, information sharing and analysis centers (ISACs) were established in the U. S. to facilitate information exchange among critical infrastructure sectors. ISAC members usually "share information in a way that preserves their anonymity while providing an overview of cyber incidents within their sector not otherwise obtained individually. "Indeed, the Commission of the European Communities notes that "urgent measures are needed to produce a statistical tool for use by all Member States so that computer related crime within the European Union can be measured both quantitatively and qualitatively. "This is important; however, there also needs to be a common methodological way to look at cybercrime, lest the quantity and quality results be slanted. Information sharing efforts, however, are hindered by national laws that deter the private sector from sharing security incident information with public sector entities. Laws such as the U. S. Freedom of Information Act and other similar national "access to information laws" cause concern within the private sector that shared confidential or proprietary information may be disclosed.

Antitrust laws also deter collaborative information sharing activities. Additional concerns are raised by the sharing of security incident information with foreign governments. U. S. Sentencing Guidelines create an additional risk. Corporations worry that by sharing security breach information and seeking the assistance of law enforcement, an investigation could reveal wrongdoing by corporate insiders which could "snap back" on the company and expose it to harsh penalties under the Guidelines. Thus, there is a need to develop a consistent international framework that encourages public-private information sharing by mitigating the risks that flow from these existing laws.

> 2. Working to this end, the UN should give recognition to the work already accomplished by the negotiating parties to the Council of Europe Convention on Cybercrime (CoE Convention). The CoE Convention would draw greater strength if all parties who participated in its negotiation process were to sign the Convention if they have not already done so, and those who have were to accelerate the ratification and transformation processes. Immediately subsequent to the entry into force of the Convention, signatories should take steps to nominate and notify their Authority for the handling of mutual assistance, to participate in the 24/7 network, and to take other steps to promote international cooperation in the defeat of cybercrime as the CoE Convention foresees.

Cybercrime defies national boundaries. Any effective strategy to prevent and combat the new types of cyber offenses and the new modalities of committing traditional offenses through technologies of cyberspace must, therefore, lead to transnational responses in criminal law and law enforcement. There must be no national loopholes; the present situation in which there are considerable differences of legal coverage, standards, and levels of protection is highly unsatisfactory. The case for a binding, universal international code of broad scope is compelling. At the same time, shared prescriptions of this nature will be unsuitable for containing and penalizing all cyber attacks. Attacks by nation states and international terrorist groups on critical societal and economic infrastructures and the defense establishment of other countries, giving rise to highly relevant threat scenarios, require different international responses, as discussed under Recommendation 3.

A number of private fora and international organizations have attempted to address the substantive, procedural, and jurisdictional challenges posed by the transnational nature of cybercrime.

The most extensive is the Council of Europe' s Convention on Cybercrime (CoE Convention), which was opened for signature on Nov. 23, 2001 and has, up to now, been signed by 36 countries, of which four signatories (U. S. , Canada, Japan, and South Africa) are "partner" countries but are not CoE members. The Convention covers substantive penal law as well as criminal procedural law and international cooperation in law enforcement, underlining the essential linkage between the three; indeed, the time-critical nature of tracking cybercrime, securing electronic evidence, and facilitating pursuit requires such linkage.

All attempts at creating a consistent and universal penal framework for dealing with the cyber challenge have to face a number of inherent problems:

(1) striking a balance between the privacy of communications in cyberspace and the freedom of expression and access to information on the one hand, and the requirements of national security and speedy law enforcement on the other;

(2) the retarding influence that will be exercised by the need to ratify a treaty containing civil and criminal provisions and administrative and procedural requirements;

(3) the need to transform treaty obligations into applicable law;

(4) the need to ensure essential equivalence of these laws in the face of very general directive language in the international texts;

(5) the time requirements for setting up functioning transnational cooperation mechanisms; or

(6) the complex problem of including content-related cyber offenses.

These difficulties notwithstanding, the CoE Convention offers great promise for moving towards a universal penal system in this field. Given the present composition of affiliated member states, it avoids the pitfall of offering a purely European focus and lends itself to a broader international audience. The ultimate objective would be to incorporate it, textually its provisions into a future Model Law on Cyberspace which is the central issue around which these Recommendations revolve.

In order to enhance the credibility and effectiveness of the CoE Convention, Recommendation 2 appeals, as a first and important step, to the parties that participated in the negotiation process to ratify and implement the Convention and to establish the necessary cooperation mechanisms for the broad geographical area which they represent.

Further steps to extend the number of signatory nation states to the CoE Convention would be welcome. Indeed, it would be highly desirable that a campaign to promote universal adherence get underway, at short notice, at the level of the United Nations, in the preparatory phase for the creation of a universal regulation of cyberspace. It would be important that response times for such an international appeal be kept as short as feasible, and that each signatory, in launching the process for transforming treaty obligations into national law, be mindful of the time-critical nature of defeating cybercrime and keeping pace with technology. If the CoE Convention can manage to create a critical momentum for the establishment of a universal legal framework and administrative organization regarding cyberspace, this momentum must not be lost.

In assessing the importance of the CoE Convention, governments should also be aware of an important complementary effort by the European Union. The EU Ministers of Justice adopted the Proposal for a Council Framework Decision on attacks against information systems on March 4, 2003. Consequently, they will now begin harmonizing their own national laws with this Decision.

The Council Framework Decision contains definitions, model articles for the criminalization of major cyber attacks, and rules for cooperation among EU countries, some of which flesh out in more detail provisions from the CoE text, some more concise, but overall, in the Framework's own professed intention, compatible with the CoE Convention.

The particular level of legal and administrative cooperation that already exists among the Member States of the EU as a common legal and judicial space, but is lacking elsewhere, means that the Framework is not suitable as a model code to the same extent as the CoE Convention. The latter preserves its quality as the overriding and most complete legal instrument particularly suited for endorsement by the present Recommendation.

3. Cybercrime, cyberterrorism, and cyber warfare activities that may constitute a breach of international peace and security should be dealt with by the competent organs of the UN system under international law. We recommend that the UN and the international scientific community examine scenarios and criteria and international legal sanctions that may apply.

Cyber activities that constitute deliberate hostile actions by nation states or non-state actors operating transnationally may threaten international peace and security, yet elude penal sanctions under current legal frameworks or a future Model Law on Cyberspace. One consideration is that, under certain circumstances, the international doctrine of sovereign immunity protects nation states against legal actions. This protection could conceivably extend to offensive cyber actions taken by nation states. Other concerns relate to (1) the lack of international cooperation on a global scale, and (2) technical considerations regarding the inability to effectively track and trace Internet communications.

The response to any scenario—whether a cyber criminal activity, an act of cyberterrorism, or an intended act of cyber warfare by a nation state – requires the ability to effectively track and trace cyber attacks. A recent report from CERT/CC at Carnegie Mellon University notes:

> The capability of a nation (or a cooperating group of nations) to track and trace the source of any attacks on its infrastructures or its citizens is central to the deterrence of such attacks and hence to a nation's long-term survival and prosperity. An acknowledged ability to track and trace both domestic and international attackers can preempt future attacks through fear of reprisals such as criminal prosecution, military action, economic sanctions, and civil lawsuits....

The anonymity enjoyed by today's cyber-attackers poses a grave threat to the global information society, the progress of an information-based international economy, and the advancement of global collaboration and cooperation in all areas of human endeavor. Technical difficulties must be addressed by international standards setting bodies. The TCP/IP protocol,which is the current standard protocol for network communications, seriously limits the ability to track and trace cyber attacks. At present, "the Internet has no standard provisions for tracking or tracing the behavior of its users. "Because the Internet protocols were designed for a trustworthy community of researchers, it is quite easy for users to hide their tracks, making it difficult to trace the communications path. For example, because there typically is no capability for cryptographic authentication of the information in IP packets, the information in the packet can be modified and the source address can be forged. "Packet laundering" involves compromising intermediate hosts along a communication path and hopping from host to host such that traceback attempts can be effectively thwarted. These vulnerabilities could facilitate, or disguise, statesponsored cyber activities or intentionally redirect a cyber criminal act to make it appear that it came from a nation state.

As noted by CERT/CC's Howard Lipson:

> It is clear that tracking and tracing attackers across a borderless cyber-world, and holding them accountable, requires multilateral actions that transcend jurisdictions and national boundaries. Tracking and tracing requires cooperation encompassing the legal, political, technical, and economic realms. ...

One of the most significant policy implications of the technical approaches to tracking and tracing... is the need for intense international cooperation at a deeply technical level. This cooperation must go well beyond simple agreements in principle to share tracking data. Present legal regimes are ineffective in deterring highly relevant threat scenarios that may violate international peace and security. Actions that are prohibited by nation states or considered terrorist or rogue acts against other countries require further deliberation by the United Nations. Internationally agreed standards of conduct are necessary if the Internet is to remain a backbone of economies and a primary means of global communication. In a thorough analysis of the uncharted waters in the area of cyberspace attacks, three renowned scholars in the field argue that:

> In particular, the status of information operations as "force" or "armed attack" is undetermined, an uncertainty which complicates diplomatic and military decision-making. In terms of the UN Charter, it is clear that a range of information attacks would constitute uses of force, and a comparable range of countermeasures would constitute legitimate self-defence....

Beyond these preliminary conclusions, there is far more work to be done on both international technical and legal fronts. Nations that choose to employ information operations, or that expect to be targeted by them, should facilitate tracking, attribution and transnational enforcement through multilateral treaties and, more broadly, by clarifying international customary law regarding the use of force and self-defence in the context of the UN Charter and the laws of armed conflict. Several scenarios support this conclusion and range from "cyber activists" to information and cyber warfare. On the less serious end of the spectrum, there is the April 1998 distributed denial of service attack launched against the U. S. Department of Defense by "cyber activists" who caused some Department computers to crash. At the other end of the spectrum are direct attacks against the critical infrastructures of one nation state by another. One of the first examples of this was seen in 1991 in Operation Desert Storm when the U. S. disabled Iraq's communications network. Other examples of cyber warfare could include:

> "Means for highly accurate spotting of electromagnetic equipment and its destruction by way of rapid identification of separate components of control, recognition, guidance and fire information systems.
>
> . Means for hitting components of electronic equipment and power supply thereof with a view to putting individual components of electronic systems out of action for short-term or irreversibly.
>
> . Means for affecting data transmission processes with a view to terminating or disorganizing operations of data exchange subsystems, by affecting signal propagation environments and functioning algorithms.
>
> . Propaganda and disinformation facilities for modifying control system data, creating a virtual picture of the situation different from the real one, changing human value systems, damaging morale of the adversary's population. "

Packet inspection and modification or rerouting through platform technologies at country gateways. In between, lay the acts of terrorists or rogue actors that can be equally destructive.

Increasingly, nation states, either individually or collectively, are acting to protect their own networks. The range of actions that are possible is considerable, and some can have broad impact on the global network and communications capabilities. It is becoming increasingly clear that companies and countries alike must shift from the reactive mode to the active mode in dealing with cyber attacks.

As noted by two World Federation of Scientists experts, "governments (and companies) need the ability to block distributed denial of service attacks, viruses and malicious worms, and protect super-critical and critical infrastructure at the core network level before they inflict their damage along backbone and customer links. "An international discussion and understanding regarding what types of proactive actions are acceptable or allowable is necessary to ensure one nation's protective actions do not unduly hinder the communications capabilities of other nations.

The international legal framework is especially murky in the area of cyber attacks and information warfare. The UN Charter was not drafted with the information age in mind and definitions lack clear meaning in the cyber context. The Charter, for example, forbids "acts of aggression" and limits the "threat or use of force" in peacetime. Article 41 grants the Security Council the power to enforce these Charter restrictions through the "complete or partial interruption of economic relations and of rail, sea, air, postal, telegraphic, radio, and other means of communication, and the severance of diplomatic relations. " Article 42 allows for action by "air, sea or land forces" as necessary to maintain or restore peace. According to one analysis, "Factors that may influence whether something is an act of force include expected lethality, destructiveness and invasiveness. "

Thus, Article 41 may be interpreted as allowing some interruption of communications, if it is not done in a manner that is not lethal, destructive or invasive, but what does that mean in the cyber sense? Certainly, some acts against communication systems could be considered quite destructive and/or invasive, such as the manipulation of dam controls or power grids. One of the preeminent authors in this area, Walter Sharp, argues that manipulations or attacks that cause an economic crisis could be deemed a "use of force. "And while one action, such as packet sniffing, rerouting, or content modification, may not be lethal or destructive, a reasonable argument can be made that it would be invasive.

Responses to attacks on information systems could conceivably be allowed under Article 51 of the UN Charter, which allows states to take actions in self-defense but requires them to report such actions. Individual responses by states could be either overt or covert, making the reporting requirement problematic in instances of covert actions. Indeed, what types of responses might be acceptable under Article 51 is vague. Moreover, nations could engage in individual or collective cyber selfdefense through NATO or other multinational alliances.

The laws of armed conflict must also be factored into any discussion regarding cyber activities of nation states. In times of war, civilian assets that support the military (such as communication systems) may be attacked in order to obtain submission of the enemy, provided that it is limited to military objectives and civilian losses are proportional to the military advantage to be gained – and provided it avoids unnecessary suffering.Possible pre-emptive actions must be also be considered and under what circumstances these might be allowed. Elaborating upon this nutshell-identification of problems, Andrey Krutskikh, reflecting a general line of thinking among Russian experts, has made a number of suggestions for further international law work that would aim at including cyberattacks more broadly into extant international law. They can be summarized as follows:

— In line with the concept of defining techniques of interfering with information security as "information weapons," despite the present uncertainty on their scope, it is suggested that new, extended criteria for the definition of weapons and armed aggression should be sought, giving emphasis to the objectives of the "aggressor," such as seeking military superiority

— Cyber attacks on other states could then be considered acts of armed aggression under the UN Charter, and, applying the principles of proportionality and necessity, thresholds for responsive actions in self-defense could be defined, taking into account the direct as well as the indirect damage cyber attacks can cause.

— Further along these lines, the author proposes to establish a list of key information systems of critical relevance for national security which, as a "zone protected by international law," would benefit of protective mechanisms, such as legitimate international emergency responses, beyond the normal rules and practices on reprisals and responses. In the list, a distinction should be made between civilian and transnational facilities, and military systems which may be subject to legitimate attacks.

— On the argument that "cyber weapons" are not currently subject to international treaties pertaining to arms control, Dr. Krutskikh advances several suggestions on a negotiated adaptation of extant treaty law designed to curb the proliferation of such weapons and providing a clear legal framework relating to the aggressive use of cyber operations.

— In an even broader sweep, Dr. Krutskikh, following from earlier official projects within the UN and bilateral diplomacy, develops the idea of a comprehensive international legal regime banning the development, production and use of the "most hazardous types of cyber weapons"for which the key ideas are spelled out in catalogue form. Part of this broad approach is the establishment of an "early warning system. " The author also advocates a sanctuary concept under which "global information systems" would be defined and protected as demilitarized zones.

Clearly, the types of cyber activities nation states may engage in, either defensively or offensively, deserve deeper discussion in a multinational forum. The PMP supports the following conclusion:

> As electronic information networks expand and military and industrial infrastructures become more dependent on them, cyber-attacks are bound to increase in frequency and magnitude. Interpretations of the UN Charter and of the laws of armed conflict will have to evolve accordingly in order to accommodate the novel definitions of the use of force that such attacks imply....

In terms of the laws of armed conflict, the potentially dangerous consequences of an unnecessary response, a disproportional response or a mistakenly targeted response argue for keeping a human being in the decision loop.

Beyond these preliminary conclusions, there is far more work to be done on both the international, technical, and legal fronts. Nations that choose to employ information operations, or that expect to be targeted by them, should facilitate tracking, attribution, and transnational enforcement through multilateral treaties and, more broadly, by clarifying international customary law regarding the use of force and self-defence in the context of the UN Charter and the laws of armed conflict. Operationally, scientific studies and scenario generation exercises should be undertaken in the international legal and technical communities, involving the General Assembly and First and Sixth Committees. The International Law Commission could be tasked with developing an appropriate legal framework defining legitimate cyber actions by nation states.

4. Within the UN framework, we recommend that a special forum undertake the synthesizing of work on cyberspace undertaken within the UN system.

Ordering cyberspace under the perspective of universality requires comprehensive involvement by the United Nations. In many ways, this challenge has already been recognized and is increasingly met by various UN offices and bodies as well as by members of the wider UN family. There are also global initiatives undertaken by the private sector that purport to work towards similar ends and could usefully be included in an over-all effort.

These manifold, widely dispersed efforts are, however, difficult to follow and to assess in their overall impact. A central focal point within the UN itself could perform a coordinating, evaluating, and synthesizing function. Without prejudice to the mandate or autonomous policy decisions of other UN branches or outside organizations, such a forum could catalogue and assess the work done elsewhere, point to inconsistencies and duplication, identify gaps and new research requirements, and stimulate coordinated approaches.

The problem is far wider than just a question of the Digital Divide.

The list of UN or UN-related actors in the field is already long. Apart from a number of resolutions adopted by the General Assembly, the UN ICT Task Force, UN Institute for Training and Research (UNITAR), the UN Center for Social Development and Humanitarian Affairs, the UN Committee on International Trade Law (UNCITRAL), the UN Conference on Trade and Development (UNCTAD), and the UN Office for Drug Control and Crime Prevention have provided inputs in their particular field of action. Other UN entities such as the World Intellectual Property Organization (WIPO), the International Telecommunications Union (ITU), and the International Atomic Energy Agency (IAEA) have made contributions, as have the International Organization for Standardization (ISO), the International Civil Aviation Organization (ICAO), the International Air Transport Association (IATA), and others.

From the private sector, activities with a global perspective are undertaken, among others, by the International Chamber of Commerce (ICC), the Global Business Dialogue on Electric Commerce (GBDe), the World Information Technology and Services Alliance (WITSA), the Global Internet Project, the Global Information Infrastructure Commission (GIIC), and the Information Technology Association of America (ITAA).

The special UN forum recommended here should, of course, also take cognizance of the ongoing work undertaken by the OECD (especially its recently updated Guidelines for the Security of Information Systems and Networks), the G8, the European Community, and the Council of Europe. Given the broad scope of cyberspace related problems, the forum would be best established as a special entity within the UN Secretariat or as body reporting to the UN General Assembly. Mechanisms should be developed to incorporate all stakeholders in the work of such a body.

> **5. In this context, we recommend the UN and other international entities examine the feasibility of establishing an international Information Technology Agency with the indicative mandate to, inter alia:**
>
> **Facilitate technology exchanges;**
>
> **Review and endorse emerging protocols and codes of conduct;**
>
> **Maintain standards and protocols for ultra-high bandwidth technologies;**
>
> **Specify the conditions on which access to such ultra-high bandwidth technologies be granted;**
>
> **Promote the establishment of effective inter-governmental structures and publicprivate interaction;**
>
> **Attempt to coordinate international standards setting bodies with the view of promoting interoperability of information security management processes and technologies;**
>
> **Facilitate the establishment and coordination of international computer emergency response facilities, including taking into account activities of existing organizations;**
>
> **Share cyber-tracking information derived from open sources and share technologies to enhance the security of databases and data sharing.**

The above list of possible attributions for the intended Agency appears to be self-explanatory and sufficient to set in motion the process of examining its feasibility. The Agency is perhaps best established within the UN system, but an institutional format on the basis of public-private partnership is not to be excluded. The PMP is mindful of current UN budget constraints and the general reluctance of governments to embark on new institutional solutions. However, given the amount of work already performed in various bodies, UN and others, in the IT field, the organization chart of the Agency could be small, and some reshuffling of personnel might be possible. The point is to create a central entity that can serve as a clearinghouse and coordination center for the various initiatives and work already undertaken or developed in this area. The initiative for a feasibility study might usefully be taken by the UN Secretary General.

Nationally and transnationally, an educational framework for promoting the awareness of the risks looming in cyberspace should be developed for the public. Specifically, schools and educational institutions should incorporate codes of conduct for ICT activities into their curricula. Civil society, including the private sector, should be involved in this educational process.

Rapid innovations of ICTs and the development of a wide variety of ICT products and applications has resulted in a permanently increasing and heterogeneous ICT-user community of all ages, skills, and intellectual and cultural backgrounds. ICT products are becoming more and more pervasive and ubiquitous resources of our life. More or less, all individuals use ICT products as part of their private, professional, and public life. ICTs are becoming such a part of everyday life, we are becoming as accustomed to using them as we are with other natural or technical resources.

With respect to this situation, all individuals have to become aware of not only the advantages of ICT applications, but also of their consequences and – sometimes hidden – risks, especially concerning safety and security. Making people aware of the risks associated with ICTs requires, at first, the development of an educational framework, and of easily accessible information systems and sources, which provide individuals with information and knowledge about data and information security risks according to their individual background, skills, and needs:

— All individuals should at least have a basic understanding of the key information security properties of an ICT system, like confidentiality, data integrity, user authentication, and access control mechanisms.

— All ICT users also have to understand that besides risks for their privacy, other risks may exist for their local environment, for a larger community, or even for the public.

— Adequate information about technical attacking techniques (e. g. viruses, trojan horses), and of non-technical attacking possibilities (e. g. social engineering)should be widely available to the public.

— An educational program should include some general procedures for intrusion prevention, intrusion detection, damage analysis, and recovery mechanisms.

— All educational curricula must incorporate codes of ethical conduct for ICT activities and begin at the primary school level and extend through secondary and tertiary levels and be incorporated into training programs in the workplace, community centers, and other venues for individual citizens.

The ISO Code of Practice for information security defines the 10 guiding principles which should be considered and presented to all ICT users according to their individual needs, skills, and background. Along the same lines, the UN publication Information Insecurity: a survival guide to the unchartered territories of cyber-threats and cyber-security presents a detailed description of the information security problems we have to face, and it includes all relevant information for prevention and actions. Together, with the cited sources and examples, it forms an excellent framework and source for assembling educational programs as discussed above.

Numerous other organizations have compiled valuable materials in this area. To provide all kinds of users with the required input on information security issues, educational curricula, as well as decision support and advisory information, this content should be distributed not only by printed articles and books, but also by the use of new media, ICT products, and/or the Internet. For example, educational curricula can be utilized in teleteaching and intelligent tutoring systems, enabling students to learn about this subject independent of time and location. Another technical approach could offer information security expertise via information bases, or knowledge bases, via an expert system interface. The expert system interface could be adapted according to a user's requirements, or skills, thus enabling goal-directed access to information and expertise.

> **7.Due diligence and accountability should be required of chief executive officers and public and private owners to institutionalize security management processes, assess their risks, and protect their information infrastructure assets, data, and personnel. The potential of market forces should be fully utilized to encourage private sector companies to protect their information networks, systems, and data. This process could include**

information security statements in filings for publicly traded companies, minimum insurance requirements for coverage of cyber incidents, and return on investment analyses.

Corporate directors and officers have a fiduciary duty of care to protect corporate assets. Since an estimated 80 percent of corporate assets today are digital,it logically follows that oversight of information security falls within the duty owed by officers and directors in conducting the operations of a corporation. Today, it is increasingly clear that officers and boards of directors have a corporate governance responsibility with respect to the security of company data, systems, and networks. Hacking, denial of service attacks, economic espionage, and insider misuse of data and systems are commonplace and threaten the profitability of every business, leaving officers and directors vulnerable to lawsuits and civil and criminal penalties.

To date, no shareholder suit has been brought against officers or directors for failure to take necessary steps to protect corporate systems and data, however, shareholders may have a valid basis for such derivative suits. The majority of U. S. jurisdictions follow the business judgment rule that the standard of care is that which a reasonably prudent director of a similar corporation would have used. The recent Delaware case, Caremark International Inc. Derivative Litigation, held that, "a director's obligation includes a duty to attempt in good faith to assure that a corporate information and reporting system, which the board concludes is adequate, exists, and that failure to do so under certain circumstances may, in theory at least, render a director liable for losses caused by non-compliance with applicable legal standards. " The recent Caremark case noted that officer/director liability can arise in two contexts: (1) from losses arising out of ill-advised or negligent board decisions (which are broadly protected by the business judgment rule so long as the decision was reached out of a process that was rational or employed in a good faith effort) and (2) from circumstances where the board failed to act in circumstances where "due attention" would have prevented the loss. In the latter situation, the Caremark court noted that:

> [I]t would, in my opinion, be a mistake to conclude that . . . corporate boards may satisfy their obligation to be reasonably informed concerning the corporation, without assuring themselves that information and reporting systems exist in the organization that are reasonably designed to prove to senior management and to the board itself timely, accurate information sufficient to allow management and the board, each within its scope, to reach informed judgments concerning both the corporation's compliance with law and its business performance. . . .
>
> Obviously the level of detail that is appropriate for such an information system is a question of business judgment. . . But it is important that the board exercise a good faith judgment that the corporation's information and reporting system is in concept and design adequate to assure the board that appropriate information will come to its attention in a timely manner as a matter of ordinary operations, so that it may satisfy its responsibility.

The Caremark case could provide a basis for a shareholder suit against officers and directors of U. S. companies for failure to implement an information and reporting system on the security of corporate networks and data such that it could :

(1) determine it is adequately meeting statutory, regulatory, or contractual obligations to protect

certain data from theft, disclosure or inappropriate use and

(2) be assured that the data critical to normal business operations, share price, and market share is protected.

There are also high risk situations where higher standards apply to directors and officers, such as acquisitions, takeovers, responses to shareholder suits, and distribution of assets to shareholders in preference over creditors. In these circumstances, directors and officers are required to obtain professional assistance or perform adequate analyses to mitigate the risks that ordinarily accompany these activities.

Some information assurance experts assert that a "higher degree of care will also be required of Directors and Officers regarding the complex nature of issues involved in information assurance. "Securities laws and regulations require public corporations to adequately disclose in public filings and public communications relevant risks to the corporation and its assets. The U. S. Sarbanes-Oxley Act requires management's attestation that information assets are protected.

Additional exposure is caused by insurance companies now routinely excluding hacking and IT-related incidents from general liability policies. Also, senior management in certain industry sectors may be subject to civil and criminal penalties for inadequate security and privacy of protected classes of data. And legal actions continue to mount against corporations for security and privacy breaches. The Independent Director put this in the context of information systems by reporting that:

Management of information risk is central to the success of any organization operating today. For Directors, this means that Board performance is increasingly being judged by how well their company measures up to internationally-accepted codes and guidelines on preferred Information Assurance practice. Additionally, when an organization is a victim of an attack on its information systems, whether from an insider or an outside bad actor, previous studies have shown that this can result in a lack of confidence in the company and even a drop in the company stock price. Consequently, shareholders may also initiate a derivative suit for loss to stock price or market share caused by inadequate attention by officers and directors to information security. According to the SANS Institute, the seven top management errors that lead to computer security vulnerabilities are:

"1. Assign untrained people to maintain security and provide neither the training nor the time to make it possible to do the job.

2. Fail to understand the relationship of information security to the business problem they understand physical security but do not see the consequences of poor information security.

3. Fail to deal with the operational aspects of security: make a few fixes and then not allow the follow through necessary to ensure the problems stay fixed.

4. Rely primarily on a firewall.

5. Fail to realize how much money their information and organizational reputations are worth.

6. Authorize reactive, short-term fixes so problems re-emerge rapidly.

7.Pretend the problem will go away if they ignore it."

8. In parallel, to the elaboration and harmonization of national criminal codes, there should also be an effort to work toward equivalent civil responsibility laws worldwide.

Civil responsibility should also be established for neglect, violation of fiduciary duties, inadequate risk assessment, and harm caused by cyber criminal and cyber terrorist activities.

Legal action taken in courts and by regulatory agencies and underwriting requirements by insurance companies are pushing civil responsibility for information security. Action taken in multinational fora is also expected to impact corporate liability and officer/director responsibility. Article 12 of the Council of Europe Convention on Cybercrime (CoE Convention) requires signatory states to establish laws that hold companies civilly, administratively, or criminally liable for cybercrimes that benefit the company and were made possible due to the lack of supervision or control by someone in a senior management position, such as an officer or director. Article 9 of the European Union's proposal for a Council Framework Decision on attacks against information systems mirrors the CoE language.

These provisions have been cited as an example of emulation for a broader international constituency in light of the need to be adapted for insertion into the new Model Law on Cyberspace.

9. Among the specific and concrete actions that should be considered is the possibility that commercial off-the-shelf (COTS) hardware, firmware, and software should be open source or at least be certified.

The concept of "open source" is now getting wide attention from a global community of users and developers. Open source does not refer to the price of software; it may be distributed free of charge or for a fee. The concept of open source or "free software" lies in the freedom associated with the code. This freedom, however, is contained within set limitations. An open source license provides freedom to any programmer to use the code, but defines the social parameters programmers must observe regarding the code. Open source generally means that:

1. The software is developed by a community of programmers, usually from around the globe.
2. The source code is distributed or easily available either without charge or for a minimal fee. 3. Improvements, changes, and corrections may be made to the software, but these must also be freely distributed without attempt to "privatize" the program. The license may require the source code to be distributed separately from modifications contained in "patch files," it may completely restrict distribution of modified source code, or it may require derived works to be distributed under a different name or version number from the original.
4. The copyright is held by the original author(s).
5. The rights attached to the program must apply to all to whom the program is distributed, without restriction that it be used for only a certain business, etc. or without restriction that any other software distributed with the program need be open source.
6. The license must be technology neutral.

In a nutshell, open source can generally be referred to as "an approach to software development with unique licensing arrangements and a community-based method of programming. "A reverse concept from commercial software licenses that restrict distribution, sale, modification, use, etc. , open source provides the global community of programmers access to source code and provides "freedom" to work within a community of accepted norms with respect to how that software code is handled, modified, distributed, used, etc. Because the term "open source" is a descriptive term, it cannot be protected by a trademark. Therefore, in order to "mark" software that is distributed under a license that conforms to the Open Source Initiative (OSI) definition, the OSI has registered a certification mark "OSI Certified" for this single purpose and has created a graphical certification mark for it. OSI maintains a list of registered licenses. The Linux operating system is perhaps the best known open source software example. Apache, BIND, Netscape, and GNU Linux which is the open source program for Red Hat, are others. The OSI definition and its certification mark are not only applicable for software programs, but also for firmware programs offering an application-oriented usage of microprocessors, and of digital control and processing units (e. g. , by means of Read-only Memory (ROM's)).

An open source approach is not as easily applied to hardware. There is no standardized definition and understanding available for open source hardware, as there is for software or firmware. One obvious reason lies in the lack of an easy or inexpensive method for copying hardware, such as exists for software or firmware programs. However, in 1997, some ICT hardware manufacturers formed an Open Hardware Certification Program as a self-certification program for hardware manufacturers whose hardware is Linux or FreeBSD ready. Hardware with an HDL-specified hardware description (which means that a hardware device is precisely specified by a Hardware-Description- Language program) enables easy copying and distribution of the hardware's specifications, but not of the hardware itself. With respect to ICT security considerations, open source or OSI certified programs could function in the marketplace to provide increased confidence in commercial off-the-shelf (COTS) products by providing:

— An approved license;

— A complete and certified description of the software or firmware and its functionalities or operations; and

— An understanding of its compatibilities and implementation.

From the COTS developers' point of view, however, traditional, commercially licensed software can have market advantages over open source. From the customer's point of view, open source enables a product's user to adjust, refine, adapt, or enlarge the product coincident with its specification and according to the customer's specific requirements.

The open source movement is gaining momentum, especially in developing countries where governments and businesses chafe against high license fees for Microsoft and other proprietary software products. The movement is still relatively young and refinements, as well as additional quality measures and specification standards, are certain to follow.

10. Information security issues should also be addressed in forthcoming multilateral meetings. Regional organizations should also add to national and international efforts to combat attacks in cyberspace in their respective regional contexts.

In addition to action taken in the UN and the Council of Europe, activities regarding information security and cybercrime should proceed in other fora, including regional and multilateral organizations and meetings. Regional efforts consistent with the global developing legal framework are encouraged. Regional activities are often very productive because consensus is easier to reach within regional organizations and linkages are typically stronger than those in international fora.

Additionally, certain actions that would promote information security and a harmonized global legal framework would be appropriate for discussion in the World Trade Organization Doha Round.

> **11. International law enforcement organizations should assume a stronger role in the international promotion of cybercrime issues. The competences and functions of Interpol and, in the European context, Europol, should be substantially strengthened, including by examining their investigative options.**

Disparities in the international legal environment greatly handicap law enforcement activities and often make it impossible to proceed in investigating cybercrime cases and bringing the perpetrators to justice. The speed and flexibility of cyber attacks (they can take place in an instant, or can be spread out over extended periods of time in a "low and slow" attack scenario that can be very difficult to detect) pose significant legal challenges to our traditional law enforcement environment. Particularly vexing legal issues include, but are not limited to: intercepting communications, searching and seizing electronic evidence, differing requirements for archiving logs of transactions and traffic generated at computer and communication systems, obtaining information from communication and Internet service providers, and ensuring validity of cybercrime evidence across a variety of legal jurisdictions. International law enforcement initiatives can leverage national efforts and create momentum for change.

The EU has addressed the cooperation of international law enforcement with respect to cybercrime through the European Police Office (Europol). Headquartered in The Hague, The Netherlands, Europol is the EU's law enforcement organization responsible for improving the effectiveness and cooperation between competent authorities in EU Member States. It was established on February 7, 1992, under the Treaty on European Union and is accountable to the Council of Ministers for Justice and Home Affairs. Europol became fully operational on July 1, 1999. Its mandate includes preventing and combating terrorism, drug trafficking, and other serious forms of international organized crime, such as immigration networks, vehicle trafficking, trafficking in human beings including child pornography, forgery of money and other means of payment, money laundering, and trafficking in radioactive and nuclear substances.

Europol has approximately 250 members on staff, all of whom have been assigned by various EU member nations. Approximately 45 of these staff members – known as Europol Liaison Officers (ELOs) – represent their nation's various law enforcement agencies such as police, customs, gendarmerie, and immigration services. Europol recently completed the phased deployment of The Europol Computer System (TECS).. The new computer system is specifically designed to facilitate the sharing and analysis of criminal data between EU member nations and law enforcement organizations in other countries. Each EU member nation has assigned two Data Protection Experts to Europol to closely monitor how personal data is stored and used. In September 2000, the EU's Council of Ministers for Justice and Home Affairs asked EU member nations to start responding to requests from Europol to investigate specific cases, and keep Europol informed about the status and results of the investigation. Since November 2000, EU member nations have been able to leverage the resources of Europol National Units (ENUs) on joint investigations in accordance with the Europol Conventionand its implementing rules. The European Police Chiefs Operational Task Forcecoordinates its activities with Europol in combating transnational crime.

The International Criminal Police Organization (Interpol) was founded in 1923 and has been located in Lyon, France since 1989. Interpol is an important link among law enforcement organizations globally. Interpol has 178 member countries and maintains close working relationships with dozens of intergovernmental bodies such as the Council of Europe and World Customs Organization. Interpol's primary mission is to promote the widest possible mutual assistance between all criminal police authorities.

Interpol has a system of offices around the world referred to as National Central Bureaus (NCBs). Each of its 178 member nations has an NCB station, generally within that nation's capital. One or more local law enforcement agencies are responsible for staffing the NCB and represent national law enforcement to Interpol. For example, in Canada, the Royal Canadian Mounted Police (RCMP) staff and support the NCB in Ottawa. Should a police officer in Montreal or Winnipeg need something from the police in Gaberone, Botswana, the Montreal police would route their request through their police computer systems to the NCB in Ottawa. The RCMP staff would then forward that request via a private encrypted computer network to the Interpol Secretariat General in Lyon, France. The bureau receiving the message at the

Secretariat would read the message and forward it to the necessary agency in Botswana. Each of the 178 countries participating in the Interpol system has access to special computer and telephone systems to facilitate the transfer of this information.

Interpol has been actively involved in combating Information Technology Crime (ITC) for a number of years. The Interpol General Secretariat has harnessed the expertise of its members in the field of ITC through "working parties" or groups of experts. Each working party consists of the Heads or experienced members of national computer crime units. Working parties are designed to reflect regional expertise and are established in Europe, Asia, the Americas, and Africa, although each is in different stages of development. In addition, Interpol has created several handbooks and computer crime manuals that it distributes to law enforcement agencies worldwide to use as best practice guides. Interpol currently has a number of ongoing projects related to high technology crime, including information sharing mechanisms for law enforcement and a 24 hour/7 day a week pointof- contact network to allow investigators in one jurisdiction to locate and communicate with their counterparts abroad.

12. The international science community should more vigorously address the scientific and technological issues that intersect with the legal and policy aspects of information security, including the use of ICTs and their impact on privacy and individual rights.

Increasingly, we realize that the globally connected network is a multidisciplinary effort that combines scientific and technological achievements with legal and policy considerations. Over the past few years, a legal and policy framework has developed that, in large part, is responsive to both the capabilities of networked communications and the vulnerabilities of Internet protocols, software, and networks. The ability of governments and private sector entities to access, gather, and retain vast amounts of information about Internet users has raised concerns of privacy groups, consumer advocates, and civil libertarians. Likewise, they have also been alarmed by government use of the Internet and ICTs in national and global surveillance and their potential government access to Internet account and traffic data.

To date, there has been little interaction and coordination between the scientific and technological communities and the legal/policy community. While generally aware of each other's endeavors, there has been minimal effort to identify critical intersection points to engage in multidisciplinary initiatives to resolve critical information security problems. It is incumbent upon the scientists and technologists to bring together stakeholders from the legal and policy realms to explain the capabilities and vulnerabilities of ICTs and to begin a dialogue to bridge the gaps in understanding. For example, legislators and policymakers are currently developing privacy and security laws, often without a clear understanding of whether they are actually addressing the issues caused by technological weaknesses and vulnerabilities or merely papering over a problem area.

A. Technologies With Significant Legal and Policy Implications

1. *Encryption, Signatures, and Authentication*

Cryptography has become an integral part of seeking to assure an acceptable level of security and privacy of communications and data storage. The development and use of sophisticated, strong cryptography has a long history as a technique used by governments to protect sensitive information. The development of public key cryptographyin 1975, and the subsequent evolution of that approach have put strong cryptography in the hands of private enterprises and the general public. Today, research and development into increasingly stronger, more efficient, and widely-usable encryption techniques continues at a high level.

For years, legal and policy conflicts swirled around the public use of strong encryption technologies. The U. S. , in particular, tried to regulate public use of encryption and the export of low-level encryption technologies and pushed legislative agendas mandating key escrow or embedded chips, arguing law enforcement would be stymied without such controls. Fierce resistance by industry, academia, scientists, technologists, and policymakers ultimately defeated these efforts and the unregulated public use of encryption became the global standard.

Today, only a few countries regulate public use of encryption, although many countries control the export of powerful, dual-use encryption technologies. A few countries, such as the U. K., require assistance with decryption or demand the encryption key be given to law enforcement upon request. Overall, governments around the globe have concluded that the benefits of encryption outweigh the negative consequences of encrypted communications by criminals. As lawmakers moved away from controlling encryption, their understanding of the importance of information security resulted in the enactment of laws and regulations that promote the use of authentication and authorization technologies.

There is little understanding, however, outside the scientific and technical communities regarding the capabilities to decrypt messages either real-time or offline. As more evidence mounts that Al Qaeda terrorists are using encryption technologies to protect their communications,the old fears surrounding encryption begin to surface once more. Because innovations are constantly changing both the state of encryption technologies and the ability to decipher these communications, a continuing dialogue between scientists, technologists, policymakers, and stakeholders is critical.

2. *Tracking and Tracing Internet Communications*

A technology issue central to deterring cyber attacks on information infrastructures is the degree to which attacks can be tracked to their origin. With the present TCP/IP protocol, there is very little ability to track and trace Internet attacks to their source. For example, information in an IP packet can easily be modified, the source address can be forged, and communications can be woven through intermediary hosts prior to reaching its destination ("packet laundering"). The critical link between technology and policy today is succinctly articulated by CERT/CC's Howard Lipson:

In this high-threat, target-rich environment, the technical ability to reliably track and trace intruders (supported by international agreements on monitoring and information sharing, and by international law proscribing attacks and specifying sanctions and punishment) is an indispensable element for enabling the continued use of the Internet to provide many of the essential services that societies depend on. Even with an accommodating policy environment, ISPs are likely to require both technical assistance and financial incentives to support tracking and tracing endeavors due to the cost and burden they impose on their operations.

Emerging next-generation standards and protocols from the Internet Engineering Task Force (IETF) promise to enable improved security and significantly greater tracking and tracing of cyberattacks.

IPsec is an emerging security standard for IP that provides for packet authentication and confidentiality and can be used to cryptographically authenticate a packet's source address. The Internet Protocol Version 6 (IPv6) is the next generation standard protocol that is slowly replacing the current version, which is IPv4. The security features of IPsec are made available in every IPv6 implementation, although the use of IPsec features is optional. Moreover, IPv6's expanded header size can enable more tracking and audit data to be stored. Its increased address space would make it possible (though not a requirement) for every network device to be assigned a static IP address, making it easier to link a particular IP address with an entity or individual. The adoption of IPv6 by the user community is proceeding slowly, however, due to high conversion costs.

Most tracking and tracing approaches are only effective against attacks that generate large floods of attack packets. However, there is promising ongoing research focused on the capability to track even single attack packets to their source. Such a tracking capability would require the storage, for some limited time, of a digest of all packets seen by participating routers. This would require very large data storage resources, even if only a small fraction of each packet is retained. Such large-scale storage has significant privacy implications, and is clouded with jurisdictional, legal, and law enforcement considerations.

Thus, the dialogue between scientists, technologists, and policymakers is all the more critical during this time of transition when cyber attacks are on the rise and our ability to track and trace them is limited. Howard Lipson wisely notes:

> The ability to accurately and precisely assign responsibility for cyber-attacks to entities or individuals (or to interrupt attacks in progress) would allow society's legal, political, and economic mechanisms to work both domestically and internationally, to deter future attacks and motivate evolutionary improvements in relevant laws, treaties, policies, and engineering technology....

However, improvements to current Internet technology, including improved protocols, cannot succeed without an in-depth understanding and inclusion of policy issues to specify what information can be collected, shared, or retained, and how cooperation across administrative, jurisdictional, and national boundaries is to be accomplished. Nor can policy alone, with only high-level agreements in principle, create an effective tracking and tracing infrastructure that would support multilateral technical cooperation in the face of attacks rapidly propagating across the global Internet. To be of value, the engineering design of tracking and tracing technologies must be informed by policy considerations, and policy formulations must be guided by what is technically feasible and practical. International efforts to track and trace cyber-attacks must be supported by intense technical cooperation and collaboration in the form of a multilateral research, engineering, and technical advisory group that can provide the in-depth technical skill and training to significantly improve the capabilities of incident response teams and law enforcement.

Anonymizer technologies can defeat tracking and tracing capabilities. These technologies are extremely controversial due to their ability to protect privacy on the one hand, while defeating the ability of law enforcement and private sector entities to track and trace attacks and illegal conduct.

3. *Response and Recovery Technologies*

Despite the theoretical and practical advances in tracking capabilities in the future, the prudent course of action for protecting information infrastructures is to adopt self-healing or self-mitigating architectures and operational procedures that are survivable in the face of sophisticated attacks. Survivability strategies include sophisticated schemes to simulate, detect, and respond to attacks whether from the outside or inside of the system. This area will require continuing technical, legal, and policy collaboration, but the rewards could be rich.

4. *Multilateral, Multidisciplinary Technical Research, Engineering, and Advisory Capability*

Many nations are beginning to understand that security of cyberspace requires a strategy that is linked to a nation's economic and national security interests. In February 2003, the U. S. released its National Strategy to Secure Cyberspace. The Strategy is intended to help the U. S. protect its critical infrastructures and to reduce vulnerabilities that can be exploited in order to "ensure that such disruptions of cyberspace are infrequent, of minimal duration, manageable, and cause the least public damage. "Other nations are similarly taking a national look at how their public and private sectors are securing critical information infrastructures and the relationship between cyber attacks and national and economic security.

Numerous technical information security activities have also been undertaken by the U. S. National Institute of Standards and Technology (NIST), resulting in several government technical standards and criteria for security products. As a forerunner, in 1995, the British Standards Institution developed British Standard 7799, a Code of Practice for Information Security Management. This standard has now been accepted as an international standard, ISO/IEC 17799.

Although international standards setting bodies, such as the IETF and IEEE,have been working closely in the area of cyber security and infrastructure protection for years, there is a lack of multidisciplinary collaboration on technical, legal, and policy issues at the nation state level. The Internet Society (ISOC), the main governing body of the Internet, presently covers some of this ground, but it is an independent, professional membership society comprised of more than 150 organizations and 11,000 individual members from 182 countries. It is not a multinational body of nation states that collectively discusses the array of issues concerned with cyber security and reaches agreements on cooperation, legitimate actions, and penal codes.

It is impossible for any country to unilaterally achieve security in a globally connected network environment. Again, CERT/CC's Howard Lipson, recognizes this void:

Regardless of the precise organizational structure, a multilateral technical research, engineering, and advisory capability is essential to (a) research and recommend the best tracking and tracing techniques and practices, (b) provide ongoing support for a multilateral tracking and tracing capability, (c) provide ongoing training and awareness for cooperating incident response and investigatory teams world-wide, (d) make recommendations to international engineering bodies, such as the Internet Engineering Task Force (IETF), for protocol improvements and standards creation in support of member states' requirements for tracking and tracing attackers, (e) interact with those creating cyber-law and policy to ensure that the technical and non-technical approaches complement and support each other, (f) help assure that the tracking and tracing infrastructures and technologies of cooperating entities can interoperate, and (g) assess the results of cooperation already undertaken by technical and law enforcement agencies, in order to provide feedback for continual improvement.

B. Examples of Technologies Engendering Potential Conflict with Human Rights

1. Data mining, profiling and biometric technologies

Of great concern since September 11, are information processing and retrieval technologies aimed at detecting and identifying terrorists from text-based and network-based databases through the identification and tracking of the actions of communities, the prototyping and profiling of suspects groups and individuals, and the matching of keywords, phrases, and patterns of expression. These technologies presuppose the existence of very large searchable databases.

The concern over the excessive use of data warehousing and mining is exemplified by the debate in the U. S. of the Total Information Awareness (TIA) programbeing promoted by the U. S. Defense Advanced Research Projects Agency (DARPA). According to DARPA, TIA is developing:

1) architectures for a large-scale counter-terrorism database, for system elements associated with database population, and for integrating algorithms and mixed-initiative analytical tools;

2) novel methods for populating the database from existing sources, creating innovative new sources, and inventing new algorithms for mining, combining, and refining information for subsequent inclusion into the database; and,

3) revolutionary new models, algorithms, methods, tools, and techniques for analyzing and correlating information in the database to derive actionable intelligence. "

DARPA is also developing Human Identification at a Distance (HumanID)which is a suite of automated biometric identification technologies to detect, recognize, and identify humans at great distances.

TIA would monitor the daily personal transactions by Americans and others, including tracking the use of passports, driver's licenses, credit cards, airline tickets, and rental cars. Privacy groups and civil libertarian organizations immediately raised 1984 Orwellian "Big Brother" concerns over such government use of these technologies. The U. S. Congress quickly became involved. Senator Patrick Leahy noted in a letter to U. S. Attorney General John Ashcroft that:

Collection and use by government law enforcement agencies of such commercial transactional data on law-abiding Americans poses unique issues and concerns, however. These concerns include the specter of excessive government surveillance that may intrude on important privacy interests and chill the exercise of First Amendment-protected speech and associational rights.

Subsequently, the U. S. Congress has blocked funding for the TIA program. However, this is but one small system out a vast array of government systems around the globe that uses ICTs to monitor, track, and keep information on the activities and movements of people inside their countries. Authoritarian regimes routinely block access to certain Internet sites, and because they are also usually the monopoly provider of communications, they have unfettered access to an array of communication traffic and content data. However, even democracies such as the U. S. have developed sophisticated systems to monitor email traffic. The "Carnivore" system, developed by the FBI, can be installed on an ISP to monitor all traffic moving through that provider. Although the FBI claims the system is designed to "filter" traffic and allow investigators to see only those packets the FBI is lawfully authorized to obtain, privacy and civil liberties groups remain skeptical.

2. *Global electronic surveillance*

The ECHELON system is an "automated global interception and relay system operated by the intelligence agencies in five nations:" the U. S. , U. K. , Canada, Australia, and New Zealand, with the U. S. National Security Agency at the helm. A provisional report of the European Parliament confirms that "the existence of a global system for intercepting communications, operating by means of cooperation proportionate to their capabilities among the USA, the UK, Canada, Australia and New Zealand under the UKUSA Agreement, is no longer in doubt. "The report further confirms that "the purpose of the system is to intercept private and commercial communications, and not military communications"This system and its potential for violating civil liberties of citizens has been the subject of inquiry by the legislatures of the Netherlands, Italy, and the United States among others.

3. *Anonymity, privacy, and freedom of expression*

Anonymity and privacy are frequently used interchangeably, especially, in colloquial speech. Anonymity, seen as a part of privacy (privacy of identity), can be an important means of preserving international human rights and freedom of expression. Lack of anonymity in an expanding world of information technology makes it increasingly easy for private sector entities (with particular regard to economic interests) to gather vast amounts of information and track Internet activity and for governments to conduct widespread surveillance on individuals and groups. Lack of anonymity, combined with "passive" monitoring techniques such as "cookies" and the more intrusive "clickstream" monitoring (a page-by-page tracking as a person wanders through the Internet) allows private sector entities to assemble detailed dossiers on individuals. This erosion of privacy is compounded by the weak privacy laws and regulations in the U. S. , but is countered by the more stringent data protection afforded by the European Union.

A countervailing consideration is that the "anonymity enjoyed by today's cyber attackers poses a grave threat to the global information society, the progress of an information-based international economy, and the advancement of global collaboration and cooperation in all areas of human endeavor. "With respect to malicious cyber attacks by individual hackers and the more ominous case of attacks by nation states (including acts of cyber warfare),the ability to deter attacks, obtain redress, or otherwise hold attackers accountable is directly linked to the ability to identify the sender and origin of the communication. Therefore, it is imperative that interests in tracking and tracing be balanced with legitimate privacy interests and rights provided under international law.

13. The international scientific community, and in particular the World Federation of Scientists, should assist developing countries and donor organizations to understand better how ICTs can further development in an environment that promotes information security and bridges the Digital Divide.

Much of the work in addressing developmental and digital divide issues is seen as falling within the purview of political and economic decisionmakers. However, the scientific community make significant contributions in this area because, among other reasons, of the rapid growth of peer-topeer scientific networks which offer low-cost opportunities and solutions for developing countries. ICTs bring both opportunities and challenges to developing countries. The G8, World Bank, United Nations (UN), and U. S. Agency for International Development (USAID) are each committed to bridging the global "Digital Divide. "The donor communityalso understands that ICTs are a powerful development tool that can help boost economies, increase competitiveness, attract foreign direct investment

(FDI), and raise the skill level of the workforce in developing countries. Developing countries also realize the potential impact of technology, and many are launching their own ICT initiatives and aggressively competing for donor funds to assist them.

Internet growth works in their favor. Today, there are approximately 600 million people connected to the Internet. However, that online population accounts for only 10% of a world population of about 6 billion people. Since 65% of Americans are already online,we can expect some of the highest connectivity increases to be in the 180 developing countries around the globe. Indeed, Forrester Research predicts that by 2007, 70% of software programming will be performed in developing countries. Thus, developing countries have an unprecedented opportunity to seize upon the advantages of ICTs to propel their progression toward industrialization, market economies, and social advancements. These opportunities, many of which are directly dependent on inputs from the scientific community, include:

— Attracting foreign direct investment to (a) build infrastructure, (b) launch ICT projects, (c) partner with donor organizations and governments on pilot projects, and (d) tap undeveloped or under-developed markets.

— Privatizing and liberalizing monopoly providers to introduce competition, lower prices, and advance the deployment and utilization of ICTs.

— Attracting data processing applications such as data entry, customer service and telemarketing operations, records processing (accounts receivable, accounts payable, general ledger, etc.), order entry, inventory control, databank development, data storage operations, remote systems administration, etc.

— Attracting Internet start-up companies, e-commerce operations, and software development centers.

— Developing telemedicine and health care centers.

— Using ICTs for distance learning, education, brokerage services, and building workforce skills.

— Using ICTs for agri-business and agricultural information and industry sector support.

— Attracting light manufacturing operations.

— Modernizing the financial sector.

— Fostering the growth of small and medium-sized enterprises (SMEs) to spur job creation, innovation, flexibility, and competitiveness.

— Reforming and automating court administration and case management and availability of judicial information.

While the contribution of the scientific community could be a force-multiplier, each of these opportunities, is largely dependent upon the development of the legal and regulatory framework to support these activities. The legal framework is one of the most important factors because it touches upon all aspects of commerce, is critical to attracting investment, and is at the core of providing certainty to business operations. The term "legal framework" also includes public policy, which forms the underlying foundation of government support for ICTs and a favorable business environment. Information and infrastructure security are two of the most important components.

With nearly 200 countries connected to the Internet, cybercrime has become a global issue that requires the full participation and cooperation of the public and private sectors in all countries, including the 180 developing countries, around the globe. A major component of information and infrastructure security is a nation's ability to deter, detect, investigate, and prosecute cyber criminal activities. Weaknesses in any of these areas can compromise security not only in that country, but around the globe. This is due to the global, interconnected nature of the Internet and the way in which countries must rely upon each other's expertise and assistance in addressing cybercrime matters.

The confidentiality, integrity, and availability of data and networks – including critical infrastructure –are central to attracting FDI and ICT operations to developing countries. The opportunities associated with ICTs are not guaranteed; they are dependent upon developing countries' ability to effectively address the additional challenge of cyber security and to take steps to actively participate in the global community in combating cybercrime.

Appropriate security laws and regulations are also important because:

— They protect the integrity of the government and reputation of the country.

— They help preclude a country from becoming a haven for bad actors, such as terrorists, organized crime, and fraud operations.

— They help prevent a country from becoming a repository for cyber-criminal data.

— They instill market confidence and certainty regarding business operations and attract foreign direct investment.

— They provide protection of classified, secret, confidential and proprietary information, criminal justice data, personal information, and certain categories of public data. . They protect consumers and assist law enforcement and intelligence gathering activities.

— They deter corruption.

— They increase national security and reduce vulnerabilities to attacks and actions by terrorists and other rogue actors.

— They help protect corporations against risk of loss of market share, shareholder and class action lawsuits, damage to reputation, fraud, and civil and criminal fines and penalties.

— They provide a means of prosecution and civil action for acts against information and infrastructure.

— They increase the chance that electronic evidence in physical-world crimes, such as murder or kidnapping, will be available when needed.

— They create an atmosphere of stability in which economic and social welfare can flourish.

For the most part, developing countries are struggling with how to use e-commerce and ICTs in everyday government and business operations.

The lack of an adequate legal framework – especially with respect to information and infrastructure security and computer crime – will diminish or prevent developing countries from grasping ICT opportunities. The reasons are clear:

— Internet and e-commerce operations require an enabling legal framework that also provides for security of data and networks.

— Data processing operations require information and infrastructure security laws for a safe operating environment and protection of data.

— Companies will not allow their data to be processed in countries that do not have adequate legal protections against economic espionage, computer crime, infrastructure attacks, and misuse of telecommunications devices and equipment.

— Certain laws, such as the EU data protection directive, require that countries afford equal legal protections against misuse of personal data.

Much of the inadequacies in addressing these critical issues in developing countries occur because of shortages in scientific and knowledge-based resources. Much is also due to scarcities in financial resources, which in turn constrict the enormous potential inherent in the large human resource base in the developing world. By helping identify and discover low-cost solutions, and by closer coordination with other relevant partners, the scientific community can unleash these human resources, and place them at the service of the developmental effort. The role of the World Federation of Scientists would be an important catalyst in this effort.

Bibliography

Carter, D., Katz, A., "Computer Crime: An Emerging Challenge for Law Enforcemen", URL: 9 Mar., 1999.

Denning, Peter J., (editor), "Computers Under Attack: Intruders, Worms, and Viruses", Reading, MA: Addison-Wesley, 1990.

Hafner, K. & Markoff, J., "Cyberpunk: Outlaws and Hackers on the Computer Frontier", New York: Simon and Schuster, 1995.

Hoffman, L., et al., "Cryptography Policy and Technology Trends", URL: 1 Dec 1993, revised 30 Jan, 1994.

McKee, Phillip C., "Remarks to the 'Consumer Protection in Electronic Commerce' Panel at The Public Voice in the Development of Internet Policy Conference of the Global Internet Liberty Campaign." National Fraud Information Center. Internet. URL: 25 Feb., 1999

Varon, Elana, "Bill Would Double Budget to Fight Internet Child Pornography", *CNN Interactive*, Internet.

Index